D1807065

The Future of the Patent System

The Future of the Patent System

Edited by

Ryo Shimanami

School of Law, Kobe University, Japan

Prepared and edited with the assistance of
The Institute of Intellectual Property

Edward Elgar

Cheltenham, UK • Northampton, MA, USA

First published in Japanese as *Kiro ni tatsu tokkyo seido*, Institute of Intellectual Property (IIP).

Translated by the Contributors.

Published by
Edward Elgar Publishing Limited
The Lypiatts
15 Lansdown Road
Cheltenham
Glos GL50 2JA
UK

Edward Elgar Publishing, Inc.
William Pratt House
9 Dewey Court
Northampton
Massachusetts 01060
USA

A catalogue record for this book
is available from the British Library

Library of Congress Control Number: 2012935314

ISBN 978 1 78100 053 3

Typeset by Servis Filmsetting Ltd, Stockport, Cheshire
Printed and bound by MPG Books Group, UK

Contents

PART III DEVELOPING COUNTRIES AND THE FUTURE OF THEIR PATENT SYSTEMS

Contributors

T.G. Agitha, Research Officer, HRD Chair on IPR, Centre for IPR Studies, Cochin University of Science & Technology, India, Ph.D.

Guy Carmichael, Examiner, Scenario Analyst, European Patent Office

Shirin Elahi, Former Scenario Project Leader, European Patent Office

N.S. Gopalakrishnan, Professor, HRD Chair on IPR, Centre for IPR Studies, Cochin University of Science & Technology, India, Ph.D.

Konstantinos Karachalios, Dr., External Relations, Scenario Analyst, European Patent Office

Jay P. Kesan, Professor & H. Ross & Helen Workman Research Scholar, Director, Program in Intellectual Property & Technology Law, University of Illinois, USA

Viviane Yumy Mitsuuchi Kunisawa, Attorney at Law in Brazil, Legal Counsel at Syngenta in Brazil; Lecturer in the Post-Graduate Course in Intellectual Property Law at the University of the State of Rio de Janeiro

Mark A. Lemley, William H. Neukom Professor of Law, Stanford Law School, Director, Stanford Program in Law, Science and Technology; Partner, Durie Tangri LLP, USA

Ciaran McGinley, Controller, European Patent Office

Kazuyuki Motohashi, Professor, The University of Tokyo, Japan

Nobuhiro Nakayama, Chairman, Institute of Intellectual Property, Professor Emeritus of The University of Tokyo, Japan

Clara Neppel, Dr., Examiner, Scenario Analyst, European Patent Office

Yoichi Omori, Executive Director, Institute of Intellectual Property, Japan

Zhang Ping, Professor, Peking University, China

Berthold Rutz, Dr., Examiner, Scenario Analyst, European Patent Office

Futoshi Yasuda, Associate Professor, National Graduate Institute for Policy Studies, Japan

Foreword

A *patent* is now talked about much as a wonder boy, but we can say that it is still in its infancy, compared to *ownership*, which has a far longer history. Although its origin dates back to the Venetian patent system in the 15th century, the patent started to gain the significance we recognize today only after the emergence of factory-based machine industry during the Industrial Revolution in the 18th century. A patent system came about as a result of a time when the conventional industrial structure changed drastically, bringing about the era of mass production and mass sales. In short, the current patent system evolved as a response to the needs of the times, backed by the machinery and chemical industries which flourished during the 18th and 19th centuries.

We must not forget that a patent is not a universal right, like ownership, which exists beyond time, but has instead arisen from an industrial structure at a certain point in time. In other words, when the industrial structure changes along with changing times, the significance or raison d'être of the patent system must also change. Once, during the period of the French Revolution, a patent was appraised as a natural human right, but such a notion was a theory elaborated in an attempt to deprive the monarchy of its authority to grant exclusive rights. In a strict sense, a patent right was born out of the climate of the industry at a certain time in history. This also applies to copyright.

However, after a system is established, it is very hard to change or abolish it. The more people or companies involved in a system, the greater the number with an interest therein, and the greater the energy that will be required to change such a system. In the case of the patent system, almost all countries in the world have their own respectable patent offices, and most companies have their own patent divisions (or intellectual property divisions), accumulating an enormous amount of patent assets to date. A huge number of people are concerned with the patent system, namely, patent attorneys, lawyers, intellectual property judges, personnel at intellectual property divisions of private companies, employees of patent research companies, and university professors specializing in intellectual property. Furthermore, there is even an international body dealing with patent issues, the World Intellectual Property Organization (WIPO). It is not an easy task to change the direction of a giant ship carrying such a large number of stakeholders.

Nevertheless, the world is currently going through dramatic changes, and in the future, the present time will be evaluated as a revolutionary period equal to or greater than the Industrial Revolution. The field of intellectual property is also being hit by violent waves of changes, such as the impact of digitization, economic globalization, and the sharp increase in the number of patent applications. In society, we can see the emergence of new concepts such as free software and creative commons, which cannot be explained or reasoned based on our conventional intellectual property system. It is not easy to achieve a drastic reform of the system as mentioned above, but sooner or later reform must be carried out. Without reform, the existence of the patent system will be in danger. The Japan Patent Office has set out to discuss a comprehensive reform of the patent system. The Institute of Intellectual Property needs to, at the very least, arm itself with a theoretical framework in preparation for responding to such reform, as this may be the mission entrusted it. From this standpoint, I believe this book will be the first step in the course of exploring the essence of the patent system on a global scale. The enormity of the patent system reform issue is vast as international aspects must also be taken into consideration. This book may not be able to give an answer, but I hope that it will, in some ways, clarify the issue and become the impetus for further discussion.

In my youth, I studied at the Max Planck Institute in Munich, Germany, and while studying there I had a dream that in the future a similar institute may be established in Japan. With this aim in mind, 20 years ago, I took the initiative to collect signatures from more than 100 scholars and attorneys in this field, pursuing the establishment of an institute specializing in intellectual property that would compare with the Max Planck Institute, submitted a written petition for the establishment of the institute to the Ministry of International Trade and Industry, and finally realizing the establishment of the Institute of Intellectual Property. I am filled with deep emotion to see the Institute celebrating its “coming-of-age” its 20th anniversary. The first chairman of the Institute was Mr. Gaishi Hiraiwa, then Chairman of the Tokyo Electric Power Co., Inc. (TEPCO) (who subsequently became Chairman of Nippon Keidanren). Next, Mr. Ichiro Kato, former President of the University of Tokyo, served as chairman for a long time, and then I myself succeeded to the post. Mr. Hiraiwa passed away in 2007, and Mr. Kato also passed away on November 11, 2008.

On a personal note, I became an assistant to Professor Kato in 1969 enabling my study at the University of Tokyo to continue. This was the starting point of my career as a researcher of intellectual property law.

Professor Kato, who was a great and prominent scholar in civil law, held important posts including the presidency of the University of Tokyo and the chairmanship of the Institute of Intellectual Property. The Institute achieved significant progress under the leadership of Professor Kato as its chair from 1991 to 2005. The Institute will be forever indebted to the contributions of Professor Kato and I would like to take this opportunity to pay tribute to his memory on behalf of the Institute of Intellectual Property.

Nobuhiro Nakayama
Chairman, Institute of Intellectual Property
March 2012

Preface: patent system at the crossroads

The Institute of Intellectual Property was established in 1989 by the Ministry of Economy, Trade and Industry as an institute specializing in intellectual property. In commemoration of its 20th anniversary in 2009, the Institute decided to publish this book with the hope of simulating multi-perspective discussion on the patent system and using the insights gained from the discussion to determine the future direction of the patent system. In this preface, I would like to briefly explain the loss of momentum in Japan's initiative to become an intellectual property power, the problems related to the patent system, and the risks that companies face as patent system users.

LOSS OF MOMENTUM IN JAPAN'S INITIATIVE TO BECOME AN INTELLECTUAL PROPERTY POWER

Since the establishment of Japan's Intellectual Property Basic Act in December 2002, Japan has annually devised an intellectual property strategic program in order to pursue the goal of making Japan an intellectual property-based nation. This concept of "making Japan an intellectual property-based nation" is said to have its origin in the administrative policy speech given in 2002, only eight years ago, by former Prime Minister Junichiro Koizumi. Nowadays, the media has already lost interest in intellectual property strategies, indicating that the "intellectual property boom" is over.

The majority of people feel that Japan should value intellectual property more highly than other countries. They argue that the patent system plays an important role in protecting and using innovations in light of the fact that Japan has few natural resources but has a relatively high level of innovation capability in the world. Thus intellectual property systems function as an important infrastructure to facilitate the free flow of human resources, goods, and money around the globe, which is vital to Japan because of its great dependence on trade.

These arguments are reasonable. Many people seem to support these arguments and consider the protection and use of intellectual property as important. If this is the case, one could wonder why the "intellectual property boom" was short-lived. If intellectual property is really important, the initiative to become an intellectual property power would automatically progress and intensify. Why has the boom subsided?

Japan established its first patent law in 1885. This is earlier than the establishment of the Constitution in 1889 and the Civil Code in 1896. However, Japan's initiative for becoming an intellectual property power did not begin until 2002 as mentioned above. Until then, the patent system had never been ranked high in national policy. What had prevented the patent system from attracting policy makers' attention?

PROBLEMS RELATED TO PATENT SYSTEM

The slowdown of the aforementioned "making Japan an intellectual property-based nation" initiative may be attributable not to the method or system of implementing the initiative but to the various problems inherent in the patent system that had prevented patent system users from making active use of the system.

In the following sections, I will discuss five problems related to the patent system. My argument is, in short, that the current patent system has failed to catch up with the changing nature of technology development.

Failure of Catching Up to Adjust to the Great Change in the Industrial Structure

The first problem lies in the failure of catching up to adjust to the great change in the industrial structure. The recent change in the industrial structure increased the value of intangible assets in the corporate world. Consequently, an increasing number of companies obtain the results of their technology development activities in the form of information goods such as software. However, such information goods are not sufficiently protected under the current system.

As a result of a gradual change in the industrial structure since the late 20th century, the tertiary industry has become more significant than secondary industry. For example, in Japan, the total percentage of the primary and secondary industries in real domestic product was 54 percent in 1965, while the tertiary industry accounted for 46 percent. In 2000, tertiary industry increased to 66 percent.

With this change, the source of value in the corporate world shifted from tangible assets to intangible ones. Today, investment funds are no longer flowing into companies owning a number of land properties and large-scale facilities, but into companies possessing superior intangible assets and business models. The same shift occurred in personal assets as well. With the percentage of tangible assets decreasing, the percentage of intangible assets (e.g., brands, corporate philosophy and other incorporeal assets, index funds, and real-estate trusts) has been on the rise.

Product manufacturers have also transformed themselves from mere manufacturers into something completely different in order to survive fierce competition. For example, Toyota has become one of the world's greatest companies not simply because it has produced great cars but because it has built up great intangible assets such as its manufacturing technique, known as the just-in-time inventory system, and its sales technique that has made Toyota renowned for its selling power. Against this background, it is inevitable that the patent system changes with the times. A new patent system should consider the results of technology development activities broadly as information goods and provide proper protection for such goods.

Failure of Catching Up to Adjust to the Change in the Significance of Technology Development

The second problem lies in the failure of catching up to adjust to the change in the significance of technology development. Today, technology development activities themselves are subject to fierce competition. Consequently, at any moment in time, many projects are being carried out around the world to develop similar technologies. The fact that inventions brought about the Industrial Revolution indicates that technology development was no less important a hundred or two hundred years ago. The difference is that technology development was not the major target of investment. At that time, investments were mostly made in land, facilities, and labor.

On the other hand, in the modern world, investment in land would not bring you great profit. For this, you need to invest in technology development which is why countries make it national policy to promote the development of cutting-edge technologies. Naturally, many development projects for similar technologies are concurrently carried out in many parts of the world, causing development costs to skyrocket. Under the current patent system, only a person who invented the world's most advanced technology is entitled to a patent right. Such a system of granting an absolute right exclusively to one person may be making other technology development efforts meaningless.

Failure of Catching Up to Adjust to the Change in the Mode of Technology Development

The third problem lies in the failure of catching up to adjust to the change in the mode of technology development. Nowadays, technology development activities are carried out not by individuals but by organizations.

In the past, technology development relied on the abilities of individuals. For example, in the age of the Industrial Revolution, both James Watt's steam engine and Robert Fulton's steamboat were invented by individuals. On the other hand, in the modern world, most inventions are made based on the knowledge accumulated by a great number of people over time. This indicates that highly advanced and complicated technologies are not something that individuals can invent by themselves. While the "linear model," which is a technology development model in which large research institutes play a major role, successfully created many flourishing products such as nylon, the linear model has lost its significance. In fact, nowadays, many of the successful companies such as Intel and Sun Microsystems do not have research institutes. Under a newly introduced model called the chain-linked model, research includes such activities as carrying out detailed surveys on consumer needs, procuring necessary funds, and having discussions with experts in a variety of fields. Technology development activities performed in accordance with the chain-linked model have produced a great number of improvement inventions, causing a dramatic increase in the number of patent applications.

Even within Japan, as many as several million claims are made for improvement proposals and the results of technology development activities. These inventions may be compared to a pyramid with its top consisting of a small number of important inventions that satisfy the strict criteria for industrial applicability and inventive step and with its bottom consisting of a large number of minor improvement proposals. The question is which part of the pyramid should be protected to what extent in order to contribute to industrial development most effectively.

Another change in the mode of technology development is that corporate technology development activities have become increasingly borderless. Many Japanese companies design their cars in the United States. For Japanese business executives, Japan is merely one of the regions targeted by their business.

National borders are dissolving not only in corporate activities, but also in the world of technologies. For instance, internet-related patents would be meaningless unless they ensure global protection. Suppose a patent is granted for a business model that designates Japan as the location of a server computer and the U.S. as the location of a terminal computer. If the patent is infringed, which country's laws should be applied to the infringement?

Failure of Catching Up to Find a New Raison d'Etre

The third problem lies in the failure of catching up to find a new raison d'être. The goal of the patent system has been to promote technology development by granting monopoly rights. However, people started questioning the purpose of the patent system after seeing the success of unpatented, uncopyrighted open source software such as Unix and Linux, which are available to any person as long as he/she follows certain rules.

People developed technologies even before the establishment of the patent system. Their motives ranged from the eradication of plagues to the mitigation of the fear of war, establishment of supremacy, attainment of honor, etc. This means that technology development goes on without the patent system. The raison d'être of the patent system is to increase an incentive for technology development by granting monopoly rights to inventors for their benefit. However, the success of Unix, etc., shows that monetary benefit and monopolistic control are not necessarily the only incentives for technology development. For some inventors in the modern world, honor and social contribution could serve as strong incentives. The existence of various incentives aside from the incentives provided by the patent system has raised a question about what role the patent system should play in the future.

Failure of Catching Up to Cope with the Ever-increasing Applications

The fifth problem lies in the failure of catching up to cope with the ever-increasing applications.

The importance of technology development is expected to further increase in the future. As a result of innovation driven technology development, such as development activities carried out based on a chain-linked model, the number of applications filed with patent offices will increase exponentially. Unless drastic measures are taken, the increasing workload would crash patent offices around the world, leading to a collapse of the patent system as a whole. It would be necessary to emphasize that the patent system is not designed to protect innovations but designed to protect inventions. The distinction between the two blurs too often, which has resulted in the grant of more than 700,000 patents in the world every year. It is estimated that the number of patents existing in the world is at least 10 times larger than the annual grants. Which provides a greater incentive to those involved in technology development, the vast number of patents or a few Nobel Prizes granted every year?

RISKS POSED TO PATENT SYSTEM USERS

The five problems described above pose business risks to patent system users in the corporate world. In this section, I will present some example cases where business risks arise.

Risk of Infringing Patents of Other Companies

The first risk is that companies could inadvertently infringe the patents of other companies. In the case of a company producing a product consisting of a large number of parts, it is very burdensome for the company to search for all of the related patents to prevent infringement. This problem is called "patent thickets" or "patent mines."

Some technology fields are filled with patent portfolios. A patent portfolio would allow the portfolio-holding company to benefit from its monopolistic control over the relevant field and to prevent other companies from entering the field. For instance, no companies can compete with Toyota and Honda in the field of petroleum-electric hybrid vehicles because the two companies own patent portfolios. Their patent portfolios are said to have prevented other companies from entering the field. On the other hand, patent portfolios could make Japanese companies suffer hardships as well. For example, the Japanese computer industry in its infancy was hit by patent infringement lawsuits filed by IBM.

In particular, in the electric and machinery industry, a single product often involves hundreds or thousands of patents. When developing a product in this industry, a company has to avoid infringing any of these patents. This is not an easy task. Economists call such a dense web of patents a patent thicket and consider it one of the impediments to R&D activities and business activities. In recent years, patent thickets have been especially problematic in the field of combined technology. For example, a mobile phone functions as an information terminal, telephone, music player, and camera. In the field of combined technology, it is impossible to develop a product without infringing any of the existing patents. In order to minimize the risk of infringement litigation, companies are taking self-defense measures such as the creation of patent pools.

Each company must make continuous efforts to avoid infringing any of the large number of patents owned by other companies because a huge number of patents exist in this world as explained above; in other words, the world is filled with patent mines. Any company conducting business in the U.S. needs to avoid infringing any U.S. patent. Any company conducting business in China needs to avoid infringing any Chinese patent. The same may be said about India, Brazil, or European countries. The globalization of economy has not globalized the world of intellectual property. For safe business operation in other countries, Japanese companies need to keep searching for patent mines that are buried in local languages and scattered across major countries and regions around the world.

An inadvertent use of another party's patent would lead to a lawsuit. In comparison with regular industrial lawsuits, patent infringement lawsuits pose much higher risks to companies. In the "pachisuro case," the Tokyo District Court ordered payment of ¥8.4 billion in damages in 2002. In a U.S. patent infringement lawsuit, the case was settled in March 1992 with a payment of ¥16.5 billion ($127.5 million) from a Japanese company, Minolta Camera, to a U.S. company, Honeywell.

Risk that the Patents Obtained Based on the Upstream R&D Activities Could Hinder Development Activities in the Downstream

The second risk is that patent protection related to the upstream R&D activities could inevitably impose restrictions on development activities in the downstream. This risk arises because current R&D activities have a multi-layered structure.

For example, in the field of biotechnology, patents granted furthest upstream include those granted for human DNA sequences and research tools to read DNA. The grant of a patent for human DNA raised considerable controversy which subsided when it was decided that human DNA may be patented with conditions. On the other hand, research tools have already been patented, imposing substantial restrictions on development activities in the downstream in some cases. Critics still argue that the grant of patents for research tools would hinder research activities around the world. The absence of a reasonable solution to this problem has made Japanese pharmaceutical companies deeply concerned.

Risk of Losing Patent Rights

The third risk is that companies could lose patents even after registering them. There are some cases where a patent registered after due examination by patent examiners was invalidated after the patent was put to use.

In general, a property right is considered stable. Once you purchase something and own it, your property right would not be invalidated unless there are very special circumstances. For instance, you might lose your property right if a war or political upheaval has erupted or if the property right has been acquired through a criminal act. In contrast, even in developed countries such as the U.S. and Japan, you could find your patent right invalidated under normal circumstances.

According to statistics, it is not rare to see a registered patent right invalidated and extinguished in judicial proceedings. Even after Japanese Patent Office (JPO) examiners grant a patent, the validity of that patent might be reexamined in a JPO trial. Even if the validity is confirmed in the trial, there is still a 55.9 percent chance of seeing it invalidated by a court (as of 2007). In short, even if the patent passes the JPO's examination and trial procedures, there is still about a 60 percent chance of patent invalidation.

This data shows that a patent right is inherently very unstable. This means that the validity of intellectual property rights cannot be confirmed unless they are fought for all the way to the Supreme Court. No other property rights would require such an ordeal.

What makes patent rights so unstable? Under the Japanese Patent Act, a patent will not be granted to an invention that has already been publicized somewhere in the world. This principle is called "absolute novelty." Although this principle requires, at least officially, prior art searches covering documents published all over the world, there is a limit to the extent of searches that can be performed for each patent application. The JPO examines about 300,000 applications every year. Therefore, it is impossible for the JPO to grant a patent for each invention after conducting a search on all of the technical documents published in various languages around the world and confirming that there is no existing technology that corresponds to the invention.

The JPO conducts prior art searches by using a database that contains around 70 million Japanese documents accumulated since the Meiji era, and the databases of the U.S. Patent and Trademark Office (USPTO) and the European Patent Office (EPO) to cover foreign documents mostly written in English.

The number of prior art documents keeps rising with time. The Japan Association for International Chemical Information (JAICI) has a database called the CAS (Chemical Abstracts Service), which specializes in chemistry-related information. The number of documents contained in this database increased exponentially: slightly less than 280,000 in 1961, 530,000 in 1971, 990,000 in 1981, 1.57 million in 1991, and 2.4 million in 2001. The number of documents grew 10 times over a period of 40 years. As of 2007, a breakdown of CAS documents by language shows that English accounts for 79.1 percent, Chinese 13.3 percent, Japanese 3.4 percent, German 0.9 percent, and French 0.2 percent. Ten years ago,

Chinese accounted for only 4.7 percent. The increase in the proportion of Chinese documents is noteworthy.[1] The most frequent users of this database are the examination departments of patent offices in various countries.

Losing a patent infringement lawsuit would cause enormous damage to business activities. This is why a defendant company makes every effort to invalidate the plaintiff's patent right. If the patent in question is vital to the survival of the defendant, the defendant would employ the best attorney it can find and spare no expense to conduct in-depth searches covering documents published in Russia, Eastern European countries, China, and in some cases other countries. Since the patent in question was usually registered based on the results of searches conducted with regular intensity, if the defendant conducts searches covering every document published around the world with the focus on the invention in question with no regard to the costs and time that such searches would take, a prior art document may be found in many cases.

As described above, the principle of absolute novelty inevitably keeps patent owners concerned about the possible existence of undiscovered prior art documents. This is one of the reasons why the chances of finding a patent right invalidated by a court are extremely high in comparison with other property rights. Another reason is the unclear definition of patent right. A patent right is defined merely as a technical idea specified in a document. In addition, the definition of "inventive step" is not clear enough because it is a concept that can be perceived only by highly-educated people. Consequently, in a patent infringement dispute, both sides make arguments over the allegedly-infringing goods based on vaguely-defined concepts. Such a shaky framework for patent infringement disputes has also increased the likelihood of patent invalidation.

CONCLUSION

In the preceding, I pointed out many fundamental problems inherent in the patent system. Despite all of those problems, the system has fully established its global presence. The number of member countries of the Paris Convention for the Protection of Industrial Property has increased to 171, while the number of the WTO member countries has grown to 153. It would be beneficial to gain insights from jurists and economists in Japan as well as from prominent experts in the U.S. and European countries, which are regarded as front-runners in the field of intellectual property. Furthermore, insights from rapidly developing countries such as China, India, and Brazil would be also beneficial.

The authors of this book include not only such jurists, economists, and experts in developed countries but also opinion leaders in China and India who are well versed in the intellectual property systems of their respective courtiers. In recent years, these countries have thoroughly examined what went wrong with the developed countries' patent systems and very carefully designed their domestic patent systems so that their systems would not suffer the same fate.

I hope this book will be useful to those who engage in designing intellectual property systems. In closing, I would like to express my deep appreciation to all of the people concerned for their kind support and cooperation rendered to the Institute of Intellectual Property over the last 20 years.

Yoichi Omori
Institute of Intellectual Property
March 2009

NOTE

1. Chemical Abstracts Services (CAS) (2008) 'CAS Statistical Summary 1907–2007'.

Introduction

Ryo Shimanami

Since it first took shape in England in the 17th century, the patent system has consistently continued to enhance its function and effects. Yet there has been no era other than today where the significance of the patent system has been questioned and calls have been made for reform. Pathological phenomena, such as the sharp increase in the number of patent applications, the decrease in the quality of patent rights, the increase in the cost of patent infringement lawsuits among other phenomena, are now common and serious issues in many countries and regions. Papers and publications with provocative titles referring, for example, to the crisis or failure of the patent system, have become too numerous to count.

This book intends to analyze different perspectives on the turning point now faced by today's patent system under the current period of reform and different visions for its future, based on its status in Japan, the U.S., Europe, India, Brazil and China, where the level of acceptance of the patent system varies, and by applying two theories, which have different approaches: jurisprudence and economics.

Part I presents the arguments of a Japanese jurist and economist and an American scholar with profound knowledge of the law and economics on the current status and vision of the patent system. The following points will be examined in this chapter: whether the patent act provides uniform norms for all technologies and disputes, and how far the patent right retains the characteristics of a traditional exclusive right.

First, Chapter 1 clarifies from a jurisprudence perspective that the uniformity and versatility of the norms that were originally a part of the patent system have been lost today and there is often a tendency to apply a temporary adjustment of interests. With regard to issues such as infringement under the doctrine of equivalents, indirect infringement, exhaustion of rights, inventions by employees, etc., the transition in the characteristics of applicable norms from rules that are formal and adequately stable to standards that are substantive and highly appropriate is described. In addition, with the increased use of the method for the substantial balancing of interests to which the aforementioned standards are applied, the standards for the balancing of interests become more important in the future. The author thus examines the standards by returning to the very beginning point, justification theory, and the consideration of the reasons why the patent system exists. On this basis, the author examines the standards for categorizing the various types of norms that are included in the patent act into rules and standards; and raises warnings about the current situation of the Japanese Patent Act where the patent act is losing its coherence as a single law as a result of the excessive use of standards. From the phenomenon in the U.S. where the U.S. Supreme Court denied the formal interpretation of the patent act provided by the U.S. Court of Appeals for the Federal Circuit (CAFC) and demanded a more flexible interpretation, it can be seen that, in fact, this standardization of the patent act is a cross-border issue.

Chapter 2 examines in a demonstrative way, from an economic perspective, what effects the reinforcement of patent rights in Japan, in other words, the amendment of the legal system in a pro-patent direction, has had on trends in innovation in Japanese companies (for instance, corporate activities, such as research and development investment, patent application, licensing, etc.). As a result of the examination, the following matters are noted: the pro-patent policy did not cause significant changes in the innovation tendencies of Japanese companies. However, it had a greater impact on high-tech industries, including the electronics and pharmaceutical industries, than on other industries, while the degree and content of the impact are different when comparing the electronics industry and pharmaceutical industry. There are previous research studies in Europe and the U.S. with respect to the effects of pro-patent policies. Their results have shown that the impact on company activities varies by country or industry field. If so, there should be reasons for the recent tendency to become mainstream in the supreme courts of Japan and the U.S. where uniform rules are not applied to all disputes, but are adjusted subtly in each case by applying standards.

Moreover, in Chapter 3 it is shown that the current status of many industries other than the pharmaceutical industry reveals how the existence of the patent right has been ignored. The author indicates that situations where a patented invention is used by others without obtaining approval from the patent right holders are rampant in practical business practices. This loss of the patent right function reveals a significant difference from other cases where it is extremely rare that tangible objects (in particular, land) are used by others without obtaining the approval of the property right holders. On this basis, the author clarifies that unlike the property right system, the operation of the patent system, where rigid right treatment is not implemented prior to the use of an object, has a certain reasonability. The author then defines a concept of an efficient patent license market located between the extremes – the rigid protection of rights as shown in the cases of property rights and the ignorance of rights – and makes concrete suggestions along with the concept, such as the disclosure of applications at an early stage, mandatory disclosure of the license term, etc. Underlying this concept is an attempt to transform the patent right from a traditional exclusive right to the right to claim value and to demand the conversion of basic characteristics of the patent system to give invention incentives by granting exclusive rights.

In Part II, issues related to patent systems in Europe, the U.S. and Japan and the path to resolving these issues are examined from the respective positions of Patent Office practitioners, jurists and economists. Japan, the U.S. and Europe are advanced countries and regions of economic development and have long histories with respect to the use of the patent system when compared with other countries. However, the trend towards reinforcing patent rights (pro-patent policy) that was adopted in these three countries and regions starting in 1980 caused pathological phenomena, such as the increase in the number of patent applications over the last quarter century and has had the adverse effect of restricting innovation in society overall. The crisis of the patent system in Japan, the U.S. and Europe may lead to a world-wide crisis in the patent system if appropriate measures are not taken now.

In Chapter 4, the current status of patent systems in Europe, four scenarios for the future and countermeasures for issues are examined from the point of EPO examiners and others. In this chapter, the strides in cross-border harmonization between patent systems for which Europe is a world leader are introduced. The author then describes the four scenarios that the European patent system may face: (i) a world where patents will function increasingly as financial means for large-scale companies and the patent system will collapse; (ii) a world where multiple regional patent systems coexist; (iii) a world where the social trust in patent systems will be lost and other ways to provide R&D incentives are explored; and (iv) a world where the patent system itself transforms along with the rapid progress in technology. In this chapter, specific strategies are also examined where the patent system stands against the issue of the sharp increase in the number of patent applications (so-called "global patent warning"), such as strategies increasing the level of progress, etc., in the four aforementioned scenarios. In conclusion, the author issues a strong warning that there is no option to take no measures now against issues that the patent system faces regardless of the scenario that the patent system will face in the future.

In Chapter 5, an American jurist describes one vision of the U.S. Patent

Act. The author indicates here how the U.S. Federal Circuit has proactively embodied abstract language in the patent act since its foundation in 1982 and developed its own theory that is different from other areas of the law; on the other hand, the U.S. Supreme Court, which is superior to the Federal Circuit, has limited excessive action by the Federal Circuit and strived to maintain homogeneity between the patent act and other areas of the law. Because of industries that are strong lobbyists to the patent system, such as pharmaceutical, biotech and IT companies, this chapter also reveals the recent state of the patent act repeating inconsistent amendments and their influences on patent practices, including the projections of the ripple effect that may arise from the Patent Reform Act of 2011, which incorporates the shift from the first-to-invent system to the first-to-file system. This analysis comes from the institutional theories that have been developed in recent years in the U.S., and it can be recognized as an attempt to question which institution (companies or nation; judiciary branch, legislative branch or administrative branch of the government; the Supreme Court or the Federal Circuit) should assume the role of building and operating the patent system.

Moreover, in Chapter 6, from the standpoints of a former examiner of the Japan Patent Office and an economist, the author discusses the behavior of Japanese companies in obtaining patents and the method to resolve the issue of slower examinations in the JPO, which has arisen due to this behavior. According to the discussion, supported by a corporate culture that has a strong desire to improve technology as well as to partake in copycat behavior, the number of patent applications per R&D expenditure or for each researcher for Japanese companies is significantly higher than for companies in other countries. Due to the behavior of these companies in obtaining patents and shortening the period of demand for examination since 2001, the slowing down of examinations by the Patent Office in Japan has become a more serious problem than in other countries. This chapter demonstrates these phenomena in conformity with the data and proposes institutional reforms as measures to overcome them, such as diversifying the length of the period of demand for examination, which is currently a uniform period, restricting the exercise of the right to seek an injunction, setting a higher bar for inventive steps, among other changes.

In Part III, current status and vision of patent systems are discussed from the perspective of economically-developing countries, such as India, Brazil and China. These three countries are members of the so-called BRICS. All of these countries have extensive national land and large populations, and are rich in national resources, including coal, iron ore and natural gas. They have achieved rapid economic development over the last ten years thanks to their rich human and material resources without relying on intellectual property. At the same time, they are also facing a growing gap between rich and poor and difficulties in national unification due to their multiethnic populations. With regard to the patent system that was formulated by the economically-advanced countries and made globally dominant or imposed by international treaties, how does it function in BRICS and what issues does it face?

In Chapter 7, India is examined first, a country which has achieved rapid economic development, mainly in the IT industry, since the start of this century. India has operated a patent system for more than a century since it was imposed by the British. According to this chapter, there has always been an attempt in India to balance conflicting goals: economic development, by strengthening patent monopolies, and the realization of the need to allow people access to patented products by attenuating their strength. With regard to technologies that have a significant impact on people's lives, such as pharmaceutical products, computer programs, traditional knowledge, etc., protection by patent has been denied from the beginning, the bar for obtaining patent has been raised, and efforts have been taken to limit the effectiveness of the right. One of the main themes in this chapter relates to how long India will retain treatments that vary by technology field or industrial field under the TRIPS Agreement, which has a "one size fits all" philosophy. The current state of India is a worthy example not only for other BRICS countries, but also for patent-advanced countries that face various kinds of problems.

In Chapter 8 the problems and perspectives of Brazil are discussed. This country had provisions to protect property rights of inventors in its first Constitution (1824) after its foundation and established a patent act very early in 1830. As a patent-advanced country, Brazil, which was one of first allied nations of the Treaty of Paris, had a patent system that remained virtually asleep from the perspective of the protection of domestic industries after World War II. However, since the 1990s, the acknowledgement and use of the patent system have been spreading rapidly in order for the country to become a member of WTO and to import foreign capital. This chapter depicts the Brazilian patent system analytically as it strides to open a new way for bio-technology inventions to obtain patents along with its restrictions on patent monopolies for inventions that relate to public health, such as AIDS medicines, by exercising compulsory licenses. How is the balance found between the development of domestic industries by the introduction of foreign technologies and the protection of public health under the impact of globalization? The approaches in Brazil will serve as a forecast for future patent systems in the world.

Chapter 9 discusses China, whose first patent act was enacted only a quarter of a century ago in 1985. China not only has a short history of operating a patent act when compared with the other countries and regions discussed in this book, but it also has the characteristic of introducing a market economy progressively while maintaining a communist government. Under this government and economic system, the patent right had poor characteristics as private property at first; however, it gained an outline that substantially conforms to the systems of other foreign countries by means of legal amendments in 2001 and 2009 in order for the country to become a member of WTO. However, in actual operation, it is impossible to say that patent rights are sufficiently protected, while industrial development that is led by protection has been seen. Therefore, the Chinese government set the goal of accomplishing the completion of the intellectual property system by 2020 in its Outline of the National Intellectual Property Strategy issued in 2008. The Outline emphasizes an instrumentalism-like idea, which is different from the aforementioned cases in India and Brazil and positions the patent system solely as a means for industrial development. This chapter portrays a major power where the patent system is still under development in terms of the balance between strengthening the execution of patent rights and preventing the abuse of rights and in terms of how it attempts to respond to today's issues, such as Patent Thickets, technical standards, and other concerns.

It has been 20 years since the Institute of Intellectual Property was established based on the model of the Max Planck Institute in Munich. This book was planned in commemoration of the 20th anniversary and the Japanese version was released in 2009. Thanks to the high level of interest in Japan, this English version is also being released. As is always the case with this type of book under joint authorship by international authors, it is particularly difficult to publish without the support of many people. It is my wish to see the international development of the patent system. I would also like to express my deepest gratitude to the authors, the publisher, and to all of the people who supported this project.

PART I

Essence and functions of the patent system

1. Current situation and vision of the patent system: from the perspective of jurisprudence[1]

Ryo Shimanami

TURNING POINT OF THE PATENT SYSTEM

Recently, debate has focused on reform of the patent system. As stated in other chapters in this book, the necessity of patent reform has been advocated in various ways not only in Japan,[2] but also in Europe and America,[3] and in developing countries.[4] These arguments include procedural issues, such as how to ensure effective examination procedures at the Patent Office, the division of roles between a trial for patent invalidation and an infringement lawsuit concerning the validity of a patent right, or issues under substantive law regarding the kind of effect that should be given to a right and to what kind of object or subject it applies. Moreover, the wide variety of problems ranges from specific and practical issues, such as requirements for the exhaustion of rights for a patented product that has been modified, to abstract and fundamental issues that concern the abolishment or reduction of the patent system, questioning why the patent system exists in the first place, or whether the patent system is effective for technological innovation.

The issues that these discussions on patent reform aim to resolve seem disparate at first glance. Therefore, each of the solutions they offer also seems different. However, as explained below, recent judgments and some revisions of the law seem to have common characteristics to the extent that they eliminate some of the traditional characteristics preserved in the patent system. In other words, the "uniformity" of norms, where the specific characteristics of each dispute are ignored and where a wide scope of legal norms is applied generally to many cases without exception, is gradually being eliminated from the patent system. The Patent Act is currently in a process of evolving from rigid regulations that disregard the specific qualities of each case to substantial regulations that make judgments by balancing the interests of each case. If the *uniformity* of regulations is indeed eliminated, and interests are therefore adjusted substantively such that the adjustment applies on a case by case basis, what would be the identity of the "Patent Act" as laws and regulations, or as a topic for academic discourse?

The discussion that has become all the more important for the Patent Act, which is now facing the turning point risking loss of its uniformity is the justification for the existence of the patent system. The more the patent system tends to balance interests substantively for individual cases instead of applying the broad scope of regulations uniformly to various disputes, the more it must seek criteria to balance interests by returning to the basics, that is, the original purposes and reasons for justifying the system, with regard not only to an actor who construes and applies the law after the occurrence of a dispute, but also to an actor who is going to act before the occurrence of a dispute. The Patent Act or patent jurisprudence will not be able to find its identity as an independent law field or present guidelines for the resolution of new phenomena or guiding principles if one is oblivious to such basics; it will eventually lose its coherence and become merely a compilation of laws and regulations lacking any uniformity.

Meanwhile, as we shall see below, with regard to the justification for the existence of the patent system, or in other words, as a logic for developing industries through incentives for inventions, there has been a recent turbulence in both theory and practice. The Japanese Government sets aside an enormous budget for science and technology, more than ¥3,500 billion every year, including a budget of approximately ¥1,500 billion for basic research intended for universities, etc.[5] Apart from the incentives for research and development, is there any reason for the government to establish a patent system that contains various social costs?[6] Moreover, does an individual doing research and development, regardless of whether he or she is an academic or an employee of a company, ever create an invention out of economic incentives, or only with non-economic motivations, such as social recognition or for the sake of scientific inquiry? While there is skepticism over these reasons for justifying the patent system, the happy period when the logic for developing an industry through incentives for invention was believed at face value is now becoming history.

In this chapter, I will review the turning point that the current patent system is facing and the future we can foresee beyond it from the perspective of jurisprudence, as preparation for describing the specific vision of the Patent Act. Specifically, based on recent major judgments by the Supreme Court, the phenomenon of the dissolution of the patent system (the loss of uniformity) will be reviewed first. Then, the skepticism concerning the reasons justifying the patent system that underlie these phenomena will be reviewed. Finally, I will provide one perspective on how far the patent system should be dissolved, which will serve as an introduction to the following chapters.

DISSOLUTION OF THE PATENT SYSTEM

Tradition of Uniformity

The patent system was basically established as a system with a high level of uniformity. The modern statutes of the patent law were developed at the end of the 18th century in a form that is almost the same as the current Patent Act in the United States, which accepted a broad range of general inventions as subjects of protection regardless of the technical field. Basically, the modern statutes of the patent law also did not distinguish the procedures for obtaining and the effect of patent rights by technical field. This "uniformity" in the original sense of treating various technical fields without distinction is now required internationally by a provision in the first sentence of Article 27, paragraph (1) of the TRIPS agreement.[7] In Japan, from the perspective of the protection and fostering of domestic industries, there were provisions that prohibited the grant of a patent to a technology in industrial fields that were undeveloped as compared to foreign countries in order to avoid technical monopolies by foreign companies.[8] These provisions have now been abolished[9] and there are no specific provisions for specific technical fields with respect to the effect of existing patent rights.[10]

The patent system is uniform in the sense that specific differences between technical fields are eliminated and various technologies are treated equally. This phenomenon is also found in disputes. In other words, although actual disputes concerning patent right infringements vary widely in terms of the degree of subjective malignancy or the interests of the infringer or, on the other hand, in terms of the degree of fault or damage to the rights holder, a public position has been maintained that the concrete conditions of interest does not affect the judgment as to whether an infringement exists or not. Under this public position, a system was adopted for assessing whether or not an infringement of a patent right exists (or whether or not an injunction should be granted) based only on two simple requirements of object and conduct, that is, basically, whether a "patented invention" has been claimed was "worked" without permission, without balancing the specific interests of the parties (see main clause of Article 68). Of course, with respect to the calculation of damages after a patent right infringement is legally determined, the conclusion depends on the individual circumstances, such as the existence of damage to the rights holder or the subjective position of the infringer (intent or negligence), according to principles of the Civil Code. The Patent Act attempts to eliminate a variety of these disputes by establishing special provisions, such as deeming or presumptive damages (Article 102) or presumptive faults (Article 103), etc.[11] This situation is considered to reflect the uniformity of the patent system in the sense that disputes, which are originally varied, are firstly abstracted to the level of assessing whether or not a "patented invention" is "worked," and then all of the common disputes at the abstracted level are handled equally.

These characteristics of the uniformity of the patent system that disregards the technical fields and disputes are considered to be established in analogy with the property system. In other words, under the property system, whether or not an infringement has occurred is judged without distinguishing the object of the right, regardless of whether it is a watch or land (uniformity that surpasses the object of a right) and is judged regardless of the existence of actual damage to the rights holder or the subjective position of the infringer. It is judged based only on two simple requirements concerning the object and conduct, such as, for instance, whether or not an object "entered" into "land" without permission (uniformity that surpasses the disputes). The patent system likens an invention that is intangible to a tangible substance, establishes proprietary rights in the invention, maintains uniformity much like the property system, and enhances the stability (or predictability) of the system operation.

Loss of Uniformity

Meanwhile, in recent years, it has been found in many countries that juridical precedents concerning the Patent Act tend to deny the above-mentioned uniformity of the patent system.

The best example is the judgment of the Supreme Court of the United States in *eBay Inc v. MercExchange, L.L.C.*[12] This judgment attracted a great deal of attention because it restricted the right to request an injunction based on an infringement of the patent right and, as a result, prevented execution of the patent right by the patent troll. From the perspective of this chapter this judgment is remarkable as a case in which the uniformity of the patent system that surpasses the disputes was clearly denied. According to this judgment, even if an infringement of a patent right is legally determined, relief by injunction shall follow the principle of equity and shall be permitted only after meeting certain requirements,[13] such as if the patent right holder suffers irrecoverable damage, etc. The judgment denies the traditional practice in which a demand for an injunction is automatically granted if an infringement of a right alone exists (in other words, the traditional practice with high uniformity that surpasses the disputes) and it approves an injunction only in cases where the injunction can be justified, taking into consideration conditions specific to the individual dispute, such as the interests of the parties or the influence on public interests, etc. It is nothing but a movement of individualization eliminating the uniformity of the patent system that surpasses the disputes, in terms of judging the existence of relief from an infringement of the patent right by balancing the substantive interests of the parties to the dispute (or those of the society that underlies the parties).[14]

In Japan, there is no judicial precedent that has approved general restrictions on the demand for injunction as stated above.[15] The only hint can be found in the argument for legislation concerning the type of right that is taken to remedy at law only through the request for indemnity of the infringement.[16] However, in cases where it is reviewed from the perspective of the loss of the uniformity of the patent system, the same movements are found in various and important issues in the recent judgments of the Supreme Court of Japan as stated below.

Infringement under the doctrine of equivalents

A year after the judgment of the Supreme Court of the United States in *Warner-Jenkinson Company, Inc. v. Hilton Davis Chemical Co.*,[17] the judgment of the Supreme Court of Japan in the *Ball Spline Bearing* case[18] directly approved the theory of infringement under the doctrine of equivalents concerning patent rights. This theory considers, with regard to technology that the patent right does not formally affect (or which is not included in the claim), that the patent right will have a substantive effect (or will consider said technology to be included in the technical scope of a patented invention) in order to protect a rights holder from unexpected technological progress after the patent application is filed.

Among the five requirements[19] for legally determining infringement under the doctrine of equivalents that were established by the Supreme Court in the *Ball Spline Bearing* judgment, the nonessential portion (first requirement), substitutability (second requirement), and being easily arrived at (third requirement) concern specific conditions (malignancy) of an infringer when manufacturing the subject products; on the other hand, requirements that the subject products shall not be able to be estimated easily (fourth requirement) and that there shall not be any special circumstances, such as when the subject product was excluded intentionally (fifth requirement), concern the specific condition (degree of fault) of a rights holder at the filing of the patent application. These concrete conditions were not considered in the judgment, at least under the provisions of the Patent Act, with respect to basic literal infringement whether it is the degree of malignancy of an infringer or the degree of fault of a rights holder. If the physical scope of protection of a patent right is substantively expanded after consideration of those conditions, it will cause considerable damage to the fundamental uniformity of the Patent Act, in other words, the characteristics of the Patent Act to see only whether a "patented invention" that has been actually claimed is "worked" when assessing an infringement claim and to eliminate variations concerning other elements by each case.[20]

These changes in the Patent Act, which are a loss of uniformity caused by the introduction of the theory of infringement under the doctrine of equivalents, focus from an ex post perspective on the concrete appropriateness of resolution of a dispute. In relation to legal stability (predictability) from an ex ante perspective, it is impossible to allow such changes without limitations. Therefore, the problem becomes where the limit on the specific conditions that should be considered shall be placed. Especially with regard to the fifth requirement, which is an open-type requirement considering specific conditions, limit setting becomes a particular problem. As the other four requirements are also full of normative judgments[21] there is concern that the legal stability may decrease excessively depending on the selection of facts that provides basis for evaluation and that support each requirement.

Limit of the exhaustion of rights

In its judgment in the *Canon Ink Cartridge* Case, the Supreme Court of Japan gave its first judgment on the limit of the exhaustion of patent rights concerning a patented product that has been modified and for which the components have been replaced.[22] This judgment first stated as follows:

> If the patent holder, or the licensee who was licensed by the patent holder (hereinafter, "patent holder etc."), assigned the patented product in Japan, the patent regarding this patented product is exhausted since it has achieved its purpose and thus, the effect of the patent does not extend to the use, assignment etc. . . . of the patented product and therefore, the patent holder is not entitled to exercise the patent in relation to this patented product.

The court adopted the exhaustion of the patent right (in Japan) for the first time as grounds of the judgment.[23] Moreover, the court also stated:

> the objects to which the exercise of the patent right is restricted because of its exhaustion, should be the patented products themselves that the patent holder, etc. had assigned in Japan. If the patented product, assigned in Japan by the patent holder, etc., has been modified or its components replaced, and as a

> result, it can be regarded as a novel production of the patented product which is not identical to the first patented product, the patent holder is entitled to exercise the patent right over this patented product.[24]

With respect to the limit of the exhaustion of the right concerning patented products that have been modified or in which components have been replaced, this judgment intentionally did not adopt the strict two-type theory[25] that was presented in the first instance.[26] The court judged according to normative requirements as to whether the modification, etc. of the patented products could be regarded as a "novel production." In other words, this judgment defined not a rule but a standard when establishing criteria for judgment of patent right infringement. This is the most significant characteristic of the judgment.[27] When looking from the perspective of the problems focused on in this chapter, since it considered specific conditions comprehensively and thereby adjusted for individual interests that are unique to each dispute when establishing exceptions to exhaustion of the right, it appears to eliminate the uniformity of the patent system from two sides: by establishing exceptions, and individualizing the judgment. In the future, the method for balancing various facts that provide the basis for evaluations with respect to the kind of modification or replacement of components in the patented products that will be recognized as a "novel product" will become gradually more sophisticated with the accumulation of specific cases; however, it will be difficult to expect the same kind of legal stability as before.

Defense of invalidation

In Japan, the judgment of the Supreme Court in the *Kilby Patent Case*[28] allowed the submission of a defense of an abuse of rights which is made against enforcement of the patent right that involves grounds for invalidation.[29] In response to this judgment, the defense of invalidation was established in statutory form under the Patent Act (Article 104-3). Thus, when "a patent is recognized as one that should be invalidated by a trial for patent invalidation" in a litigation, an alleged infringer was found to be relieved of the responsibility for infringement of the patent right without going through the procedures of a trial for invalidation at the Patent Office.

Meanwhile, the decision by the Patent Office as to whether to grant a patent or to make a decision for invalidation is absolutely effective and, therefore, the patent right can be *erga omnes* right. However, under the circumstances today, where a defense of invalidation is permitted in an infringement lawsuit, it is institutionally approved that an evaluation of patent rights (or judgment of validity) can differ between the procedures (for invalidation or correction) used by the Patent Office and an infringement lawsuit. In addition, this situation generated the possibility that various judgments will be given depending on the quality of the claims or proof by an alleged infringer concerning the grounds for invalidation[30] or the purpose for the advancement of the allegations and the evidence for them,[31] such as, for example, that one patent right is valid in relation to company A, but is denied in relation to company B. This means that a conclusion concerning the existence of patent right infringement varies in response to the characteristics of the dispute. The uniformity of the patent system is thereby, to a certain extent, eliminated, where the same right or the same act of working leads to the same conclusion.[32]

Applications for new drug approval and the working patented inventions for experiment and research

With regard to Article 69, paragraph (1) which stipulates that the effect of a patent right shall not extend to the working of the patented invention for experimental or research purposes, the appropriateness of its effectiveness has been judged by whether the working of the patented invention is for the purpose of further technical improvement by additional experimentation or is solely for profit.[33] However, the judgment of the Supreme Court[34] deemed the following case to be the working of a patented invention "for experimental or research purposes": producing chemical substances or drugs that are in the technical scope of the patented invention during the patent right term, and implementing experiments necessary for obtaining references to be attached to an application for approval of manufacturing by using said chemical substances or drugs, in order to file an application for manufacturing approval pursuant to Article 14 of the Pharmaceutical Affairs Act, for the purpose of manufacturing and selling generic drugs after the end of the patent right term that have the same effective ingredients, etc. as drugs pertaining to the patented invention. The court judged that the working of a patented invention for an application for manufacturing approval of drugs is lawful pursuant to Article 14 although it is usually unavailable for the development of future technology, although its purpose is more for profit after obtaining manufacturing approval.

This judgment first established a limit that is the working of a patented invention for an application for approval of drug manufacturing and then deemed any work within the limit to be equally lawful. Therefore, the judgment seems to be highly conventional and uniform within that limit. However, the grounds for the judgment were not the intention of the system as provided for in Article 69, paragraph (1) of the Patent Act. The judgment held that the substantive extension of the protection period (for the period necessary for an application for approval of drug manufacturing) should not be permitted according to "the basis of the patent system" (quoted from the judgment) whereby a patent right is a right with a restriction on its term. Therefore, the interpretation of Article 69, paragraph (1) became less clear. In other words, the conclusions of the judgment did not derive from a particular criterion, whether the purpose of the work is technical improvement or profit, as inherent in Article 69, paragraph (1), but were derived from the principle of "the basis of the patent system" which exists outside that provision. Therefore, when applying an interpretation of a specific provision, it is necessary to evaluate individually whether the working violates the general principle of the patent system, which is beyond the specific provision having regard to many specific conditions. Since individual provisions are part of the patent system as a whole, the standpoint of the Supreme Court seems understandable. However, individual provisions have already included the general principle of the Patent Act and concretized it. Therefore, that judgment holds a construction that prevents the uniform operation of the Patent Act in a way that surpasses the characteristics of each case when compared with the conventional understanding that it is only necessary to interpret and enact each provision faithfully based on the intention of the system as provided for by each provision (for instance, in the case of Article 69, paragraph (1), it is only necessary to judge the appropriateness of the application by focusing solely on the purpose of the working in terms of whether it is for technical improvement or for profit).

Request for a misappropriated patent holder to return the patent right

The Patent Act in Japan does not stipulate a right to request the return of a patent right as a relief against a misappropriated application.[35] Before the misappropriated application is registered as a patent, the true rights holder can take measures to amend the name of the applicant[36] only after winning a lawsuit to confirm that the right to obtain the patent belongs to the true rights holder.[37] However, once the patent is registered due to an incorrect examination involving the confirmation of the right to obtain the patent, the return of a patent right that has been approved has traditionally been refused. Of course, the true rights holder can invalidate a patent right held by a misappropriated patent holder by means of a trial for patent invalidation (Article 123) and can claim damages from the misappropriating person based on a torts claim (Article 709 of the Civil Code). Meanwhile, the true rights holder can no longer obtain a patent even if he/she files a new application, due to lack of novelty (Article 29, paragraph (1), item (iii)).[38] Therefore, the conditions were insufficient for the relief of the true rights holder.

However, a recent Supreme Court ruling upheld the request of a true rights holder that a holder of misappropriated patent rights return the patent right for reason of the unjust enrichment gained by the infringer in its judgment in the *Garbage Disposer Case*.[39] Since multiple specific conditions were listed as grounds for approving the request to return the patent right,[40] this judgment still leaves unsolved questions concerning its scope.[41] In any case, as far as adopting the reasoning of unjust enrichment gained by the infringer, the circumstances of the true rights holder and those of the holder of the misappropriated patent rights will be compared and balanced comprehensively from an equitable perspective.[42] In this way, the uniformity of the patent system that surpasses the disputes was eliminated and relief was determined by the circumstances inherent to each case, such as whether the true rights holder voluntarily filed an application or not.[43]

Invention by employees

A series of revisions of laws and lawsuits concerning inventions by employees was among the recent moves related to the Patent Act that had the most impact on business activities. Although not a direct consequence of the judgment of the Supreme Court, the revision of Article 35 of the Patent Act was implemented based on the desire of the business community that had felt the pinch from the judgment of the Supreme Court in the *Olympus case*.[44] In this revision, when calculating a reasonable value to be paid to an employee by an employer who succeeds to rights pertaining to an invention by an employee (Article 35, paragraph (3)), procedures in cases where stipulations are provided in advance in the company (paragraph (4)) or the costs from the invention paid by the employees (paragraph (5)) were also taken into consideration. The revision follows in the direction of valuing the characteristics of each dispute because the circumstances to be considered in the calculation of a reasonable value increased after the revision. Therefore, the revision can be included as part of the movement to eliminate the uniformity of the Patent Act.

Moreover, according to the judgment of the Supreme Court in the *Hitachi, Ltd.* case,[45] this method of calculating reasonable individual value applies not only to patent rights in Japan, but also to patent rights overseas, if there is an agreement (express or implied) concerning the application of Japanese law.[46] If so, compared with English law, under which a request by an employee who is an inventor for his/her employer or company to pay the value of an invention is usually not approved, American law, under which such a request is not approved without prior agreement, or German law, under which the approved request amount is stipulated in detail as a prior rule, with regard to disputes over the value of an invention between employers and employees in Japanese companies at least, this judgment permitted a broad application of Japanese law and considerably extended the scope of subject patent rights for which circumstances inherent to the disputes should be reviewed in detail and various circumstances should be balanced comprehensively. The judgment also raised the amount to be paid for the value of an invention.

Summary

As stated above, we have found that all of the prominent judicial precedents of the Supreme Court in recent years concerning the Patent Act and legislation related thereto have been decided in the direction of individualization in which the uniformity of the patent system is eliminated. This trend can be seen both in cases where the rights of patent rights holder are strengthened in a lawsuit over patent right infringement ((1) infringement under the doctrine of equivalents and (2) limit of the exhaustion of rights) and where the right is weakened by a lawsuit ((3) defense of invalidation and (4) working of patented inventions for experiment and research). It is also observed widely in cases of adjusting the interests of various subjects other than in infringement lawsuits ((5) a true rights holder and a holder of misappropriated patent rights and (6) an employee and an employer). As reviewed above, the loss of the uniformity originally found in the patent system is a phenomenon now underlying the entire Patent Act. On the other hand, these moves to facilitate a close correspondence in individual disputes will generate the risk of harming the predictability of parties and, at the same time, raise a fundamental issue over interpretations that support the balancing of individual interests or guidelines for legislation. The question is, put simply, why does the patent right exist?

RECONSIDERATION OF THE GROUNDS FOR JUSTIFICATION

Background

Although the uniformity of the Patent Act has been lost and the ad hoc balancing of interests is implemented in response to various disputes, a conclusion cannot be reached without establishing criteria or in an impromptu manner when selecting the factors to be balanced and when adding weight to each of those selected factors. When balancing interests, we must return ultimately to the reasons for the justification or the intention behind of the system, in other words, why each system and, eventually, the entire Patent Act, exists. Besides the fact that there has been more interest in the basic theory of the Patent Act in recent years, it is considered that there is a dissolution phenomenon (or a loss of uniformity) of the Patent Act, as we reviewed above.

Current theories concerning the reasons justifying the Patent Act are divided roughly into two categories: natural rights theory or incentive theory that facilitates justification from the origin of patent rights protection; and utilitarianism that argues based on the consequences of patent rights protection. An outline of each of these two categories will be reviewed next, and we will then examine the criticism leveled at them and the future direction of patent jurisprudence.

Justification from the Origin

The classic method of justification for the granting of patent rights is a justification from its origin based on ideas, such as fairness or justice. This method includes a natural rights theory and an incentive theory as seen below.

First, the justification of granting a patent right from the perspective of the natural rights theory is as follows: all individuals equally have exclusive control over an invention that is a result of work originated by the exercise of his/her brain as an extension of his/her exclusive control by nature over his/her own body, life, and freedom, which is, in turn, an extension of "self-ownership." Just as a person should have ownership of the result of work done by using his/her own body – for instance, a reclaimant should have the property rights to the harvest for which the reclaimant cultivated wasted land – a person who finds a new technology through research and development should have a patent right to the result. The above-mentioned natural rights theory is supported by two negative reasons: no one can reasonably claim a right to the invention other than the inventor; and since the invention is novel, if exclusiveness is granted to the invention, it does not harm others who did not have the technology. On the other hand, it is difficult to find better reasons that proactively justify that exclusive control over the invention "should" be permitted than the fiction that the invention is the extension of the body. Moreover, questions arise from these two negative reasons. First, with regard to the first reason, there are few instances where an invention is based entirely on the inventor's own creativity as it will more or less be dependent on the contributions of predecessors. Considering these cumulative characteristics[47] of inventions, there is some doubt over the appropriateness of considering an inventor as the only person who can reasonably claim a right to an invention. A question also arises from the perspective of economic equality with regard to the second reason. Suppose that no matter how excellent a technology is, someone is bound to achieve it someday. If the person who first invented it (or filed an application for it) is the only person who can dominate the invention, while this does not mean that an inventor will directly take something away from someone at the time when the patent right is granted, it will relatively degrade the future position (or possibility) of other persons. In addition, it is difficult for the natural rights theory as an extension of self-ownership to lead to a principle of restriction, at least from the theory itself. Instead, it is easier to understand as a lasting and absolute right like the right to a human body. Therefore, it has the drawback that no criteria for balancing come when balancing the individual interests as required for resolution of a dispute. The affirmation at the level that "the inventor shall be protected as a natural right to such an extent" cannot be persuasive in itself.

Next, the justification based on the incentive theory holds that since an inventor who brought a useful invention to society by enduring certain burdens to the inventor (such as work or investment) obviously deserves reward for the invention, it is in the interests of justice that the society reward the inventor by granting him/her a patent right. Unlike the natural rights theory, this theory has two possibilities for establishing a denotation of a patent right and providing guidelines for balancing individual interests. One of the possibilities is to establish a patent right as a reward to the extent appropriate for the "burden (work or investment)" that an inventor provided. The other is to establish a patent right as a reward to the extent appropriate for the "contribution" that an invention provides to society. However, the first possibility does not conform to the fundamental structure of the current law under which a patent right is granted regardless of the degree of work or investment into research and development preceding the invention; for instance, a patent right can be provided to an incidental invention. On the other hand, if the same result is generated, it is better that the burden required to obtain the same result is small. There is a doubt over the assumption that it is the burden, not the result that should be deserving of reward (without adopting the theory of invention incentives which is the justification based on consequence, as we will see later). Moreover, even if an inventor performs an activity that carries with it a burden, such as research and development, in cases where such performance is a means for self-actualization, such as an inquiry into knowledge of science and technology, it is not normal at least that this activity deserves reward from the society (in particular, if the reward is not a mental reward, such as approbation, but a proprietary reward like the patent right).

Based on the reasons stated above, the only remaining theory feasible for justification from the origin with respect to a patent right is considered to be a "reward for contribution." The conclusion that society should repay contributions to society and that the content of the reward should correspond to the contribution has an effect on our legal consciousness. Backed by this incentive theory, the current Patent Act defines a condition to patent registration as the measurement of the degree of contribution to society by the standard of non-obviousness of the invention, and scales the scope of protection afforded to the patent right in its operation depending on the degree of non-obviousness. As a result of seeking a way for patent rights that is suitable to contributions, one study[48] recommends that a defense of independent inventions should be allowed for suspected infringers, etc. The balancing of contribution and reward as seen in the study is a leading perspective for identifying patent jurisprudence, in which dissolution of uniformity in favor of a balancing of individual interests is advancing, again from a unified perspective.

Justification Based on Consequences (Utilitarianism)

The justification from the origin as seen above states that, for either the natural rights theory or the incentive theory, an inventor "should" have a right from the perspective of fairness or justice regardless of the consequences that granting of a patent right brings to society. On the other hand, the justification based on utilitarianism, as stated below, focuses on the advantages brought by the patent system to society as a result of the invention. This theory constructs the patent system as a means or a tool for realizing an ideal society. In such cases, the conditions for an ideal society are the promotion of inventions and the development of industry (or economic growth) as a result of the promotion.

I have already mentioned that the uniformity of the patent system is analogous to the ownership system. With regard to the reason why the patent system was established, utilitarianism uses the reasons of the ownership system. Just as setting the ownership of a tangible object becomes an incentive for investments, improvements, and transactions with that object,[49] if a patent right, which is a property right, is granted to invention information, it will promote the creation, improvement, and utilization of inventions.[50] Precisely because the grant of a property right brings with it exclusivity not only in relation to the other party of the contract, but also in relation to all other people, this can lead to an appropriate amount of investment into research and development and their improvement, the effects of which are packaged in a manner efficient for the transfer and licensing of patent rights.

Moreover, there is a belief that when the individual research and development and the effects from the promotion of using the information are accumulated, the whole country can benefit from the advantages, such as in the development of industry (in the form of economic growth).

This belief is another reason why the patent system exists based on the framework of ownership. The conclusion of the Cold War between East and West in the beginning of 1990s was, from an economic perspective, a victory for free transactions in markets and a victory for the private property system that supported these transactions. Later, this trend spread not only into domestic economic systems, but also into international transactions. In 1995, the WTO Regime was established for the liberalization of trade. The TRIPS system was created as part of this trend. The reason why the TRIPS system adhered to the transplanting of the intellectual property rights law system into developing countries is that the capitalist countries were confident that establishing information as private property (as well as the establishment of a private ownership system) would facilitate economic growth in each country.

This justification based on the consequences, which paints the Patent Act as a means to realize an ideal society has, however, recently become the object of various criticisms. The first is a historical theory that considers what inspired the creation of a certain invention. According to this theory, the only invention that is considered to come from the patent right among other prominent inventions created during the industrial revolution in England is the steam engine invented by Watt who was keen to obtain and extend patent rights. From a technical perspective, Watt's invention does not occupy an important place in the development of internal combustion engines.[51] Moreover, among the three inventions within the greatest and most innovative fields of invention after the World War I – nuclear fusion technology, biotechnology, and the internet – nuclear technology was the result of national research institutions and the other two technologies were the fruits of research and development in universities. There is, for instance, a study[52] which shows that the patent system does not have any better effect on cultivating research than equipment that is in a "university." This study has the following disadvantages, which are inherent to historical study: there is the risk that the inventions subject to the analysis are selected to favor those proponents who deny the effectiveness of patent rights; and even if there are examples where patent rights were not effective, it does not necessarily logically lead to the conclusion that the patent system is meaningless. However, historical study has the power to appeal to our instincts because it does provide examples.

The second criticism observes changes in business behaviors between the periods before and after a system change in a particular country. For example, one study[53] investigated the changes in companies' investments into research and development as a result of the enforcement of the Patent Act revision of 1987 in Japan. This revision strengthened the protection of patent rights by introducing a revised multiple claims system. However, no significant change was observed. Another study[54] verified the effects of measures taken to strengthen drug patents in Italy that were introduced in 1978. It also concluded that there were no apparent changes in investment into research and development by pharmaceutical companies. Moreover, another experimental study[55] concluded that companies that acquired many software patents after the number of software patents increased in the United States had decreased their investment into research and development by a greater proportion than their investment into sales, meaning that the patent rights acted as anti-incentives to investment into research and development. These studies are not persuasive in their evaluation of the absolute effectiveness of the patent system. However, they do illustrate, at least, that enhancing the protection of patent rights more than the current level does not stimulate companies' research and development, and as such, there is no reason to change the system by increasing the social costs required by exclusive possession.

The third is a theory that compares multiple countries. This is a study which, by using statistical procedures such as regression analysis, investigates which element most affected economic growth in each country. According to the study, the establishment of the ownership system correlated positively with economic growth as well as with a liberal economic system, political stability, enhancement of education systems, etc., but these results could not be found with respect to the intellectual property system, including the Patent Act.[56] If the degree of development of the intellectual property system or strength of the intellectual property system in a country does not greatly affect the economic development of the country, the correlation between the intellectual system and economic development that is generally observed today could be just a result of lobbying activities by major companies that are enthusiastic to maximize their own profits in rich and developed countries.[57] Such a study will provide an effective viewpoint on which system should be provided the limited social resources for its development as a trade-off. (For example, it may be more effective to direct the resources towards the development of education system rather than on the enhancement of the intellectual property system.)

If the Patent Act does not play such a large role in the promotion of inventions and the development of industries, as these studies show, it means they are not successful in providing a justification based on consequences. Patent jurisprudence in the future must promote accurate experimental studies based on these studies and develop "consequences" other than the promotion of inventions and the development of industries with an open mind without ignoring the possibilities that can be accomplished by means of the patent system.

VISION BEYOND THE TURNING POINT: HOW FAR DOES THE DISSOLUTION GO?

If it is necessary for the patent system to lose its original uniformity and to be dissolved into an individual comparison and balancing exercise, one of the roles required of patent jurisprudence is to seek a convenient "scale" for comparison and balancing and to provide it to practical business. This activity conforms to a traditional method of jurisprudence (case study) that compares judicial precedents and establishes their correlations.

However, there are also new issues for patent jurisprudence not only in relation to short-term contribution to business practices, but also studies at a meta-level: why was this dissolution phenomenon generated? What function does the phenomenon perform? And what is the extent of the phenomenon (in other words, how far should the uniformity of the patent system be maintained)? Not all of them can be examined in this chapter, so in closing, I would like to provide a view on the function that the dissolution phenomenon of the patent system should perform among those new issues as well as the limit of the dissolution.

The fact that the patent system is advancing in the direction of solving disputes by comprehensively considering various circumstances, such as the responsibilities or malignancies of the parties, in addition to the convenient indices of the object of rights (patented invention) and infringement (working), means that there are changes in the forum (stage) and timing for establishing the rules necessary for dispute settlement.

According to the public position of current law in which an invention is defined, the requirements to provide a patent for an invention are clearly specified, and a catalog of the types of working is limited and listed; the political sector will establish rules and the timing of the establishment should be prior to the act of the parties to disputes (before reaching the result). Meanwhile, according to modern phenomenon in which a dispute is settled by taking into account various circumstances inherent to each case, the forum which establishes rules through a comprehensive balancing of various facts is the judiciary and the timing of the establishment should be after the act of the parties to disputes (after reaching the result).

While the predictability of parties will increase if the Diet establishes rules in advance, the concrete appropriateness of dispute settlement will increase if the courts establish rules that correspond to each case ex post facto. As seen above, the forum and timing for the establishment of rules can vary. Therefore, the trade-off situation arises between "predictability (or legal stability) by uniform rules" and "concrete appropriateness by individual rules." In other words, how far the dissolution of the Patent Act should proceed (or under which conditions uniform rules or individual rules should be selected) depends on the standard that is selected concerning the forum and the timing for the establishment of rules.

The judgment as to which forum should be used for the establishment of rules, the Diet or the courts, will be affected by the decision whether democratic control by majority vote should be extended to the establishment of rules. In cases where it is necessary to protect the interests of minorities, or of majorities that are difficult to consolidate, it is preferable to establish rules in the courts where the principle of majority rule cannot reach. If the Patent Act is a law exclusively for business and there are few requests to protect minorities, etc., the recent trend where rules are established boldly by only five justices of the Supreme Court without going through the democratic process still brings discomfort even when considering, for instance, the delinquency of the political sector (legislation and government) that assumes the role of creating and integrating the will of the people. Furthermore, if we emphasize the utilitarianism that says that the Patent Act exists to realize industrial policies including the promotion of inventions, etc. and that the patent right is a means that the government established exceptionally for the realization of such policies, it would be fundamental that the will of the political sector should be reflected strongly with respect to the content of the industrial policies and the means of their realization, which should be respected by the judiciary.

On the other hand, with regard to the judgment on whether the timing of the establishment of rules is before or after the act of the parties, the frequency of application of the rules will affect them. Rules with a high frequency of application can better reduce social costs than establishing individual rules for each dispute, if the content of these rules is established in advance. On the contrary, if rules with low frequency of application are established in advance on the assumption that disputes rarely occur, it increases the cost of collecting information. With regard to the high frequency type of dispute, from a social perspective, such as the limit of the exhaustion of modified products or the appropriateness of parallel imports, the political sector should start legislative activity proactively at the time when a certain amount of disputes have accumulated at the level of the lower courts. In addition, with regard to the value of succession to an employee's invention, a legislative response has been made in recent years. However, the normative requirement for "reasonable" value, which has many of the characteristics of a general clause, still remains a very heavy burden for the court.[58]

As we have seen, from both the perspectives of the forum and the timing for the establishment of rules, as a whole, there is an impression that the recent trend of decline in the uniformity of the patent system has been excessive. Will the future of the patent system remain on course for dissolution and continue to move in a direction where the court establishes detailed and complicated rules for each case? Following that course for the patent system will force us to make a conscious choice to accept the social inefficiency of the decreasing predictability of parties while increasing the burden on the courts.

NOTES

1. This chapter reflects the discussions of the "Investigation and Research Committee for an Ideal New Patent System" (February 2008 to March 2009) at the Institute of Intellectual Property, in which the author participated. The ultimate responsibility for this article lies with the author. In writing this chapter in 2009, the author obtained aid for scientific research from the Ministry of Education, Culture, Sports, Science and Technology (No. 21730105).
2. See Chapter 6 of this book.
3. See Chapter 4 regarding Europe and Chapter 5 regarding the United States.
4. See Chapter 7 regarding India, Chapter 8 regarding Brazil, and Chapter 9 regarding China.
5. In the 2009 national budget of Japan, the budget for science and technology was ¥3,554.8 billion, including ¥1,476.9 billion for fundamental expenses for universities, etc. and basic research expenses, such as aid for scientific research, etc.; ¥1,686.9 billion for policy issue model research and development expenses (budget for eight key promoted fields), and ¥391 billion for system reform related to government-industry-academia collaborations, etc.
6. With regard to the social costs inherent to the patent system that are not included in the budget for science and technology, there are monopoly costs, which prevent general public from the free working of inventions, the costs of setting up the Patent Office, etc.
7. As an exception to uniformity, Article 27, paragraph (3) of the TRIPS agreement allows member states to exclude the following two kinds of technologies from patentability: (a) diagnostic, therapeutic and surgical methods for the treatment of humans or animals; and (b) plants and animals other than micro-organisms, and essentially biological processes for the production of plants or animals other than non-biological and microbiological processes.
8. The following substances were excluded from patentability as unpatentable inventions: three items have been unpatentable since the former Patent Act (enactment in 1921): food and drinks or sweets and luxury items, medicines or mixtures, and chemical substances. Nuclear transformation substances are unpatentable under Article 32 of the current Patent Act (1959).
9. Provisions specific to these technology fields were deleted from Article 32 of the Patent Act by the revisions in 1975 and 1994; provided, however that the Patent Office still does not permit a patent registration today with regard to any of the following technologies, which are permitted exclusion from patentability under Article 27, paragraph (3) of the TRIPS agreement for the following reasons: (a) treatment of humans because it has no industrial applicability (Article 29, introductory clause) and (b) parts of biological related inventions because granting patents to them violates public order and morality (Article 32).
10. Although it is not a subject of stipulation for a specific technology field alone, there is a system to extend the duration of patent rights (Article 67, paragraph (2) and thereafter of the Patent Act) as a system under the Patent Act, which is presumed in fact to apply solely to inventions concerning medicines and agricultural chemicals.

11. The provision for attributing damage (Article 102, paragraph (1)) is interpreted so that it does not judge an occurrence of damage itself, but the amount of damage that has occurred. Since the occurrence of a certain effect is deemed in a uniform way under the given requirement, the provision eliminates variety for each case concerning the amount of actual damages. Moreover, presuming faults (Article 103) is only a presumption of a fact under the provision, but is applied as a provision for assessing negligence. Therefore, it eliminates individual circumstances for each infringer and handles them in a uniform way.
12. *eBay Inc v. MercExchange, L.L.C.*, 547 U.S. 388 (2006).
13. This judgment followed the traditional four-factor test applied by courts of equity and held that a request for injunction shall be allowed only when a plaintiff demonstrates: (1) that he/she has suffered an irreparable injury; (2) that remedies available by law are inadequate to compensate for that injury; (3) that considering the balance of hardships between plaintiff and defendant, a remedy in equity is warranted; and (4) that the public interest would not be disserved by a permanent injunction. This four-factor test is a requirement under common law that is not stipulated in the Patent Act.
14. Moreover, in the United States, there are theories that proactively argue for constructing sub-rules for each technology or industrial field. For instance, Merges and Nelson focus on how the manner and speed of technological advances are different by the following four types: the individual invention field, cumulative invention field, chemical invention field, and academic invention field. And then they advocate establishing the scope of protection of patent rights in accordance with a doctrine that is different for each field (Robert Merges & Richard Nelson, "On the Complex Economics of Patent Scope," 90 *Col. L. Rev.* (1990), p. 839). Moreover, Burk and Lemley state that the following theories, among five typical and existing theories concerning the ideal effects of patent rights and the reasons for their justification, should apply their respective fields: the prospect theory should apply to the pharmaceutical industry; the competitive innovation theory to business methods; the cumulative innovation theory to the software industry; the anticommons theory to biotechnology; and the patent thicket theory to the semi-conductor industry (Dan Burk & Mark Lemley, "Policy Levers in Patent Law," 89 *Vir. L. Rev.* 1575 (2003). For a Japanese translation, Noboru Yamasaki trans. "Tokkyohou ni okeru seisaku rebaa (1) and (2)," *Intellectual Property Law and Policy Journal* Vol. 14 and 15 (2007)). These arguments have also drawn the attention of researchers who are interested in basic theories in Japan (as an example of one of the most ambitious reviews, see Yoshiyuki Tamura, "Patent Protection of Biotechnology in the Information Age (1), (2) and (3)," *Intellectual Property Law and Policy Journal* Vol. 10, 11, and 12 (2006)). From the perspective of this chapter, they are noteworthy in terms of the movement of individualization that eliminates the uniformity of the patent system that surpasses technologies and industries; however, they are not reviewed due to the limited length of this chapter.
15. See note 28 below and the main text corresponding to the note, with regard to the judgment of the Supreme Court in the *Kilby's Patent* Case.
16. For instance, this issue was set as the first agenda of the "Patent System Study Group," which is a private study group of the Commissioner of the Japan Patent Office and was established under the Patent Office in order to return to the starting point of the ideal way for the patent system and to review it comprehensively at the 50th anniversary of the enactment and promulgation of the current Patent Act. A summary of the second meeting of the Patent System Study Group of the Patent Office can be found at (Japanese only): http://www.jpo.go.jp/shiryou/toushin/kenkyukai/tokkyoseidokenkyu02_giji.htm (last accessed July 6, 2012).
17. *Warner-Jenkinson Company, Inc. v. Hilton Davis Chemical Co.*, 520 U.S. 17 (1997).
18. Judgment of the Supreme Court, February 24, 1998, *Minshu* Vol. 52, No. 1, p. 113.
19. If there is a part which is different from the subject products, etc. in the construction as indicated by the scope of the patent claims, (a) this part is not the essential part of

the patented invention (first requirement); (b) the purpose of the patented invention can be achieved by replacing this part with a part in the subject products and an identical function and effect can be obtained (second requirement); (c) a person who has an average knowledge in the area of technology where this invention belongs could easily come up with the idea of such a replacement at the time of the production of the subject products, etc. (third requirement); (d) the subject products, etc. are not identical to the technology in the public domain at the time of the patent application for the patented invention or could not have been easily conceived at that time by a person who has an average knowledge in the area of technology to which this invention belongs (fourth requirement); and (e) there were no special circumstances such as the fact that the subject products had been intentionally excluded from the scope of the patent claim in the patent application process.

20. Nobuhiro Nakayama, *Kogyoshoyukenhou Jou Tokkyohou* (Industrial Property Act I, The Patent Act) (2nd expanded edition), Koubundou 2002, pp. 404–406. In this book, Nakayama clearly stated that these changes in the Patent Act by introduction of infringement under the doctrine of equivalents are a transition from a system such as a real right that is similar to the ownership of land to a system such as a competition law to maintain economic order.
21. In particular, requirements such as being essential or easy strongly reflect this tendency. Therefore, their interpretation and best form of operation have been argued. (See for example, Yoshiyuki Tamura, "Kintouron ni okeru honshitsuteki bubun no youken no igi – Kintouron ha 'Shin no hatsumei' wo kyusai suru seidoka? (1) (2)" (Significance of Requirements for Essential Parts under the Doctrine of Equivalents – Is the Doctrine of Equivalents a System to Relive 'True Inventions'? (1) and (2)), *Intellectual Property Law and Policy Journal* Vol. 21 (2008), p. 1, and Vol. 22 (2009), p. 55.)
22. Judgment of the Supreme Court, November 8, 2007, *Minshu* Vol. 61, No.8, p. 2989.
23. Among the judgments of the Supreme Court, the exhaustion of the patent right in Japan was already approved as obiter dicta in the judgment of the final appeals court in the *BBS* case concerning the parallel import of patented products (judgment of the Supreme Court, July 1, 1997, *Minshu* Vol. 51, No.6, p. 2299). The grounds for the judgment are that the international exhaustion of the patent rights was denied, while it approved restricting the enforcement of patent rights by agreement and indication. With regard to the exhaustion of copyrights (distribution rights), see the judgment of the Supreme Court, April 25, 2002, *Minshu* Vol. 56, No.4, p. 808 (the judgment of the final appeals court in the Used Game Software Case).
24. Then, the judgment stated the following as facts that provide a basis for evaluation of these normative requirements, which is "novel production": "Whether the product can be regarded as a novel production of this patented product or not should be determined by taking into consideration the characteristics of the patented product, the content of the patented invention, the manner of modification and the exchange of components as well as the circumstances involving the transaction in a comprehensive way. As characteristics of the Patented Product, the function of the product, structure and materials, application, usable life, mode of use, and as the manner of modification or replacement of components, the state of the Patented Product at the time of modification, the content and extent of the modification, the usable life of the replaced components, the technical function and the economic value of the component within the Patented Product should be taken into account."
25. Under this theory, the patent right will not be exhausted (therefore, patent right infringement for the patented product will exist) in the following two cases: (i) the patented product is reused or recycled after it has finished its service along with the lapse of its ordinary life as a product (Type 1); and (ii) a third party has made a modification or replacement to all or part of the components that constitute an essential part of the patented invention of the patented product (Type 2).
26. Judgment of the Intellectual Property High Court, January 31, 2006, *Minshu* Vol. 61, No.8, p. 3103 (the court of the second instance in the Cannon Ink Cartridge case).

27. See Ryo Shimanami, "Kenriseigen no Rippoukeishiki" (Legislation Form for Restriction of Rights), *Chosakuken kenkyu* No.35 (2008), p. 93. With regard to general differences between rules and standards, for a classic discussion, see Louis Kaplow, "Rules versus Standards: An Economic Analysis", 42 *Duke L. J.* 557 (1992); and for an example of application of the discussion to the Copyright Act, see also Shimanami, above.
28. Judgment of the Supreme Court, April 11, 2000, *Minshu* Vol. 54, No.4, p. 1368.
29. Note that many judicial precedents before this judgment also did not permit an enforcement of patent rights that involved grounds for invalidation in their conclusions by interpreting claims narrowly by excluding publicly known technologies or by limiting working, etc. (For a judgment excluding publicly known technologies: the judgment of the Supreme Court, December 7, 1962, *Minshu* Vol. 16, No.12, p. 2321 (judgment of the final appeals court in the *Derailment Prevention Equipment for Coal Tub* case); and judgment of the Supreme Court, June 28, 1974, *Kinyu-Shouji Hanrei*, No.420, p. 2 (judgment of the final appeals court in the *Single-lens Reflex Camera* case). For a judgment of limiting working: the judgment of the Supreme Court, August 4, 1964, *Minshu* Vol. 18, No.7, p. 1319 (judgment of the final appeals court in the *Liquid-Fueled Combustor* case).)
30. Since geographical standards for novelty are global in nature (items of Article 29, paragraph (1)), the quality of the claims or proof concerning the grounds for invalidation will be influenced by the size of the available investment resource through a prior art search.
31. Article 104-3, paragraph (2) of the Patent Act allows the court to dismiss the lawsuit when it finds that the purpose for the advancement of allegations and evidence concerning a defense of invalidation is to delay the proceedings unreasonably.
32. Today, first instance jurisdiction over patent infringement lawsuits is held by the Tokyo District Court and the Osaka District Court, and appellate jurisdiction is integrated into the Intellectual Property High Court (Article 6, paragraphs (1) and (3) of the Code of Civil Procedure). Under this system, it is considered highly likely that a judgment on the validity of a patent by the former adjudication will have a practical impact on the latter court. Therefore, the loss of uniformity among disputes may not be as bad as feared. However, since res judicata of judgment is effective only with parties in principle (Article 115, paragraph (1), item (i) of the Code of Civil Procedure), the uniformity of judgments of patent validity in courts that handle infringement lawsuits is not legally guaranteed.
33. See Nobuhiro Nakayama, note 20, p. 318 et seq.
34. Judgment of the Supreme Court, April 16, 1999, *Minshu* Vol. 53, No.4, p. 627
35. On the contrary, stipulations that allow a true rights holder to request that a misappropriated patent holder return the patent right are Article 8 of the German Patent Act and Article 611-8, paragraph (1) of the French Intellectual Property Right Act.
36. The name of the applicant can be changed only by a successor (Article 12 of the Ordinance for Enforcement of the Patent Act, and Form 18 of said Ordinance) on submission of a document to prove the succession of the right (Article 5, paragraph (1) of said Ordinance). With regard to changing the name of the applicant by a misappropriated applicant, which is not an original succession of rights, the Patent Office also treats the judgment of a successful lawsuit to confirm the right to obtain a patent as a document proving the succession and accepts applications for change.
37. For examples of judicial precedents concerning misappropriated application from the beginning, see the judgment of the Tokyo District Court, July 22, 1983, the *Hanrei Times* No.514, p. 289 (the *Vehicle Vibration Alarm Device* case). For examples of judicial precedents concerning changing the name of applicants without permission after filing a lawful application, see the judgment of the Yokohama District Court, March 29, 1985, *Mutaishu* Vol. 17, No.1, p. 116 (the *Thermoset Molding Process* case).
38. Publication of misappropriated applications falls under "publication against the will" (Article 30, paragraph (2)) of the true rights holder. However, usually six months has

elapsed from the publication at the time of registration of the patent which was made by the misappropriated application so that a true rights holder cannot be relieved through his/her own application by exemption of loss of novelty.

39. Judgment of the Supreme Court, June 12, 2001, *Minshu* Vol. 55, No.4, p. 793.
40. For instance, where the name of the applicant is changed without permission after an application is lawfully filed; where a right to obtain a shared patent is infringed; or where a true rights holder has filed a lawsuit to confirm a right to obtain the patent, etc.
41. For examples of a judgment in which a request to return a patent right was not permitted after said judgment since the case was different from the *Garbage Disposer* case in consideration of concrete circumstances, see the judgment of the Tokyo District Court, July 17, 2002, *Hanreijihou* No.1799, p. 155 (the *Brassiere* case).
42. It does not conform with the intention of the judgment of the Supreme Court in the *Garbage Disposer* case to judge the appropriateness of returning a patent right from a misappropriated patent rights holder to a true rights holder by whether it is a case of changing the name on the application without permission after the lawful application or a case of misappropriation from the beginning. See Hisayoshi Yokoyama, "Hatsumeisha no Kenri" (Rights of Inventors), *Hougaku Kyoushitsu* No.322 (2007), p. 153.
43. Following revision of the Patent Law in 2011, which took effect in April 2012, when a patent right is granted on a misappropriated application, the legitimate right owner is now able to demand transfer of the patent right from the usurpers based on the legitimate owner's right to receive a patent for the invention. This revision was taken to resolve the uncertainty of a Supreme Court ruling in the Garbage Disposer Case.
44. Judgment of the Supreme Court, April 22, 2003, *Minshu* Vol. 57, No.4, p. 477.
45. Judgment of the Supreme Court, October 17, 2006, *Minshu* Vol. 60, No.8, p. 2853.
46. For a critical review of this stance, see Ryo Shimamura, "Gaikoku tokkyoken ni motozuku shiyousha rieki ni tsuite nihon tokkyohou 35jou no ruisuitekiyou ga kouteisareta jirei" (a case study on the judgment where analogical application of Article 35 of Japanese Patent Act is affirmed with regard to an employee's interests based on foreign patent rights), *L&T* No.34 (2007), p. 42.
47. Suzanne Scotchmer, "Standing on the shoulders of Giants: Cumulative Research and the Patent Law", 5 *J. Econ. Persp.* (1991), p. 29; Clarisa Long, "Patents and Cumulative Innovation", 2 *Wash U. L. & Pol'y* (2000), p. 229.
48. Carl Shapiro, "Patent Reform: Aligning Reward and Contribution", 8 *Innovation Policy and the Economy* (2007), p. 111.
49. Steven Shavell, *Foundations of Economic Analysis of Law* (2004), pp. 11–22.
50. Ibid., pp. 138–144.
51. Christine MacLeod, "James Watt, Heroic Invention and the Idea of the Industrial Revolution", in Maxine Berg and Kristine Bruland ed., *Technological Revolutions in Europe: Historical Perspectives* (1998), p. 96.
52. Peter Drahos & John Braithwaite, *Information Feudalism* (2002), pp. 212–213. Drahos and Braithwaite state that the prosperity of science and technology in the United States after World War II was the result of its university system being the best in the world at the time.
53. Sakakibara Mariko & Lee Branstetter, "Do Strong Patents Induce More Innovation? Evidence from the 1988 Japanese Patent Law Reform", 32(1) Rand *J. of Econ.* (2001), p. 77.
54. F.M. Scherer & S. Weisburst, "Economic effect of strengthening pharmaceutical patent protection in Italy", 26 *International Rev. of Industrial Property and Copyright Law*, (1995), p. 1009.
55. James Bessen & Robert M. Hunt, "An Empirical Look at Software Patents", 16(1) *J. of Econ. & Management Strategy* (2007), p. 157.
56. David M. Gould & William C. Gruben, "The Role of Intellectual Property Rights in Economic Growth", 48(2) *J. of Development Econ.* (1996), p. 323; Juan Carlos Ginarte

and Walter G. Park, "Determinants of Patent Rights: A Cross-national Study", 26(3) *Research Policy* (1997), p. 283.

57. In other words, economic growth is considered to be not a result of the development of the intellectual property system, but one of causes of its development.
58. This system design which is focused on the forum and timing is effective not only for substantive rules, but also for procedural rules. For example, there is an issue with regard to the judgment of the validity of patent rights on how a trial for patent invalidation and an infringement lawsuit should share their roles. This is nothing but an issue of selecting the forum and timing of the judgment of validity. If the requirements for patent registration are too clear with no room for other interpretations and an inventor has the complete information concerning prior technology documents, etc., the inventor could judge the validity by him/herself at the time of application. However, in reality, the inventor does not have this complete information. Therefore, it is found that the issue concerning the procedure of judging validity is a part of the issue of selecting the timing in which a subject, such as an inventor, the general public, the Patent Office, the court, or, even, the Diet (that establish substantive rules), etc. should bear the cost for judging validity.

2. Current situation and vision of the patent system: from the perspective of economics

Kazuyuki Motohashi

INTRODUCTION

The purpose of the Japanese Patent Act is stipulated as follows: "The purpose of this Act is, through promoting the protection and the utilization of inventions, to encourage inventions, and thereby to contribute to the development of industry" (Article 1 of the Act). I would like to suggest what the patent system should be like in order "to contribute to the development of industry" after organizing issues from an economics perspective in this chapter.

Philosophy of the Patent System

As stated in Article 1 of the Japanese Patent Act, the patent system has two sides: "protection" and "utilization" of the inventions. With regard to the "protection of inventions," it is a factor in favor of the inventor that incentives for research and development will be secured by providing exclusive rights to the achievements of an invention for a certain period. If the invention is not protected by patent right, the achievements of research and development will be copied by other companies so that research and development would be wasted. If such were the case, it would be economically advantageous to copy the achievements of other companies, which would result in reducing speed of research and development in overall society. In order to prevent such a situation, the patent system is an important system for creating innovation.

On the other hand, people who engage in the "utilization of the inventions" are not limited to inventors. The content of a patent application is published within 18 months under the laid-open publication system and becomes information in the public domain. If the patent system did not exist, the achievements of research and development would not be publicized and that information would be protected as a company secret. This situation would generate some social losses. One of the losses would be duplicated investment into the same research and development. For instance, suppose two competing companies happened to be engaged in research and development on the same subject. If one of the companies files a patent application and the information is publicized, it enables another company at that time to decide whether it should take a different approach to research and development or stop the development and change its strategy to license the patent of the other company. If there is no patent system, the achievements of research and development will be kept as a company secret and companies will not notice the fact that they have duplicated each other's investments until their products are commercialized. Another result is the loss of the improvement of social welfare as a result of being able to use other companies' technology through licenses. This function does not become available without the patent system. Therefore, there will be a downgrade in social welfare.

Current Status of the "Protection" and "Utilization" of Inventions

As stated above, the patent system has two sides, the "protection of rights" and the "promotion of effective use of the invention." Recently, however, there have been cases in which these two sides contradict each other. The patent system in some countries has been modified to strengthen patent rights, and this modification is known as pro-patent system reform; however, this strengthening of rights may have the effect of interfering with the promotion of the exploitation of the achievements of an invention.

For example, there is an argument in pharmaceuticals that since gene-related patents were registered one after another, there are now more patents that require one to obtain a license to pursue research and development. As a result, there is a decrease in the efficiency of research and development (Heller and Eisenberg (1998)). This is called the "Tragedy of the Anticommons," which is where if patents that are upstream in the innovation process are strengthened when cumulative innovation is implemented, then innovations that are downstream will be disturbed. Moreover, in the electronics manufactures, "Patent Thicket Problems" were identified because the number of patents increased drastically. The technical structures of electronics products, such as semi-conductors and home appliances, have become more complicated and it has become difficult for a single company to develop all of the technologies. Consequently, major electronics companies develop and sell products by cross-licensing. However, it is necessary to obtain many patents in order to negotiate the cross-licensing advantageously. Meanwhile, it is often seen that a patent is applied in order to ensure the flexibility of a company's own research and development or business strategy. Based on these conditions, the number of patent applications in the electronics manufactures increased sharply and created the phenomenon where the upsurge in patents formed "patent thickets" and the patent thickets constrained the flexibility of research and development between patents (Motohashi (2006)).

Globalizing Company Activities and the Patent System

Furthermore, an important issue for considering the future of the patent system is how it should correspond to the development of the globalization of business activity. The patent system has adopted the "principle of territoriality"; therefore, it is necessary to obtain patent rights in each country or region where the patent right should be claimed. International application systems have been developed, such as the Paris Convention, PCT (Patent Cooperation Treaty) Rules, etc.; however, they eventually require examination by the Patent Office of each country and the difference in the examination rules of each country and region sometimes leads to significant problems. Recently, with regard to business model patents and patents related to gene function, the trilateral Patent Offices (the Japan Patent Office (JPO), European Patent Office (EPO) and United States Patent and Trademark Office (USPTO)) unified their examination standards. Before this agreement was reached, the USPTO granted patent approval according to its own rules, which led to confusion. Another important issue is how we should establish a system for examining patents under common international rules when a new technological field appears.

Organization of this Chapter

In this chapter, I will present recent issues concerning the abovementioned patent system from an economic perspective and propose my ideal way for the future. In the next section, the patent system in Japan will be reviewed and the past approaches to system reform will be organized from the perspective of balancing the "protection of rights" with the "promotion of the exploitation of an invention." System reform in the past has promoted a pro-patent position that places greater emphasis on the "protection of rights." Next, documents relating to the connection between pro-patent system reform and innovation will be surveyed. The results of an analysis using the content of a survey conducted with Japanese companies will be given. The following section will focus on the electronics and pharmaceutical industries, which are particularly impacted by changes in the patent system. Since the issue was not clarified in the survey, interviews were conducted concerning the relationship between the patent system and innovation. And finally, the results of this analysis will be reviewed and the ideal way for the patent system to contribute to the development of industry, given these results, will be proposed. (The statistics of the survey can be found in an appendix to this chapter.)

PATENT SYSTEM REFORM IN JAPAN

Background of the Establishment of the Japanese Patent System and Motives for System Reform

The history of the patent system in Japan goes back to the "Patent Monopoly Act" that was passed in 1885. The Patent Act at the time was based on acts in France and the United States and adopted the "first-to-invent principle." Thereafter, the Act was modified several times. The "first-to-file principle" was adopted in the former Patent Act of 1921. The current Patent Act was passed in 1959, after World War II, and enacted in April 1960. This Act meets the requirements of a modern patent act, for example in clarifying the requirements for invention, such as a non-obviousness clause, and adopting a principle in which publication by official notice must be distributed elsewhere in the world, as requirements for lack of novelty (Sumida and Tatsumi (2000)).

System Reforms Related to the Current Patent Act

Table 2.1 shows a summary of the major system reforms to the current Patent Act of 1960. One major trend in patent system reforms is in the direction of enlarging the scope of patent rights or strengthening patent rights themselves. In Table 2.1, the major system reforms are organized into four categories: (1) reforms to expand subjects of protection by patent into new technology field; (2) reforms to expand the patent scope for all technologies; (3) reforms to strengthen the enforcement of patent rights; and (4) reforms to make the patent system easier to use.

System reforms are divided into the following: reform along with technology development, reform related to system operation and reform related to pro-patent measures.

The JPO named its actions as pro-patent measures and has been engaging in enhancing the protection of rights by means of the patent right since the late 1990s. These actions in support of a "strong" patent right developed into actions by the entire government. In 2003, the Intellectual

Table 2.1 Patent system reforms in Japan

	Patents in new fields	Scope of protection expansion	Strengthening protection	Reviewing operation of the system
1970s	Microorganism patents (1979)	Substance patents (1976)		Laid-open publication (1971) Request for examination (1971)
1980s	Animal patents (1988)	Improved multiple claims system (1988) Exception of patent term extension (pharmaceutical products, 1988)		
1990s	Clarification of the scope of the subject of software (1993) Electronic money patents (1995) Software medium patents (1997) (Gene-related patents) (Business model patents)	Application of the doctrine of equivalency (Ball Spline case, 1998)	Opposition after granting a patent (1996) Compensation raised (1999) Improvement of dispute settlement system (1999)	Responding to electronic applications (1990) Applications in foreign languages (1995)
2000s	Software patents (2002) Medical treatment patents (2005)		Improvement of litigation and interpretation proceedings (2000) Establishment of Intellectual Property High Court (2005)	Shortening of period of request for examination (from 7 years to 3 years, 2001) Expeditious patent examinations

Table 2.1 (continued)

	Patents in new fields	Scope of protection expansion	Strengthening protection	Reviewing operation of the system
			Strengthening of dispute settlement function (2005)	(setting a goal, increasing the number of examination officers, etc.)

Source: Kazuyuki Motohashi (2005) "Chitekizaisanseido no henka to sono kokusaitekina doukou" (Changes in the Intellectual Property System and International Trends) in Akiya Nagata and Kouichi Sumikura (eds), *MOT Chitekizaisan to gijutsukeiei (MOT, Intellectual Property and Technology Management)*, Maruzen; Table 14.1 in Chapter 14 has been modified.

Property Strategy Headquarters, which is in charge of intellectual property strategies for the entire government, was established; and the Intellectual Property Policy Outline, which indicates the basic strategy for Japanese intellectual property measures, defined the Japanese government's policy as "an intellectual property-based nation." Until now, the intellectual property system has been reformed in accordance with the "Intellectual Property Strategic Program" that is established every year.

Expanding the Subjects of Patent Protection in New Areas

Software and biotechnology are important fields for the expansion of subjects of patent protection into new areas.

The measures for protecting software include protection by copyright and protection by patent right. Protection by copyright was established when the Copyright Act was modified in 1985 to clarify that software is protected as a work. Meanwhile, with regard to the protection by patent right, software still has patentability problems, and therefore not all software can be the subject of this protection. However, since the Copyright Act aims to protect "expression" only and does not protect "ideas," it is considered that the protection by copyright alone is insufficient and the system has been reformed by expanding its treatment under the Patent Act.

What becomes a problem when considering software as the subject of a patent, is its relevance to a "technical idea that uses the laws of nature" that is a requirement for invention under the Patent Act. Up until the early 1990s, software itself was considered to be just a statement of a computation method and not to be the subject of a patent. However, patents were granted to the software that implemented functions along with hardware; for instance, patents were granted to software of a Kana-Kanji conversion system for word processors along with the hardware.

As the importance of software has increased in society, operations by the JPO have gradually been eased. In 1993, requirements for software-related inventions to correspond to inventions under the Patent Act were presented as criteria and the requirements of a relationship with hardware were drastically eased. Moreover, since the amount of packaged software that was not embedded in hardware increased, the JPO presented a guideline to approve patents for software recorded in media, such as FD (Floppy Disks), in 1997.

Furthermore, treatment of software under the Patent Act also changed. In 2000, software itself became a subject of protection under the Patent Act, and patent protection was extended to software distributed via internet in 2002.

Like software patents, patents were recently granted to business models, such as auctions, settlement systems, etc. in electronic commerce. Many patents applications have been filed in Japan for business models related to inventions in response to the increasing number of patented business models in the United States. In Japan, they are regarded as software inventions related to business methods and patents were granted to part of them by an examination in accordance with the criteria for software inventions.

Today, precedent cases are put into a database and "unobviousness" is examined more strictly. In Japan, as well as in Europe, operating standards for business model patents must have technical aspects; therefore, granting a patent to a business method alone, which is not related to software, is not allowed. In this regard, Japan has adopted stricter standards than the United States, where patents are granted to a broader scope of subjects if the invention has usability, regardless of the technical aspects. Meanwhile, with regard to standards for approving patents for a business model as a form of software, according to the results of a comparative study by Patent Offices of the JPO, EPO and USPTO, it is confirmed that differences among them are not significant.[1]

As for the field of biotechnology, it started with microorganism patents in 1979 and the scope of subjects for patent has been widened along with development of technology. In the 1980s, patents related to pharmaceutical products and plants and animals obtained through genetic modification were granted. In the 1990s, patents related to the analysis of gene functions and research tools were granted. Regarding gene fragment patents, Japan, the United States and Europe reached an agreement in 1999 that patents shall not be approved for them if they do not have special functions or usability; however, one problem is that concrete judgment of the function and usability varies for each Patent Office.

In Japan, the requirements for patents were clarified by the examination standards for gene related patents that were established in 1999. These standards have been updated, including, by adding cases concerning screening methods in 2000. In addition, a guideline for patent protection for medical-related treatment was established in 2005. The guideline states clearly that the "pharmaceutical inventions that will be specified by treatment conditions, such as the combination of multiple medicines, dosage interval, dosage amount, etc." or the "method of movement of medical equipment," which were not previously subjects of patent protection, are now subject to protection.

Cross-sectional Expansion of the Scope of Patent Protection

The expansion of the scope of patent protection is not limited to new areas, such as IT and biotechnology. Cross-sectional measures to expand protection, such as substance patents (since 1976), an improved multiple claims system (since 1988), patent term extensions for pharmaceutical products (since 1988), the doctrine of equivalents (since 1998), etc., are also important.

Before substance patents were permitted, patents were not granted to the manufacturing method of new compounds used for pharmaceutical products. From 1976, the substance itself has been protected by a patent. Before that, it was impossible to prevent another company from using different manufacturing methods to avoid using the patent. Therefore, the system to provide incentives for the development of new drugs was flawed. Through the introduction of substance patents, the achievements of the development of pharmaceutical products based on new compounds become appropriately protected. This is considered to have had a great impact to the research and development of pharmaceutical products.

The improved multiple claims system that was introduced in 1998 is a system under which multiple inventions can be applied for as one patent. The Japanese patent system had operated under the principle of one claim per patent and it was necessary to apply for multiple related patents separately. Since it became possible to apply for those multiple related patents as one patent, it also became possible to protect a broader range of inventions.

Exceptional special measures to extend the patent protection period to cover the time required to obtain government permission to manufacture products, such as pharmaceutical products and agricultural chemicals, were introduced at the same time as the introduction of the improved multiple claims system. The patent term is 20 years; however, the exceptional measures enabled an extension of up to five years.

Furthermore, there is the idea of a doctrine of equivalency concerning the range of inventions (claims) that are protected by patent. In this doctrine, an act replacing a part which is not essential to a patent claim with something else infringes the original patent, if the patent claim has the same functional effect as the original patented invention. In the appeal of the Ball Spline Case in 1998, the doctrine of equivalency was also supported in Japan. If the doctrine of equivalency comes to be supported generally in patent disputes, it will have the effect of broadening the range of inventions that are protected by the patent right.

Strengthening Enforcement of the Patent Right

Along with these expansions of the scope of inventions subject to protection by patent rights, the system has also been modified to strengthen enforcement of the patent right itself. Major modifications include an increase in compensation payment for patent infringement that was applied from 1999 to 2000, the improvement of the patent dispute settlement system and the improvement of litigation and interpretation proceedings.

In particular, the most important modification among the pro-patent measures is the "establishment of an Intellectual Property High Court," to improve the patent dispute settlement system. The court was established for the purpose of improving the speed of dispute settlement and of heightening the predictability of judgments on intellectual property disputes, which have become technically more sophisticated (unification of criteria at an early stage). The court is expected to improve the stability of intellectual property rights.

At the same time, necessary measures were undertaken for enhancing dispute settlement functions, such as strengthening the protection of trade secrets during patent examinations, facilitating proof of infringement, and the development of public administration (invalidation trials by the Patent Office) and justice (litigation in court) for patent disputes, etc. These system reforms have secured stable protection of inventions for various kinds of intellectual property rights, including patent rights, and have improved the reliability of the system.

Revision of System Operation

The movement to review the operation of the system, which aims to establish a more convenient patent system, has a close relationship with the "strong" patent trends. Many measures were introduced to improve the speed of patent examination. For instance, in 1996, the period necessary for granting a patent was accelerated by setting the opposition period, which until then had been set before granting a patent, after the patent grant. The fee for patent applications, requests for examination, registrations, etc. was raised in the early 1990s; however, it was reduced in both 1998 and 1999. These measures were made in order to promote making the achievements of technical development, etc. into patent rights. However, the period from application to request for examination was shortened from seven to three years in 2001 so that a large number of requests for examination were made temporarily. In response, the fee for requesting the examination was raised in 2003. Moreover, in order to respond to the rapid increase in patent examinations, the goal was set to reduce the applicants awaiting patent examination to zero eventually and necessary measures were undertaken in order to reduce the backlog of examinations according to the plan by assigning fixed-term examination officers.

Measures Concerning Creation and Utilization

In addition, it is not stated in Table 2.1 that various kinds of measures concerning the creation and utilization of intellectual properties are included in the annual Intellectual Property Strategic Program. It is important for intellectual creation to promote inventions at universities or public research institutes. In these research institutes, a TLO (Technology Licensing Office) has been set up along with necessary measures, such as the establishment of the Japanese Bayh-Dole Act, in order to attribute the rights pertaining to the results of research funded by the national government to an institute that received the funding, such as universities. With regard to the exploitation of intellectual properties, in addition to strengthening the distribution business of patent information, etc., the Trust Act has been modified to cover intellectual properties, and the Bankruptcy Act has also been modified in order to strengthen the position of licensees when a licenser becomes bankrupt, and so on.

PRO-PATENT SYSTEM REFORM AND INNOVATION IN JAPANESE COMPANIES

U.S. Pro-patent System Reform and its Evaluation

As a backdrop to the political activities that have been promoted by the entire Japanese government and the aim to establish an "Intellectual

Property-based Nation," is the long stagnant Japanese economy following the bust of the bubble economy. These political activities are based on the importance of giving an impulse to companies' innovation activities in order to break out of such a sluggish situation. An oft-cited background argument is that the pro-patent measures undertaken in the United States in the 1980s when it suffered a decline in competitiveness served as a motivation for the revitalization of its current competitiveness. Representative examples of the pro-patent measures that were promoted in the 1980s in the United States are the establishment of the CAFC (Court of Appeals for the Federal Circuit), which exclusively handles patent infringement appeals, and the expansion of the scope of patent protection in the biotech and software fields. This expansion and strengthening of patent rights stimulated innovations in companies and led them to strengthen their competitiveness. Recently in the United States, the compensation amount for patent disputes has been rising. It is possible to say that this situation also led them to strengthen rights.

However, there is also controversy in the United States over whether the pro-patent measures, which extend and strengthen patents further, have a tangible effect on the innovation activities of companies. Incentives for companies to invest in research and development and to develop new products will receive impacts from various factors, such as the expansion of technological opportunities or systematic factors other than the intellectual property system (i.e. safety regulations for pharmaceutical products), in addition to the economic environment for companies. According to analyses focused on past cases in the United States, most results indicated that pro-patent measures only had a marginal impact on the innovation activities of companies (Kortum and Lerner (1999); Hall and Ziedonis (2001) and Lerner (2002)). In addition, the issue of anticommons has become a criticism of pro-patent measures. For instance, one argument states that gene-related inventions in pharmaceuticals were patented one after another so that the number of patents necessary to obtain licenses for research and development increased and the efficiency of research and development was diminished (Heller and Eisenberg (1998)). It is also important to promote the distribution of technologies, as a purpose of intellectual property right measures, by clarifying the rights of established technologies, as well as securing incentives for innovation in companies. There is a possibility of disturbing the distribution of technologies if excessive exclusive rights are granted to specific technologies.

Pro-patent System Reforms in Japan

What relationship then does the above-mentioned pro-patent system reform in Japan have with the innovation activities of companies? As examined above, the Japanese patent system has enhanced and strengthened patent rights both on the side of a "broader" patent range that has the effect of granting patents to new technology fields and of expanding the scope of protection (breadth of claims) of patent rights, and on the side of a "strong" patent, as is seen in raising the compensation amount. How do these measures influence innovation activities, such as the research and development of companies?[2] Patent rights give incentives to research and development by granting exclusive rights to economically efficient inventions for a certain period. Therefore, pro-patent measures have the effect of promoting the innovation activities of companies. However, we cannot forget the perspectives of patent users when considering the efficiency of innovation for the whole of society. Regular research and development is conducted cumulatively by standing on the shoulder of scientific knowledge that has been acquired. Consequently, if knowledge that is useful from the perspective of users is excessively protected by patent rights, the cumulative innovation will be disturbed. The number of gene patents and patents related to research tools in the field of biotechnology is increasing; however, this condition may become an obstacle to research and development in the lower stream of the development of pharmaceutical products. Moreover, in the field of software, there are cases where multiple patents combine and complete a single technology. In this case, it is necessary to negotiate with multiple patent right holders in order to use the patents, which leads to significant transaction costs. As stated above, when considering the relationship between the patent system and innovation activities, it is necessary to note not only one side, incentives to inventors, but also the interaction with the innovation of users. An efficient way to view the relationship between pro-patent measures and technology spillover is to observe licensing trends, which are an index of the condition of the technology market.

Moreover, as a purpose of the patent system, it is important that technology spillover be promoted in a way other than licensing, by disclosing the content of technologies. It is possible that new ideas will derive from disclosed patent information or that duplicated investments into research and development may be avoided by disclosing the content of technologies developed by other companies. As was obvious with the establishment of the open publication system in 1970, the patent system in Japan focuses on the disclosure of technologies and its spillover system.[3]

Survey Outline

A survey concerning the economic analysis of pro-patent measures was implemented at the end of 2001 by the Institute of Intellectual Property

(Institute of Intellectual Property (2002)), in order to evaluate the relationship between the abovementioned pro-patent system reforms and the innovation activities at Japanese companies. This survey was restricted in size to 1,398 subject companies (number of respondents: 373 companies; response rate: 26.7 percent); however, a detailed survey was conducted on both sides, including items on patent application and research and development from the perspective inventors and items on obtaining patent licenses from other companies from the perspective of users, and the survey provides effective information. In this survey, pro-patent measures are classified in the following three items and the influences on the innovation activities of companies are studied by type:

- broad protection (expansion of the scope of protection to new areas): for example, microorganism patents, gene fragments, software, business model patents, etc.;
- broad protection (expansion of the scope of protection of individual patents): for example, improved multiple claims system, application of the doctrine of equivalency, etc.;
- strong protection: appreciation of compensation amounts, expeditious dispute settlement, etc.

Influences of Pro-patent Measures on Company Actions

Table 2.2 indicates by industry the percentage of companies corresponding to an "increase of research and development expenses," "increase of patent applications" and "adverse effects were imposed" as influences for each measure. The table enables a comparison of the average of all industries and the trends of major companies in the pharmaceutical industry and electronics industry and small- and medium-size research and development type companies (small- and medium-size venture companies). The most distinctive point in Table 2.2 is that a high percentage of companies in the pharmaceutical industry responded that there is some influence. The pharmaceutical industry is an industry where patents are particularly effective to secure the exclusivity of technology; it is therefore natural that the pharmaceutical industry would be influenced by the system reform.[4] With regard to especially broad patents (new areas), nearly half of the companies in the pharmaceutical industry saw an increasing number of patent applications and approximately one-third of the companies viewed the increased research and development expenses as an influence of the system reform. However, at the same time, the percentage of companies that answered that an "adverse effect was imposed" is higher than in other industries. This indicates that if a company has

Table 2.2 Influences from pro-patent measures to patent and research and development activities

		All industries	Pharmaceutical industry	Electronics industry	Small- and medium-size venture companies
Broad range of patents (new areas)	Increase of research and development expenses	8.0%	34.6%	2.2%	15.8%
	Increase of patent applications	24.1%	46.2%	26.1%	11.8%
	Adverse effect was imposed	6.2%	23.1%	4.3%	3.9%
Broad range of patents (expansion of protection)	Increase of research and development expenses	5.9%	19.2%	0.0%	11.8%
	Increase of patent applications	11.3%	23.1%	8.7%	10.5%
	Adverse effect was imposed	11.5%	23.1%	6.5%	3.9%
Research with strong patents	Increase of incentives	27.3%	30.8%	30.4%	19.7%
	Increase of research and development expenses	14.7%	19.2%	17.4%	9.2%
	Enforcing patent rights more actively	17.4%	11.5%	23.9%	11.8%
	Adverse effect was imposed	7.5%	11.5%	4.3%	1.3%

Source: Kazuyuki Motohashi (2005) "Chitekizaisanseido no henka to sono kokusaitekina doukou" (Changes in the Intellectual Property System and International Trends) in Akiya Nagata and Kouichi Sumikura (eds), *MOT Chitekizaisan to gijutsukeiei (MOT, Intellectual Property and Technology Management)*, Maruzen; Chapter 14.

higher exclusivity with its technologies, the same applies to other companies at the same time.

Pro-patent measures have not affected the electronics industry as much as the pharmaceutical industry. The influence of broad patents (new areas) on research and development expenses is slightly higher than all industries. This is considered to be due to the expansion of the patent scope for software. The influence on patent application is lower than the average of all industries. It is interesting that many companies cited "enforcing patent rights more actively" as being an influence of strong patents. This indicates a company that attempted to exploit existing patents actively by licensing other companies due to the strengthened force of patent rights by raising the compensation amount.

Finally, with regard to small- and medium-size venture companies, they have not been influenced by changes in the patent system compared to larger companies. The percentage of companies that answered "research and development expenses were increased" by broader patents is higher than the average of all industries. Since the samples from the survey consist of small- and medium-size research and development-type companies, it is possible that they intend to pursue research and development despite the pro-patent measures.

Factors for the Change in the Number of Patent Applications and Pro-patent Measures

Figure 2.1 takes a more detailed look at the companies' trend of patent application and the factors for its change, including pro-patent measures. Of the companies responding to the questionnaire, 120 of 373 answered that the number of patent applications in 2000 had increased from those in the past three years. An "increase in inventions" accounted for approximately one-third of the reasons for the increase.

In the pharmaceutical industry, the percentage of companies that pointed to the "strengthening of patent rights," which is an influence of pro-patent measures, is small. As reviewed in Table 2.2, this indicates that there are influences from intellectual property right measures, but the comparative influence with other factors, such as an "increase of inventions" or "preventing other companies from obtaining patents," etc., is small. In the electronics industry, "aiming for cross-licensing" is relatively large. Table 2.2 showed the companies' attitude towards exploiting existing patents actively. However, it indicated that companies are more likely to aim for strengthening their bargaining power with other companies anticipating cross-licensing rather than increasing incomes from licensing.

Licensing Activities and Pro-patent Measures

The questionnaire undertaken by the Institute of Intellectual Property also surveyed the influences of pro-patent measures on companies' licensing

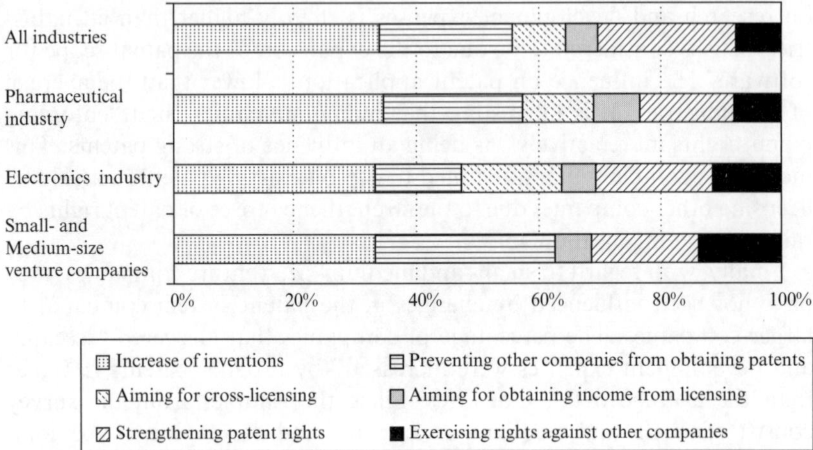

Source: Kazuyuki Motohashi (2005) "Chitekizaisanseido no henka to sono kokusaitekina doukou" (Changes in the Intellectual Property System and International Trends) in Akiya Nagata and Kouichi Sumikura (eds), *MOT Chitekizaisan to gijutsukeiei (MOT, Intellectual Property and Technology Management)*, Maruzen; Chapter 14.

Figure 2.1 Factors in increasing the number of patent applications (excluding no responses)

activities. Pro-patent measures that aim to realize "strong" patents, for example by raising compensation amounts and realizing expeditious dispute settlements, etc., will enhance the bargaining ability for licensing of licensors who hold patent rights. In addition, the shift to "broader" patents may work more advantageously for patent holders during disputes on the breadth of patent claims. This is also considered to have the effect of raising licensing fees.

The results of a survey concerning the influences of pro-patent measures on licensing are summarized in Table 2.3. They indicate that licensing fees tend to increase both in cases of licensing-in and -out. Many companies, both in the pharmaceutical industry and electronics industry, pointed to the increase in licensing fees particularly in the case of licensing-in. Meanwhile, among small- and medium-size venture companies, there is little recognition that the measures have the effect of increasing licensing fees.

There are many companies forecasting that the number of both licensing-out and –in will increase; however, the forecasting patterns vary between the pharmaceutical industry and the electronics industry. Many companies forecast that the amount of licensing-in will increase in the future in the pharmaceutical industry, while many companies forecast that the amount of licensing-out will increase in the electronics industry.

Table 2.3 Influences of pro-patent measures on licensing

		All industries	Pharma- ceutical industry	Electronics industry	Small- and medium- size venture companies
Increase of licensing fees	Licensing-out	14.7%	15.4%	19.6%	2.6%
	Licensing-in	15.0%	26.9%	28.3%	1.3%
Increase of licensing-out in the future	Increase of licensing needs	18.7%	30.0%	6.1%	37.0%
Reasons: (responses of companies, which responded that licensing-out will increase in the future)	Aiming to obtain income from licensing	57.8%	45.0%	61.2%	54.3%
	Due to necessity of cross-licensing	23.6%	25.0%	32.7%	8.7%
Increase of licensing-in in the future	Increase of licensing needs	13.3%	31.0%	6.0%	11.8%
Reasons: (responses of companies, which responded that licensing-in will increase in the future)	Outsourcing research more proactively	15.7%	17.2%	12.1%	26.3%
	Development of new business	50.5%	44.8%	42.4%	47.1%
	Due to necessity of cross-licensing	20.4%	6.9%	39.5%	14.7%

Source: Kazuyuki Motohashi (2005) "Chitekizaisanseido no henka to sono kokusaitekina doukou" (Changes in the Intellectual Property System and International Trends) in Akiya Nagata and Kouichi Sumikura (eds), *MOT Chitekizaisan to gijutsukeiei (MOT, Intellectual Property and Technology Management)*, Maruzen; Chapter 14.

High percentages of "development of new business" and "increase of licensing needs" are given as reasons for the increase in licensing-in in the pharmaceutical industry. This shows that research and development in the pharmaceutical industry is expanding into new areas, such as the exploitation of gene information and bioinformatics, and is required to cooperate externally in order to respond to new technologies.

In addition, in the electronics industry, high percentages of "aiming to obtain income from licensing" and "due to necessity of cross-licensing" are given as reasons for the increase of licensing-out. This shows that when the scope of patents expands, companies use existing patents actively and find strategies to strengthen their bargaining positions for cross-licensing since other companies also use their existing patents proactively.

As for small- and medium-size venture companies, more companies forecast that licensing-out will increase than in electronics industries. This shows a strategy of venture companies, which do not have their own manufacturing process or distribution channel, to promote their technologies proactively.

In this way, the influences of pro-patent measures on licensing vary according to the situation of the industry and the type of company. This means that the influence in the pharmaceutical industry is directed towards increasing licensing-in because of the need to develop new technology fields in which the companies have no technologies. In that process, licensing fees have risen. It is believed that this situation is caused by lowering the bargaining position as a licensee since the licensing-in of technology in new research and development areas is essential. In relation to the patent system, this situation is related to the fact that patent subjects have been extended to new areas, such as gene function, screening technology, etc.; however, we consider that there is a significant influence from the expansion of technological opportunities, such as the exploitation of genome information for drug-discovery, etc., which becomes a prerequisite to the situation.

On the other hand, in the electronics industry, it is seen that they are approaching the proactive use of patents as well as the strengthening of patent rights. Moreover, with regard to software-related patents, for which the number of applications is now rapidly growing, since they have technical characteristics requiring multiple patents in order to develop a single product, the ability to conclude beneficial licensing agreements with other companies becomes key for the competitiveness of product development. In contrast, it is highly possible that a company's own technologies will be used by other companies. Therefore, licensing agreements are often concluded in the form of cross-licensing as a working solution (Grindley and Teece (1997)). Consequently, there is a movement to obtain patents proactively for technical achievements in order to prepare for cross-licensing with other companies.

With respect to small- and medium-size venture companies, since there are many cases where each company specializes in its own technology,

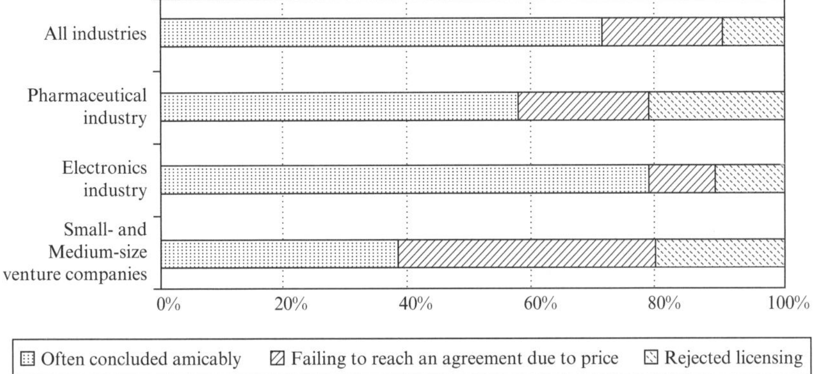

Source: Kazuyuki Motohashi (2005) "Chitekizaisanseido no henka to sono kokusaitekina doukou" (Changes in the Intellectual Property System and International Trends) in Akiya Nagata and Kouichi Sumikura (eds), *MOT Chitekizaisan to gijutsukeiei (MOT, Intellectual Property and Technology Management)*, Maruzen; Chapter 14.

Figure 2.2 Conditions at closing licensing agreement (excluding no responses)

there are limited possibilities that pro-patent measures will impose a situation in which the patents of other companies will disturb their technical development. Rather, it is considered that pro-patent measures, which strengthen patent rights, are an advantage to research and development type venture companies in the following points: they allow the venture companies to protect their own rights and to implement their licensing strategy more advantageously.

Licensing Fees and Pro-patent Measures

Licensing fees have become more expensive than when receiving a patent license in the late 1990s (Nagaoka (2002)). At the end of this section, I will investigate the issue of whether the appreciation of licensing fees creates obstacles to the distribution of technologies. In Figure 2.2, the results of licensing negotiations are summarized. There are many cases of "often concluded amicably." The spill-over effect, which is from the distribution of patented technologies, is one of the advantages of the patent system. There are no adverse effects on technology market from the appreciation of licensing fees at this stage. Meanwhile, cases of "failing to reach an agreement due to price" are increasing among small- and medium-size venture companies. This indicates that financial constraints are significant in those companies. However, as examined in Table 2.3, since small- and medium-size venture companies have less awareness of the increase of licensing fees by pro-patent measures, it is considered that the increase in the abovementioned case indicates only general financial shortage among small- and medium-size companies; therefore, it does not have a significant relationship with the patent system.

DETAILED ANALYSIS OF THE ELECTRONICS MANUFACTURERS

As examined in the previous section, pro-patent measures had a significant influence on high-tech industries, such as the electronics and pharmaceutical industries. However, just investigating these two industries shows that the relationship between the intellectual property system and innovations is very different depending on the field of technology and the industry. In this section, I will analyze an interview survey with companies and patent data in order to examine in detail the condition of these two high-tech industries respectively.[5]

Interview Responses of the Electronics Manufacturers

First, an interview survey was conducted with four major electronics manufacturers on their relationship with patent system reform and innovations. The results are as shown below.

Influences of pro-patent measures on patent activities (application, registration, licensing, etc.)

- The expansion of patent protection to new areas, such as business model patents, etc. has had an effect on innovation. Other system changes are issues concerning patent procedures. The modification of the procedures for software patents is appreciated to the extent that it facilitated the preparation of patent claims; however, it only has an effect on deciding whether existing technologies should be patented.
- With regard to the improved multiple claims system, few companies mention that it broadens the scope of patents; however, they recognize that it enables them to describe the scope of single invention from a variety of angles by means of claims so that it has the effect of clarifying the scope of an invention.
- With regard to effective patents, it is important to improve the dispute settlement system. If a dispute is not settled promptly, the

effect of an "injunction" will become virtually meaningless in fields with dramatic technological innovation.

Influences of pro-patent measures on research and development or licensing

- The intellectual property department has become more important for company-wide innovation strategies; however, it has not reached a level where it influences the direction or amount of investment in research and development. Therefore, it is hard to consider that the change in the intellectual property system directly affects research and development.
- With regard to licensing strategies, they involve the development department (division) rather than the research section; intellectual property departments, which know about the patent conditions of other companies, take a more active role than other departments.
- For IT companies, multiple patents are necessary for the development of a single product so that it is a regular occurrence for them to form an alliance that covers a broader range of technologies than cross-licensing. Therefore, there may be patent strategies in order to form more dominant future alliances.
- Recently there has been an increase in the number of companies which do not have a manufacturing department. This increases the number of cases where the correspondence with cross-licensing becomes difficult. However, this situation will not disrupt research and development except in unusual cases where the technology of a certain company must be used since it has become a de facto standard.

International patent strategies

- Since the United States Patent and Trademark Office has been responding promptly to patent protection requests for new areas, the proportion of international patent applications mainly in the United States has increased.
- In the United States, a broad range of patents are granted first and then the limits of the patent right are determined by the court when exercising the patent right. Therefore, patent applications for technology that will lead to global business have to be filed in accordance with the standard in the United States.

Trends of research and development or patent applications in the late 1990s and their background

- The number of patent applications increased in the 1980s for many companies, while it decreased drastically in the 1990s. This is because each company closely examined each invention for which they would apply for a patent due to the collapse of the bubble economy. Since the number of international patent applications has been increasing, it is possible that patent applications in Japan have been decreasing relatively under the budget constraints.
- However, there are companies that increased the number of patent applications in the 1990s, or companies that increased the number of patent applications again in the late 1990s. As stated above, the number of patent applications fluctuates according to the company's strategy regardless of its output of innovations.
- The number of cross-licensing, warnings concerning patent infringement, etc. have tended to increase. Patent applications have also taken technology strategies or patent portfolios into account and have a clearer direction.
- With regard to research and development, it is important to predict new waves of new technologies in the IT field. For example, the development and content, etc. of PDAs in the broadband period, cell-phone semiconductor chips, etc. are important; however, there is no relationship between these technology trends and the intellectual property system.

As seen above, the expansion of patents into new areas, such as software, business models, etc. in the patent system takes an important role in relation to the innovation activities of major electronics manufacturers. On the other hand, with regard to other patent systems, such as cross-sectional and broad patents or strong patents that are seen in the improvement of the dispute settlement system, their influence is not considered to be significant. In addition, as seen with business model patents, patents in the United States often serve as pioneers in the protection of new technologies by patent. Consequently, major global electronics manufactures establish patent strategies based on patent trends in the United States.

In relation to research and development, patent information has been used as invaluable information in order to learn the research and development strategies of other companies in the IT field, where cross-licensing and strategic alliances with other companies have become important. Nevertheless, none of the companies that participated in this survey felt that pro-patent measures promoted their research and development. Their research and development policies were directed under initiatives from their research institute or business division. The intellectual property department has become more important in providing information; however, it does not take an active role in driving the company's research strategy.

Summary of the Results of Interviews with the Electronics Manufacturers

I would like to list several points that are considered to be important for examining the ideal route that the patent system should follow in the future based on the interviews with major electronics manufacturers. First of all, there is the evaluation of the expansion of patent protection to new areas. In the United States, it is said that many venture companies involved in semiconductor design were created because of the strengthening of patent rights due to the expansion of the scope of the rights (Hall and Ziedonis (2001)). It is important for fabless companies which do not have a manufacturing department to have their intellectual property rights strengthened. Cross-licensing is often used in the IT field where many patents are required for the development of a single product. If the counterparty is a venture company, licensing-in is necessary. In that case, are there any barriers against licensing as there are in the pharmaceutical industry? In the IT field, at least in the companies which participated in the interview survey, it is not seen to be a significant issue. In cases where the necessary patent is a fair price, new patents, which are generated by the expansion of the scope of protection by patent rights, are useful from the perspective of their spill-over effects.

Next, there are the differences between the patent systems of Japan and the United States. Throughout the interviews, it was felt that examination by the United States Patent and Trademark Office is relatively loose and actual patent rights are determined by patent disputes, while the Japan Patent Office determines patent rights via a more severe examination. In this situation, it is natural for the USPTO to take the initiative on patent protection of new areas and it is normal for companies developing their business globally to establish patent strategies based on filing applications in the United States. The business model patent has been adjusted at Trilateral Patent Office Meetings between Japan, the United States and Europe. This approach will become efficient if a certain number of cases are reached where business models are patented in new areas; however, it cannot be a countermeasure against cases where protection for new areas is too late. If this issue is pursued, it will affect more fundamental issues, such as differences in judicial systems and personnel between Japan and the United States. However, short-term measures, such as conducting patent examinations at the Patent Office more strategically, etc., should also be examined.

Investigation into Granting Patent Rights to Software

The relationship between the intellectual property system and innovation has been examined by focusing on major electronics companies in the above paragraphs. Next, the influence of software patents on pure-software companies will be investigated. Patent rights have been expressly granted to software, an intangible property, since the late 1990s. Before this system reform, patent rights were granted to software by describing it as an integral function of hardware. Consequently, it was possible for hardware manufacturers, such as electronics companies, to receive patent protection for inventions concerning software by formulating claims. However, it was difficult for pure-software companies to obtain patent rights. Software has been regarded as a subject of protection under the Copyright Act; however, copyrights protect "expression," such as programs, but not inventions (or ideas) themselves. Therefore, the expansion of patent rights to software has a large influence, particularly on pure-software companies.

The data used for the investigation into this issue comes from a database (Motohashi and Kani (2009)) connecting the Survey of Selected Service Industries (Ministry of Economy, Trade and Industry), the Basic Survey of Japanese Business Structure and Activities (Ministry of Economy, Trade and Industry) and the IIP Patent database (Goto and Motohashi (2007)). The Survey of Selected Service Industries is data from business offices related to the software industry. The subject offices that belong to the same company in this data were gathered; then, the data was sorted by company and connected to the Basic Survey of Japanese Business Structure and Activities, for which the data is given by company. Patent data by the applicant's name in the IIP Patent database is linked to this connected data. In order to limit the subjects to pure-software companies, the subjects of the analysis are only companies whose ratio of software in their total revenue is 80 percent or more. Then, we have the panel dataset within the five-year period from 2001 to 2005 and the sampling number is approximately 550 companies per year. Since IIP Patent database includes all patents filed in 1964 and beyond, past data on patent applications filed by the subject companies can be used.

Content of the Innovation Technologies of Software Companies and the Number of Patent Applications

The content of the technology constituting the innovation of software companies is reviewed. Patent applications are categorized in accordance with their technological classification and the fields in which many applications were filed are listed in the following (Motohashi and Kani (2009)):

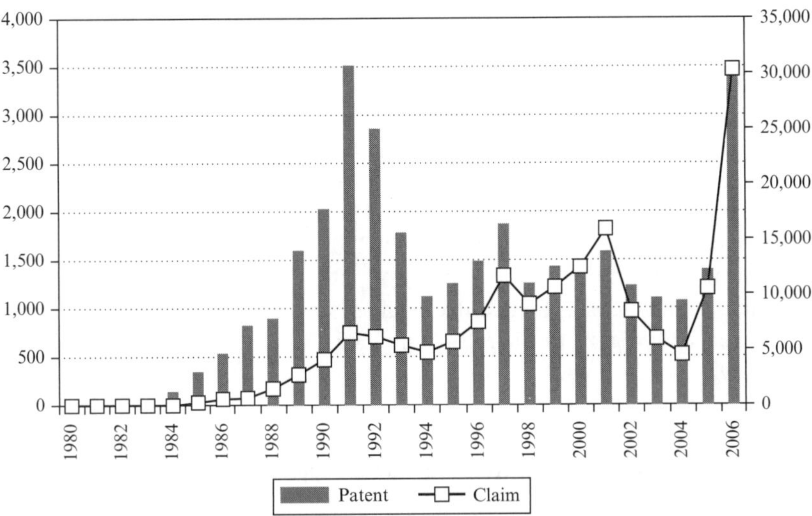

Source: Motohashi and Kani (2009) "Propatento seido kaisei ga haiteku sangyou no inobeishon katsudou ni ataeru eikyou bunseki" (Analysis of the Influence of the Pro-Patent System Reform on the Innovation Activities of High-Tech Industries), *Heisei 20 nendo Tokkyocho Ukeoijigyo: Heisei 20 nendo Wagakuni ni okeru sangyou zaisankentou no shutsugandoukoutou ni kansuru chousahoukokusho (Contract Project of the Patent Office in Fiscal Year 2008; Report on the Survey of Trends, etc. in Industrial Property Rights, etc. Applications in Japan in Fiscal Year 2008)*, p.162, Institute of Intellectual Property.

Figure 2.3 Number of patent applications and claims filed by software companies

- data processing systems conformed to a managerial purpose, commercial purpose, financial purpose, etc. (including patents for e-commerce and business models): G06F17/60, G06F15/20, 21 (Version 4);
- information systems and control inside the computer: G06F12/, G06F13/;
- information search and database structure for the search: G06F17/30, G06F15/40 (Version 4);
- program control: G06F9/;
- general digital computers: G06F15/;
- error detection: G06F/11.

Figure 2.3 shows the status of these patent applications in chronological order. The number of patent applications hit a peak in 1991, and then decreased once until 2006, when a large number of patent applications were filed again. However, the improved multiple claims system was introduced in 1989 and the number of claims for a single patent increased. Therefore, it is appropriate to look at the total number of claims to examine the changes in invention. The total number of claims as shown in the line plot tended to increase until 2001, dropped once to 2004 and recently began to increase again. Major system reforms concerning software patents were implemented in 1997, 2000 and 2002. With regard to the reforms in 1997 and 2000, the number of patent applications increased and the increase includes influences from the system reform, while the number decreased with regard to the reform in 2002. As stated above, it is difficult to analyze the influence of the system reforms based on the number of patents at the macro level.

Impact of Japanese System Reforms on the Application Actions of Software Companies

The above-mentioned number of applications at macro level may be changed by the trend of companies that file a large number of patent applications. Therefore, the DI (Diffusion Index: annual trends in the number of patents and claims are counted by setting the index as follows: Increase = 1; No change = 0; and Decrease = −1) is calculated. Transition of DI is shown in Figure 2.4. The DI of the total number of claims remains in positive figures until 1997. This indicates that there are more companies for which the number of claims is increasing than companies for which the number of claims is decreasing. The DI became negative once in 1998. This is considered to be a recoil reduction from increase in 1997. As mentioned above, it is highly possible that the reason why the number of patent applications increased temporarily is because of the influence of the system reform (for software media patents). Meanwhile, the DI fluctuated drastically in 2000 and after, so it is difficult to argue that the change in the number of patent applications is related to system reform. Software companies are considered to have been influenced by the IT bubble and its collapse in 2000 and 2001. It appears that this change in the macroeconomic environment had the impact of changing the number of patent applications.

Impact of Japanese System Reforms on the Time Software Companies Start Filing Applications

Next, with regard to approximately 550 subject software companies, the distribution conditions in the initial year when they filed a patent

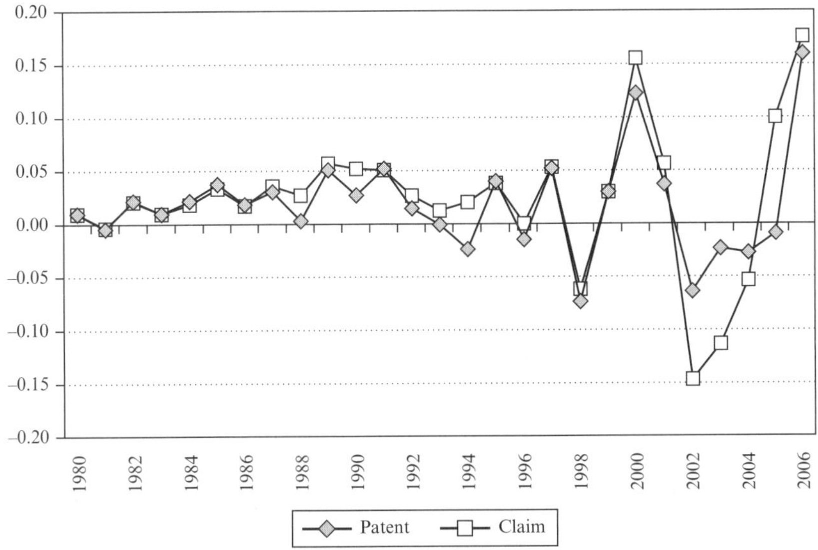

Source: Motohashi and Kani (2009) "Propatento seido kaisei ga haiteku sangyou no inobeishon katsudou ni ataeru eikyou bunseki" (Analysis of the Influence of the Pro-Patent System Reform on the Innovation Activities of High-Tech Industries), *Heisei 20 nendo Tokkyocho Ukeoijigyo: Heisei 20 nendo Wagakuni ni okeru sangyou zaisankentou no shutsugandoukoutou ni kansuru chousahoukokusho (Contract Project of the Patent Office in Fiscal Year 2008; Report on the Survey of Trends, etc. in Industrial Property Rights, etc. Applications in Japan in Fiscal Year 2008)*, p.163, Institute of Intellectual Property.

Figure 2.4 Diffusion Index of the number of patent applications and claims

application (the initial year of the patent application) will be examined. The following mechanism is assumed with respect to the relationship between software patents and innovations: (1) Expansion of the scope of patent rights to software → (2) Increasing incentives for investment in innovations at software companies → (3) Activation of innovations. If reality follows the mechanism, the pattern will emerge that the number of companies for which patent applications became possible by means of the system reform will increase. The results are as shown in Figure 2.5. The number of companies that started filing patent applications increased smoothly until the middle of the 1990s and there are no spikes from the system reform. The number of companies that started filing patent applications jumped up in 2000 and 2001. It is likely that this is due to the influence of the IT bubble and the boom in business model patents, as stated before. As mentioned above, the results do not show a clear relationship

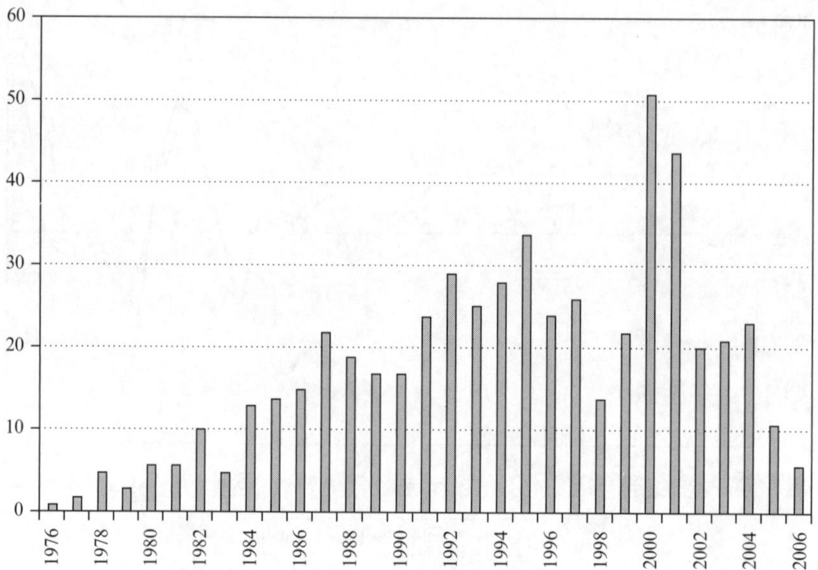

Source: Motohashi and Kani (2009) "Propatento seido kaisei ga haiteku sangyou no inobeishon katsudou ni ataeru eikyou bunseki" (Analysis of the Influence of the Pro-Patent System Reform on the Innovation Activities of High-Tech Industries), *Heisei 20 nendo Tokkyocho Ukeoijigyo: Heisei 20 nendo Wagakuni ni okeru sangyou zaisankentou no shutsugandoukoutou ni kansuru chousahoukokusho (Contract Project of the Patent Office in Fiscal Year 2008; Report on the Survey of Trends, etc. in Industrial Property Rights, etc. Applications in Japan in Fiscal Year 2008)*, p.164, Institute of Intellectual Property.

Figure 2.5 Distribution of companies by initial year of patent application

with the initial year of patent application and system reform for software patents.

Detailed Analysis of the Patents and Innovations of Software Companies

Motohashi and Kani (2009) analyzed in detail the relationship between patents and innovations at software companies by using regression analysis. The software industry in Japan is characterized by its multilayered structure. A mechanism has been established in the Japanese software industry so that an original contractor receives an order for the development of extensive software, an intermediate subcontractor receives an order from the original contractor and then sends it to a small-sized subcontractor. Minetaki and Motohashi (2008) analyzed the productivity of various software companies in this structure and showed that independent software companies that do not belong to the hierarchy had the highest productivity. In general, these companies often positioned themselves as distinct from other companies through their own technology and provided software as packaged software. As an index of innovation, the percentage outside subcontracting (percentage of orders from companies other than software companies in revenue) and the percentage of packaged software (percentage of packaged software in revenue) were considered. As a result of the analysis, we found that holding patents is deeply connected to whether a subcontractor escapes from the subcontracting structure, which consists of contracting software companies, and shifts to an independent-type software company. In addition, this relationship is particularly seen with companies that started filing patent applications in the late 1990s and after. Therefore, it is possible that the patent system reform concerning software, which started in the late 1990s, has influenced the relationship.

DETAILED ANALYSIS OF PHARMACEUTICALS

Pharmaceuticals Interview Replies

With regard to pharmaceuticals, an interview survey was conducted with five major pharmaceutical companies. The results are as follows.

Influence of pro-patent measures on patent activities (application, registration, licensing, etc.)

- The system reforms that had a significant impact are the substance patents in 1975 and the patent term extension for pharmaceutical products in 1987.
- In particular, substance patents were essential for securing incentives for research and development for drug discovery. Research and development for pharmaceutical products are usually implemented over a long period, covering 10 to 15 years. Therefore, when a drug is launched that uses compounds patented at an early stage of the research and development, several years may have passed after the patent was granted. To that extent, the measures to extend patent term pertaining to pharmaceutical products have had a great significance.
- The patent term from application to request for examination was reduced from seven to three years; however, it imposed adverse restrictions, such as requiring an applicant to make a judgment as to

whether the examination should be requested at a stage where it is unknown whether the invention would lead to a new drug.

- Other measures are not recognized as having a particularly significant influence. The impact from the improved multiple claims system and promoting expeditious patent examinations was not significant. If litigation is brought, various expenses will be incurred and the important question becomes whether they win or lose. Therefore, these companies do not feel much influence from the increase in the amount of compensation.
- With regard to the expansion of the scope of protection to new fields, such as gene patents, etc., pharmaceutical companies aspire to enter into the global market. Patent applications are filed according to the patent standards in the United States, which responds to new fields faster than Japan and Europe. There is no significant impact from change in the Japanese patent system.

Influence of pro-patent measures on research and development or licensing

- When developing a new drug, the intellectual property department works closely with the research and development department from an early stage. Therefore, if more fields are protected by patents, it may affect research and development. However, the impact is not as great as changing the total expenses for research and development.
- The patent system was mainly for substance patents and was simple; however, new technologies have become patented. Moreover, the operating policy of the Patent Office has been changed more often. Therefore, the patent system has become unstable. Research and development strategies have become more complicated, which has led to an increase in cost. Meanwhile, in the United States, cases in which patents are granted to the use of pharmaceutical products without limitation on the compound structure have appeared. Consequently, these companies consider that the scope of patent protection is too broad.
- Since patents situated upstream in the drug discovery process, such as drug target quests or screening based on gene information, have been increasing, licensing fees for research and development have also increased.
- Licensing fees are rising sharply; however, they do not affect research and development strategies. A company's research and development strategy comes first and then the necessary technologies are licensed-in according to the strategy.

- Licensing with universities and venture companies is also increasing. Licensing-in is mainly implemented as a whole, while licensing-out of the company's own technologies merely happens.

International patent strategies

- Major pharmaceutical manufactures develop drugs with a view to entering the global market, while the pharmaceutical market in Japan is growing slowly. Therefore, patent strategies are established based on international patents. PCT systems have been improved. When filing an international application, in principle, the PCT system is used. However, some companies file an international patent depending on the type of invention.

Trends in research and development or patent application in the late 1990s and their background

- With regard to drug discovery using gene information, many companies have increased research and development expenses. However, some companies are reducing other fields. Therefore, whether total research and development expenses increase or not depends on the company. There are more companies whose overall number of patent applications has increased than those where it has decreased, while there are companies focusing on more narrow patent applications. Therefore, patent strategies vary by company.
- One of the reasons behind the increase in research and development expenses and in the number of patent applications is not the influence of the patent system, but stems from the fact that research and development has expanded into new fields and the subject matter of patent protection has diversified. However, these patent applications are for internal use, not for licensing-out in the future.

Other

- Research and development departments and intellectual departments in the pharmaceutical industry work closer together than in other industries. Recently, this trend has become stronger.
- With regard to the reduction of patent fees, it has not had a significant influence since the number of patent applications is not large to begin with.

Summary of the Results of Pharmaceuticals Interviews

During the interview survey, the patent system reforms implemented in 1970 and after are commonly cited as having the most significant influence on innovation activities are the substance patents that were introduced in 1975 and the patent term extension of pharmaceutical products that was introduced in 1988. Meanwhile, it was found that other measures were not considered to have had a significant influence. In the questionnaire from the previous section, 30 percent or more of the companies in the pharmaceutical industry responded that pro-patent measures contributed to an increase in research and development or patent applications; however, no companies commented that there was an obvious influence.

Meanwhile, when examining in detail the content of patent applications in the pharmaceutical industry, in addition to patents on technology concerning the traditional development process of pharmaceuticals products, such as chemosynthesis, the percentage of patents related to biotechnology, such as genetic modification, analysis of gene function, etc. has recently been increasing. This increase is considered to be influenced by the fact that the subject areas for patent protection under the patent system have been expanding to biological patents, gene-related patents, etc. The pharmaceutical industry has become global and, as shown in the results of the interview, it is common for companies to file an international patent application through the PCT system for most inventions. Since the United States market is particularly important in the international pharmaceutical market (Motohashi (2007)), patent system operation in the United States has a significant influence.

It is not seen, at least among major pharmaceutical companies, that pro-patent measures in Japan clearly contribute to the promotion of innovation activities in companies. On the other hand, concerns are heard from many companies about the "tragedy of the anticommons" of patents for gene fragments and research tools, which are found mainly in the United States. It is a feature of research and development in the pharmaceutical industry that they are implemented in close coordination with the intellectual property department; and this relationship currently tends to be stronger. This is because intellectual property strategies have become important at an early stage of research and development due to the increase in patents upstream in the drug discovery process, while substance patents were focused and patented fields were clear in the past.

Moreover, the number of licensing-in of patents has increased and licensing fees are rising as drug discovery technology that uses gene information expands and the achievements are patented. In theory, even if patent rights are strengthened, there will be no problems if a licensee negotiates a licensing agreement before investing sunk costs, such as research and development (Green and Scotchmer (1995)). In the case of pharmaceutical products, the intellectual property department is involved with research and development at the early stages and research proceeds by checking a patent map. Therefore, in theory it is close to an ideal condition. However, patent examination standards for new areas are reviewed one after another and standards for some fields remain ambiguous, such as judgments on whether patents on screening tools affect end products. Therefore, we cannot deny the possibility that strengthening patents for upper-stream technology disturbs innovation in lower-stream technology. Although it is rare that research and development are discontinued due to the rejection of licensing, there are many cases where expensive licensing fees are paid in order to avoid such a situation. Many of the companies that have become counterparties to this licensing are overseas venture companies, mainly in the United States. Consequently, the pharmaceutical industry has a structure that can be significantly influenced by the United States patent system, even more than the patent system in Japan. During the interview survey, there was an indication that patents which cover a broad range of final pharmaceutical products focusing on the functions of gene and proteins (functional medical-use patents) were recently approved in the United States. It is important to promote a clarification of the patent standards and to encourage strict control over the operation of the patent system at the Trilateral Patent Offices Meeting, etc.

SUMMARY OF PRO-PATENT SYSTEM REFORMS AND COMPANY ACTIONS

We have reviewed the transitions of the patent system and the trends of companies' innovation activities in Japan after World War II. Under the current Japanese Patent Act, which came into force in 1960, numerous system reforms have been conducted due to international harmonization of the intellectual property system and pro-patent measures. The patent right was established as a "broader" and "stronger" right through the expansion of patents into new areas in the IT and biotech fields, substance patents, patent term extensions, increase of compensation amounts for patent disputes, improvement of procedures, etc. These system reforms have been implemented in order to secure incentives for companies' innovation activities, which can be regarded as a source of economic development in Japan. Moreover, the Japanese patent system focuses not only on securing incentives for investors, but it also on providing advantages to the users of patented technologies, for example by adopting the laid-open publication system at an early stage.

With regard to the relationship between the patent system and companies' innovation activities, there were no signs that research and development expenses or the number of patent applications made by companies obviously increased due to the system reforms. The patent system has been reviewed intermittently in response to the prevailing conditions of the time; therefore, it is possible to say that it is difficult to portray the effects of individual system changes. However, it is appropriate to consider that research and development investment is influenced by various factors, such as trends in long-run demand for target products or rival companies, expansion of technological opportunities, etc. and the patent system is just one of many factors. Bransteter and Sakakibara (2001) implemented quantitative analysis by using data classified by company on the influence of the system reform in 1987, during which the improved multiple claims system and the extension of patent terms for pharmaceutical products were implemented, and stated that there was no influence on research and development. Moreover, in cases in the United States, Kortum and Lerner (1998) analyzed the causes of the recent rapid growth in patent applications and also concluded that the causes were the expansion of technological opportunities mainly in IT and biotech fields rather than the influence of the patent system.

Regarding changes in the number of patent applications in Japan, the number of applications in the IT and biotech fields have been increasing since the late 1990s. Moreover, when examining in detail technology fields in which the number of patent applications has dramatically increased, one finds the greatest increases in the new patent areas, such as software, etc. With respect to the overall economy, it would appear that the influence of the patent system on innovation activities is limited, while the influence on high-tech fields, such as the IT and biotech fields, is relatively significant. According to the result of the company survey carried out by the Institute of Intellectual Property, the percentage of companies that have felt an impact from recent pro-patent measures is high in the electronics and pharmaceutical industries. However, it is necessary to note that the content of pro-patent measures that have an impact on them is different for the electronics industry and for the pharmaceutical industry. Companies in the electronics industry consider exploiting patents that they hold proactively for cross-licensing and are therefore greatly aware of the influence of the system reforms concerning "strong" patents. On the other hand, companies in the pharmaceutical industry are active in licensing-in in the field of biotechnology-based pharmaceuticals, and they are thus more sensitive to the expansion of patent rights into new fields, such as gene-related patents.

In this chapter, I have investigated in detail the incentive structure for innovations in companies through company interviews in the electronics manufactures and pharmaceuticals respectively. With regard to the electronics manufactures, each of the major electronics manufacturers has attempted to activate its own patent properties strategically. Trends in the number of patent applications vary by company since some companies have focused on more narrow patent applications. With regard to software patents, each company has increased the number of patent applications, the reason being that the available scope of software patents was broadened. However, it is found that the influence from pro-patent measures is limited to patent strategies, but does not reach research and development activities.

Meanwhile, with regard to the pharmaceutical industry, the term for research and development of their products is 10 years or more and the right protection by patent is very important. However, there was no sign that pro-patent measures obviously affected companies' research and development or innovation activities, such as patent applications, etc. It is necessary to note that patent applications in new areas have been activated through the expansion of technological opportunities in research and development, such as drug discovery studies using genetic recombination technology or gene information. In addition, Japanese pharmaceutical manufacturers have engaged in licensing-in activities with overseas venture companies. If rights are not protected by patent, new technologies held by universities or venture companies will not be disclosed and it is possible that the speed of research and development of pharmaceutical products will be reduced. On the other hand, if they are protected by patent, research and development may be disturbed by an upsurge in the number of patents. In particular, the patent system in the United States has adopted a first-to-invent system. Therefore, expensive licensing fees may be demanded due to submarine patents. In that case, there are no advantages for patent users. It is also considered that rising licensing fees or increasing patent disputes may heighten the uncertainty of research and development and reduce investment. These may be seen as issues concerning the operation of the patent system in the United States and they have become particularly important issues in the pharmaceutical industry, although they do not concern the subject of this report, the patent system in Japan.

INTERVIEWS ON GLOBALIZED COMPANY ACTIVITIES

Globalizing Company Patent Activities

In the company interviews, there were many indications that it is essential to respond not only to the trends of the patent system in Japan, but also to those in Europe and the United States. Since the patent system has adopted a principle of territoriality, in which rights are valid only in the area where they are obtained, if a business field develops into other countries, rights must be obtained in accordance with the patent system of countries where the business field is developed. In particular, due to the size of its market and its growth potential, the influence of the intellectual property system in the United States has increased. Many share the opinion that companies have to establish their strategies based on the United States patent system because patents have expanded into new areas and rights are strengthened under the United States patent system to a more advanced degree than in other areas since the patent system shifted to pro-patent measures in the 1980s.

Development of the International Application System by the PCT

The number of international patent applications from Japan has increased sharply since the late 1990s. With regard to international patent applications, convenient methods, such as applications based on the Paris Convention and PCT system, etc., have been developed. In particular, the number of patent applications by using the PCT system has recently been rapidly increasing. The PCT (Patent Cooperation Treaty) is a system that came into effect in 1978 and over 110 countries participate in the PCT today. Under the PCT system, an applicant must list the countries where a patent application is going to be filed and then the individual applications can be filed as a single "bundle."

International Harmonization of the Patent System

As mentioned above, a convenient international patent application system has been organized. Global companies have a greater advantage to see patent systems harmonized internationally and finally become a single, global patent system. With regard to the international harmonization of patent systems, the TRIPS Agreement of the WTO came into effect in 1995 and stipulated minimum protection levels for intellectual property rights, such as copyright, trademark, geographical indication, design, patent, etc.; moreover, there were procedures for exercising rights and dispute settlement procedures. WTO member countries are required to comply with the agreement. Many of the previous patent system reforms in Japan were in response to the TRIPS Agreement.

Comparing patent systems in Japan, the United States and Europe, the systems in Japan and Europe are very similar, while the United States has adopted a different system. The biggest difference is that Japan and Europe have adopted a "first-to-file system" (timing of application supersedes) for determining the priority date of a patent, while the United States has adopted a "first-to-invent system" (timing of invention supersedes). Under the patent system in Europe, just like in Japan, if an application is filed, it will be published after 18 months and the subject will be examined only when an examination is requested. Meanwhile, under the patent system in the United States, since the laid-open publication system or examination request system do not exist, others can learn the information only when the patent is registered. This problem is called a "submarine patent." In response to this issue, the United States Patent Act was modified in 1999 and an early laid-open publication system was adopted. However, an invention for which a patent application is not filed in countries other than the United States is not subject to this system. Therefore, this system does not match the patent systems in Japan and Europe. In contrast, if a Japanese company claims priority based on the patent application in Japan and files a patent application in the United States, the invention shall be disclosed and the 18-month period starts from the priority date, the content of the invention will be disclosed in a comparatively short time from the date of application in the United States. Consequently, this system is disadvantageous to foreign companies.

Adjustment of Patent Examination Practices

Along with the above-mentioned system adjustments, it is important to adjust patent examination practices. For instance, the issue of how far to grant patents in new technological fields, such as business model patents, gene function patents, etc., has been adjusted between Japan, Europe and the United States based on case studies. As a whole, it is said that the standards used in the United States are not strict. It is also indicated that the standards for "novelty" or "inventive step," which are requirements for a patent, are low in the United States and low-quality patents are mass-produced. Jaffe and Lerner, leading scholars of the United States intellectual property system, indicate in their book that the United States Patent and Trademark Office granted low-quality patents unnecessarily in a way that disturbed innovation (Jaffe and Lerner (2004)). According to their analysis, after the CAFC was established in 1982, the percentage of judgments that upheld the validity of a patent in a lawsuit claiming the invalidity of a patent increased from approximately 30 percent to 55 percent. On the other hand, the United States Patent and Trademark Office adopted an incentive system, in which a greater number of patents are examined in a certain period of time in response to an increasing number of patent applications. This caused a situation where many patents with questions over their novelty or with an overlapping scope of patent rights were granted and patent disputes increased rapidly. In this way, when the instability of patent rights or the future risk of disputes increases, it can cause particular disturbances to the innovations of companies that have less bargaining ability, like venture companies. In order to respond to these problems, Jaffe and Lerner state that it is essential to heighten the quality of patent rights through opposition to a patent before granting the patent or through a reexamination system after granting the patent.

IDEAL FUTURE FOR THE PATENT SYSTEM

Optimizing Ideal Patent Protection

The Intellectual Property Strategy Basic Plan, which was established in June 2003, emphasized strengthening the intellectual property right system by patents, etc., under the theme of an "intellectual property-based nation." As elements for strengthening the protection of intellectual properties in a specific plan of action, measures for "strong" patents, such as expeditious patent examination, establishment of a "patent court" function, strengthening the compensation system, etc., were accentuated.

However, according to the results of this analysis, the effects of measures taken in consideration of "strong" patents, as seen in improvement of the patent dispute settlement system or the increase in compensation amounts, were marginal. Rather, it is important to establish proper patent protection in high-tech fields, such as IT and biotechnology, etc. In this regard, it is important not to promote the expansion of rights protection, but to establish a balanced protection of rights in consideration of the distribution of technology as well.

The contents of proper rights protection may vary for each individual field. For instance, if the rights protection of patent holders is strengthened with regard to a field, such as biotechnology-based pharmaceuticals, where pioneer patents are held by companies and universities in Europe and the United States, it is highly possible that it would have the effect of controlling the innovations of Japanese pharmaceutical manufacturers.

Meanwhile, whereas the exploitation of scientific knowledge has become important in pharmaceutical research and development, the patent system plays an important role in properly distributing research achievements at universities and public research institutes. Consequently, it is appropriate to obtain a patent for an invention, strengthen its protection and enhance exemptions for patent exploitation simultaneously.

Progress in Harmonization

The Patent Offices of Japan, the United States and Europe hold regular meetings and have been adjusting the intellectual property system or examination standards through cooperation in patent examination. With regard to the global harmonization of patent systems, WIPO (World Intellectual Property Organization) adopted the Patent Law Treaty in 2000 in order to promote international harmonization. The treaty stipulated mutual exploitation of investigation on prior art of patent or examination results and the goal of achieving international harmonization ("deep harmonization") not only in the system, but also at the operational level. Mutual exploitation of investigation on prior art or examination results are important for adjusting operational examination standards and providing greater advantages to the Patent Offices of each country where the operational burden has increased due to the increase in patent applications. Moreover, it is expected that activities for realizing global patents will be undertaken in the future by expanding the modified actual condition investigation (with respect to internationally applied patents, a system in which other countries accept the results of the examination conducted by a country in order to eliminate duplicated examinations).

NOTES

1. Examination standards in Europe are considered to be the strictest because business models are expressly not included among patent subjects. However, many business model patents are originally realized in software; therefore, a patent has been granted to them based on the technical requirements of software (Aita et al. (2001)).
2. With regard to the relationship between pro-patent measures and innovation activities in the United States, Jaffe (2000) conducted a wide ranging survey of both theoretical studies and experimental studies. In addition, Nakayama (2002) conducted a survey focused on an issue of anticommons that is caused by pro-patent measures.
3. On the other hand, a laid-open publication system was established in the United States in 1999 as a result of the international harmonization of patent systems. However, there is criticism, for example if a technology is disclosed, it will disadvantage small- and medium-size companies that have a smaller bargaining capacity (Gallini (2002)).
4. The Yale Survey is famous as a survey concerning the exclusiveness of technology. An investigation of Japanese companies was conducted using the same survey slips by the

National Institute of Science and Technology Policy. This feature of pharmaceutical industry is confirmed by both investigations conducted in Japan and the United States (National Institute of Science and Technology Policy (1997)).

5. This interview was conducted from December 2002 to February 2003. Meetings with companies have been continued intermittently and it is confirmed that there are no significant changes in the results of the interview.

REFERENCES

Aita, Y., R. Hirashima and K. Sumikura (2001), Sentankagakugijutsu to chitekizaisanken (Advanced Science and Technology and Intellectual Property Right), Japan Institute of Invention and Innovation

Branstetter, L. and M. Sakakibara (2001), "Do Stronger Patents Induce More Innovation? Evidence from the 1998 Japanese Patent Law Reforms," *RAND Journal of Economics*, **32**(1), 77–100

Gallini, N. (2002), "The Economics of Patents: Lessons from Recent US Patent Reform," *Journal of Economic Perspectives*, **16**(2), 131–154

Goto, A. and K. Motohashi, "Construction of a Japanese Patent Database and a first look at Japanese patenting activities," *Research Policy*, **36**(9), 1431–1442

Green, N. and S. Scotchmer (1995), "On the division of profit in sequential innovation," *RAND Journal of Economics*, **26**(1), 20–33

Grindley, P. and D. Teece (1997), "Managing Intellectual Capital: Licensing and Cross-Licensing in Semiconductors and Electronics," *California Management Review*, **39**(2), 8–41

Hall, B.H. and R.H. Ziedonis (2001), "An Empirical Study of Patenting in the US Semiconductor Industry, 1979–1995," *Rand Journal of Economics*, **32**(1), 101–128

Heller, M.A. and R. Eisenberg (1998), "Can Patents Deter Innovation? The Anticommons in Biomedical Research," *Science*, **280**(5364), 698–701

The Institute of Intellectual Property (2002), Heisei 13 nendo Kougyoushoyukenseidomondai chousa houkokusho (Fiscal Year 2001: Report on the Survey on Industrial Property Issues), Tokkyo to keizai ni kansuru chousakenkyuhoukokusho (Report on Research on Patent and Economy)

Jaffe, A.B. (2000), "The US Patent System in Transition: Policy Innovation and the Innovation Process," *Research Policy*, **29**, 531–557

Jaffe, A.B. and J. Lerner (2004), *Innovation and its Discontents: How Our Broken Patent System is Endangering Innovation and Progress, and What to do about it*, Princeton University Press

Kortum, S. and J. Lerner (1998), "What is Behind the Recent Surge in Patenting?" *Research Policy*, **28**, 1–22

Lerner, J. (2002), "Patent Protection and Innovation over 150 Years," NBER Working Paper Series, No. 8977

Minetaki, K. and K. Motohashi (2008), "The Software Industry's Multilayered Subcontracting Structure: Empirical analysis of innovation and productivity," RIETI Discussion Paper Series 08-J-002

Motohashi, K. (2005) "Chitekizaisanseido no henka to sono kokusaitekina doukou" (Changes in the Intellectual Property System and the International Trends) in Akiya Nagata and Kouichi Sumikura (eds), *MOT Chitekizaisan to gijutsukeiei* (MOT, Intellectual Property and Technology Management), Maruzen

Motohashi, K. (2006), "Tokkyo no yabu to kigyo no chizaisenryaku ni kansuru Kenkyu" (Research on Patent Thickets and Companies' Intellectual Property Strategy), *Heisei 17 nendo Tokkyochou sangyouzaisannken seido mondai chousak-enkyuuhoukokusho "Anchikomonzu no higeki" ni kansuru shomondaino bunseki-houkokusho* (Fiscal Year 2005: Research Report on Industrial Property System Issues, Analysis Report of Issues on the "Tragedy of the Anticommons"), March, Institute of Intellectual Property

Motohashi, K. (2007), "The Changing Autarky Pharmaceutical R&D Process: Causes and Consequences of Growing R&D Collaboration in Japanese Firms," *International Journal of Technology Management*, **39**(1/2), 33–48

Motohashi, K. and M. Kani (2009), "Propatento seido kaisei ga haiteku sangyou no inobeishon katsudou ni ataeru eikyou bunseki" (Analysis of the Influence of Pro-Patent System Reform on the Innovation Activities of High-Tech Industries), Heisei 20 nendo Tokkyocho Ukeoijigyo: *Heisei 20 nendo Wagakuni ni okeru sangyou zaisanken tou no Shutsugandoukoutou ni kansuru chousahou-kokusho* (Contract Project of the Patent Office in Fiscal Year 2008; Report on the Survey of the Trends, etc. in Industrial Property Rights, etc. Applications in Japan in Fiscal Year 2008), March, Institute of Intellectual Property

Nagaoka, S. (2002), "Gijutsuhyoujun eno Kigyoukankyouryoku: Patentopuulu no Keizaigaku" (Collaboration among Competitors for Innovating Technical Standards: Economics of the Patent Pool), Hitotsubashi University Institute of Innovation Research Working Paper 02-02, Paper 02-J-019

Nakayama, I. (2002), "'Propatento' to 'Anchikomonzu': Tokkyo to inobeishon ni kansuru kenkyu ga shisasuru 'propatento' no igi, kouka, kadai" ('Pro-patent' and 'Anticommons': Meaning, Effects and Issues of 'Pro-patent' Indicated by Research on Patents and Innovation), RIETI Discussion Paper 02-J-019

National Institute of Science and Technology Policy (1997), Technological Opportunities and Appropriating the Returns from Innovation – Comparison of Survey Results from Japan and the U.S., NISTEP REPORT No.48

Patent Office (2000), Sofutowea kanren hatsumei no kakudai to hatsumei no teigi (Expansion of Software-relate Invention and Definition of Invention)

Sumida, M. and N. Tatsumi (2000), Chitekizaisanhou (Intellectual Property Act), Yuhikaku Arma

APPENDIX: STATISTICS OF THE SURVEY

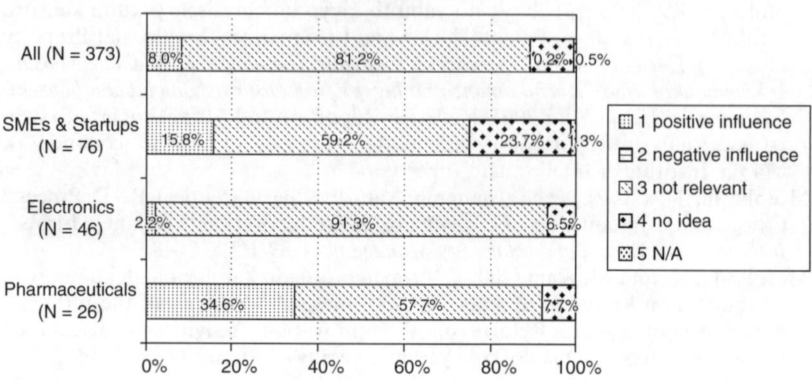

Figure 2A.1 *Influences of broad protection (expansion of the scope of protection to new areas) on amount of investment in research*

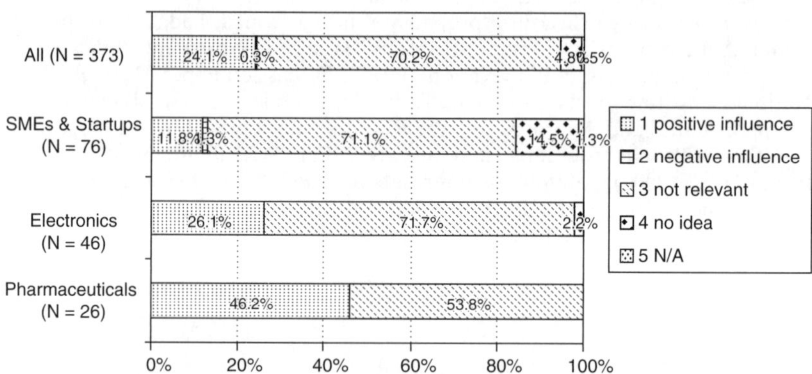

Figure 2A.2 *Influences of broad protection (expansion of the scope of protection to new areas) on the number of patent applications*

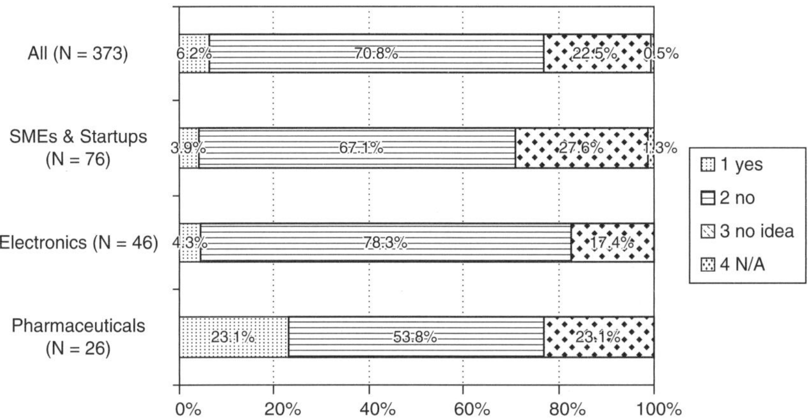

Figure 2A.3 *Existence of adverse effects from broad protection (expansion of the scope of protection to new areas)*

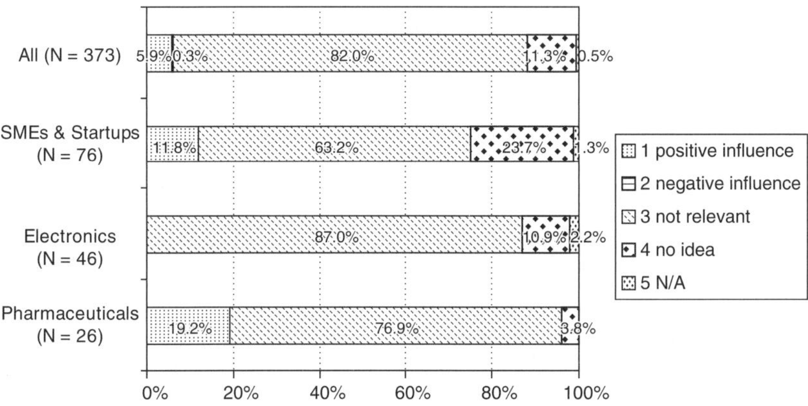

Figure 2A.4 *Influences of broad protection (expansion of the scope of protection of individual patents) on amount of investment in research*

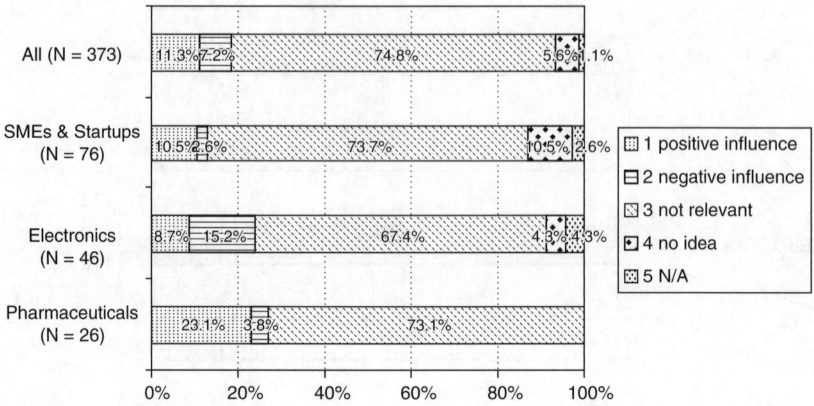

Figure 2A.5 Influences of broad protection (expansion of the scope of protection of individual patents) on the number of patent applications

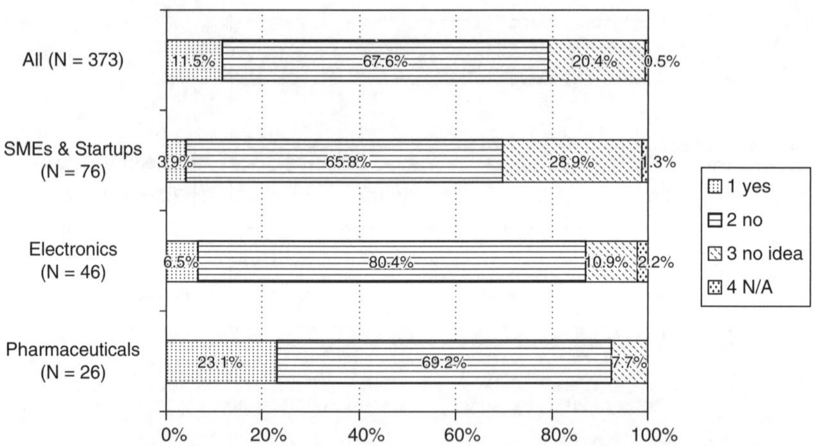

Figure 2A.6 Existence of adverse effects from broad protection (expansion of the scope of protection of individual patents)

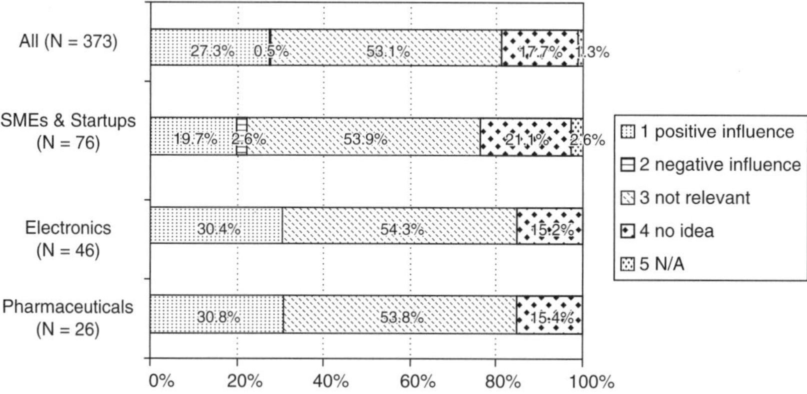

Figure 2A.7 *Influences of strong protection to incentives for research*

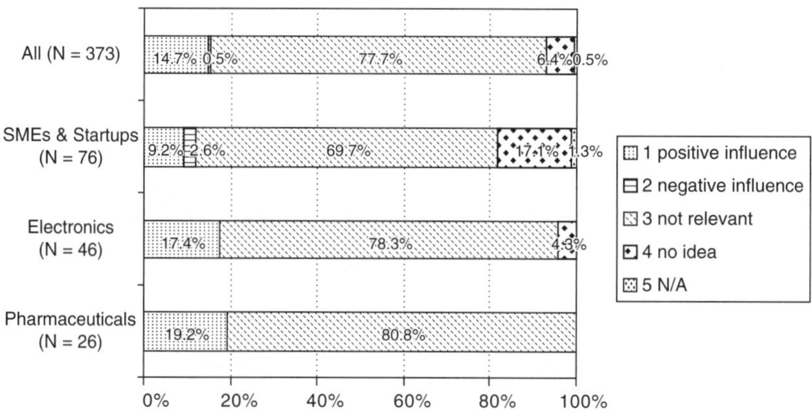

Figure 2A.8 *Influences of strong protection on the number of patent applications*

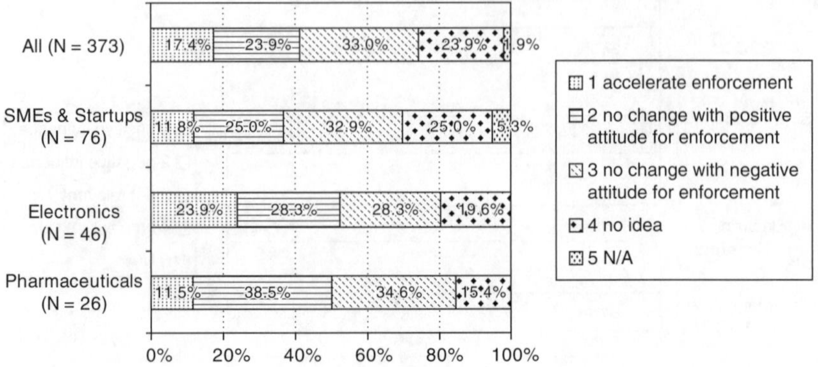

Figure 2A.9 Influences of strong protection on policies for enforcing patent rights

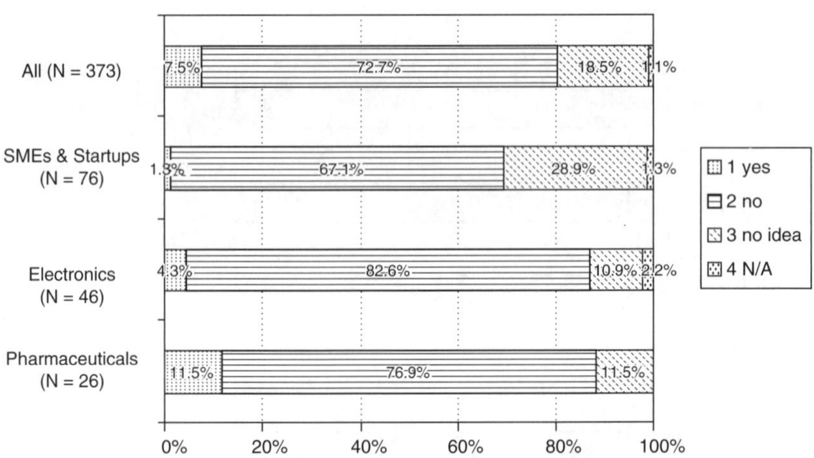

Figure 2A.10 Existence of adverse effects from strong protection

3. Ignoring patents*

Mark A. Lemley**

More than 2.5 million United States patents have been issued in the last 20 years.[1] While these patents are spread across all industries, a large percentage is concentrated in the information technology (IT) industries and others in biotechnology.[2] The prevalence of patents in these industries has caused a number of people to worry about an "anticommons" in patent law, in which companies that want to make a product find it impossible to acquire all the rights they need from many different owners.[3] This is a particular problem for semiconductor, telecommunications, and software companies, which must aggregate hundreds or thousands of different components to make an integrated product. Each of those components may be patented, some by many different people.[4] The threat that any one of those patent owners can obtain an injunction shutting down the entire integrated product allows them to extort settlements well in excess of the value of their patent.[5] The patent damages rules similarly permit excessive recoveries, such as the recent $1.5 billion jury verdict against Microsoft for infringing one of many patents covering just one of many features of an add-on to the Microsoft Windows product.[6] Patent law permits these product manufacturers to be found to be "willful" infringers liable for treble damages and attorneys' fees, even if they were unaware of the patent or even the patent owner at the time they began selling the product.[7] And even if the manufacturer can avoid any of these risks by invalidating or proving non-infringement of each of these patents, doing so would cost millions of dollars per case in legal fees.[8] Given these problems, it's a wonder companies make products in patent-intensive industries at all.

And yet make products they do. Both my own experience and what limited empirical evidence there is suggest that companies do not seem much deterred from making products by the threat of all this patent litigation.[9] Intel continues to make microprocessors, Cisco routers, and Microsoft operating system software, even though they collectively face nearly 100 patent-infringement lawsuits at a time and receive hundreds more threats of suit each year.[10] Companies continue to do research on gene therapy, and even make "gene chips" that incorporate thousands of patented genes,[11] despite the fact that a significant fraction of those genes are patented.[12] Universities and academic researchers continue to engage in experimentation with patented inventions despite the now clear rule that they are not immune from liability for doing so.[13] John Walsh's study suggests that threats of patent infringement are not in fact responsible for deterring much, if any, research.[14]

What's going on here? The answer, I think, is straightforward, if surprising: both researchers and companies in component industries simply ignore patents. Virtually everyone does it. They do it at all stages of endeavor. Companies and lawyers tell engineers not to read patents in starting their research, lest their knowledge of the patent disadvantage the company by making it a willful infringer.[15] Walsh et al. similarly find that much of the reason university researchers are not deterred by patents is that they never learn of the patent in the first place.[16] When their research leads to an invention, their patent lawyers commonly don't conduct a search for prior patents before seeking their own protection in the Patent and Trademark Office (PTO).[17] Nor do they conduct a search before launching their own product. Rather, they wait and see if any patent owner claims that the new product infringes their patent. Even then, it is common in many industries characterized by a significant number of "patent trolls"[18] to ignore the first cease-and-desist letter one receives from a patent owner, secure in the knowledge that patent litigation is expensive and uncertain and that some letter-writers will never follow up with a serious threat of suit.[19] Finally, and most significantly, companies in component industries who in fact get sued for patent infringement never pull their product off the market pending the outcome of the suit. Rather, they decide to take their chances in court and hope that they can avoid infringement or invalidate the patent. Even if they embark upon a product redesign to avoid infringing the asserted patent, the redesign rarely replaces the original product unless and until the patent is held valid and infringed.[20] This intentional ignorance of patent rights in the hands of others has led some to label major manufacturers in the IT industries "patent pirates."[21]

To get a perspective on how strange this might seem to an outsider to the patent system – or even to an outsider to the component industries in which this behavior is common – compare it to the world of real property. If I want to build a house, I'd better be darn sure that I own the land on which the house is built. In fact, it would be foolhardy to begin construction before I owned the rights to the land, in the hopes that I would be able to obtain the rights later. Nor would a prospective homebuilder put up with significant uncertainty about the boundaries of the land on which she was building. People don't often build houses that might or might not be on their land, hoping that they would ultimately win any property dispute.

And even if a few people were so reckless as to want to do one of these things, banks won't fund construction without certainty in the form of a title insurance search report indicating that the builder unambiguously owns all the rights she needs.

It is currently very much in vogue to talk about patent rights as a form of property, and in particular to draw analogies to real property.[22] So let's engage in a thought experiment: what if we took the analogy seriously and actually behaved with patents as we do with real property? Product manufacturers would have to stop ignoring patents. No venture capitalist or bank (or shareholder, should Intel fund the project internally) would give Intel the money to build a new manufacturing plant (or "fab") unless it could demonstrate that it had conducted an exhaustive search for patents it might infringe in manufacturing its chips and had obtained irrevocable or at least long-term licenses[23] to use any patent that anyone might conceivably later assert against the chips or the manufacturing plant. Intel, in turn, would look to a group of "patent insurance" firms that would spring up and that would conduct the search and determine what patents needed to be licensed. Unless and until all of this had happened, Intel could not start construction of its fab, much less make or sell chips produced by that fab. If there were significant disagreement over whether a party legitimately owned patent rights, perhaps Intel could bring a declaratory judgment action to try to clarify those rights, but it would hold construction in abeyance until it got an answer.[24] And since there is no experimental use defense to patent infringement, scientists at both universities and corporations would have to conduct a similar search and wait to get permission from all possible interested parties before they began their research, lest they infringe a patent in the lab.

Would this world be desirable? I'm skeptical. Let's begin with the benefits of such a world. Patent owners would get paid early and often. Patent litigation would decrease, or maybe even disappear entirely, because anyone who wanted to make a product would find the patent owner and enter into a deal up front, or else not make the product. And patent owners who compete in the marketplace, and rely on the patent to preserve exclusivity, would not face competition during the often-protracted period during which the patent is being litigated.

At the same time, these benefits would come at significant cost. First, both research and the manufacture of products would be regularly delayed for years and perhaps decades as potential defendants identified and cleared rights. The problem is not simply the time and cost required to find and evaluate the patents, contact the patent owner, and negotiate a license, though those costs may be significant. Rather, the legal rights in question may not even exist at the time Intel needs to make its investment decision. Many, perhaps most, patent lawsuits are filed against independent developers who themselves came up with the idea, generally at about the same time the patentee did.[25] The fact that it takes over three and a half years for the PTO to issue a patent, and that for at least 18 months of that time the application is not published,[26] means that the wait to identify the relevant rights may be significant indeed. The problem is even worse because of the common practice of filing continuation applications, which permit applicants to change their claims in an application for up to 20 years after the application was filed and even after a patent has issued on that application.[27]

A true title-search system would require Intel to wait until we knew for sure whether a patent would issue on any existing continuation application. Nor would the uncertainty end then; 10 years of claim construction litigation have made clear that we rarely know for sure what a patent covers even after it issues.[28] So it is not clear that we will know even then which patents Intel must license. The significant delay of a title-search system harms consumer welfare because both innovation and product deployment occur later than they otherwise would.[29]

Second, a real-property patent system would replace competition with central coordination in a significant number of cases. So far we have assumed that the patent owners will be willing to license their patents. But that is likely not to be true in many cases. Patent owners who compete in the marketplace want exclusivity, and there is no license price an equally efficient competitor will be willing to pay that will compensate for the loss of monopoly rights. Even patent owners who do not compete in the marketplace may find it more lucrative to grant an exclusive rather than a non-exclusive license to someone who does make a product, for the same reasons. Nor will a competing company be particularly sympathetic to efforts by outsiders to engage in research on the invention if the effect of that research will be to design around or improve that core invention. The effect of a real-property or title-search system is to replace competition in the shadow of a patent while it is being litigated with single-firm markets whenever the patentee participates in the market, either directly or by proxy. Researchers who could not obtain a license would direct their scientific efforts into different fields, and potential competitors would do the same, meaning that the owner of a core patent could control who, if anyone, worked on a particular technology. If you believe, as I do, that the evidence suggests that competition is often a better spur to innovation than monopoly,[30] removing that contingent competition is a potentially significant cost.[31]

Third, and perhaps most important, a significant percentage – maybe as many as three-fourths[32] – of these patents turn out to be either invalid or not infringed. It is this probabilistic nature that most critically distinguishes patents from real property.[33] Under the current system in patent-ignoring industries, consumers benefit from competition during the time before those patents are invalidated or held not to be infringed. Under a real-property patent system, the owners of invalid patents can capture supracompetitive profits during the time before their patents are invalidated, profits made at the expense of consumers and that they will never have to disgorge.[34] That extra profit, in turn, would create significant incentives to obtain and enforce dubious patents. Indeed, the problem is even worse: in a title-search system in which researchers and manufacturers must clear rights before beginning work, accused infringers may be unlikely to take the chance of challenging the patent at all, agreeing to pay a license even for a weak patent.[35] I identified reducing patent litigation as a benefit of the real-property approach; the flip side is that ignoring patents promotes patent challenges. If you believe, as a number of scholars suggest, that challenges to bad patents are a public good that is undersupplied today,[36] the real-property approach will make that undersupply problem worse.

Finally, people usually build a house on a single plot of land, while as I have noted, there may be hundreds or thousands of rights that must be aggregated to build a multi-component product. As Carl Shapiro and I have argued elsewhere, this fact exacerbates the patent holdup problem and leads to systematic overpayments by manufacturing companies, because individual patent owners won't discount the royalty they charge to account for the complementary rights owned by others.[37] It's not that nothing of that sort ever happens with land; commercial builders often face a holdout problem when they need to buy numerous plots of contiguous land for a new building. But the problem is much, much worse in the patent system, because the number of rights that must be aggregated is greater, the scope of those rights (and therefore which ones need to be included) is less clear, and courts may be unable to grant injunctive relief tailored to protect only the patent in question without interfering with the non-infringing uses.[38] The result is that bargaining breakdown, already a risk in real property (and the justification for the use of eminent domain in support of private projects),[39] will be much more of a risk.[40] And in this hypothetical world, without successful bargaining no one will build products or engage in research.

There is, to be fair, one industry in which the patent system does bear some resemblance to the world of my thought experiment: the pharmaceutical industry. Patent owners in that industry identify all the patents they have covering a drug by listing them in the Orange Book.[41] Entry by generic pharmaceutical companies is strictly regulated by the FDA. Once the FDA grants approval, the generic must tell the patent owner it plans to enter and give the patent owner an opportunity to sue. If they do – and they essentially always do – patent owners are entitled to automatic preliminary injunctions pending the outcome of patent litigation.[42] Even once that automatic preliminary injunction expires, generic entrants are often afraid to enter "at risk" without a final determination that the patent is invalid or not infringed, just as people are afraid to build houses on land they don't own. If a title-search system works in the pharmaceutical industry, why won't it work just as well in other industries?

The answer is two-fold. First, the characteristics of the pharmaceutical industry are quite different from the component industries in which it is common to ignore patents. The need for strong patent rights is greater in that industry because of the cost and delay associated with FDA approval.[43]

Virtually all patent owners in the industry are market competitors who rely on the exclusivity of the patent system coupled with the exclusivity that FDA approval provides.[44] The scope of the patents is generally quite clear, as they are defined in terms of chemical structure, and disputes over what the patent means are less common than in information technology. Pharmaceutical innovation is rarely cumulative, so the need for further research on a particular drug after FDA approval, while not zero,[45] is not particularly high. Further, the patent owner identifies up front the patents that cover a particular product. It can do that because market entry is delayed for years and even decades by the FDA approval process, with the result that all parties involved will generally know what patent rights exist before the generic seeks to enter. All of these characteristics, particularly those that flow from the FDA regulatory structure, make the need for strong patent protection greater and the costs of that protection less.

Second, notwithstanding those characteristics, it is worth noting that the title-search approach creates significant problems even in the pharmaceutical industry. Patent owners have strong incentives to extend the life of their patents, whether by "evergreening" – obtaining multiple patents covering the same product[46] – or by "product-hopping" – changing the product they sell and restarting the regulatory clock once their patent on the existing product expires or is invalidated.[47] Because generic entry is regulated, they have significant incentive to enter into side deals with generics to keep them from competing, and indeed it is quite common for patent-owning pharmaceutical companies to pay their only possible competitors to stay out of the market.[48] And generic companies increasingly agree to such monopoly-sharing settlements, rather than invalidating the patents in question. As a result, we rarely see generic entry much before the natural expiration of an original patent on a drug, and in fact, generic entry often doesn't even occur once that patent expires.

In short, the real-property characteristics of pharmaceutical patents are a function of the FDA regulatory process. Even there, it is not clear that the costs of delayed competition are worth the candle. We might still get pharmaceutical innovation if generic companies were permitted to ignore patents as well. But outside the regulated industry context, it seems likely that treating patents like real property would significantly delay entry and improvement without conferring many of the benefits asserted for the real-property approach. In those other industries, having patents but operating as if they don't constrain behavior may be better than treating the patent right as sacrosanct.[49]

That doesn't mean that ignoring patents is the best of all possible worlds either. In industries that ignore patents, patent owners can generally get paid only if they threaten to sue. In a real-property world, manufacturers can make products only if they pre-clear all the rights. There ought to be a middle ground between these extremes. Imagine a functioning, efficient market for patent licenses, one that incorporated the possibilities of patent invalidity and non-infringing alternatives and avoided licenses based on holdup, but which also inculcated in manufacturers norms of paying for the rights they use. Patentees could get paid a reasonable amount for their rights, but without the risks and uncertainty of the current system.[50] And companies interested in using innovations could seek out new ideas embodied in patents, rather than burying their heads in the sand and developing inventions entirely on their own.[51]

What would it take to get to such a world? Patent law would have to change in significant respects. First, we would need greater certainty about the nature and scope of patent rights much earlier than we have it today. This would require the PTO to devote substantial additional resources to processing patent applications more quickly,[52] but it would also require strict caps on the ability of patentees to delay prosecution using continuation applications.[53] Requiring publication of applications in all cases, and encouraging it to occur earlier than 18 months after filing, would help.[54]

It might also be desirable to implement peer-review,[55] post-grant opposition,[56] gold-plating,[57] or some other mechanism for determining the scope and validity of rights earlier rather than later. Second, we might want to implement an independent invention defense or at least some form of prior user right,[58] both as a matter of equity – manufacturers can reasonably object to paying for technology they developed themselves and did not copy – and because even with a quicker patent grant it will be hard to find and negotiate over patents in cases of simultaneous invention. Third, we would need to ensure that the rules that target willful infringement do not discourage people from reading patents.[59] Fourth, we need to change the patent remedy rules to reduce or eliminate the problem of holdup. The *eBay v. MercExchange*[60] decision is a significant step in this direction, but reform of the reasonable royalty calculation will also be necessary.[61]

Having restructured patent law in significant ways to reduce the need for component-industry manufacturers to keep their heads in the sand, two further changes in the law would be appropriate to discourage them from doing so. First, manufacturers in this world should be required or at least strongly encouraged to conduct a reasonable search for patents and to enter into good-faith negotiations to license patents that cover their technology. A failure to search and negotiate should trigger enhanced damages and perhaps other remedies, such as an award of attorneys' fees, or perhaps even incline the court to grant injunctive relief to non-manufacturing patent owners. Second, to facilitate an efficient market for patent licenses, the law should require the publication of patent license terms.[62] The goal would be a world in which manufacturers can find relevant patents and in which there is an efficient market for the licensing of such patents.[63] In such a world, patentees can get paid for their inventions, but would lose the ability to engage in holdup. Manufacturers would not be entitled to a free ride, but they would also be free from the significant risks of the patent anticommons.

The steps required to move from our world to this ideal one are radical, and it seems unlikely that they will happen. In the absence of fundamental changes, it is likely that companies will continue to muddle through. But they will do so in significant part by ignoring patents.

NOTES

* This chapter was first published in the Michigan State Law Review. Mark A. Lemley, *Ignoring Patents*, 19 MICH. ST. L. REV. (2008).

** Thanks to Tim Bresnahan, Andy Coan, Paul Goldstein, Rose Hagan, Paul Heald, Daniel Ho, Roberta Morris, Laura Rosenbury, Chiaki Sato, Al Sykes, and participants in workshops at Michigan State University, St. Louis University, Stanford Law School, and Washington University for discussions or comments on an earlier draft and Sarah Craven for research assistance.

1. There were 2,524,321 patents issued between March 18, 1987 and March 18, 2007. To get an idea of how big this number is, consider U.S. Patent No. 4,651,345 issued March 24, 1987, and U.S. Patent No. 7,191,469 issued March 13, 2007. In other words, more than a third of all the patents issued in 217 years of U.S. history were issued in the last 20 years. Note that this doesn't include design, plant, or reissue patents. Not all of those patents are still in force, however. *See* Kimberly A. Moore, *Worthless Patents*, 20 BERKELEY TECH. L.J. 1521, 1526 (2005) (53.7 percent of patents "expire for failure to pay . . . maintenance fees").
2. *See*, e.g., John R. Allison & Mark A. Lemley, *Who's Patenting What? An Empirical Exploration of Patent Prosecution*, 53 VAND. L. REV. 2099, 2148 tbl.1 (2000) (in the

1990s, 24.2 percent of the patents issued were computer-related, 9.3 percent were semiconductor patents, 7.7 percent were electronics patents, and 3.7 percent were biotechnology patents); Mark A. Lemley & Bhaven N. Sampat, *Is the Patent Office a Rubber Stamp?* 31 (Stanford Pub. Law & Legal Theory Working Paper Series, Research Paper No. 999098, 2007), available at http://ssrn.com/abstract=999098 (one half of all patent applications filed in January 2001 were in the IT industries).

3. For a discussion of the anticommons, see Michael A. Heller, *The Tragedy of the Anticommons: Property in the Transition from Marx to Markets*, 111 HARV. L. REV. 621 (1998) and Michael A. Heller & Rebecca S. Eisenberg, *Can Patents Deter Innovation? The Anticommons in Biomedical Research*, 280 SCI. 698 (1998). The origin of the term and the concept dates to Frank I. Michelman, *Property, Utility, and Fairness: Comments on the Ethical Foundations of "Just Compensation" Law*, 80 HARV. L. REV. 1165 (1967).
4. For a number of examples involving hundreds or thousands of patents covering a particular technology, *see* Mark A. Lemley & Carl Shapiro, *Patent Holdup and Royalty Stacking*, 85 TEX. L. REV. 1991, 2025–29 (2007) (documenting the stacking problem in 3G wireless phones, WiFi, DVD players, and other industries).
5. *Id.*
6. *See*, e.g., Robert A. Guth & Nick Wingfield, *Microsoft Hit With $1.52 Billion Verdict in MP3 Suit; Ruling in Alcatel's Favor May Have Broad Impact on Digital-Music Firms*, WALL ST. J., Feb. 23, 2007, at A3. That verdict was later vacated, but Microsoft remains on the hook for an unspecified amount of damages. On the general problem of overcompensation by reasonable royalty awards in component industries, see Lemley & Shapiro, *supra* note 4, at 2017–25.
7. *See*, e.g., Underwater Devices Inc. v. Morrison-Knudsen Co., 717 F.2d 1380 (Fed. Cir. 1983), *overruled by In re* Seagate Tech., LLC, 497 F.3d 1360 (Fed. Cir. 2007) (en banc). On the odd definition of willfulness and its problems, see Mark A. Lemley & Ragesh K. Tangri, *Ending Patent Law's Willfulness Game*, 18 BERKELEY TECH. L.J. 1085 (2003). The *Seagate* decision by the Federal Circuit significantly tightened up the standard for proving willfulness. *See In re* Seagate Tech., 497 F.3d 1360 (Fed. Cir. 2007) (en banc). The revised standard still permits companies that independently developed the invention to be found willful, but only if they were "objectively reckless" in responding to the patent once they learned of it. *Id.* at 1384.
8. AIPLA, Report of Economic Survey 2007, at 21–22 (cost of a high-stakes patent case is $3 million per side in legal fees pre-trial, and $5 million if the case goes to trial).
9. While empirical evidence on this question is hard to come by, the 2003 IPO survey of IP managers found that only 23 percent said that competitor patents played an important role in companies deciding to abandon later-stage development of otherwise promising technologies. Iain M. Cockburn & Rebecca Henderson, *Survey Results from the 2003 Intellectual Property Owners Association Survey on Strategic Management of Intellectual Property* D.2 (Oct. 2003).
10. There were 2,720 patent suits filed in 2005. Univ. of Houston Law Ctr., Patent, All P-T-C, and All Civil Actions – 1970–2007, at 2 (Jeffery Johnson et al., eds), available at http://www.patstats.org/Historical_Filings_PatentSuits_OtherSuits.rev2.doc (last visited May 4, 2008).
11. Affymetrix, for example, makes a "genome on a chip" that incorporates all the genes in the human body. Affymetrix, http://www.affymetrix.com (last visited May 4, 2008).
12. More than 4,000 of those genes are patented. Stefan Lovgren, *One-Fifth of Human Genes Have Been Patented, Study Reveals*, NAT'L GEOGRAPHIC NEWS, Oct. 13, 2005, available at http://news.nationalgeographic.com/news/2005/10/1013_051013_gene_patent.html. *But cf.* David E. Adelman & Kathryn L. DeAngelis, *Patent Metrics: The Mismeasure of Innovation in the Biotech Patent Debate*, 85 TEX. L. REV. 1677 (2007) (mapping the density of patents in biotechnology fields and finding relatively little concentration).
13. *See* Madey v. Duke Univ., 307 F.3d 1351 (Fed. Cir. 2002).

14. John P. Walsh et al., *Effects of Research Tool Patents and Licensing on Bio-medical Innovation, in* PATENTS IN THE KNOWLEDGE-BASED ECONOMY 285 (Wesley M. Cohen & Stephen A. Merrill eds, 2003) [hereinafter Walsh et al., *Effects*]; *see also* John P. Walsh et al., *Where Excludability Matters: Material v. Intellectual Property in Academic Biomedical Research*, 36 RES. POL'Y 1184, 1188–90 (2007) [hereinafter Walsh et al., *Matters*] (finding that even after *Madey*, patents didn't deter academic researchers).
15. *See*, e.g., Edwin H. Taylor & Glenn E. Von Tersch, *A Proposal to Shore Up the Foundations of Patent Law that the* Underwater *Line Eroded*, 20 HASTINGS COMM. & ENT. L.J. 721, 737 (1998) ("As matters now stand many companies discourage employees from reading patents. This presumably lessens the chance that the company will be found to have knowledge of a patent. However, this defeats the basic purpose of the patents [sic] laws, dissemination of information."); Dennis Fernandez, *Move Over Letterman: Top 10 Most Common IP Management Mistakes for New Companies*, PAT. STRATEGY & MGMT., July 1, 2003, at 3 ("Additionally, in many cases it may be appropriate for companies, as a matter of policy, to discourage looking at issued patents owned by other entities so as to avoid awareness of potentially infringed patents."); Lemley & Tangri, *supra* note 7, at 1100–102.
16. Walsh et al., *Matters*, *supra* note 14, at 1189. Empirical research suggests that scientists don't in fact gain much of their knowledge from patents, turning instead to other sources. *See*, e.g., Wesley M. Cohen et al., *R&D Spillovers, Patents and the Incentives to Innovate in Japan and the United States*, 31 RES. POL'Y 1349, 1362–64 (2002).
17. Cockburn & Henderson, *supra* note 9, at F.6 (a survey of IP managers found that 53 percent disagreed with the statement "[w]e always do a patent search before initiating any R&D or product development effort").
18. These are chiefly the computing and electronics industries. *See* Mark A. Lemley & Nathan Myhrvold, *Tracking Patent Trolls* (Working Paper 2008) (on file with author) (documenting the rates of litigation by "non-practicing entities" in those industries).
19. A number of in-house counsel in technology companies have told me privately that this is their policy. It is worth distinguishing the practice of cross-licensing among large companies, which involves "ignoring" patents only in a different sense. Large companies in the IT industry often cross-license each other, usually on royalty-free terms, because each company knows that it infringes the other's patents, so that asserting its own patents against the other would be self-destructive. One could argue that this is not ignoring patents, but in the sense I mean here I think it is. Companies in cross-licenses generally do not assert their patents or use them to generate revenue; they enter into symmetric deals that allow both sides to clear patents out of the way.
20. In several high-profile patent cases in 2006, the adjudged infringer asserted that it had developed a non-infringing alternative but did not implement it pending final resolution of the case, instead either settling or fighting the injunction. *See* eBay Inc. v. MercExchange, L.L.C., 547 U.S. 388 (2006); NTP, Inc. v. Research in Motion, Ltd., 418 F.3d 1282 (Fed. Cir. 2005).
21. Wikipedia offers this meaning in the first three citations for the term. Patent Pirate, Wikipedia, http://en.wikipedia.org/wiki/Patent_pirate (last visited May 4, 2008). Interestingly, the term has also been used for those on the other side, particularly patent trolls. *Id.*
22. *See* Frank H. Easterbrook, *Intellectual Property is Still Property*, 13 HARV. J.L. & PUB. POL'Y 108, 112 (1990) (maintaining that a "right to exclude in intellectual property is no different in principle from the right to exclude in physical property"); *see also* Stephen L. Carter, *Does It Matter Whether Intellectual Property is Property?*, 68 CHI.-KENT L. REV. 715 (1993); Kenneth W. Dam, *Some Economic Considerations in the Intellectual Property Protection of Software*, 24 J. LEGAL STUD. 321 (1995); John F. Duffy, *Intellectual Property Isolationism and the Average Cost Thesis*, 83 TEX. L. REV. 1077 (2005); Trotter Hardy, *Property (and Copyright) in Cyberspace*, 1996 U. CHI. LEGAL F. 217; F. Scott Kieff, *Property Rights and Property Rules for Commercializing*

Inventions, 85 MINN. L. REV. 697 (2001); Edmund W. Kitch, *Elementary and Persistent Errors in the Economic Analysis of Intellectual Property*, 53 VAND. L. REV. 1727 (2000); Edmund W. Kitch, *Patents: Monopolies or Property Rights?*, 8 RES. L. & ECON. 31 (1986); Edmund W. Kitch, *The Nature and Function of the Patent System*, 20 J.L. & ECON. 265 (1977); David McGowan, *Copyright Nonconsequentialism*, 69 MO. L. REV. 1 (2004); *cf.* Wendy J. Gordon, *An Inquiry Into the Merits of Copyright: The Challenges of Consistency, Consent, and Encouragement Theory*, 41 STAN. L. REV. 1343 (1989) (discussing similarities between copyright law and common law property). In other cases, property theorists don't focus on intellectual property (IP) but use IP examples as part of a broader theory of property. *See* Thomas W. Merrill & Henry E. Smith, *Optimal Standardization in the Law of Property: The* Numerus Clausus *Principle*, 110 YALE L.J. 1, 3–9, 19–20 (2000) (arguing that the principle of numerus clausus is virtually omnipresent in many areas of property law, including IP, although recognizing that it "is probably at its weakest in . . . [this] area"). Of the property scholars, Richard Epstein's work is perhaps the most thoughtful. He believes that the characteristics of IP largely but not entirely parallel real property, and he focuses on the distinctions between the two to justify limits on IP law. *See* Richard A. Epstein, *Liberty Versus Property? Cracks in the Foundations of Copyright Law* 26–27 (U. Chi. L. & Econ., Working Paper No. 204, 2004), *available at* http://ssrn.com/abstract=529943; *cf.* Adam Mossoff, *Is Copyright Property?*, 42 SAN DIEGO L. REV. 29 (2005) (arguing for the property position while distinguishing IP from real property); Michael A. Carrier, *Cabining Intellectual Property Through a Property Paradigm*, 54 DUKE L.J. 1 (2004) (endorsing the real property analogy but focusing on the limits imposed on real property to justify limits on IP). But Epstein still begins with the baseline assumption – adopted implicitly from the real property model – that someone ought to own an invention. Other scholars have lamented the rise of property rhetoric and its effects, while acknowledging its growing significance in the debate. *See*, e.g., Rochelle Cooper Dreyfuss, *We Are Symbols and Inhabit Symbols, So Should We Be Paying Rent? Deconstructing the Lanham Act and Rights of Publicity*, 20 COLUM.-VLA J.L. & ARTS 123, 140 (1996) (speaking of the "privatization" of words and symbols); Shubha Ghosh, *Deprivatizing Copyright*, 54 CASE W. RES. L. REV. 387, 389 (2003) ("To conceive of copyright as essentially private property . . . is to ignore the important historical and realist tradition that has envisioned real property as an instrumental construct designed to pursue certain social and political goals . . . ."); Mark A. Lemley, *Romantic Authorship and the Rhetoric of Property*, 75 TEX. L. REV. 873, 895–903 (1997) (reviewing JAMES BOYLE, SHAMANS, SOFTWARE, AND SPLEENS: LAW AND THE CONSTRUCTION OF THE INFORMATION SOCIETY (1996) and concluding that the "propertization" of IP law "is a very bad idea"); Robert P. Merges, *Property Rights Theory and the Commons: The Case of Scientific Research*, SOC. PHIL. & POL'Y, Summer 1996, at 145, 146–47 (discussing the "creeping propertization" in the pure sciences); Neil Weinstock Netanel, *Copyright and a Democratic Civil Society*, 106 YALE L.J. 283, 314–21 (1996) (tracing the connection to the preeminence of the Chicago School of economic analysis); Kenneth L. Port, *The Illegitimacy of Trademark Incontestability*, 26 IND. L. REV. 519, 552 (1993) (noting that "courts generally use property rhetoric to describe trademarks" and arguing that this "is quite problematic because there is, in actuality, no property right in the trademark itself"); Arti Kaur Rai, *Evolving Scientific Norms and Intellectual Property Rights: A Reply to Kieff*, 95 NW. U. L. REV. 707, 710–13 (2001) (discussing propertization in academic science); Pamela Samuelson, *Information as Property: Do* Ruckelshaus *and* Carpenter *Signal a Changing Direction in Intellectual Property Law?*, 38 CATH. U. L. REV. 365, 396–97 (1989) (hoping that "the first amendment's protection of free speech interests will serve as some check on the reach of the information as property doctrine"); *cf.* Dan Hunter, *Cyberspace as Place and the Tragedy of the Digital Anticommons*, 91 CAL. L. REV. 439 (2003) (noting the effects of analogizing the internet to real property). One measure of the extent to which the parallel has filtered through the legal academy is that first-year property casebooks now include significant discussions of IP. *See*, e.g., JOHN P. DWYER & PETER S. MENELL, PROPERTY LAW AND POLICY: A COMPARATIVE INSTITUTIONAL PERSPECTIVE 502–43 (1998). I should note that I think the property analogy is seriously flawed, for reasons I have explained elsewhere. *See* Mark A. Lemley, *Property, Intellectual Property, and Free Riding*, 83 TEX. L. REV. 1031 (2005); Mark A. Lemley, *What's Different About Intellectual Property?*, 83 TEX. L. REV. 1097 (2005).

23. While the vast majority of people who build houses own the land on which they are built, there are exceptions, notably in Hawaii and at Stanford, where a central entity owns the underlying land but grants long-term renewable leases of that land to the people who build improvements on it. For a discussion of this background, see *Hawaii Housing Authority v. Midkiff*, 467 U.S. 229 (1984).
24. Until 2007, such a suit would have been impossible because the Federal Circuit limited declaratory judgment relief to cases where the plaintiff could show a "reasonable apprehension of imminent suit." *See*, e.g., Teva Pharms. USA, Inc. v. Pfizer, Inc., 395 F.3d 1324 (Fed. Cir. 2005). The Supreme Court flatly rejected that standard in *MedImmune, Inc. v. Genentech, Inc.*, 127 S. Ct. 764 (2007), in favor of a more liberal – though not yet clearly defined – standard for declaratory relief.
25. Chris Cotropia and I are currently conducting an empirical study of the extent of independent development, but it seems to be present in the overwhelming majority of patent cases.
26. 35 U.S.C. § 122(b) (2000). Some applications may be secret for much longer because the statute permits those who file applications only in the United States to delay publication for up to five years. *Id.*
27. See Mark A. Lemley & Kimberly A. Moore, *Ending Abuse of Patent Continuations*, 84 B.U. L. REV. 63 (2004) (discussing the problems with abuse of continuations); Lemley & Sampat, *supra* note 2 (documenting substantial use of continuations in this decade).
28. Kimberly Moore's work has documented the high and increasing reversal rates in patent claim construction cases. *See* Kimberly A. Moore, *Judges, Juries, and Patent Cases – An Empirical Peek Inside the Black Box*, 99 MICH. L. REV. 365 (2000) [hereinafter Moore, *Black Box*]; Kimberly A. Moore, Markman *Eight Years Later: Is Claim Construction More Predictable?*, 9 LEWIS & CLARK L. REV. 231 (2005). Indeed, Dan Burk and I have suggested that this uncertainty is to a large extent inherent in the claim construction process. Dan L. Burk & Mark A. Lemley, *Quantum Patent Mechanics*, 9 LEWIS & CLARK L. REV. 29 (2005).
29. Cf. John F. Duffy, *Rethinking the Prospect Theory of Patents*, 71 U. CHI. L. REV. 439 (2004) (arguing that one advantage of patent races is to accelerate the discovery and disclosure of new inventions).
30. For a sense of the literature on this long-running economic debate, see Kenneth J. Arrow, *Economic Welfare and the Allocation of Resources for Invention, in* NAT'L BUREAU, ECON. RESEARCH, THE RATE AND DIRECTION OF INVENTIVE ACTIVITY: ECONOMIC AND SOCIAL FACTORS 609, 620 (1962) (concluding that "preinvention monopoly power acts as a strong disincentive to further innovation"). *See also* MORTON I. KAMIEN & NANCY L. SCHWARTZ, MARKET STRUCTURE AND INNOVATION 16 (1982) (discussing various theories of the effects of economic structures on the rate and form of innovation); F.M. SCHERER & DAVID ROSS, INDUSTRIAL MARKET STRUCTURE AND ECONOMIC PERFORMANCE 660 (3d ed. 1990) (criticizing Schumpeter's "less cautious" followers for advocating monopoly to promote innovation). In the specific context of IP, the canonical argument from both theory and empirical evidence is Robert P. Merges & Richard R. Nelson, *On the Complex Economics of Patent Scope*, 90 COLUM. L. REV. 839 (1990). *See also* Kenneth W. Dam, *The Economic Underpinnings of Patent Law*, 23 J. LEGAL STUD. 247, 252 (1994) (noting that in the computer industry, for example, companies coordinate improvements by broad cross-licensing because of "the pace of research and development and the market

interdependencies between inventions"). For discussions of particular industries in which competition appears to spur innovation, see, for example, Mark A. Lemley & Lawrence Lessig, *The End of End-to-End: Preserving the Architecture of the Internet in the Broadband Era*, 48 UCLA L. REV. 925, 960–62 (2001) (the internet); Rai, *supra* note 22, at 709–10 (biotechnology); Howard A. Shelanski, *Competition and Deployment of New Technology in U.S. Telecommunications*, 2000 U. CHI. LEGAL F. 85, 85 (telecommunications). For an argument that part of the goal of antitrust law is to spur innovation, not merely static competition, see, for example, Jonathan B. Baker, *Beyond* Schumpeter vs. Arrow*: How Antitrust Fosters Innovation*, 74 ANTITRUST L.J. 575 (2007); Mark A. Lemley, *A New Balance Between IP and Antitrust*, 13 SW. J. L. & TRADE AM. 237 (2007).

31. For a discussion of the importance of transaction costs in setting patent policy, see Paul J. Heald, *Transaction Costs and Patent Reform*, 23 SANTA CLARA COMPUTER & HIGH TECH. L.J. 447 (2007).
32. See Paul M. Janicke & LiLan Ren, *Who Wins Patent Infringement Cases?*, 34 AIPLA Q.J. 1, 1–6 (2006). Forty-six percent of patents litigated to judgment are invalid. John R. Allison & Mark A. Lemley, *Empirical Evidence on the Validity of Litigated Patents*, 26 AIPLA Q.J. 185, 205 (1998). And while patentees win most infringement and inequitable conduct issues, they lose some of those as well, even at trial. Moore, *Black Box*, *supra* note 28, at 390 tbl.4. Because the patentee must win on each of these issues to prevail, the total number of cases they win can be quite small.
33. See Mark A. Lemley & Carl Shapiro, *Probabilistic Patents*, J. ECON. PERSP. Spring 2005, at 75, 76. *See also* Sivaramjani Thambisetty, *Patents as Credence Goods*, OXFORD J. LEGAL STUD. 707, 708 (2007) (arguing that patents don't represent sufficiently clear exclusive rights to promote bargaining).
34. For an economic explanation of why even antitrust claims against fraudulent patents won't permit the recovery of these gains, see Christopher R. Leslie, *The Role of Consumers in* Walker Process *Litigation*, 13 SW. J. L. & TRADE AM. 281 (2007).
35. *See* Joseph Farrell & Robert P. Merges, *Incentives to Challenge and Defend Patents: Why Litigation Won't Reliably Fix Patent Office Errors and Why Administrative Patent Review Might Help*, 19 BERKELEY TECH. L.J. 943, 968–69 (2004); Joseph Farrell & Carl Shapiro, *How Strong Are Weak Patents?*, 98 AM. ECON. REV. (forthcoming 2008). *Cf.* Christopher R. Leslie, *The Anticompetitive Effects of Unenforced Invalid Patents*, 91 MINN. L. REV. 101 (2006) (on the harms that even unenforced patents can do).
36. *See* John R. Thomas, *Collusion and Collective Action in the Patent System: A Proposal for Patent Bounties*, 2001 U. ILL. L. REV. 305, 333–36; Joseph Scott Miller, *Building a Better Bounty: Litigation-Stage Rewards for Defeating Patents*, 19 BERKELEY TECH. L.J. 667, 688–89 (2004); Farrell & Merges, *supra* note 35, at 946–47.
37. This is known as the Cournot complements problem. *See* Lemley & Shapiro, *supra* note 4, at 2013–16.
38. On this last point, see Mark A. Lemley & Philip J. Weiser, *Should Property or Liability Rules Govern Information?*, 85 TEX. L. REV. 783, 793–94 (2007).
39. See Kelo v. City of New London, 545 U.S. 469, 489 n.24 (2005).
40. Scott Kieff claims that "predictability is essential in facilitating private ordering." F. Scott Kieff, *Coordination, Property, and Intellectual Property: An Unconventional Approach to Anticompetitive Effects and Downstream Access*, 56 EMORY L.J. 327, 418 (2006). But no one could argue that the validity and scope of patent rights is remotely predictable.
41. 21 U.S.C. § 355(b)(1), (c)(2) (2000).
42. 21 U.S.C. § 355(j)(2)(A)(vii)(I) to (IV) (certification and disclosure requirements); 21 U.S.C. § 355(j)(5)(B)(iii) (30-month stay).
43. See Dan L. Burk & Mark A. Lemley, *Policy Levers in Patent Law*, 89 VA. L. REV. 1575 (2003) (providing estimates of the cost and delay associated with regulatory approval, and arguing that they justify stronger patent protection in pharmaceuticals than in other industries).

44. This stands to reason, since patent owners who do not participate in the market would be unable to get revenue without licensing the patent up front to someone who would invest the time and effort of obtaining FDA approval. For a discussion of how FDA approval creates rents alongside the patent system, see William E. Ridgway, Note, *Realizing Two-Tiered Innovation Policy Through Drug Regulation*, 58 STAN. L. REV. 1221 (2006).
45. *See*, e.g., 21 U.S.C. § 355a (providing for additional exclusivity to encourage clinical investigation of the safety of already-approved drugs for use by children).
46. *See*, e.g., Lara J. Glasgow, *Stretching the Limits of Intellectual Property Rights: Has the Pharmaceutical Industry Gone Too Far?*, 41 IDEA 227, 233–35 (2001) (pointing out the loopholes in the Hatch-Waxman Act that pharmaceutical companies exploit to extend the life of their patents); Christine S. Paine, Comment, *Brand-Name Drug Manufacturers Risk Antitrust Violations by Slowing Generic Production Through Patent Layering*, 33 SETON HALL L. REV. 479, 497 (2003) (defining the tactic of evergreening as a strategy to extend monopoly); 2 HERBERT HOVENKAMP ET AL., IP AND ANTITRUST § 33.9 (perm. ed. & Supp. 2008) (discussing cases involving this practice).
47. Abbott Labs. v. Teva Pharms. USA, Inc., 432 F. Supp. 2d 408 (D. Del. 2006) (permitting an antitrust cause of action to proceed against product hopping); 1 HOVENKAMP ET AL., *supra* note 46, § 12.5 (analyzing the issue).
48. For disparate legal treatment of those cases, see, for example, *In re* Tamoxifen Citrate Antitrust Litig., 466 F.3d 187, 212 (2d Cir. 2006) (treating exclusion payments as per se legal); Valley Drug Co. v. Geneva Pharms., Inc., 344 F.3d 1294 (11th Cir. 2003) (inquiring into the validity of the underlying patent); *In re* Cardizem CD Antitrust Litig., 332 F.3d 896 (6th Cir. 2003) (treating them as per se illegal); *In re* Schering-Plough Corp., No. 9297, 2003 WL 22989651 (Fed. Trade Comm'n Dec. 8, 2003), *vacated*, 402 F.3d 1056 (11th Cir. 2005) (treating them as presumptively anticompetitive).
49. One might reasonably question whether, if companies in many industries deal with the patent system by ignoring patents, we would be better off simply eliminating the patent system in those industries. While the argument has some appeal, I think that conclusion is unwarranted. Not only would it require industry-specific line drawing of the kind that creates problems for legislatures, *see* DAN L. BURK & MARK A. LEMLEY, BEND OR BREAK: HOW OUR PATENT SYSTEM FOUND ITSELF IN CRISIS AND HOW INDUSTRY TAILORING CAN SAVE IT (forthcoming 2009), but it wrongly assumes that the patent system has no effect merely because companies ignore particular patents. In fact, it may be that the existence of the patent system deters outright copying of inventions even if it doesn't prompt companies to search for patents that might cover their independently-developed inventions. And the current system does provide a reward and therefore an incentive to many patentees, though they may have to litigate to get it. That incentive may be particularly important for small inventors who could not otherwise commercialize their ideas.
50. James McDonough argues that patent trolls are good for society because they serve as efficient arbitragers, *see* James F. McDonough III, Comment, *The Myth of the Patent Troll: An Alternative View of the Function of Patent Dealers in an Idea Economy*, 56 EMORY L.J. 189, 204–20 (2006), but that is not true in a world in which patent owners can engage in holdup and capture a greater share of the value than they contribute. Amy Landers argues that increasingly sophisticated efforts to monetize patents are at odds with the public interest, *see* Amy L. Landers, *Liquid Patents*, 84 DENV. U. L. REV. 199 (2006), but I think that's true today only because existing patent rules encourage holdup. Change those rules so that what patentees can recover bears a reasonable relationship to what they contribute and McDonough's factually incorrect argument becomes correct: the monetization of patents becomes a good, not a bad, thing.
51. Several scholars have noted the importance of patents as signals. *See*, e.g., Heald, *supra* note 31, at 455; Clarisa Long, *Patent Signals*, 69 U. CHI. L. REV. 625 (2002). But the

point here is more direct – patents are supposed to confer information to scientists, but they can't do that if scientists ignore patents; *cf.* Benjamin Roin, Note, *The Disclosure Function of the Patent System (Or Lack Thereof)*, 118 HARV. L. REV. 2007 (2005) (noting that the patent system doesn't achieve this disclosure goal).

52. Despite PTO efforts to hire more examiners and speed the processing of applications, the time an application spends in the PTO has grown from an average of 2.23 years in the 1970s to 2.77 years in the 1990s to well over three years today. *See* John R. Allison & Mark A. Lemley, *The Growing Complexity of the United States Patent System*, 82 B.U. L. REV. 77, 98 (2002); Lemley & Sampat, *supra* note 2, at 4. That trend would have to be reversed – and reversed dramatically – if prior licensing of patents were not to unduly delay innovation.
53. For a variety of proposals along these lines, see Lemley & Moore, *supra* note 27. The PTO issued regulations that would limit applicants to three continuations (plus an unlimited number of divisionals) as a matter of right, a rule that would take a very modest step towards solving the problem. Changes to Practice for Continued Examination Filings, Patent Applications Containing Patently Indistinct Claims, and Examination of Claims in Patent Applications, 72 Fed. Reg. 46,716 (Aug. 21, 2007). At this writing it is far from clear that even these watered-down rules will go into effect, however; they are currently enjoined. *See* Tafas v. Dudas, 511 F. Supp. 2d 652 (E.D. Va. 2007).
54. 35 U.S.C. § 122(b) (2000) currently requires publication at eighteen months in some but not all cases. Our best estimate is that by 2004, about 86 percent of all U.S. applicants chose to publish their applications. *See* Lemley & Sampat, *supra* note 2, at 47 n.64. Patent reform efforts proposed in the last Congress would have required publication of all applications at 18 months. *See*, e.g., Patent Reform Act of 2005, H.R. 2795, 109th Cong. (2005).
55. See Beth Simone Noveck, *"Peer to Patent": Collective Intelligence, Open Review, and Patent Reform*, 20 HARV. J.L. & TECH. 123 (2006). The PTO has recently established a pilot project to implement peer review. *See* Dennis Crouch, *USPTO's Patent Peer Review Pilot Project*, PATENTLY-O: PATENT LAW BLOG, May 8, 2006, http://patentlaw.type-pad.com/patent/2006/05/usptos_patent_p.html.
56. For a sense of the academic debate, see Mark D. Janis, *Rethinking Reexamination: Toward a Viable Administrative Revocation System for U.S. Patent Law*, 11 HARV. J.L. & TECH. 1 (1997); Robert P. Merges, *As Many as Six Impossible Patents Before Breakfast: Property Rights for Business Concepts and Patent System Reform*, 14 BERKELEY TECH. L.J. 577 (1999); Craig Allen Nard, *Certainty, Fence Building, and the Useful Arts*, 74 IND. L.J. 759 (1999); J. H. Reichman, *From Free Riders to Fair Followers: Global Competition Under the TRIPS Agreement*, 29 N.Y.U. J. INT'L L. & POL. 11 (1997); Thomas, *supra* note 36. Patent reform efforts proposed in the last two Congresses would have created a post-grant opposition procedure. *See*, e.g., Patent Reform Act of 2007, S. 1145, 110th Cong. (2007); Patent Reform Act of 2005, H.R. 2795, 109th Cong. (2005).
57. *See* Doug Lichtman & Mark A. Lemley, *Rethinking Patent Law's Presumption of Validity*, 60 STAN. L. REV. 45 (2007).
58. For proposals for an independent invention defense, see Samson Vermont, *Independent Invention as a Defense to Patent Infringement*, 105 MICH. L. REV. 475 (2006); Carl Shapiro, *Prior User Rights*, AM. ECON. REV., May 2006, at 92, 95; *cf.* Mark A. Lemley, *Should Patent Infringement Require Proof of Copying?*, 105 MICH. L. REV. 1525 (2007) (noting the benefits of but also some potential problems with such an approach); Samson Vermont, *The Angel is in the Big Picture: A Response to Lemley*, 105 MICH. L. REV. 1537 (2007).
59. For a proposal along these lines, see Lemley & Tangri, *supra* note 7, at 1116–24.
60. 547 U.S. 388 (2006).
61. Lemley & Shapiro, *supra* note 4, at 2039–42; Mark A. Lemley, *Distinguishing Lost Profits From Reasonable Royalties* (Working Paper 008).

62. For a defense of this proposal, see Mark A. Lemley & Nathan Myhrvold, *How to Make a Patent Market* (Stanford Law & Econ. Olin Working Paper No. 347, 2007), available at http://ssrn.com/abstract=1012726.
63. An efficient market for patent rights would require intermediaries that could provide information about market value and engage in arbitrage to smooth out purchases based on inadequate information. But such intermediaries are already starting to develop, *see* Peter N. Detkin, *Leveling the Patent Playing Field*, 6 J. MARSHALL REV. INTELL. PROP. L. 636, 642 (2007), and there is enough money at stake that I think if the legal prerequisites for a patent market existed, we would see even more.

PART II

Trilateral area and the future of their patent systems

4. The future of IP in Europe[1]

Clara Neppel, Berthold Rutz, Guy Carmichael, Konstantinos Karachalios, Shirin Elahi and Ciaran McGinley

PATENTS: A EUROPEAN INVENTION

> The [first important historic event] was the invention of patenting itself – the creation of a system whereby a monopoly was created, and simultaneously the knowledge made accessible for everyone. This accessibility is in my opinion an important issue. The alternative way – protecting knowledge by keeping it secret – is a disastrous way of using knowledge.
>
> Dr J. Staman, Director, Rathenau Institute, Netherlands – EPO Interview

Unlike many other ground-breaking inventions where it is often difficult or even impossible to tell where they actually originated, it can be said with some certainty that patents were invented in Europe, more precisely in Italy. The first patent letters (from the Latin word *patere*: to stand wide open) were issued in the city of Florence in the 14th century followed by the first written patent law in the State of Venice in 1474. However, the patent law of those days only roughly resembled today's modern patent system. The state awarded a limited monopoly right to an artist or craftsman with the intention to attract foreign knowledge and know-how.

The modern patent system can probably be said to have first appeared in Britain in the reign of King James I with the Statute of Monopolies of 1623. In many other European countries patent systems were introduced much later and, often, following fierce discussions. For example in Germany many industries resisted the introduction of patents at the end of the 19th century while, in the Netherlands, patents were abolished altogether in 1869 and only reintroduced in 1911. At the end of the 19th century the chemical industry in Switzerland opposed patents while actively imitating their foreign competitors. Italy had no patent protection for pharmaceuticals from 1939 until 1978. Many other European countries only introduced patents on chemical products as such – in particular for pharmaceuticals – rather recently (e.g. Greece and Spain after 1992).[2, 3, 4]

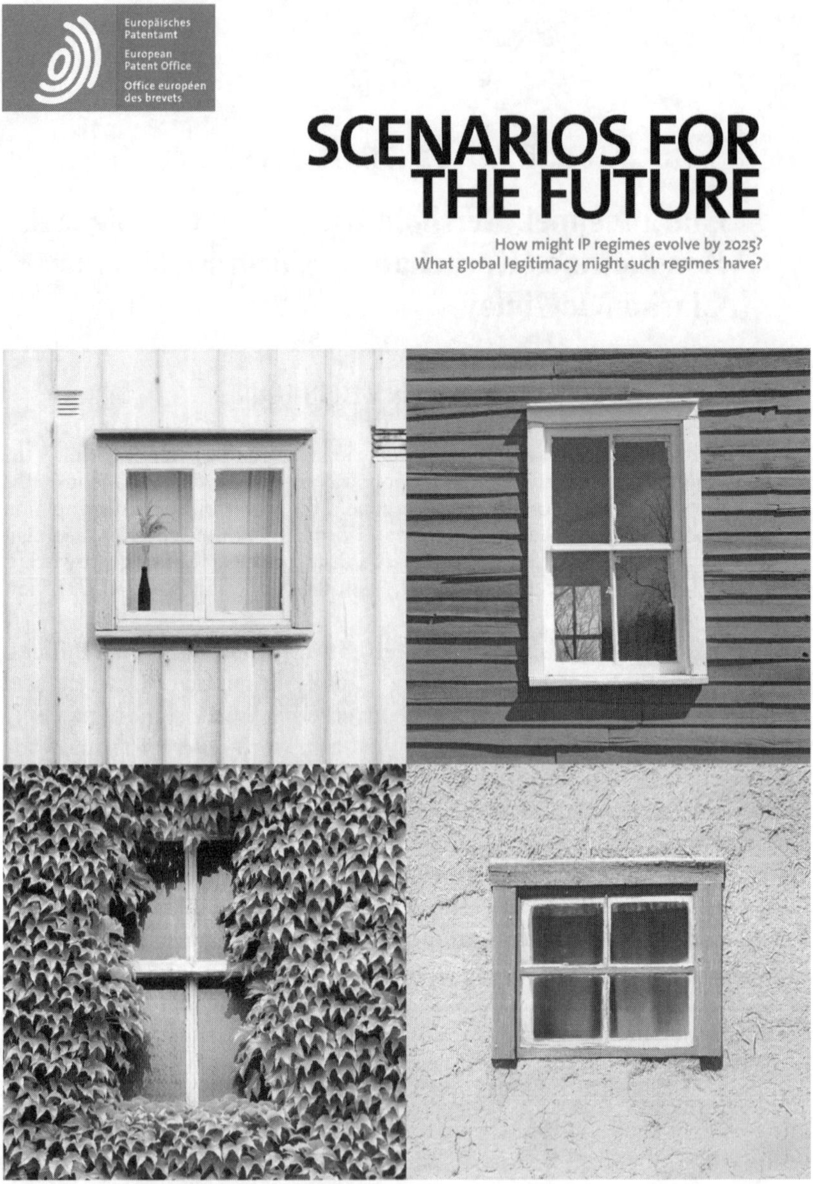

SCENARIOS FOR THE FUTURE

How might IP regimes evolve by 2025?
What global legitimacy might such regimes have?

Figure 4.1 EPO scenarios for the future

GLOBALISATION OF PATENTING

With the industrialisation and rising global trade in the 19th century, patent applicants were interested in filing patent applications for the same invention in different countries. This, however, was difficult to achieve in a time of messengers and horse-drawn carriages. The 1883 Paris Convention for the Protection of Industrial Property was designed to encourage inventors of the day to show their inventions without fear of theft. The initial membership was small: only 11, mostly European, members – the industrialised world of the time. Today there are 174 member states across the world. The Paris Convention allows an inventor to file a first application in any member state and to enjoy for 12 months a right to priority from that first application in any other member state. This was a major improvement on the situation before where the patent applicant had to file in different countries on the same date to avoid a filing in one country to become detrimental to the novelty of the filing in another country.

The other truly global patent treaty, the Patent Convention Treaty (PCT), was signed in 1970 in Washington and came into existence in 1978. It allows an applicant to file a single application for some or all member states (currently 146) and to select an International Search Authority (ISA) and an International Preliminary Examination Authority (IPEA) to provide a search report accompanied by a written opinion on patentability, and to possibly conduct a preliminary examination. In addition to efficiency gains through a unified application procedure, the PCT procedure also allows an applicant to delay his final decision as to in which countries to continue with the application from the original priority period under the Paris convention (12 months) to an overall 30 to 31 months.

THE CREATION OF THE EUROPEAN PATENT ORGANISATION

> Before 1940 there were multiple national economies, each with its own national patent system. After 1945, as the European Economic Community was established and the economy spread territorially, so a regional patent system was developed. This European patent system was characterised by one office, one procedure and one standard of quality. We now have a situation within Europe where the German population trusts a European patent granted by an Irish or Italian examiner of the European patent system. This has been a major innovation.
>
> The late Johannes Bob van Benthem, one of the founding fathers of the EPO

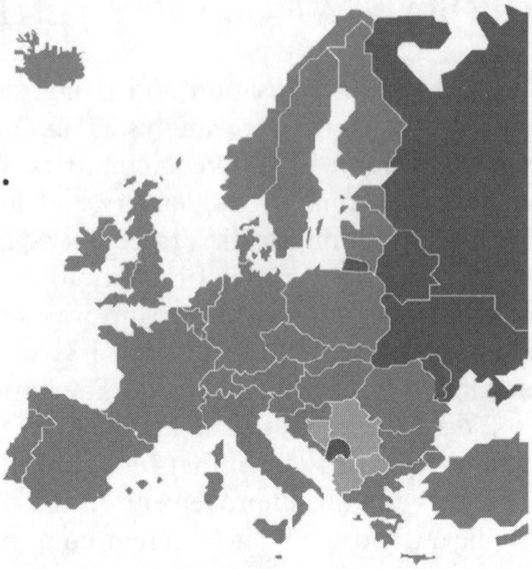

Austria • Belgium • Bulgaria • Croatia • Cyprus • Czech Republic • Denmark • Estonia • Finland • France • Germany • Greece • Hungary • Iceland • Ireland • Italy • Latvia • Liechtenstein • Lithuania • Luxembourg • Malta • Monaco • Netherlands • Norway • Poland • Portugal • Romania • Slovakia • Slovenia • Spain • Sweden • Switzerland • Turkey • United Kingdom

European patent applications and patents can also be extended at the applicant's request to the following states:

Albania • Bosnia-Herzegovina • Former Yugoslav Republic of Macedonia • Serbia

Figure 4.2 34 member states

European law in general has two main legal traditions: the Roman-Latin branch of detailed codified law as exemplified for example by the Code Napoleon in France (1804) or the Bürgerliches Gesetzbuch in Germany (1900) on the one hand and the Anglo-Saxon case law tradition on the other hand which relies less on codified positive law but on antecedents and earlier court decisions. These differing European legal traditions were of course reflected in the European national patent laws in the middle of the 20th century when plans for a common European patent system first appeared. The founding fathers of the European Patent Convention (EPC), which was agreed upon by 16 signatory states in 1973, had to find a compromise between the different existing legal patent systems. They did so by devising a system which created a central authority (the 'European Patent Organisation') for the granting of a single European patent, comprising a bundle of patents that are valid in all the designated EPC contracting states. This task to grant European patents is carried out by the European Patent Office (EPO) which was inaugurated in 1977. The transfer of sovereignty rights from the contracting states to the European Patent Organisation was generally limited to the pre-grant phase. As an exception the EPO also carries out opposition, limitation and revocation proceedings for patents granted under the EPC. Decisions of the examination and opposition divisions can be appealed before the EPO Boards of Appeal. The EPC contracting states retain their competence regarding the enforcement of the European patents, including infringement and revocation proceedings.

The EPO is supervised by the Administrative Council (AC) of the European Patent Organisation which is made up of representatives of its contracting states. It appoints the President and the Vice-Presidents of the Office and adopts the budget of the Office and the Organisation. The Organisation is an autonomous and independent intergovernmental organisation which is neither financially nor institutionally connected to the European Union. Eleven of the currently 38 EPC contracting states are not member of the European Union.[5]

The EPC can only be amended by a diplomatic conference and the resulting changes have to be ratified by all contracting states, although time limits laid down in the Convention, the Implementing Regulations of the EPC, the Rules, and a number of other Regulations can be modified by the AC.

Since the adoption of the EPC in 1973, there has only been one major revision. This took place in 2000 and led to the EPC 2000, which came into force in December 2007. The most important amendments to the EPC have included the introduction of a limitation and revocation procedure after grant, the possibility of the Enlarged Board of Appeal to review decisions of the Boards of Appeal (so called 'petition for review'), the legal basis for the new combined search and examination practice, the formalisation of the allowance of further medical use claims and a number of smaller procedural changes. In terms of the systematic legal framework, the EPC 2000 transferred a number of provisions from the EPC itself to the Implementing Regulations thus allowing for more legislative flexibility in the future.

PLANS FOR FURTHER EUROPEAN HARMONISATION

The European Community Patent (ComPat) was first proposed in the 1960s – the Community Patent Convention (CPC) which should establish a Community patent was signed in 1975, but has never entered into force. The Community patent would overcome the limited territorial effects of the national and European patents and would establish a unitary patent covering the entire territory of the European Union including a common litigation system. However, it has so far not materialised due to a number of contentious issues, such as the language question and the choice of an appropriate court system. Other solutions to deal with these are set out below.

The issue of language has been a thorny one within the European patent world. Most of the EPC contracting states require that European patents be translated into their national languages in order to take effect on their territory. This has major cost implications for European business. A major breakthrough on the route to more moderate translation related costs was achieved in 2008 with the entry into force of the London Agreement.[6] The London Agreement either limits the requirement for translation of the patent after grant into an official language of the contracting state at stake to a translation of the claims (in countries which have no official language in common with one of the three official languages of the EPO) if the European patent is available in the designated EPO language prescribed by this state, or dispenses completely with the translation requirement (in signatory countries which have an official language in common with one of the three official languages of the EPO). The London Agreement has so far entered into force for 18 EPC member states including Germany, France and the UK.[7] It is estimated that it will reduce the cost of a European patent by approximately 40 per cent.

The other important aspect of the European patent system still missing is a uniform patent litigation system. Several EPC contracting states elaborated the so called draft European Patent Litigation Agreement (EPLA) which would establish a common European patent court for its contracting states outside of the EU framework. The draft EPLA could, from a technical perspective, be submitted to a diplomatic conference for adoption. However, such a conference has not been convened so far convened due to the ongoing negotiations within the EU for a Community patent including an EU patent court. This issue is therefore still under debate.

EUROPEAN AND GLOBAL WORK SHARING

Patent offices worldwide struggle under steadily rising numbers of patent applications.[8] Since a big share of this workload is made up of applications which are filed in several patent offices in parallel, the first and most obvious response to such development is to seek to avoid duplication of work. In the early 1980s the three biggest patent offices established the project of Trilateral cooperation which aimed at improving collaboration and enhancing the exchange of information between offices:[9]

> Trilateral cooperation is of historic significance because reciprocal acceptance on the same grounds was introduced into the frameworks of the different patent systems . . . The fact that they have cooperated in their examination phases and standardised some procedures in their systems has demonstrated the ability of the patent system to operate in a more harmonised way. (Kazuo Wakasugi, Counselor, Japan Petroleum Exploration Co, and formerly Commissioner, JPO)

However, today about half of all worldwide patent applications are filed outside the Trilateral Offices.[10] The group of Trilateral Offices has therefore started to extend their collaboration to include the Chinese and South Korean patent offices in a group called 'IP5' which together account for about 80 per cent of all worldwide patent filings. In order to tackle the workload the five biggest patent offices agreed to explore the possibility of work sharing and consequently that unnecessary duplication of work among the offices should be eliminated, that the efficiency and quality of patent examination is enhanced and that the PCT shall be the privileged platform for work sharing and it needs to be developed to reach its full potential.

Ten 'Foundation projects' have been agreed upon by the IP5 which aim to harmonise the global environment for patent searches and examination in order to enable better work sharing and use of common resources.[11]

A number of projects are currently under way to improve work sharing. At the European level, a Utilisation Pilot Project (UPP) was started in 2007. Applicants take part on a voluntary basis and the aim is to make available to an EPO examiner any search report and/or preliminary opinion on patentability already generated by a participant office of first filing (so far the patent offices of the UK, Germany, Austria and Denmark are participating). The EPO examiner can decide to what extent the information gained can be used for drawing up a European Search Opinion on Patentability. PCT applications are excluded from this programme. In November 2008 the European Patent Office submitted a proposal to the Administrative Council recommending a full-scale implementation of the UPP process.

On a more global level three main projects in which the EPO participates can be distinguished: 'Strategic Handling of Applications for Rapid Examination' (SHARE), 'Patent Prosecution Highway' (PPH) and 'Triway'. SHARE has as its aim to give procedural priority to first filings in all trilateral offices (EPO, JPO, USPTO), to allow the office of second filing to make efficient use of the results obtained by the office of first filing. The Trilateral Offices started a pilot for SHARE in a number of technical areas in 2008.[12] The PPH allows an applicant to achieve rapid processing of his application in the other participating offices once he has already obtained a positive opinion on patentability in the office of first filing. The EPO is currently participating in a PPH comparable pilot project with the USPTO and is in discussions with the JPO about a similar pilot project.[13] The 'Triway' project is designed to leverage the search expertise of the other of the Trilateral Offices (European Patent Office (EPO), Japan Patent Office (JPO) and USPTO) for the benefit of both applicants and the Offices. Under the Triway scheme, each Office conducts a search on a corresponding application filed under the Paris Convention in each of the Offices in a sufficiently early time period. The search results from each Office would then be shared among the Offices in order to help improve the resulting examination quality of any patents issued on the corresponding applications by each of the Trilateral Offices.

The TRIWAY pilot was launched in July 2008.

CHALLENGES AHEAD

Times have changed, however, and IP policies and strategies are no longer solely issues for a restricted circle of legal and technical experts. The IP system has increasingly been recognised as the currency underpinning the global knowledge economy. Partly as a consequence of the successful strategy pursued by industrialised countries to link IP through TRIPS with broader issues such as trade, IP has become intertwined with diverse political subjects.

However, a second, more fundamental challenge to IP is that it has become linked to the wider global challenges humanity faces. Escalating tensions around natural resources, such as water, food and energy, are already being overshadowed by a fundamental challenge to humanity: the attempt to delimit and possess knowledge, a fundamentally different type of resource. Knowledge is *potentially* non-exhaustible and non-rival, yet due to the advent of the information and communication technologies, its very nature and availability is changing. This is resulting in a 'knowledge paradox': if the rules around access, management, production and ownership of knowledge are not chosen properly, more information could even equal less knowledge – and less innovation.

As a consequence, and despite the views of the 'traditional' IP community, the number of new stakeholders is rapidly growing: new voices who demand a say about IP and how it impacts everyday life. In particular the new, 'always on' internet generation has a very different stance towards monopolies in the creative and educative sphere – and these attitudes could possibly spill over into other areas.

The issue of reputation and societal goodwill is paramount when contemplating future perspectives of a system that underpins advances in technology, and has such major impact on both the economy and society as the patent system. For any such framework with a global reach and in order for the concept of the patent system to survive and thrive, it must proactively make its case. In today's world, it will not suffice simply to react or defend traditional positions.

Since the publication of the EPO Scenarios for the Future[14] in 2007, some of the challenges which were recognised have become even more dominant:

- The new and emerging technologies, including ethically contested ones: as the patent system expands to cover them, it also raises and some believe tacitly condones the moral minefields that they bring.
- Climate change and the technology transfer needed to tackle the huge challenges: are patents enabling or inhibiting (as a result of high royalties and their long timeframe) this vital process that requires immediate concerted global action?
- The increasingly conflicting trajectories of industrial, in particular ICT, standards and patents: these conflicts are now no longer only business versus business, but more often business+state versus business+state. The outcome of this clash would lead to geopolitical convulsions.
- The development gap: does IP help to bridge this divide and if so, under which conditions? Related to this question is also the issue of access to affordable medicines for the poor people of the world. Health access issues could even spill over to industrialised countries, if the current financial crisis mutates to a long-term economic one.
- Finally, what might the consequences of the erosion of the Washington Consensus[15] be in the wake of the global financial crisis on something as intangible as intellectual property? Could this include the waning dominance of intangible assets and of a deregulation ideology?

These challenges ahead are of course not European; they are global in nature. But Europe, despite its strong internal integration, remains a very open and thus exposed player to such global factors. Therefore, Europe, with its unique regional patent granting authority, and including its national and EU institutions, has started to grasp the scale and nature of these imminent global changes and attempt to develop and implement strategies to cope with them, in a genuinely creative European way, utilising the EPO Scenarios set out below as the building blocks for discussion. As well as solving operational and internal problems of the patent system (no easy task since the issues encroach on broader issues such as transparency), the strategies and actions adopted will ultimately determine the ability of the European patent system to not only survive the coming storms, but to thrive and remain a factor of stability and social wealth for the world beyond Europe.

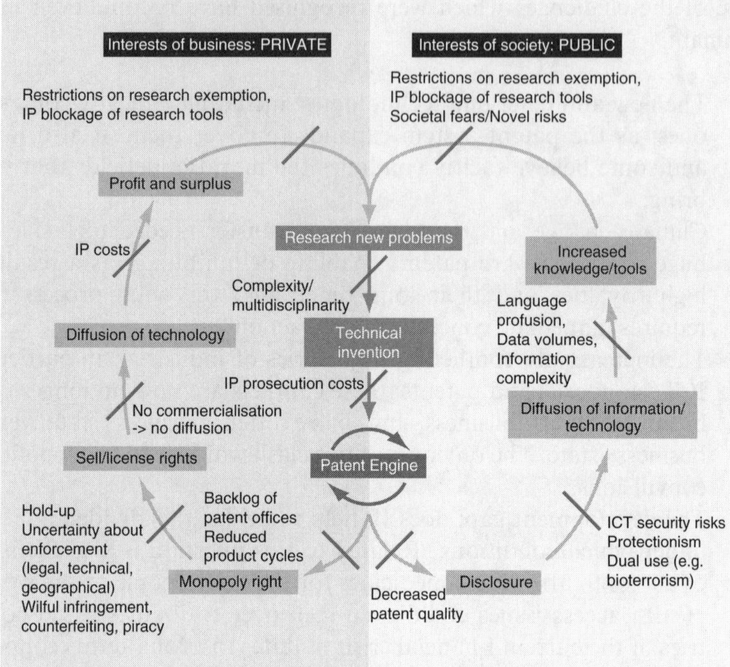

Source: EPO Scenarios for the Future (2007), p.17.

Figure 4.3 Blockage of the classic patent system

THE EPO SCENARIOS FOR THE FUTURE

Alain Pompidou, the former European Patent Office President initiated the EPO Scenarios for the Future project, when he took office in 2004. The project was initially intended to determine what the future of the EPO might be, but it soon became apparent that the future of the EPO, a legal/technical organisation tasked to grant Europe-wide patents, would be critically tied up with the future of intellectual property issues in Europe and, indeed, worldwide. The project was then re-aligned to examine the external context of the global knowledge economy and its potential impacts on the fate of the EPO.

Why did the EPO choose a scenario methodology? All too often, decision-makers base their decisions on an official future, or even just what they would like the future to be. This linear forecasting is based on the assumption that tomorrow's world will look like today and it makes little allowance for possible discontinuities. In contrast, the scenarios' approach accepts uncertainty and is therefore a powerful tool with which to explore complexity.

The open scenarios created are relevant, challenging and plausible stories of what might happen in the future. They form a collective mental model formed from contrasting worldviews and assumptions and explore the contextual world beyond the organisation, the world over which institutions normally have little or no control. They study the interaction between the most important and most uncertain political, economic, societal, technological, historical and environmental factors that might impact the system. The decisions made today create the future to be faced tomorrow. Like 'wind-tunnels' used to test strategic thinking, the scenarios provide a useful decision-making tool which can test how robust different strategies for the future might be. They need to be used as a single set of alternative options to explore consequences into the future in order to make sound, accepted decisions today.

The EPO interviewed around 150 key players – including critics – from all over the world from the fields of science, business, politics, ethics, economics and law, seeking their opinions on how intellectual property might evolve to 2025.[16] The scenarios were then developed in a series of workshops, setting up a framework allowing disparate groups to see across multiple dimensions and within a wider context. The four drivers identified dominate their own scenario (business, society, geopolitics and technology) and they enable the examination of possible discontinuities, caused by the dynamics in the battlefield of codified knowledge, and allow the drawing of new landscapes resulting from such tectonic shifts.

These stories are by no means the EPO's scenarios and do not represent its views or visions. Rather, they are designed to challenge conventional thinking and examine the potential challenges to the future of the system – one that impacts the EPO, both its European and global stakeholders as well as the worldwide environment in which it operates. In order to do so, several trajectories were followed by separately analysing the dynamics of four main drivers in the current globalisation era: strategies of flagship corporations, agendas of major geopolitical players, emancipative societal movements and aspirations of the techno-scientific complex.

While the immediate future may be possible to predict with a reasonable degree of certainty, the longer term is far harder. But, as the scenarios will show, it is by no means certain that the continuation of the IP system as it is now is inevitable. Thus it is important to consider the question 'What if . . .?' and to consider what challenges the particular dominant drivers might bring about if they were to shape the future. There are four scenarios, which together present a set of futures that might unfold over the next 20 years. These four scenarios can be described as:

- market rules: the grey world where business is the dominant driver;
- whose game: the red world where geo-politics is dominant;
- trees of knowledge; the green world where status-quo critical, societal groups are the dominant driver;
- blue skies: the blue world where techno-science is dominant.

Market Rules: The Grey World where Business is the Dominant Driver

The world of today is the starting point and in the first scenario developed by the EPO, Market Rules, the future is one in which the primary driving of the IP system lies in the hands of big business – in particular the multi- or trans-nationals (MNCs or TNCs). Some might argue that this is merely a continuation of today's world. The current IP system produces one of the few legal monopolies, if not the only one, which a company or an individual can obtain in a liberal economy, although, of course, patent rights are not monopolies per se, since they are rights to exclude rather than rights to act and are subject to restrictions imposed by regulatory bodies and competition laws.

In the business environment, the 'use' of patents is a relatively recent phenomenon. Historically, patents have been a primarily defensive tool; a means to prevent others from entering an area of technology and a means to obtain legal redress to maintain a commercial advantage. Indeed it was only in the mid-1990s that a significant change in the management of intellectual property began as Xerox and IBM applied a more proactive approach. IBM was faced with great financial difficulties and identified unused patents as one potential source of income. Instead of leaving the rights gathering dust in a drawer, why not seek a potential buyer or licensee? The success of this is well documented[17] and has been an inspiration to others but studies show that the exploitation of such rights is by no means a certainty.

Of course, these successes have not gone unnoticed. There is a clear incentive to enter a system which can produce seemingly easy but also highly profitable rewards. The publicity surrounding cases which produce large financial gains, such as the award of $625m to NTP in the so-called Blackberry case, has attracted the attention of investors at a time when other areas of investment are less profitable. While the 1980s saw the opening of western financial markets, the 1990s saw the dot.com boom and the early 2000s have seen property and exotic financial products gather investments; the end of these booms has left investors such as

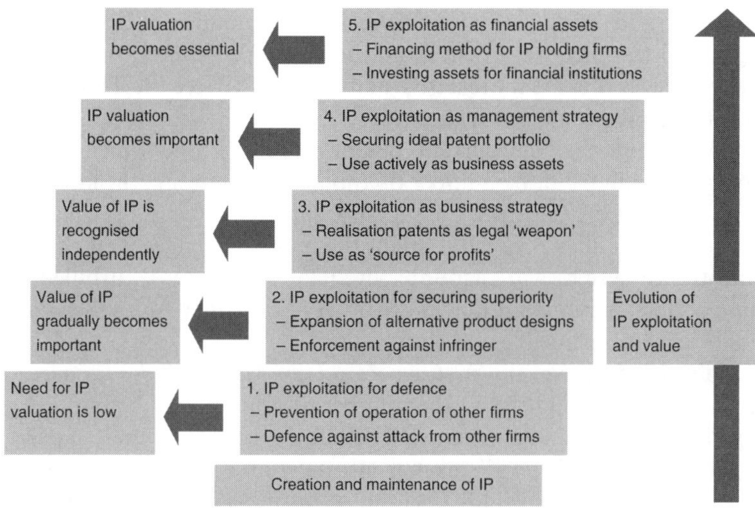

Source: Otsuyama (2003).[18]

Figure 4.4 An illustration of the evolution of IP exploitation and demand for valuation

venture capitalists looking for new areas for investment. The world of IP represents a potential gold-mine for those with the ability and initiative to exploit the opportunities.

This potential value has stimulated pressure for more IP rights. As a consequence, the scope of patentable subject matter has been extended and there has been an unprecedented rise in patent applications. This has led to concerns regarding the ability of the system to cope with the challenge of 'global warming of the patent system',[19] The main users of the system do not stand to gain from such a failure yet nor do they appear to be in a position to curb their own filing behaviour.

At the same time, it is also worth recognising that the global IP system is changing as the world's economies have changed.[20] Global trade has seen a rise in the activities and breadth of geographic footprint of the larger companies. Outsourcing of innovation, production and sales to many more countries has also led to a need for more protection. The advance of the BRICS countries (Brazil, Russia, India, China, South Africa) has led not only to an increase in filing numbers in those countries from multinationals but also to an increase in domestic filings as the populations of those countries become more technologically developed. Given the large populations involved, engagement with the global IP system can be expected to add significantly to the already large number of IP rights being sought and the encouragement from the developed countries for the rest of the world to become more active in matters of IP (see the TRIPS agreement) has done nothing to restrain this.

In *Market Rules*, the current patent system is one which is under increasing strain from the number of applications entering the system and in this world of big business, the pressure simply escalates. So what might this future look like? And what might the main challenges be if this is the future the IP system will encounter in 2025? And, after a turbulent economic period – with potentially more or worse to come – does the scenario remain relevant, plausible and challenging?

As discussed above, the first aspect of the *Market Rules* scenario for 2025 was a continuing rise in the number of applications being filed globally. This arose from the increasing demand for IP rights and, in particular, a broadening of the IP market into new areas, both geographically and technologically. The globalisation of business means that companies from the developed world need protection in areas where business has been out-sourced or where new markets are being developed. At the same time, new innovators or, at least, new users of the IP system are rapidly gaining ground, perhaps most importantly in China. The desire to export innovation is as yet relatively limited in the number of applications[21] but the growth in domestic filings and the rate of this growth reflect a significant trend. Certainly, Market Rules starts from the assumption that this is inevitable.

IP rights have also attracted the attention of investors, in particular the Venture Capitalists (VC), who have identified this as a new area for investment. Their influence in IP matters has become apparent since 2007 when a group of VCs intervened with the US Senate regarding patent reform bills which the VCs considered to negatively affect their business models with regard to the area of enforcement.[22] IP rights form the nucleus of the VC business model, and some VCs focus solely on the exploitation of these rights, much to the dismay of others who describe them as trolls or sharks who merely seek to leverage income, either ethically or not, from the innovations of others.[23] The current global economic crisis appears, at first glance, likely to put a brake on such activities but commentators are already predicting the opposite trend, particularly if the purchase of IP rights were to become cheaper[24] as failing companies are forced to discount and sell their IP rights to remain solvent. The ability to enter a market at a financial trough is a significant attraction for all investors and, as the *Market Rules* posits, even a long recession should not be considered to be permanent within the context of scenarios that have a 20-year time horizon.

At the heart of *Market Rules* is the shift of IP rights from a legal identity instrument to a financial tool. The ability to trade IP rights has become more popular and forms the very business model of some of the 'inno-mediaries' or innovation intermediaries such as the American company, Ocean Tomo. While not being their only form of intermediation, IP auctions are one area for which such companies have become prominent, with auctions having been held throughout the US and Europe over the past few years.[25] The market in tradable IP rights is thus developing and bringing buyers and sellers of IP rights together more efficiently. As more companies enter this market, the trend points to a greater awareness of the opportunities and profits to be made. As other markets collapse, the relatively unknown world of intellectual property is becoming an attractive bolthole. And, of course, these new players need ever more IP rights to use as the tools of their trade.

The increasing sophistication of this area of asset management has led to the introduction of a new Commercial Code by the German accounting authorities, whereby certain aspects of the value of patents will be required to be included on company balance sheets.[26] While Germany has taken the first step on this path, reports suggest that others are following suit.[27] Of course, the accurate valuation of IP rights remains problematic but Market Rules poses the question: 'What if such valuations are in fact possible in the IP system of 2025?' As IP collateralisation becomes more popular, the need to use a standardised accredited methodology can only increase and the recent financial industry problems related to the valuation of collateral can only intensify this requirement in order to avoid similar problems to those faced by the financial industry occurring in the world of IP.[28]

The most prominent facet of the *Market Rules* scenario is the drive for harmonisation within the patent system. To date, there have been numerous attempts to reach agreement on a European Community Patent – a unitary patent valid in all member states of the European Union. This was first proposed at the initial 'Convention for the European Patent for the common market', or (Luxembourg) Community Patent Convention (CPC), which was signed at Luxembourg on 15 December 1975, but without success. In 2004, the European Commission stated that:

> The Community patent (Compat) system will exist alongside patents for individual Member States available through the European Patent Office or national patent offices. Applicants will be able to choose what kind of patent they end up with for any particular invention, whether a unitary Community patent covering the whole of the EU, or individual patents for separate EU Member States.[29]

And again, in November 2008, reported that 'Generic [pharmaceutical] companies and originator companies are in agreement over the need for a single Community patent and the creation of a unified and specialised patent judiciary in Europe.'[30] Despite these multiple efforts, the issue of the different languages of the member states and the requirements for translations has proved too difficult to overcome. Simultaneously, attempts to form a European Patent Litigation Agreement have met with problems of cross-border jurisdiction such that all moves, despite widespread support even from European IP judges themselves, have failed. At a meeting in Venice in November 2008, the judiciary reiterated their support for both measures, concluding:

> If it will not be possible to win the support of all EU-member states for the proposed court system and the Community Patent, both projects should be realised by using the possibilities of an Enhanced Cooperation foreseen by the EC-Treaty. Considering the developments of a Patent Judiciary in countries like Japan and China, the time is ripe for an effective and high quality unified European Patent Judiciary with a decentralised First Instance and a centralised Appeal Instance.[31]

While mutual recognition still appears a distant mirage which is unlikely to become plausible within the time-frame of these scenarios, the joint activities of the Big 5 or IP5, the five major patent authorities – USPTO, JPO, SIPO, KIPO and EPO – has accelerated the process of work-sharing. This harmonisation of practices related to the different elements of patent prosecution,[32] is continuing with the most recent instance being between the USPTO and the EPO, as a pilot programme.[33] The aim of these programmes is to share data and so improve efficiency and consequently to accelerate the patent grant (or refusal) procedure.

The Venture Capitalists mentioned earlier stressed that for the proper functioning of investment in smaller innovative entities, a system which produces strong patents is required in order to be able to defend against infringement. Strategies such as the EPO's Raising the Bar,[34] support such certainty in the IP system and this particular strategy is one of the joint activities which is encouraging the harmonisation moves.

The *Market Rules* scenario thus remains relevant as a plausible and relevant possible future for the IP system and the challenges it raises remain the same – will the patent system be able to cope with ever-increasing numbers of applications and how will issues of global enforcement affect future of IP rights as a financial tool?

Whose Game? The Red World where Geo-politics is Dominant

If the scenarios were a time machine and the Transnational Corporations (TNC) button of the *Market Rules* scenario were to be dimmed, it would be possible to consider an IP system used as a critical pawn in a world with open conflict in the face of changing geopolitical balances and competing ambitions. In this scenario, geopolitics is the dominant driver and the players have changed. Whose game is this?

An article in a European newspaper[35] commented that the 'western' world had not yet fully grasped the historical importance and dimension of the opening of China and its repositioning on the world scene, a process which started three decades ago and is proceeding at an ever faster rate. However, according to the same article, if these developments and their potential benefits for humanity are misunderstood and misjudged, this might lead to a new era of protectionism, nationalism and isolationism – and not only in the West.

Intellectual property and industrial standards are not secondary issues in this global game; unfortunately, they have already become key assets. The German Chancellor Angela Merkel put forward in her speech during her visit to the premises of the EPO for the occasion of the public launch of the *Scenarios for the Future* work, a proposal for the creation of a new single transatlantic market, including the EU and US. In an article describing her proposal, it was stated that 'The plan, described in a confidential 12-page outline, lists four areas – intellectual property, energy and environment, industry standards and capital markets – where the US and EU should co-operate more.'[36] The US has since reacted favorably at the highest level to this plan and the Transatlantic Economic Council meets regularly.[37]

As the western capital markets go through their most critical phase post-World War II and Asia emerges as a region that could undermine the current western factual and ideological hegemony, it is of paramount importance to see what could happen in the three other areas listed by Merkel. These areas – energy and the environment, industry standards and capital markets – are all interrelated, linked together by patented, cutting edge technology. What unites them is the ultimate reward, the golden fleece of our time: the 'golden patent'. This treasure is embedded in a widely used standard, with the potential for technological lock-in and lucrative licensing returns.

At the dawn of the 21st century, IP arbitrage provided large global corporations with powerful incentives to engage in progressive innovation outsourcing and off-shoring. They invested in overseas R&D in countries with weak valorisation of intangible assets and could therefore tap into the intellectual resources of lowly paid scientific researchers. Such 'global sourcing'[38] has evolved as flagships to global innovation networks, with novel organisational models very different from the more hierarchical traditional MNC forms. Underpinning these investments was a belief that these R&D innovation networks were uniquely placed to take advantage of an under-utilised human capital and its innovative capabilities, while not being exposed to excessive risk of imitation.

Samuel Palmisano used the term 'Globally Integrated Enterprise' to identify this radically mutating business landscape and the new corporate strategies for innovation and R&D, based on global sourcing.[39] He described the contemporary shift of the perspective as follows:

> When everything is connected, work flows. In the era we are now entering, the key to success will be whether you can get work to flow to you. That will depend not on how big you are or where you are located, but on how you differentiate yourself through innovation, within a much larger and more open arena. Today, these same criteria – and opportunities – apply to the small as well as the large. We are surrounded today by vast new possibilities, but they bring with them an unprecedented complexity to social and economic life. Yet, for all its challenges, hundreds of millions of entrepreneurs, professionals and 'new global citizens' seem eager to take this journey. [40]

However, this cosy landscape has been dramatically challenged by the fall of Lehmann Brothers and the subsequent erosion of the Washington Consensus. The emphasis of the state has changed: it is a very worried actor seeking long-term solutions. What counts in the new era is no longer profits or shareholder value, but national interests and hegemony. It is not the power of the market rules that prevails, but rather the rule of state power. At the same time, this is the story of a boomerang effect which strikes today's dominant patent players. Contrary to the intentions of the West, globalisation is now backfiring as things turn around. Nations and cultures compete and IP has left the private and business domain to become a powerful weapon in a game for world hegemony.

Kenneth Cukier, Technology Editor of *The Economist,* put it bluntly in the 2007:

> Within the next 40 years, some of the most major innovations will come from elsewhere – outside the west. For the moment, the West is lucky that they don't have IP protection. But within 40 years you can imagine that the great scientific cures and great IT innovations are going to come from other regions. (EPO Interview)

Driving this stunning change are the relentless efforts of hundreds of millions of people who feel that the time has come to secure their share of prosperity and self-respect. East and southeast Asia crystallise as the geopolitical epicentres of this unstoppable movement, both demographically and in terms of economic power. Sensitive technological know-how moves rapidly eastwards, driven by the short-term shareholder demands of western TNCs trying to retain value through increased outsourcing and off-shoring of R&D and by the strategies of venture capital.[41] This epochal transfer of sensitive knowledge (unique in human history – and all without war or submission) is further facilitated by the long term strategies of the receiving states, skilfully playing off rivalry between western corporations and between geopolitical blocks, and of course by the continuous rise in production and technical skills in Asia.

Fatally, the West 'manages down' its basic scientific research, failing to use IP to maintain technological superiority. In contrast, the new entrants become increasingly successful at shaping the evolution of the global technical architecture. They use the weapon of IP and industrial standards to establish geopolitical advantage, adapting and changing the existing rules. Over time their IP offices become fully fledged political regulatory agencies, with an official remit to use patents effectively to promote national interests and to restrict 'abuses' by foreign patent owners.[42]

The situation therefore facilitates the course for technological catch-up, launched by the Chinese *zizhu chuangxin*.[43] The remaining gap is closed by inner-Asian alliances, realising one of the worst nightmares of the intelligence report editors in the early years of the 21st century:[44] a curb on the overwhelming techno-military supremacy of the West. The threshold countries of 2007 have become the top innovators in 2025 and defend a strong global patent system. Their revenues from IP licensing abroad are now huge, but – back home – they follow a different strategy, experimenting with a variety of models, including collaborative, open innovation and flexible enforcement rules. This is not the world of *dura lex sed lex*;[45] based on their pragmatic, non-legalistic tradition, this experimenting enables them to find systems best suited to their needs and helps their economies grow even faster.

In response to the rising competition from newcomers, the West reacts with additional protection mechanisms. It revives the earlier plan of the German conservatives and eventually establishes a Transatlantic Free Trade Union – a new single market that includes both Europe and North America. In addition to the harmonisation of norms and standards and liberalisation of trade within the zone, imports from outside the zone are submitted to new environmental and labour standards. This means that product specifications based on HOW a product is produced determine its eligibility for import and consumption within TAFTA. Combined with a new ACTA++[46] protocol requiring a heavily bureaucratic IPR clearance before importing a certain product into TAFTA, a new super-*Limes*[47]

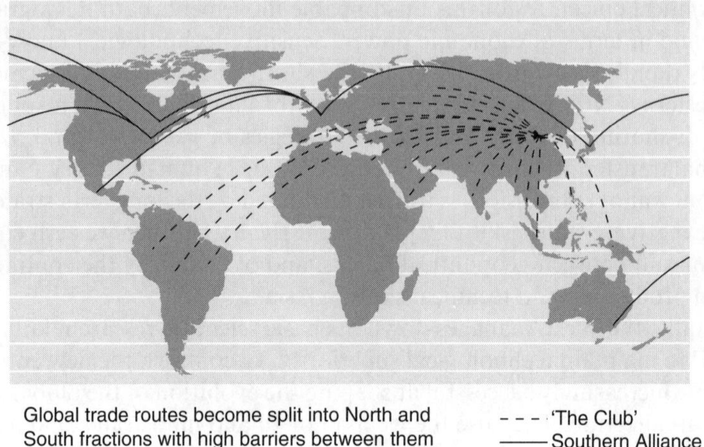

Source: EPO.

Figure 4.5 How the trade and IP systems could fragment into two blocks

is erected. Asia responds with a Free Trade area for the Asia Pacific (FTAP), linking key Asiatic countries with Latin American and African countries.[48]

Thus, two dominant trading blocs emerge by 2025 – the Transatlantic and the Asia/Pacific. Competing trade zones battle for skills and knowledge with rival IPR regimes. The appearance of competing and almost mutually exclusive trade blocs eventually leads to rejection or abrogation of IP rights. Under these circumstances TRIPS loses virtually all relevance, as 'national treatment', its proud pillar, collapses; first de facto and ultimately de jure. Within these blocs, however, depending on the prevalent system, enforcement can be quite powerful.

Within the western block, a de facto Americanisation of the patent-related litigation system occurs, as legal norms in the Web 2.0 era are superseded by the reality of global litigation emanating from American MNCs. In terms of IP enforcement this means a de facto global outreach of US jurisdiction, as Michael Geist[49] had predicted in 2005, when asked whether nations still had the option of determining their own patent law:

> Unlike harmonization initiatives, the Americanization of IP law is not achieved at the negotiating table but instead through the aggressive assertion of jurisdiction. To put a new spin on an old phrase, much like 'if Mohamed does not come to the mountain, the mountain will come to Mohamed,' in today's world of IP law, if the U.S. approach to IP law is not adopted by foreign jurisdictions, then the United States will bring its laws to those jurisdictions.

He concluded that 'today, we increasingly find that IP policy around the world does indeed emanate from the United States, coming from U.S. courts, from the U.S. Congress and from national legal codes.' [50, 51]

By the time TAFTA is formally established, this de facto harmonisation includes the fully fledged de jure Americanisation of the whole patent system. This Americanisation is balanced in part by Europe's rise as the dominant legislator in competition and regulatory issues such as in health, consumer protection, environment and labour standards.

Within the Transpacific zone several enforcement traditions initially co-exist, as there is no normative power strong enough to impose itself on the rest. Although in 2008 Tian Lipu[52] had predicted that China would need several generations to understand the meaning of IP, this view was proven to be too pessimistic. As a matter a fact, by 2025 most Chinese exporting entrepreneurs will have successfully embraced the system and be pressing for effective and harmonised IP enforcement throughout the Transpacific trade block.

Stronger 'outsider' nations cut their own deals, poorer ones simply bypass IP or use open source as the only route past the digital divide. Many developing countries are excluded from the process and work instead within a 'communal knowledge' paradigm or focus on collective intellectual rights to manage their biodiversity heritage. However, the split in two blocs brings back a configuration similar to the 'iron-curtain' era, where smaller countries with natural resources or a favourable geopolitical placement can benefit from the antitheses between the two blocs, creating a space of arbitrage and greater choices, also regarding selective enforcement of IP rules.

All in all, the fragmentation of the world into blocs throws global challenges, for example climate change and scarce natural resources, into stark relief making globally co-ordinated actions almost impossible to achieve. This highly competitive, often brutal, world is not one we and our children would choose to live in.

Trees of Knowledge: A World where Status-quo Critical, Societal Groups are the Dominant Driver

In this story, diminishing societal trust and growing criticism of the IP system result in its gradual erosion. The key players are popular movements – often coalitions of civil society, businesses, concerned governments and individuals – seeking to challenge existing norms. This 'kaleidoscope society' is fragmented yet united – issue by issue, crisis by crisis – against real and perceived threats to human needs: access to health, knowledge, food and entertainment. Multiple voices and multiple world views feed popular attention and interest, with the media playing an active role in encouraging and steering the debate.

This loose 'knowledge movement' echoes the environmental movement of the 1980s, initially sparked by small, established special interest groups but slowly gaining momentum and raising wider awareness through alliances such as the A2K (Access to Knowledge) movement. The paradigm change is also taking place in a time of pressure exerted by a series of public health and agricultural disasters, not only in the south but increasingly also in the north. In particular, the reluctance of the owners of patented technology to make it readily available, either free of charge or under strong FRAND (Fair, Reasonable, Non-Discriminatory) conditions, comes under heavy fire. Moreover, patents are held accountable for the failure of the pharmaceutical industry to respond to the public health crises and to deliver new, innovative and affordable medicaments.

> The challenge is going to be ensuring that developing countries have access to generic medication. We are also going to see challenges in the developed countries, around the expense of drugs that cost tens of thousands of dollars or more annually or this will create pressure to modify patent laws to generic versions of these drugs. (Professor Joel Lexchin, School of Health Policy and Management, York (EPO Interview))

At the 61st World Health Assembly in 2008 the World Health Organisation (WHO) concluded its resolution WHA 61.21. 'Global strategy and plan of action on public health, innovation and intellectual property'[53] which included critical views on the patent system. For example, it underlined the importance of compulsory licenses and other flexibilities of the TRIPS agreement as a last resort to provide affordable medicines in developing countries. Countries like Thailand and Brazil had already made use of compulsory licenses, in particular for AIDS medication, but in 2008, for the first time, cancer medicines were also covered by compulsory licenses.[54] The WHO resolution referred to prize funds as a possible stimulus for innovation into neglected diseases and other areas where market mechanisms appeared insufficient. Prize funds are a way to uncouple the investment into R&D of a product from the later sales of said product by providing a prize to the inventor in exchange for the invention to be released into the public domain (examples include the X-prize foundation[55]). Influential figures such as the Nobel Prize laureates Joseph Stiglitz (Economics) and John Sulston (Medicine) who have raised general concerns about the commercialisation of science support the introduction of prize funds to address important public health issues.[56]

These hostile views pose great problems for the pharmaceutical industry, which has based its entire business model on patents. Civil society groups and development organisations demand affordable medicines, but also question increasingly the patent-based innovation model with increasing vigour. Governments and health insurers try to manage the rising health costs by putting caps on medicament prices, by favouring generic medicines or by demanding clear proof of improved efficacy for new medical products (e.g. British NICE programme[57]). The industry itself acknowledges that the output of novel chemical entities (NCEs) is decreasing while R&D efforts and the number of patent applications are still rising. There are many good reasons for this, but in terms of public perception of the industry it certainly does not resonate well, particularly in the light of the considerable marketing activity undertaken by the industry. Generic manufacturers have claimed for some years that the pharmaceutical industry (which in some cases have their own generics branch) limits their market entry through strategic use of IP rights (e.g. patent 'evergreening'), regulatory procedures ('market or data exclusivity') and strong marketing.[58] The European Commission in January 2008 raided headquarters of some pharmaceutical companies for an inquiry into possible anti-competitive practices in the pharmaceutical sector which was published in 2009.[59]

The other big industry where patents have been a contested issue for a while now is Information and Communication Technology (ICT). Here the trend of open and collaborative innovation finds more and more acceptance not only amongst programmers and pro-sumers (consumers generating products), but also in managing boards. 'Power of Collaborative Innovation' was the central topic of the 2008 World Economic Forum in Davos. How these new forms of innovation fit the model of intellectual property and patents depends very much on the context and the respective business models. Some companies, in particular in the software industry, use two tier strategies: on one level they promote open (source) software to create a platform on a second level for services or proprietary add-on products. Others rely completely on advertising revenues for providing free services and products thus following the powerful model of Google. The entertainment content industry (music, movies, games) is also increasingly looking into alternative business models that could replace the traditional out-dated record selling paradigm. Ever decreasing respect for IP on the internet has been identified in several studies (e.g. UK Olswang Consumer Convergence Survey 2007, Gowers review). A study commissioned by the European Commission underlined the economic importance of Open Source[60] and many government agencies now actively promote the use of open source software (e.g. City of Munich). Many companies, even outside ICT, run open or collaborative innovation initiatives (e.g. Procter & Gamble, Lego, BMW). The intellectual property issues in these initiatives are handled differently: some companies use IP as a tool to build a safe and fair negotiation platform between all partners, others rely on secrecy or other means to recoup their investment. In the ICT sector competition authorities no longer bow to the system of patents: Microsoft was convicted by the ECJ in a competition law case partly concerning its use of patents.[61]

Other areas where crises are looming are the food and the energy sectors. The year 2008 saw extremely volatile prices in both sectors. The food sector is impacted by patents via the increasingly widespread use of genetically modified plants. These GM plants are often protected by patents and there are concerns that they are aggravating the existing monopolisation tendencies.[62, 63] In the energy sector fears are raised that patents on 'clean technologies' might prevent their widespread use.[64, 65] Climate change is likely to have a major impact on all areas of society and to lead to more government intervention in crucial areas. The world-wide financial crisis in 2008 has already shown how a critical sector can come under such extreme pressure that government intervention and bail-outs are considered the only solution. It remains to be seen how this retreat to 'Keynesian economics' will spread to other industries.

In 2008 a young, charismatic and internet-savvy Democrat was elected President of the USA. IP Watch reported that: 'IP and technology experts such as Duke University law professor Arti Rai, former Federal Communications Chairman Reed Hundt, and MIT computer scientist Daniel Weitzner [W3C Technology and Society Domain Leader and Chair of the W3C Patent Policy Working Group] have been part of Obama's inner campaign circle, according to sources.'[66] In his patent reform statement Obama said:

> A system that produces timely, high-quality patents is essential for global competitiveness in the 21st century. By improving predictability and clarity in our patent system, we will help foster an environment that encourages innovation. Giving the Patent and Trademark Office (PTO) the resources to improve patent quality and opening up the patent process to citizen review will reduce the uncertainty and wasteful litigation that is currently a significant drag on innovation. [. . .] As president, Barack Obama will ensure that our patent laws protect legitimate rights while not stifling innovation and collaboration.[67]

So how will these trends unfold in the Trees of Knowledge scenario until 2025?

Powerful foundations and mighty 'flagship' corporations, the business models of which are based on integrating diverse technologies on patent-free platforms, ally themselves with those movements and help decisively shift the balance. Knowledge is supposed to remain a common good, while acknowledging the legitimacy of reward for innovation plays less and less a role.

Thus the patent system is shrunk drastically, only a few patents are granted, and only in some classical areas such as mechanics and chemistry, while enforcement is avoided where possible. As a result of the A2K movement, copyright is also drastically limited.

Government interventions will limit the profits of the pharmaceutical industry drastically and reduce their role mainly to production and some involvement in clinical trials. Cultural flat fees and advertising are dominating the entertainment industry. Focus on prize funds and advance purchase agreements in health sector leaves the resulting drugs in the public domain, that is, open to generic producers. Political prioritisation of open source in ICT provides space for collaborative innovation but shifts focus to branding, speed-to-market and close customer relations.

Understandably, there is a growing use of trade secrets and valuable knowledge remains in a 'black box' as many companies move backwards to increased secrecy, which might also be viewed as an indirect, but quite efficient form of 'enforcement'. However, the shift to branding, geographic indications, trademarks and design rights leads consumers ultimately to ask for stricter enforcement in these areas to ensure quality of luxury articles, but also of essential goods such as drugs and food and safety sensitive products such as airplane parts.

Unfortunately, human nature being what it is, some examples lead to complaints that societal input has not delivered the promised removal of constraints on the free flow of people, ideas and tacit knowledge, rather to capture by certain loud voices and design by committee.

Also, over time the promised freedom is revealed to be more a freedom of the markets than of the citizens. Following a successful epic[68] battle to control the mass media by the on-line advertising and service provider giants, the legalisation of detailed profiling of on-line systems' users[69] enables unprecedented levels and intensity of ubiquitous, individually customised and timely optimised advertising, offered through on-line 'free platforms'. Besides serving clients, these technologies promote new forms of subtle manipulation and it becomes extremely difficult to separate personal desire from the relentless and well timed 'offers' of the system: it appears that the *nomen* 'Android'[70] threatens to become an *omen*.[71]

Blue Skies: The Blue World where Techno-science is Dominant

The world of *Blue Skies* is, by contrast, a world where technicians take the lead. Their credo: where there is a problem, there is a technical solution. This is a world where techno-science is the dominant driver; the key players are techno-politicians and futurists. Not to do what appears doable in order to reach super-humanity or at least trans-humanity through 'generic and evolutionary computation, evolvable hardware, neural nets and computational neuroscience',[72] is considered as a cardinal sin. These complex new technologies are based on highly cumulative innovation processes and – beyond futurist promises – they are also seen as the key to solving systemic problems.

Such problems include climate change, desertification, epidemics, access to health care, food security and the preservation of biodiversity. History shows that human society has usually turned to technology, the application of science to the solution of practical problems, as one of the principal means for dealing with threats and difficulties confronting society. Policies designed to stimulate the creation and diffusion of technology are thus directly relevant to the consideration of the ways in which the global community can respond to the problems. Here, intellectual property plays an important role – however, the 20-year timescale of a patent is increasingly at odds with the changing nature and pace of technology.

A problem arises however from the fact that the trajectories of the intellectual property needs of complex new technologies are in conflict with the ones of classic, discrete technologies. Discrete technologies are characterised by a relatively strong product-patent link, for example in pharmaceuticals or chemistry, whereas in complex industries products are likely to build on an intricate web of multiple technologies, all protected by a large number of patents held by various parties.

In some complex high technology industries the process of research and development is comparable to the continuous extension of a pyramid through the addition of new building blocks at the top. Here, the pyramid serves as a metaphor for the cumulative nature of scientific research in complex product industries. Firms increasingly protect their contributions to this pyramid with patents. As a result several high technology industries are now affected by 'patent thickets'. In a patent thicket many rival firms hold patents protecting components of a single technology. Whenever a firm uses such a technology it is vulnerable to challenge, delay and capitulation by firms holding blocking patents. The threat posed by blocking patents frequently induces firms to build up a large portfolio of patents. This creates a strong bargaining position for the firm owning the portfolio in any disputes with rivals. In a patent thicket all firms face the prospect of hold up and have strong incentives to patent, which perpetuates the patent thicket. Studies[73] indicate that patent thickets exist in nine of the 30 technology areas in Europe.

Patent thickets are also a good environment for 'sharks' or 'trolls' that have no intention of engaging in the production of the technology underlying their patents. For sharks, revenue comes from royalty payments they obtain directly from their licensees or indirectly in terms of damage awards. In contrast to 'classic' licensors, however, sharks use surprise tactics to facilitate their attempts to force manufacturers into unexpected licensing fees ex post after the victim has a successful product on the market. The relevance this topic has assumed over time is dramatic, being reflected in a series of disputes, mainly in the United States. But recent decisions by the US Supreme Court have created a somewhat less hospitable environment for sharks. For example, these decisions have eliminated automatic injunctions for patent infringements. But current laws do not prevent sharks from orchestrating infringements on patented technologies embedded in complex products, possibly resulting in increased patent shark activity not only in the US but also in Europe.

Without doubt, sharks create uncertainty for innovators and their activities may lead to damage awards which are a multiple of what the shark's victim, as a legitimate licensee, would have been willing to pay ex ante.[74] The future situation may be aggravated by the current financial crises and the resulting bankruptcies of many small high-tech companies leaving large piles of patents and patent applications for sharks.[75]

Another important aspect of this world is the convergence of technology and standards. This aspect encompasses the need for IT systems to be able to exchange information, as well as to allow consumers to piece together systems based on products from different suppliers. Both the rise of the Internet and network computing have reinforced this trend, to the point where it is now very difficult to sell a product that does not easily interact with other complementary products. Thus, there is a strong market need for collaboration in the development of 'platform' products and in particular for coordination among rights holders in the form of cross-licences, patent pools and package licences.

Standards are a major stumbling block for the growing requirements for interoperability, particularly due to the mismatched lifecycles of patents and IT products. Unlike copyright, there is no interoperability derogation provision in patent law – which could mean growing reliance on competition law to compel patent owners to license for interoperability purposes. In this context the rulings of the European Commission against Microsoft cements Europe's role as the lead international regulator of dominant companies.[76] This has also a major impact on global markets, since many developing countries are beginning to model their laws after the EU's more restrictive regime. Thus, the ruling may also lead to tougher legal regimes in developing countries such as China and India, which are just beginning to develop their antitrust laws.[77] However, again the mismatched timescales create problems, as the pace of technology outstrips the legal system.

So the world of *Blue Skies* grapples with different problems:

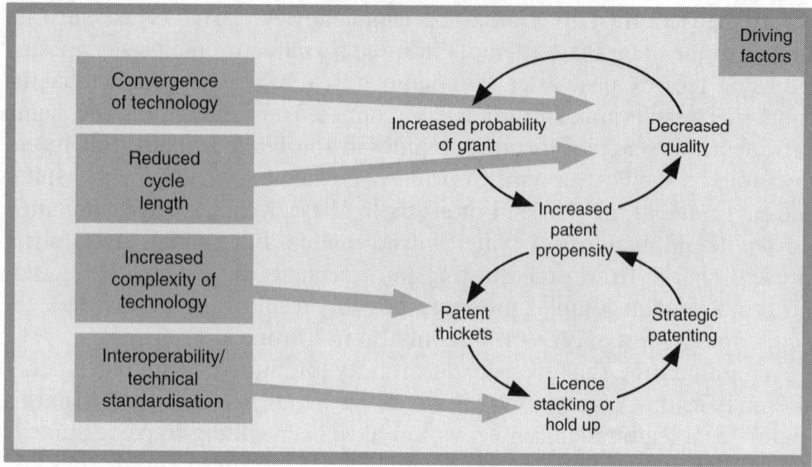

Source: EPO Scenarios for the Future (2007).

Figure 4.6 The patent bubble

interoperability, increasing privatisation of knowledge, patent thickets and sharks. In this world, the pace of technology is quickening. Clearly, there are different attitudes to exclusive rights among industries with product life cycles of only a couple of months or several years. A mobile phone might encompass a thousand patents – and just one patent can block it – while in the pharmaceutical field one or two patents can completely protect an idea.

So how would this world evolve by 2025? Technology is likely to materially transform the IP world of the future, as it has already forced the music industry and other industries to adapt their business models in order to survive. The delocalisation of transactions and use of software has meant that the territorial nature of intellectual property rights can be compromised. The increased access, in particular automated delivery (downloading) means that the traditional model of licensing needs to be reconfigured to ensure that the licences granted are compatible with the law of the user, particularly where they are consumers. One major issue here is the legal position online, and as technology changes the nature of business transactions, what happens as ever more products acquire an online service component? How will policies be impacted by enforcement and what are the potential unintended consequences? The licensing model is now developing on two fronts – the development of free and open source licences[78] is occurring at the same time as proprietary developers are starting to take full advantage of licence models.

The patent world itself is also continually trying to adapt to the challenges coming from rapid technological change, such as the processing and enforcement of complex interdisciplinary inventions. Even in discrete technology fields, such as in pharmaceutical drug discovery, there has been a shift away from the traditional model based on the vast screening of molecules to a more sophisticated model that relies on advanced IT systems and innovative computational models. Today major software developers have departments dedicated to providing IT solutions for healthcare, as well as an emphasis on growing partnerships with life-science companies aimed at introducing new products to the market, such as innovative diagnostic tools, delivery systems and personalised medicines.[79]

For such complex industries, there is a growing consensus that something needs to be done to minimise technology blocking and that mechanisms have to be put in place in the legal regime to adequately address the situation where a patent owner may be using a patent to block a technical standard, for example by charging excessive royalties.

Different versions of 'soft IP' have been proposed,[80] which vary from a property-based system towards a 'liability-based' one. In these cases, although right holders were entitled to compensation for the use of their proprietary assets, their ability to prevent third parties from using these assets or to determine what the monetary compensation for such use should be would be considerably restricted. These proposals effectively represent a shift from a fierce debate on what kind of inventions should be patentable and what should not – the debate on pre-grant criteria of substantial law of patentability – towards a discussion on modifications of the post-grant effects a patent should have. Also, compulsory licenses were presented as a necessary and a preferable mechanism for the transfer of knowledge, especially in the case of developing countries.

Looking back from 2025, the decisive momentum can be seen to have come after the failure of the Conference of the UNFCCC to agree on the basic terms for a post-Kyoto Convention. Developed and developing countries failed to agree whether high customs tariffs or high royalties for patenting technology looming large represented the biggest obstacle to a resolution. Negotiations were blocked by a 'poisonous'[81] atmosphere around the issue of patents within the UNFCC bodies.

As the consequences of climate change started to be felt in developed countries, politicians decided to act. Unfortunately for the patent system, but actually quite predictably after the heated debates in Bali in 2007,[82] the system became a convenient scapegoat; its exclusivity, the Holy Grail for innovative investors, was sacrificed in several key technological sectors.

Under these circumstances, a split of the patent system across industrial sectors occurred, ending the era of one-size-fits-all.

By 2025, the 'soft IP' regime with licenses of rights and other compensatory liability regimes has become the norm in almost all standard-related technological fields for Telecoms, Audio-Video-Media and Computers at the global level. In key environment-related technologies flexible forms of IP protection have also been adopted, enabling differentiated FRAND regimes to be priced according to the level of development of a country/region, in analogy to lessons learned from the pharmaceuticals sector. The IP commons has become the resource connecting the successful technological responses to those facing similar challenges, thereby benefitting the global environment.[83] IP has become the glue that holds these global innovation networks together.

The former patent regime still applies to classic technologies with discrete innovation dynamics. Patents still confer top down exclusive monopoly rights there and are rigorously enforced, as the reputation of the patent system is reinforced and societal tolerance towards infringers is rapidly diminished.

Within the patent world, there is also increasing reliance on technology. New forms of knowledge search and classification emerge and a global knowledge infrastructure is established, comprising public, freely available databases of technological and scientific information and operating on common standards for data interchange.[84]

As IP rights in several technological sectors have lost their most powerful weapon, the monopoly right, enforcement in its classic sense has become obsolete. Patent owners in these sectors cannot prohibit copying but can demand licence fees, with arbitration and court actions if parties cannot agree on terms.

Not surprisingly, serious problems arise. Drawing a legal line between strongly converging but still diverse technological sectors opens interminable legal debates about where how and by whom the lines should be drawn. So, to the despair of the engineers who initiated this paradigm change in intellectual property; the lawyers triumph once again.

Another important problem is the social acceptance of such a global, technocratic solution. Moral questions on 'fair value' are repeatedly asked and the concept of IP gets intertwined with catchy policy issues such as globalization and public health.

But, most importantly, the techno-fix ideology that prevails in this era struggles in vain to address the menacing environmental problems, because it fails to recognise the mental attitude at the root of the causal chain: that nature is still perceived as a *natum*, for instance an inert object, and not as *physis*, that is a process sensitive to changes in its boundary conditions.

Scenario Overview

These four scenarios illustrate the divergent ways the world of patenting and intellectual property could evolve. Each of these four worlds represents a series of trade-offs that will be made, and each will have winners and losers, advantages and disadvantages. In *Market Rules*, the interests of business will be paramount, and societal concerns are likely to be ignored most of the time. Occasionally, the odd excess in the system will be rooted out, but the business world will soon try and find new ways to exploit the use of their granted rights, while continually lobbying for greater IP protection. Patents will become established as a key financial asset, a critical means to maximise profits and support emerging lines of business.

In the world of *Whose Game?* the dynamics will be determined by the changing geopolitical and technology landscape as patent money flows eastwards. As the West reacts, global structures will give way to regional trade blocks, with their differentiated IP systems. Since IP is viewed as a tool of national competitiveness, the winners will be the new players who are increasingly able to flex their geopolitical and technological muscle; the losers will be existing players forced to surrender their dominance. The fate of less developed economies will depend on how successfully they manage to use open source and their collective intellectual property rights.

In *Trees of Knowledge*, the decline of societal trust in multinational corporations and governments in an increasingly connected digital world will lead to the growing power of popular movements, a rainbow alliance of coalitions including civil society, businesses and governments. Although the issues and crises vary, the underlying theme remains access to health, knowledge, food and entertainment. New methods are devised to try to provide incentives to innovate while keeping knowledge in the public domain. The winners and losers will be defined by the results: who is able to innovate what – with the answer dependent on the quality of governance.

The world of *Blue Skies* will see the tensions between the novel technology sectors and the classic technological fields come to a head; there are likely to be many conflicts around the boundaries created between sectors and systems. Societal reliance on complex technological systems, in particular solutions to global ecological crises, will create a world that provides great opportunity for certain innovators. IP is acknowledged as the means to share technological solutions to complex problems, so the winners will be those able to adapt to the changing nature of knowledge and the speed of change – and survive in a global jungle.

HOW TO RESPOND TO THE CHALLENGES?

The four scenarios are regularly used for setting the scene within very diverse contexts: in intensive workshops linked to public conferences, as keynote speeches in conferences and symposia, for reports destined for governments and legislators and for developing future strategies, including by key policy makers and IP-related foundations as a tool to deal with fundamental uncertainty: 'not just what we don't know but, more importantly, what we don't know we don't know'. They have moved the debate from single issue adversarial positions to the wider context. Besides the fact that the scenarios extend the reach of informed debate beyond the grey horizons, they hint at inherent global challenges looming large in all their examined configurations.

These global challenges are likely to become more concrete for the world of IP institutions. Thus, the continued growth of patent application filings worldwide has led some observers to conclude that patent offices are in danger of no longer being able to handle their workloads. The growth in filings is sometimes referred to as 'global patent warming'. As demonstrated in a recent publication, global patent warming exists only in those places where three factors coincide – globalisation, pendency and woolly boundaries.[85]

In the context of the four scenarios, it is worth reflecting on how IP institutions could respond to these three concrete challenges in order to reduce this negative phenomenon.

As described before also in the grey and red worlds (*Market Rules* and *Whose Game?*), globalisation has led to increased levels of cross-regional patent filings as well as strongly increased levels of patent propensity in a number of countries (e.g. China, South Korea and USA). The strongest growth for most patent offices has been trade related. For example, Europe's patent propensity as measured by the volume of first filings has slowly increased by just 1 per cent per year since the 1990s. However, the proportion of these first filings that European companies have sent to the EPO, USPTO, Japan etc. has exploded since the 1980s. Europe now sends more than 40 per cent of its annual 110,000 first filings to the United States. Trade and globalisation are therefore the dominant drivers behind rising numbers of patent filings.

If globalisation were the only factor, then patent offices and the systems they serve could probably cope. However this is not the case. Pendency is also an important and growing factor. Traditionally pendency has been expressed in terms of timeliness. For example, the so-called Paris Criteria in Europe and USPTO pendency targets are both expressed as a number of years. Regrettably, this focus on timeliness hides a growing problem in

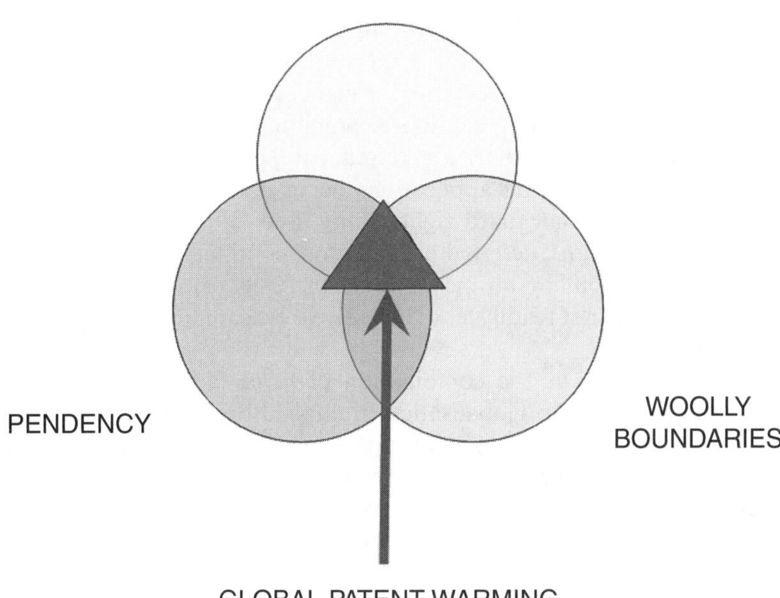

Source: EPO.

Figure 4.7 Global patent warming

terms of volumes. In 2000, three years pendency in Europe would have been equivalent to 300,000 potential patent rights waiting in the system. Today, that figure would be closer to 600,000 and it is growing fast. The patent system is permanently flooded by the volume of pending applications. Today, the volume of patents pending is probably greater than the volume of patents granted and still valid.

In some industrial sectors, especially those where the life cycle of patents is less than 8–10 years, the ratio of pending patents to patents in force is completely distorted, and will remain so for the foreseeable future. This again is a good environment for patent thickets and trolls, as described in the blue scenario. Given this situation, patent offices are increasingly confronted with applicant behaviour aimed at exploiting the situation by adopting strategies to generate additional pendency.

Together, globalisation and pendency represent powerful drivers. A third can usefully be added – that of woolly boundaries.

Property boundaries between individual patents have become

increasingly vague or woolly across the patent systems. Some patent systems have more problems than others, but global interdependency means that these problems are duly shared across the patent systems of the world. Again most commentators tend to focus on granted patents in the IT sector. But this is not necessarily the main area of concern.

Woolly boundaries are much more common, and perfectly legitimate, among pending applications. As a consequence, patent offices see increasing examples of incoming applications being drafted in 'special' ways; rules established to safeguard rights being used 'differently'; non-unity; divisional applications; deferred examination; continuation-in-part applications and, last but by no means least, the emergence of patenting in useful arts that do not readily lend themselves to clear intellectual property boundaries.

To summarise, it is the combination of three factors that leads to global patent warming: globalisation multiplied by pendency multiplied by woolly boundaries. This situation is generating two unwelcome consequences: greater uncertainty and greater risk. High volumes, high pendency and woolly boundaries are fertile ground for different, potentially uncompetitive, behaviour. Some of this behaviour is planned and some of it is opportunistic. As one observer reported, the intentions of patent sharks and patent trolls are unclear to themselves until an opportunity arises. One person's risk is another's opportunity.

Within the patent system, the main patent offices are seeking solutions, although not always to the same problem. The EPO's assessment of the situation has revealed four major strategic directions that form the basis of different thinking.

Merging the Islands

On one end of the merger framework is better co-operation between patent offices through simply sharing information. At the other end of the merger framework is federalism; this means, for example, accepting each other's decisions. Ultimately, such a strategic direction is not so much about improving the different patent systems – it is about unifying them. This is a difficult strategic direction to take, with some intrinsic risks as set out in the grey scenario. The arguments can get quite heated –witnessed at times amongst EPO member states. Even with a political goal of federalism, the question arises: 'Can we get there without taking certain interim steps?' And if federalism is not the political goal, how can we pursue the strategic direction while keeping control of the final outcome?

As for the current state of affairs, the main global patent offices are partners and they will increasingly co-operate. In the United States, the line is drawn at exchanging and making maximum use of each other's work, but falls short of substantive recognition. China has also defended this line. In Europe, the majority of countries also draw the line in the same place. As usual in Europe, there are always one or two outliers who do not feel that attached to the mainland and they join Japan in being somewhat more federalist, albeit with certain nuances.

So we can expect to see increasing levels of work sharing, increasing alignment of the timing of outputs of different steps in the patent process and increasing sharing of knowledge and decisions. We may even see common development of tools – or at least common use of the same tools such as classification schemes, communication drafting tools, e-tools and prior art search tools, yet the ultimate federalist merger framework appears to be quite unlikely at present.

Raising the Bar

Inventors and consumers alike depend on high-quality patents. On the other hand, as described in the blue scenario, the volume of technical literature is increasing rapidly, and whereas patent applications were traditionally focused on one main technical field, over time technological fields have converged, as is the case with computers and mobile phones. Dealing with the volume of material, and reorganising patent and non-patent literature in a manner that promotes efficient and complete searching and examination, has become increasingly difficult. As a result of these internal stresses, combined with criticism from some applicants, member states, and academics, together with the results of the Scenarios project, the view within Europe has concluded that current quality standards are inappropriate for the needs of today's society and that the value of patents has decreased.

Therefore, the strategic aim is to make the application of existing rules stricter and more rigorous. Eventually, it is desirable to grant less than patent offices would today by increasing the level of inventive step required to obtain a patent. Efficient and streamlined processes that promote best practice and involve interested parties are also important factors in the provision of high quality services.

There are three main aspects to raising the bar and increasing patent quality. First, create a better status quo by establishing quality standards across all European patent offices and by tightening up current practice. Second, it is the intention of the EPO to fine tune certain entry and process rules, and to remove (or limit) opportunities for abuse such that sharper boundaries are established earlier on in the procedure. Third, although this may take more time, the EPO intends to raise the bar itself by changes to existing practices within the legal framework with a main focus on inventive step. The aim is to grant patents only for innovations with sufficient inventive merit meeting the needs of society. The move towards making patents harder to obtain is backed up by evidence that the allowance rate is falling, with the number of granted patents falling in relation to previous years.

Shine a Light

The purpose of this strategy is to create certainty in the area of pending applications. In essence, the strategy of shining a light acknowledges the current situation within the patent systems and tries to work within this framework to create greater certainty.

Questions to be answered could be: how and when is uncertainty created in the patent filing, search and examination process? Who are the responsible players and what is their motivation? How might certain applicants and attorneys be increasingly exploiting uncertainty in the system and in which ways do they use the system in a counterproductive way?

One end of this strategy is to make information about uncertainty available. At the other end, patent offices could actively prioritise and create certainty. Alternative methods to measure these elements of uncertainty, as well as assess their economic consequences, are focal points of the discussion.

For the time being this is an emerging strategic direction. For example, the EPO has made a proposal[86] that could improve competition conditions and thus directly benefit consumers through a better exchange of information and collaboration between competition agencies and patenting authorities:

> The EPO believes that a better understanding of the competitive implications of companies exploiting otherwise perfectly logical and legitimate provisions in secondary patent legislation can lead to improvements.
>
> The focus of the EPO is therefore not in ex post individual competition cases – this is not the vocation of the EPO. Although if the EPO is able to shine a light on the growing mass of (pending) IP rights then this will definitely be considered.
>
> Instead the focus of the EPO is in ex ante measures, from various regulatory bodies including the patent offices themselves, in order to correct rules and procedures whose original intentions are open to uncompetitive distortions.[87]

The EPO is also trying to intensify its outreach efforts to address more directly and explicitly transparency and clarity issues. In parallel, strong cooperation with the other major patent offices is necessary to enter this arena and join forces. For instance, one possible European answer to the problem of patent thickets and sharks can be seen in the exclusion of sensitive fields from patentability. In patent circles, there are probably no more controversial subjects than software and business method patents. In October 2008, the US Federal Circuit excluded abstract methods from patentability.[88] At the same time in Europe, a referral to the Enlarged Board of Appeal of the EPO has been made relating to the deeply contentious question about how to assess the patentability of software-related inventions.

Invent a Better Mousetrap

The final strategic direction is to redesign, reconfigure or streamline the patent processing workflow. The 'mousetrap' refers here to the metaphor derived from a popular quote ascribed to the 19th-century American essayist and poet Ralph Waldo Emerson (1803–1882), a shortened version of which reads: 'Build a better mousetrap, and the world will beat a path to your door.' While the literary correctness of the quote has never been fully established, the 'mousetrap approach' has become a commonplace English expression referring to the ability to improve a concept or design without changing its original purpose and does not convey any derogatory meaning about patents and /or the patenting process.

The purpose of this strategic direction is to redesign, reconfigure or streamline the workflow. So whereas merging the islands was about making the different patent systems into one, inventing a better mousetrap is about making them function better as a process. One end of this strategy is simply to make the current system better. However, this smacks too much of business as usual – the emerging insider view is that it will not be sufficient to meet the challenges of the future. At the other end, patent offices across the globe could co-produce certain key steps in the intellectual property rights process that are fit for purpose in their own regions. In between, reconfiguration could create a situation whereby current distorting incentives (fees, rules . . .) are removed and positive incentives are created.

There are many angles to inventing a better mousetrap. Singly or jointly, they would impact on each of the three elements driving global patent warming. Two specific concrete actions are worthy of special mention.

The first is co-production, a critical way to overcome the problem that like the gas turbine or aircraft industry, major development costs and risks can no longer be borne by a single company or institution. As an example, the USPTO has installed an in-house electronic filing, scanning and workflow system with the help of the EPO. The system installed was based on the EPO's own in-house system – Phoenix. What is important to note is that both the EPO and the USPTO had experienced major project failures for similar systems before Phoenix was finally developed and tested by the EPO. The resources – financial, human as well as intellectual – required for this project were, when properly calculated, enormous.

As a consequence, the heads of five intellectual property offices announced the adoption of the vision statement of work-sharing initiative among the five offices: 'The elimination of unnecessary duplication of work among the offices, enhancement of patent examination efficiency and quality, and guarantee of the stability of patent right.' The five offices also elaborated on this cooperative framework in the form of 10 Foundation Projects. These projects have been devised to harmonize the search and examination environment of each office and to standardize the information-sharing process. The projects are expected to facilitate the work-sharing initiative by enhancing the quality of patent searches and examinations and building mutual trust in each other's work.[89]

A second action worthy of note under the inventing a better mousetrap strategy is the redesign of the fee system. There seems to be general agreement that having cost-covering procedural fees could be one appropriate means to limit further global patent warming. But how might this work? One of the more frequent objections to this proposal is that procedural fees that covered upfront costs could reduce the propensity to patent, especially among SMEs, a valid concern. However, a French example shows that governments will always look for ways to subsidise first filings as a basic part of their innovation policy. In this case, the EPO charges the French government an indexed cost-covering procedural fee for performing searches for French national first filings, while the French government uses national renewal fee income to reduce drastically the actual search cost to the French applicant. This example indicates that it is questionable whether full cost coverage of procedural fees could reduce the global propensity to patent, but it could, however, be used as a policy to address second filing levels.

More importantly, full cost coverage of procedural fees could be used to influence behaviour of applicants. If one takes as a starting point the obvious economic statement that behaviour is influenced by costs, because costs include fees, the evidence suggests that fee levels on their own might influence behaviour. Generally, low fee levels are perceived as an incentive for certain types of behaviour and high fee levels as a disincentive. Sometimes the incentive offered by fee levels combines with rules to reinforce behavioural patterns with negative systemic consequences. Examples that could be cited are poor initial drafting; abuse of divisional mechanisms; delay tactics; strategic patenting (i.e., filing with no intention of obtaining a grant) and systematic opposition. These examples directly contribute to global patent warming by creating uncertain boundaries and increasing pendency. If full-cost coverage of procedural fees were to inhibit such behaviour, it would have a positive impact. Overall, just like shining a light, the possibilities of inventing a better mousetrap are only just emerging.

CONCLUSION

To conclude, the patent offices impact and are impacted by different external factors as set out in the scenarios. For some of the challenges, like the global patent warming, there are strategies that might help. Some strategies, such as merging the islands and inventing a better mousetrap, lie well within the scope and capacity of patent systems themselves, but the same cannot be said for raising the bar and shining a light. Raising the bar, specifically that element that would make it more difficult for a technological advance to be deemed inventive by the patent system, has a clear economic dimension. Shining a light goes further, it requires a greater understanding by patent offices as to what is going on in the real economy.

But could any of these strategies be implemented, effectively and on time? The cost of inaction would be very high. The very metaphor global patent warming suggests an element of despair, of helplessness. But does that make it impossible to deal with? Tell that to Al Gore or the IPCC; they would certainly not agree.

The same applies to the patent system. Global inaction on this issue is one of the major drivers behind the emergence of some of the Scenarios developed by the EPO. As presented, we can have a green or a blue scenario whereby the patent system is abolished or replaced by alternative models such as a license of rights scheme. We can have a red scenario, whereby different states set up regional patent system fortresses in order to protect themselves against foreign onslaughts. We can have a grey scenario, whereby the intellectual property bubble is finally burst by the financial sector. So, just as with real global warming, doing nothing has a price. Some people seem to be willing to wait and take the risk, but for the eco-system as a whole, or in our case the IP system, this is obviously not a wise option.

There is an increasing recognition across the leadership of major patent offices that action is required and a growing determination to tackle these thorny issues. Awareness of the difficulties has been encouraged by serious public debate backed up by strategic reviews in Europe (for example, European Commission consultation process, the EPO strategy debate and the EPO Scenarios project), Japan[90] and the United States. As a consequence, there seems to be a growing willingness among patent offices to put serious energy into more fundamental, but controversial, issues. A further consequence is to be found in a renewed energy for large-scale, inter-patent office co-operation, such as the development of the Foundation Projects.[91]

In general, some strategies, or aspects thereof, are much easier to implement than others. Traditionally, the biggest consideration has been whether the various practical elements for a given policy are under the control, or direct influence, of a patent office. This is changing. The changing political landscape has led to some practical breakthroughs that support the strategies of merging the islands (at least the initial steps) and inventing a better mousetrap. The strategy of raising the bar has now become very explicit inside the European Patent Organisation – a major project with this title and scope is well underway. And finally growing public and political awareness about the importance of pendency volumes and woolly boundaries may bring the necessary courage to all stakeholders to shine a light on what is happening.

The patent system has a long history, and its greatest strength is that, like the technologies it has served, it has adapted to change. Today, it is important to ensure that the patent system, and the offices that serve its needs, are sufficiently realistic to the challenges of the future and aware of the need for flexible strategies. This is essential if this historic system is to remain resilient and adaptable in the face of further challenges imposed on it by the future, for instance the recent financial crisis. This means that any strategic renewal process will have to be a continuous, iterative one, involving most of the many stakeholders determined to shape its future.

NOTES

1. This chapter builds on the 'EPO Scenarios for the Future', published by the EPO in April 2007, (available at http://www.epo.org/topics/patent-system/scenarios-for-the-future/download.html). This chapter was written in English and translated into Japanese in 2008. Except for some minor adaptations, the content does not reflect possible changes since. For example, the plan for a 'Community patent' has developed into a proposal for a unitary patent involving 25 member states of the European Union, for details see: http://www.epo.org/news-issues/issues/eu-patent.html.
2. Dominique Guellec, Bruno van Pottelsberghe de la Potterie, *The Economics of the European Patent System: IP Policy for Innovation and Competition*, Oxford University Press, 2007.
3. Peter Drahos, 'Information Feudalism: Who Owns the Knowledge Economy?', Earthscan Ltd, 2002.
4. Josh Lerner, 150 Years of Patent Protection (August 1999). Available at SSRN: http://ssrn.com/abstract=179188 or DOI: 10.2139/ssrn.179188.

5. See http://www.epo.org/about-us/organisation/member-states.html.
6. The London Agreement came into force on 1 May 2008.
7. See http://www.epo.org/patents/law/legal-texts/london-agreement/status.html.
8. Study 'Future Workload' of the Board of the AC of the EPO, available at http://www.epo.org/topics/news/2007/20071214.html.
9. http://www.trilateral.net/background/.
10. Trilateral Statistical Report, Edition 2007, http://www.trilateral.net/tsr/tsr_2007/ and WIPO, World Patent Report: A Statistical Review, August 2008, available at http://www.wipo.int/ipstats/en/statistics/patents/.
11. See http://www.epo.org/about-us/press/releases/archive/2008/20081031.html.
12. See http://www.epo.org/topics/news/2008/20081107.html.
13. See http://www.epo.org/about-us/press/releases/archive/2008/20081114a.html.
14. See http://www.epo.org/topics/patent-system/scenarios-for-the-future.html.
15. This term was initially meant to describe a set of specific economic policy prescriptions by institutions such as the International Monetary Fund (IMF) and the World Bank. However, the term was used more broadly to characterise market fundamentalism (deregulation) and the hegemony of intangible over tangible assets.
16. See http://www.epo.org/focus/patent-system/scenarios-for-the-future/interviews.html and http://www.epo.org/focus/patent-system/scenarios-for-the-future/detailed.html.
17. L.V. Gerstner, 'Who Says Elephants Can't Dance? Inside IBM's Historic Turnaround', Collins, New York, 2002.
18. H. Otsuyama (2003) 'Patent Valuation and Intellectual Assets Management', in Samejima, M. (ed.) *Patent Strategy Handbook*, Chuokeizai-sha, Tokyo, Chapter 5.
19. Ciaran McGinley, 'Taking the heat out of the global patent system', *Intellectual Asset Management*, August/September 2008.
20. 'Sharper Focus on Intellectual Property', *Financial Times*, 18 November 2008.
21. PCT Yearly Review: Developments and Performance; available at http://www.wipo.int/pct/en/activity/pct_2007.html (Section 3.1).
22. 'Venture capitals slam patent reform bill', Eileen McDermott, New York, 1 November 2007, available at www.managingip.com.
23. Joachim Henkel & Markus Reitzig (2008) 'Patent Sharks', *Harvard Business Review*, June, pp. 129–133
24. Joff Wild, 'Why sinking markets could mean real opportunities for patent acquirers and licensees', Intellectual Asset Management blog, 7 October 2008, available at http://www.iam-magazine.com/blog/Detail.aspx?g=8790d519-e2e9-48d3-9605-d74eab9d3125.
25. Joff Wild, 'Ocean Tomo success underlines the growing market for IP', Intellectual Asset Management blog, 7 April 2008, available at http://www.iam-magazine.com/blog/Detail.aspx?g=2988d4a2-edfb-4d6f-a401-b01de13d1236.
26. Corporate Germany, Newsletter of Simmons & Simmons, July 2008, available at http://www.elexica.com/download.aspx?area=crms&resource=D5CorporateGermany200807eng.pdf. The new Commercial Code was introduced in early 2009.
27. Dr. Matte Köllner, 'Developing a patent valuation standard', *Intellectual Asset Management*, Feb/March 2007, p. 5.
28. Proposal submitted by DIN (Germany) on patent valuation, available at http://publicaa.ansi.org/sites/apdl/Documents/News%20and%20Publications/Links%20Within%20Stories/NWIP%20(Patent%20Valuation).pdf.
29. European Commission, DG Internal Markets, Community Patent FAQs, May 2004, available at http://ec.europa.eu/internal_market/indprop/docs/patent/2004-05-faq_en.pdf.
30. European Commission, DG Competition, Pharmaceutical Sector Inquiry, Preliminary Report, 28 November 2008, p. 6, available at http://ec.europa.eu/comm/competition/sectors/pharmaceuticals/inquiry/preliminary_report.pdf.
31. 'Resolution Venice IV', Fourth European Judges' Forum, Venice (IT), 15 November 2008, available at http://www.iam-magazine.com/blog/articles/VeniceRes08.pdf.
32. 'Blueprint Laid Out for Work-sharing Among Five IP Offices', EPO Press Release,

Munich (DE), 31 October 2008, available at http://www.epo.org/about-us/press/releases/archive/2008/20081031.html.
33. 'Patent prosecution Highway Pilot Programme Between the European Patent Office and the United States Patent and Trademark Office', EPO press Release, 26 September 2008, available at http://www.epo.org/patents/law/legal-texts/InformationEPO/archiveinfo/20080926.html.
34. 'Raising the bar on patent quality', EPO Annual report 2007, available at http://www.epo.org/about-us/office/annual-reports/2007/focus.html.
35. 'Die beruhigende Nutzlosigkeit der grossen Mauer', *Neue Zürcher Zeitung*, 17 September 2007, available at http://www.nzz.ch/nachrichten/kultur/aktuell/die_beruhigende_nutzlosigkeit_der_grossen_mauer_1.556363.html.
36. 'Merkel's transatlantic plan gains ground', *Financial Times*, 26 January 2007, available at http://www.ft.com/intl/cms/s/0/40f1702e-ace1-11db-9318-0000779e2340.html.
37. 'Transatlantic talks "to tackle barriers"', *Financial Times*, 27 June 2007.
38. See Dieter Ernst & David Hart, 'Governing the Global Knowledge Economy: Mind the Gap!', 2007 Atlanta Conference on Science, Technology and Innovation Policy, Georgia Tech, October 2007:

> Finally, an important new development is that smaller U.S.-based high-tech companies, and even start-ups, are facing considerable pressure to engage in innovation offshoring. In fact, venture capitalists in Silicon Valley now require start-ups to present an 'offshore outsourcing' plan as a precondition for receiving funding . . . According to one of Silicon Valley's best-known venture capitalists, 'We see innovation all over the world. We don't just want to sit here in Silicon Valley, only making investments in companies we can drive to.'

39. Samuel Palmisano, CEO of IBM, *Financial Times*, 6 May 2008:

> Unlike the multinational – which created miniversions of itself in markets around the world – this new kind of organisation locates work, skills and operations wherever it makes sense, based on access to expertise, on superior economics and on the presence of open environments and technologies.

40. Regarding the fundamental 'egocentric' shift in the way we perceive the world (the Google Earth syndrome, i.e., the world should come to us *immediately* and not vice versa, a journey is not necessary anymore), see also the works of Paul Virilio in *Speed and Politics: An Essay on Dromology*, New York: Semiotext(e), 1986 [1977].
41. Ernst & Hart, *supra* note 37.
42. See the proposed rule change for foreign patent filings in China: available at http://www.ft.com/cms/s/0/524dc6ac-4852-11dd-a851-000077b07658.html.
43. 'Development of indigenous national innovative activities': see Richard P. Suttmeier, Xiangkui Yao & Alex Zixiang Tan (2006) 'Standards of Power? Technology, Institutions, and Politics in the Development of China's National Standards Strategy', The National Bureau of Asian Research.
44. Global Trends 2025: The National Intelligence Council's 2025 Project, available at http://www.dni.gov/nic/NIC_2025_project.html.
45. Latin: 'the law is harsh, but it is the law'.
46. Anti-Counterfeiting Trade Agreement (ACTA) is a proposed plurilateral trade agreement that would impose strict enforcement of IPRs, mainly related to internet activity and trade in information-based goods.
47. *Limes:* the long wall built by Caesar Hadrian across the borders of the Roman Empire to protect it from 'barbarian' incursions.
48. See 'Australia set to join trade pact', *Financial Times*, 20 November 2008.
49. See Industry Canada Study, first published 5 October 2005, Discussants' Comments, Session I, available at http://strategis.ic.gc.ca/epic/internet/inippd-dppi.nsf/en/ip01414e.html.

50. Geist emphasizes that his comments should not be viewed as U.S. bashing, quite the contrary, as 'the Industry Canada study provides a compelling case for the US to act in a very rational manner by pursuing a policy that affords maximum IP protection'.
51. 'Britons could be extradited over gambling', *Financial Times*, 18 July 2006, available at http://www.ft.com/intl/cms/s/0/cf492eb8-1699-11db-8b7b-0000779e2340.html.
52. Tian Lipu, SIPO Commissioner, commented at the press information centre of the 17th CPC National Congress (18 October 2007) that 'Chinese people did not have the idea of intellectual property in their minds for several thousands of years and the term "intellectual property" was included in Chinese authoritative dictionary in 2000'. He said further that 'frankly to resolve the problem, China needs to make efforts of several generations'.
53. WHO resolution WHA 61.21, available at http://www.who.int/gb/ebwha/pdf_files/A61/A61_R21-en.pdf.
54. US Chamber of Commerce, Thailand Compulsory Licenses Briefing, 24 April 2008.
55. See http://www.xprize.org/.
56. Universities Allied for essential Medicines, Updated Signatory List, 'Eminent Academics: IGWG Delegates Should Explore New Mechanisms to Correct Current Deficiencies in Medicine System', 28 April 2008, available at http://essentialmedicine.org/story/2008/04/28/updated-signatory-list-eminent-academics-igwg-delegates-should-explore-new-mechanis.
57. See http://www.nice.org.uk/.
58. European Generic Medicines Association (EGA), 'Patent-related Barriers to Market Entry for Generic Medicines in the European Union: a review of weakness in the current European patent system and their impact on the market access of generic medicines', July 2008, available at http://www.egagenerics.com/ega-barriers_rpt.htm.
59. European Commission, DG Competition, Pharmaceutical Sector Inquiry, Preliminary report, 28 November 2008, available at http://ec.europa.eu/comm/competition/sectors/pharmaceuticals/inquiry/preliminary_report.pdf.
60. Study on the: Economic impact of open source software on innovation and the competitiveness of the Information and Communication Technologies (ICT) sector in the EU, available at http://ec.europa.eu/enterprise/ict/policy/doc/2006-11-20-flossimpact.pdf.
61. See http://ec.europa.eu/comm/competition/antitrust/cases/microsoft/index.html.
62. ETC report, 'Who owns nature', November 2008, available at http://www.etcgroup.org/upload/publication/pdf_file/707.
63. Geoff Tansey & Tasmin Rajotte (eds), 'The Future Control of Food: A Guide to International Negotiations and Rules on Intellectual Property, Biodiversity and Food Security', Earthscan/IDRC 2008, available at http://www.idrc.ca/openebooks/397-3/.
64. European Patent Forum 2008, 'Inventing a cleaner future: Climate change and the opportunities for IP', available at http://www.epo.org/about-us/events/archive/2008/epf2008/forum-1.html.
65. Beijing High-level Conference on Climate Change: Technology Development and Technology Transfer, 7–8 November 2008, available at http://www.ccchina.gov.cn/bjctc/en/index.asp.
66. IP Watch, 'Who Will Advise Obama On IP? Let The Name Games Begin', 6 November 2008, available at http://www.ip-watch.org/weblog/index.php?p=1304.
67. Barack Obama: Connecting and empowering all Americans through technology and innovation, available at http://cairns.typepad.com/blog/files/fact_sheet_innovation_and_technology_plan_final.pdf.
68. See the fictive EPIC story (*Evolving Personalized Information Construct*): http://mccd.udc.es/orihuela/epic/.
69. See Google's patent application in 2007 'Using information from user video game interactions to target advertisements, such as advertisements to be served in Video', Patent number WO2007041371.

70. See http://www.openhandsetalliance.com/android_overview.html.
71. Bruce Sterling, *When Blobjects Rule the Earth*, Los Angeles, August 2004, available at http://www.viridiandesign.org/notes/401-450/00422_the_spime.html.
72. John Smart, *Brief History of Intellectual Discussion of Accelerating Change*, available at http://www.accelerationwatch.com/history_brief.html.
73. Dietmar Harhoff, Georg von Graevenitz & Stefan Wagner (2008) *Incidence and Growth of Patent Thickets – The Impact of Technological Opportunities and Complexity*, SSRN, CEPR Discussion Paper No. DP6900, July.
74. Markus Reitzig, Joachim Henkel & Christopher Heath, *On sharks, trolls, and their patent prey – Unrealistic damage awards and firms' strategies of 'being infringed'*, Elsevier, February 2007.
75. Brian Kahin: *The Patent Bubble . . . Still Growing*, September 2008, available at http://www.huffingtonpost.com/brian-kahin/the-patent-bubble-still-g_b_129232.html.
76. In 2004, the EU requires Microsoft to disclose complete and accurate interoperability information to developers of work group server operating systems on reasonable terms. In failing to do so, the European Commission imposes in 2008 a penalty payment of €899 million for non-compliance with its obligations. The international scope of the EU's role was reflected in the Microsoft case in that it was a US-based multinational, Sun Microsystems Inc., rather than a European company, that brought the initial complaint in Europe.
77. A ruling of the Supreme Court in China in the year 2008 stated:

> Regarding the current reality that China's standard setting organizations have not yet established patent information public disclosure and use systems for standards, where the patent right holder participates in the standard setting or following his consent, where the patent is included in the national, industry or local standard, it is deemed that the patent holder licenses others to implement the standard and concurrently use the patent, relevant behaviour of others using the standard is not regarded as a patent infringement behaviour as stipulated in Article 11 Patent Law. The patent holder can request the implementing person to pay a certain usage fee, but the paid amount must be clearly/obviously lower than a normal licensing fee; where the patent holder has promised to waive the patent usage fee, it shall be proceeded according to his promise.

See http://www.chinaiprlaw.cn/file/2008073013379.html for more insight.

78. M. Swaine, 'Saving Open Source', *Dr. Dobb's Journal*, November 2008.
79. Dr. Meir Pugatch, 'If it ain't broke, don't fix it', *Stockholm Network*, 2008.
80. Joff Wild, 'IBM IP chief outlines patent plan for Europe', *Intellectual Asset Management*, 1 July 2007.
81. Communication by a high ranking UNFCCC official at the margin of the meetings of subsidiary bodies under the United Nations Conference on Climate Change (UNFCCC) and the Kyoto Protocol in Bonn, Germany, June 2008.
82. Joff Wild, 'Events in Bali heap further pressure on all IP owners', *Intellectual Asset Management*, 16 December 2007.
83. World Business Council for Sustainable Development: Eco-Patent Commons, 2008, see http://www.wbcsd.org/Pages/EDocument/EDocumentDetails.aspx?ID=13650.
84. Francis Gurry, Acceptance speech to the WIPO General Assembly on his appointment as Director General, 22 September 2008, available at http://www.wipo.int/about-wipo/en/dgo/speeches/dg_gurry_acceptance_speech_2008.html.
85. C. McGinley, 'Taking the Heat out of the Global Patent System', *Intellectual Asset Management*, August/September 2008.
86. 'Patenting and competition', an issue paper by the European Patent Office for the OECD Competition Committee, October 2008.
87. An issue paper by the European Patent Office for the OECD Competition Committee (23 October 2008).

88. See http://www.cafc.uscourts.gov/opinions/07-1130.pdf.
89. Press Release, 'Blueprint laid out for work-sharing among five IP offices', available at http://www.epo.org/about-us/press/releases/archive/2008/20081031.html.
90. Japanese Patent Office, 'Towards a Global Harmonization, High Transparency/Predictability, Promoting Innovation-Sophisticating the Pro-Patent Policy responsive to Changes', January 2008, available at http://www.jpo.go.jp/iken_e/pdf/iken_e_innovation_wg/english.pdf.
91. See http://www.epo.org/about-us/press/releases/archive/2008/20081031.html.

5. Taking stock and looking ahead: the future of U.S. patent law

Jay P. Kesan

INTRODUCTION

During the 1970s, the federal courts' conflicting interpretations of the Patent Act threatened to pull the patent system apart. While patentees rushed to get into the Fifth, Sixth, and Seventh Circuits, infringers did anything they could to go anywhere else.[1] In 1982, Congress reacted by creating the Court of Appeals for the Federal Circuit (CAFC), which has national appellate jurisdiction over all patent cases.[2]

Now over 25 years old, the Federal Circuit has come to the fore as a tremendous force. The court has shaped patent law and patent policy against a backdrop of the three major revolutions: the IT space dramatically changing people's everyday life, the biotechnology and genetics explosion in the life sciences, and the effects of globalization.

The Federal Circuit's next 25 years holds many possibilities in the patent arena.[3] For example, one patent possibility is that the Patent Act will gradually morph into different doctrines and laws for different technologies. The Patent Act would then resemble the Copyright Act's patchwork of different protections for different media.[4]

This review does not endeavor to imagine all the patent possibilities. Similarly, this review does not purport to look into a crystal ball to decipher the future of patent law and policy. Rather, this review surveys recent developments in patent law and patent policy to highlight four trends that will inform upon the trajectory of developments in patent law – continued active shaping of patent law by the Federal Circuit; the U.S. Supreme Court's recent, significant interest in patent law; legislative reform of the patent system (including judicial and statutory reform) recently passed by Congress; and the ripple effects caused by these significant developments. First, Part II of this review discusses active shaping of patent doctrine by the Federal Circuit. Next, Part III analyzes the U.S. Supreme Court's increased interest in patent law. Third, Part IV examines legislative patent reform as evidenced by the passage of the America Invents Act. Finally,

Part V demonstrates how recent developments have ripple effects on the patent system.

ACTIVE SHAPING BY THE FEDERAL CIRCUIT

Before the Federal Circuit was created, Howard T. Markey, who would become the first Chief Judge of the court, stated that "the fundamental problem in patent law in this country" was that "nonstatutory slogans are employed and grow into mindless decisional rules for all cases."[5] After the Federal Circuit was created, the court's first active shaping exercise was eliminating nonstatutory slogans from the heart of patent law doctrine, the obviousness standard under § 103. Indeed, the court anchored its obviousness jurisprudence to the statutory language and the decision in *Graham v. John Deere Co.*[6] The Federal Circuit continues to actively shape patent law doctrine and patent policy and these exercises have expanded significantly beyond merely policing statutory text.

Three themes emerge in the Federal Circuit's contemporary, active shaping of patent law doctrine and patent policy. First, the court is willing to deal with difficult issues. Second, the court is willing to be instrumentalist when making decisions.[7] Finally, the court is willing to shape and re-shape patent doctrine when it does not get it right the first time. Importantly, these shaping themes are present in both high profile and nuanced doctrinal and policy issues.

This chapter illustrates these three themes by examining some of the Federal Circuit's recent decisions in two doctrinal areas. The next section reviews the court's recent decisions in the area of patent eligibility. These Federal Circuit decisions include both panel and *en banc* opinions that have attracted public attention and been the subject of U.S. Supreme Court petitions for certiorari. The following section briefly reviews the court's recent decisions regarding joint infringement of method claims. Unlike patent eligibility decisions, these decisions represent a line of panel opinions that have not attracted widespread public attention. The final section reviews the court's recent decision regarding contributory and induced infringement of method patents. Along with the other decisions discussed in this section, this Federal Circuit decision highlights the evolving difficulties presented by method patents and how method patent issues are particularly fertile ground for analysis on the basis of the illustrated shaping themes discussed above.

Recent Patent Eligibility Decisions Illustrate the Three Shaping Themes

The Federal Circuit's recent decisions in *In re Comiskey*,[8] *In re Nuijten*,[9] *In re Bilski*,[10] and *Assoc'n for Molecular Pathol. v. United States Patent & Trademark Office*[11] illustrate the three shaping themes. This section briefly summarizes these cases with the goal of providing pertinent information for illustrating the shaping themes. The following section explains how these decisions illustrate that the Federal Circuit is willing to deal with difficult issues. The next section explains how these decisions illustrate that the Federal Circuit is willing to be instrumentalist. The final section explains how these decisions demonstrate that the court is willing to shape and re-shape when it does not get things right the first time.

Summarizing *In re Comiskey*, *In re Nuijten*, *In re Bilski*, and *Molecular Pathology*

In *In re Comiskey*, the applicant filed a patent application which essentially disclosed a process for online alternative dispute resolution. The applicant claimed, among other things, the mental process of resolving a legal dispute between two parties by a decision of a human arbitrator. The PTO rejected the claims because the prior art rendered them obvious under § 103. The Federal Circuit invoked the *Chenery* doctrine[12] to raise patent eligibility under § 101 *sua sponte* to affirm the claim rejection without considering the PTO's claim rejection under § 103. The court held the applicant's claims were not eligible subject matter, because mental processes are abstract ideas.

The Federal Circuit's *en banc* opinion vacated the original panel decision and remanded the case to the panel to revise their opinion. Three judges dissented from the court's *en banc* order, arguing, among other things, that the *Chenery* doctrine does not allow the panel to direct the examination of a patent applicant's application.[13] The original panel revised its opinion by removing dicta that apparently suggested that adding routine features to subject matter that is not eligible usually creates a prima facie case of obviousness.[14]

In *In re Nuijten*, the applicant filed a patent application which disclosed a method to construct watermarks that can be inserted into signals wherein the inserted watermark had reduced signal distortion. The applicant claimed the process for creating the new signals, "a storage medium having stored thereon"[15] the new type of signal, and the signal itself. The PTO rejected the signal claim under § 101 and the Federal Circuit affirmed the PTO. In a 2–1 panel decision, the Federal Circuit held that the applicant's signal, a transient electromagnetic transmission, was not a "manufacture" within the meaning of § 101, because the signal was not a tangible article or commodity. The majority relied on the 1895 dictionary used by the *Chakrabarty* court.[16] In opposition, the dissent argued that the signal was a "manufacture" using a 1768 dictionary.

In *In re Bilski*, the applicant filed a patent application, which disclosed a hedging scheme for fuel-oil. The applicant claimed, among other things, a process for hedging the price of commodities. The PTO rejected the claim as constituting ineligible subject matter under § 101. The Federal Circuit *en banc* affirmed this decision. The court held the applicant's claimed subject matter was not a "process" within the meaning of § 101, because the method was neither tied to a particular machine nor did it transform an article. To reach its holding, the majority expressly abandoned the *Freeman-Walter-Abele* test and expressly overruled the *State Street Bank* "useful, concrete, tangible result" test.[17] While there were various concurring and dissenting opinions, only one of the 12 judges argued the applicant's claim was patent eligible.[18]

In *Molecular Pathology*, Myriad Genetics held a patent on the composition of the isolated DNA molecules that compose the human genes BRCA1 and BRCA2. The patent also included claims to methods for detecting alterations in the BRCA1 gene and for screening potential cancer therapeutics using the BRCA1 gene. A number of physicians brought suit for declaratory judgment on the grounds that these patents were invalid. The district court found for the plaintiffs for all three claims. As for the composition of the BRCA genes, the court reasoned that the genes existed in nature and were thus unpatentable under § 101. The method claims as well were held to be unpatentable under § 101 as they merely stated scientific principles.

The Federal Circuit reversed the district court on two of the three claims, holding that isolated DNA molecules are patentable compositions of matter and that method for screening potential cancer therapeutics involved transformative steps, rendering the claim more than just a statement of a scientific principle. For isolated DNA molecules, the court explained that whether the molecules were generated in a laboratory or isolated from naturally occurring DNA strands, either molecule is subject to patentability. Although one looking at a segment of a DNA strand with a "magic microscope" would notice the same atomic/molecular pattern as one looking at the molecule of the isolated gene, a chemical compound's nature and behavior is dependent on covalent bonding.[19] Thus, since covalent bonds are broken in isolating the gene, the resulting molecule is an entirely different thing from a DNA molecule with the atomic/molecular pattern of the gene within its chemical makeup. Then, for the method of screening potential cancer therapeutics, the court used the machine-or-transformation test to affirm the claim on the grounds that the method includes transformative steps.[20]

Willing to deal with difficult issues

Patent eligibility is a difficult issue, because it is the threshold patentability question in both patent law and patent policy. As for the statute, § 101 provides "whoever invents or discovers any new and useful process, machine, manufacture, or composition of matter . . . may obtain a patent therefor."[21] So, § 101 necessarily excludes some activities from patent protection even if those activities are inventive. Yet, the 1952 Patent Act legislative history shows Congress intended patent eligible subject matter to "include anything under the sun that is made by man."[22]

The § 101 categories implicate patent policy. Deciding which activities (specifically, which types of claims) to exclude from patent protection is exceedingly difficult. The English language is a blunt instrument to describe technology features and attributes. Certain kinds of invention are inherently difficult to describe. In addition, claims directed to inventions that are too fuzzy create problems. First, the Patent and Trademark Office (PTO) cannot meaningfully examine the scope of protection sought by such applications. Second, even if the patent issues, the public has poor notice regarding what technology falls within the purview of such patents. On the other hand, the patent system serves an important economic role by rewarding human innovation and ingenuity. There are also problems when § 101 excludes too much activity from patent protection. Such exclusion erodes the incentives created by the patent system that permit inventors and firms to pay for (or recover) the cost of technology creation, permit coordination of activities in the value chain, and encourage investment and financing of technology creation and entrepreneurship. Broad exclusions may also run afoul of the broad Congressional intent in defining eligible subject matter in patent law.

Because patent eligibility is the threshold issue in both patent law doctrine and policy, the Federal Circuit's recent decisions in *In re Comiskey*, *In re Nuijten*, *In re Bilski*, and *Molecular Pathology* illustrate that the Federal Circuit does not shy away from dealing with difficult issues.

Willing to be instrumentalist

The Federal Circuit is instrumentalist when it makes things up out of whole cloth to justify decisions that it believes produces desirable outcomes for the patent system. Among the court's recent patent eligibility decisions, *In re Bilski* best illustrates that the Federal Circuit is willing to be instrumentalist for two reasons.

First, the *Bilski* concurring opinion and three dissenting opinions expressly debate whether the "machine-or-transformation" test was made up out of whole cloth by the majority. As a threshold matter, the majority opinion asserts the "machine-or-transformation" test was first articulated in *Gottschalk v. Benson* and reaffirmed in *Diamond v. Diehr*.[23] The concurring opinion supports the majority's assertion by tracing the history of § 101 back to English patent law and practice that was incorporated into the 1790 Patent Act.[24] Moreover, the concurring opinion concludes it is not the majority but the dissenters "who would legislate" under § 101.[25] On the other hand, the dissenting opinions accuse the majority of "usurp[ing] the legislative role" and of "venture[ing] away from the statute," arguing, among other things, that the word "transformation" is not expressly found in the Patent Act.[26]

Second, two *Bilski* dissenting opinions expressly make value judgments about desirable outcomes in the patent system. For example, Judge Newman, the only judge who considered the applicant's claim to be patent eligible, stated that processes like the applicant's process "contribute to the vigor and variety of today's Information Age."[27] At the other end, Judge Mayer noted that "[b]usiness method patents offer rewards that are grossly disproportionate to the cost of innovation."[28]

In rejecting the Federal Circuit's "machine-or-transformation" test, the Supreme Court highlights both indications of instrumentalism.[29] They approve of the Federal Circuit's interest in making value judgments to affect desirable outcomes; however, they reprimand the court for going too far, relying solely on a test made from whole cloth. Similar to the dissenting opinions mentioned prior, the Supreme Court refused to approve of a test that is "inconsistent with the statute's purpose and design."[30] On the other hand, they recognize, without a "high enough bar . . . when considering patent applications" the outcome would be that "patent examiners and courts could be flooded with claims."[31] On that basis, the Court does not disparage the Federal Circuit's instrumentalism; they only caution them not to take it too far.[32]

While *Molecular Pathology* exemplifies the Federal Circuit's new approach, continuing to use the machine-or-transformation test in a more limited capacity,[33] there are also strong elements of instrumentalism brought to issue between the concurring and dissenting opinions in the case. On one hand, Judge Moore contended that it is necessary to extend patent protection to isolated human genes so as not to "punish those companies who made the reasonable decision to invest large amounts of time and money into the identification, isolation, and characterization of genes."[34] In his dissent, Judge Bryson disagreed, claiming that this is an instance in which too much patent protection will impede the progress of science, instead of promoting it.[35] Either way, it is clear that Judge Moore and Judge Bryson show instrumentalist tendencies in factoring in analyses that expressly take creating desirable outcomes into account.

Willing to shape and re-shape

The Federal Circuit re-shapes patent law doctrine and patent policy when it does not "get it right" the first time. *State Street Bank & Trust Co. v. Signature Financial Group, Inc.*[36] and *In re Biliski* and to a lesser extent *In re Comiskey* illustrate that the Federal Circuit is willing to shape and re-shape doctrine and is not afraid to sit *en banc* to rectify panel opinions.

In *State Street Bank*, a potential licensee of a patent filed a declaratory judgment action against the patentee seeking a declaration of invalidity. The patent was directed to a data processing system for implementing a mutual fund comprised of many mutual funds. The district court held the patent claims to be invalid. A Federal Circuit panel comprising Judges Rich, Plager and Bryson reversed. The court reasoned that the claimed subject matter produced a "useful, concrete, and tangible result." Moreover, the court stated business methods should be treated just like any other process.

In 1998, the *State Street Bank* court cleared the way for patenting certain types of information technology innovation. For example, PTO class 705 (business method) had less than 1,000 applications filed in 1997. By 2007, in class 705, patent application filings increased to over 11,000 per year.[37] Although more applications do not necessarily lead to more issued patents,[38] the Federal Circuit thought it needed to re-shape § 101. The *Biliski* majority, which included Judge Plager and Judge Bryson, expressly overruled the *State Street Bank* "useful, concrete, and tangible result" test.

Similarly, the revised *Comiskey* opinion illustrates that the Federal Circuit will sit *en banc* to re-visit panel decisions. Indeed, the original panel probably revised its opinion, removing dicta that apparently linked patent eligibility to obviousness, to avoid doctrinal confusion.

Lastly, *Molecular Pathology* shows that the Federal Circuit will also re-shape doctrine when it is overturned by the Supreme Court, rather than starting from scratch. When the Supreme Court overturned *In re Bilski*, the Court indicated that the problem was that the machine-or-transformation test was not a dispositive test for method patentability, but that it could be useful. Focusing on that point, the Federal Circuit in *Molecular Pathology* and other cases[39] continued to make use of the machine-or-transformation test as a useful, yet non-absolute test. So, for example, when a method passes the machine-or-transformation test, the Federal Circuit uses this as a strong indication that the method is patentable.

Recent Joint Infringement Cases Illustrate the Federal Circuit's Shaping Themes

The Federal Circuit's recent decisions in *BMC Resources, Inc. v. Paymentech, L.P.*[40] and *Muniauction, Inc. v. Thomson Corp.*[41] illustrate the three shaping themes within the context of a line of panel decisions expounding a doctrinal and policy issue which has yet to receive widespread public attention.

Direct infringement occurs when every element of a properly construed claim is met by the accused product or service.[42] Typically, prima facie infringement requires the patentee to accuse one person or entity of infringing a claim. In addition, indirect infringement – both contributory infringement and induced infringement – strikes at actors who help the single infringer.[43] Nevertheless, advances in information technology in an internet environment, with merchants, software application providers, and consumers all interacting online with each other (sometimes globally) often creates the need for multiple parties to commercially interact, particularly impacting patented methods or processes. In such an environment, patentees argue joint infringement liability, a species of direct infringement, to cover multiple parties who collectively infringe a single claim, but who, nevertheless, individually execute only a subset of the steps in a method claim.

In *BMC Resources, Inc. v. Paymentech, L.P.*, the Federal Circuit first recognized joint infringement liability. The court observed a mastermind, one who has "control or direction" over multiple parties, may be liable for joint infringement. Nevertheless, the *BMC Resources* court held the defendant did not infringe the plaintiff's claimed four-step method for processing debit transactions without a pin number. The court reasoned that the defendant did not have direction or control over the multiple parties, particularly debit networks and financial institutions, who may have collectively practiced the claimed method.

In *Muniauction, Inc. v. Thomson Corp.*, the Federal Circuit expanded on the *BMC Resources* "control or direction" test for joint infringement. Indeed, the *Muniauction* panel opinion stated that this test is satisfied "where the law would traditionally hold the accused direct infringer vicariously liable for the acts committed by another party that are required to complete performance of a claimed method."[44] Nevertheless, the *Muniauction* court held that the defendant did not infringe the plaintiff's claimed method for conducting original issuer municipal bond auctions over an electronic network. The court reasoned that the defendant did not have direction or control over the multiple parties, particularly the bidders, who may have collectively practiced the claimed method.

The Federal Circuit's recent joint infringement decisions illustrate the three shaping themes. First, joint infringement is a difficult issue. Information technology advances and globalization incentivizes multiple parties to commercially interact. Patented methods and processes continue to be a valuable component of the global economy. Under the narrower rules for proving joint infringement, multiple parties may infringe a process claim with some impunity, and process patent owners are not incentivized to disclose their technology in exchange for unenforceable patent protection. Accordingly, process owners may substitute trade secret protection for patent protection. Yet, this undermines the "[p]rogress of . . . useful [a]rts,"[45] because the public does not receive the benefit of disclosure. By outlining the rules of joint infringement, the Federal Circuit is forging ahead and shaping patent doctrine in this arena.

Second, the joint infringement decisions illustrate that the Federal Circuit is willing to be instrumentalist. The *BMC Resources* court nearly states as much when it reasons that the "control or direction" test arises merely from fairness and has no statutory basis.[46] Likewise, the *Muniauction* court moves farther afield by injecting vicarious liability – a province of tort law – into direct infringement.[47] Thus, the *BMC Resources* court's statement that "it would be unfair" to justify joint infringement is a value judgment comparing process claims to globalization. Indeed, the *BMC Resources* court felt that incentivizing process owners to disclose their processes by recognizing joint infringement was outweighed by the harms to globalization resulting from expanding direct infringement liability.

Finally, the joint infringement decisions have the potential to illustrate that the Federal Circuit is willing to shape and re-shape patent doctrine. Both *BMC Resources* and *Muniauction* recognize joint infringement liability but they did not hold the defendants liable for joint infringement. Thus, the Federal Circuit may, in the future, conclude that its "control or direction" test is inadequate or too restrictive and re-shape joint infringement doctrine by modifying its "control or direction" test to newer factual situations. In this patent possibility, all hope is not lost for patentees with process claims. For instance, the *BMC Resources* court points out that "a patentee can usually structure a claim to capture infringement by a single party."[48] Patentees have been successful in structuring their claims to capture single party infringers;[49] however, this approach leaves patents issued before *BMC Resources* vulnerable to multiparty infringement.

Further Illustration of the Federal Circuit's Shaping Themes and their Centrality in the Court's Approach to Method Claims

Method patents have become the most complicated and controversial area of patent law. *In re Comiskey*, *In re Nuijten*, and *In re Bilski*, are all cases that consider what constitutes a patentable method. Later, it will be shown that even the Supreme Court has had trouble clarifying what processes are and are not patentable.[50] In *BMC Resources* and *Muniauction,* the court struggled with how to protect method patent owners from infringement by multiple parties acting together. Indeed, there seems to be a fundamental difference between method patents and other utility patents.

The court in *Cardiac Pacemakers, Inc. v. St. Jude Med., Inc.*[51] came to precisely this conclusion, that there is a "fundamental distinction" between "claims to a product, device or, apparatus" and "claims to a process or method."[52] The case discusses Section 271(f)[53] which extends infringement liability to makers and sellers of components to assemble a patented invention, even if the assembly takes place outside the United States. The legislation was passed in direct response to a Supreme Court ruling that such activity did not constitute patent infringement.[54] After the legislation's passage, the Federal Circuit in *Union Carbide Chems. & Plastics Tech. Corp. v. Shell Oil Co.*[55] ruled that exporting a catalyst necessary to perform a patented method for producing ethylene oxide violated 271(f). In short, the court applied 271(f) to method patents.

Cardiac Pacemakers expressly overruled *Union Carbide*, holding that 271(f) does not apply to method patents.[56] Therefore, when St. Jude exported implantable cardioverter defibrillators programmed to detect and treat a plurality of heart arrhythmias, no infringement was found, because the method for detecting and treating arrhythmias was not practiced inside the United States.

The court's decision exemplifies the three shaping themes. First, whether or not to treat method claims the same as other utility patent claims is a difficult issue. As noted, method claims and how to define and protect them is a perplexing matter as it stands. Going on to decide that these difficulties make method claims fundamentality different from other utility patent claims opens the gates for all manner of distinction between method and apparatus claims to be drawn at every level of patent law. Second, there is evidence of instrumentalism. True the court argues that its position comes from the language of the statute, explaining that "components" of a method cannot be "supplied"; however, the essential idea of distinguishing apparatus claims from method claims in the first place is an invention of the court.

Connected to its instrumentalism, the court shows its clear willingness to shape and reshape patent doctrine. Not only does *Cardiac Pacemakers* change the law, removing 271(f)'s application from method claims, it does so by altering the relationship between method patents and other utility patents with other types of claims. *Cardiac Pacemakers* may represent a turning point in the court's approach to method patents in general. Having noted all of the specific and unique issues that method patents seem to raise, it may be that the court is moving towards a general model of applying different rules to method patents that better suit such patents, while at the same time not interfering with the rules that govern other utility patents with apparatus claims, perhaps leading to more appropriate and thus more desirable outcomes in either circumstance.

THE U.S. SUPREME COURT'S INTEREST IN PATENT LAW

As recently as 2001, the Supreme Court was "invisible" in patent law.[57] Even when the Court did take a rare patent case, the Court avoided addressing difficult doctrinal issues. Instead, the Court based its decisions on legal principles or regimes it felt comfortable with. For example, the U.S. Supreme Court in *Markman* affirmed the Federal Circuit by interpreting the Seventh Amendment.[58] Similarly, the *Zurko* Court reached its decision by applying the Administrative Procedures Act to the Federal Circuit's appellate review of findings of fact made by the PTO.[59] Further still, the *J.E.M.* Court affirmed the Federal Circuit by statutorily interpreting the Plant Variety Protection Act and the Plant Patent Act of 1930.[60]

Today, the U.S. Supreme Court is visible in patent law. The Supreme Court's interest in patent law cannot be overstated in any patent possibility and the Federal Circuit no longer has the *de facto* final word in patent law. Three themes emerge from the U.S. Supreme Court's interest. First, the Court is increasingly getting involved with difficult doctrinal issues. Second, the Court is determined to ensure patent law is like any other area of the law. Finally, the Court is aware of the Federal Circuit's national appellate jurisdiction.

This part illustrates these three themes by examining some of the recent Supreme Court decisions in patent law. First, Part III.A explains how *KSR Intern. Co. v. Teleflex Inc.*,[61] *Bilski v. Kappos*,[62] and *Microsoft Corp. v. i4i LP*[63] demonstrate that the Court is comfortable getting involved with difficult doctrinal issues. The next section explains how *Ebay, Inc. v. MercExchange, L.L.C.*,[64] *MedImmune, Inc. v. Genentech, Inc*,[65] and *Global-Tech Appliances, Inc. v. SEB S.A.*[66] illustrate the Court is determined to ensure that patent law is like any other area of the law. The final section explains how the Court's recent decisions indicate that the Court is aware of the Federal Circuit's national appellate jurisdiction.

Comfort in Getting Involved with Difficult Doctrinal Issues in Patent Law

Obviousness is the most important patentability condition. Indeed, obviousness is a significant gatekeeper in the patent system, as failing the other conditions, such as utility and novelty, is rare in practice. Like negligence and scienter, obviousness is a difficult issue because it requires fact intensive case-by-case balancing of several factors.[67]

The Supreme Court recently confronted the core issue of obviousness. In *KSR Intel. Co. v. Teleflex Inc.*, the respondent, an exclusive licensee of a patent claiming a mechanism for combining an electronic sensor with an adjustable automobile pedal, brought suit against the petitioner, a competitor. The Federal Circuit held that the patent claims were not rendered obvious by the prior art because there was no teaching, suggestion, or motivation to combine the prior art references. The U.S. Supreme Court reversed, because a person having ordinary skill in the art did have a reason to combine the relevant prior art.

The *KSR* Court did more than just touching on the issue of obviousness. The Court, in a 9–0 vote, set aside the Federal Circuit's teaching, suggestion, or motivation (TSM) test, as rigidly applied and overly formalistic. The Court was not bothered by discarding the TSM test even though the Federal Circuit had applied this test for over 15 years.[68] Indeed, the TSM test was a central component of the Federal Circuit's obviousness jurisprudence. The Court concluded the Federal Circuit, over time, had developed the TSM test into too high a barrier for evaluating the obviousness of a patent claim.

The contours of the Court's new "reason to combine" test are not yet fully explored. Recent Federal Circuit cases have indicated, as the Supreme Court itself noted, that the TSM test was not entirely scrapped; rather, it was only modified to include known problems with predictable and finite solutions to the overall list of what is obvious.[69]

The standard for what defines a "process" also goes to the very core of patent law. To be eligible for a patent under § 101, the subject matter of the patent must be a "process, machine, manufacture, or composition of matter."[70] Any series of steps could be defined as a process, so getting to the bottom of what constitutes a patentable process is one of the most difficult doctrinal issues in modern patent law.

The Supreme Court has shown its strong interest in getting to the very bottom of precisely what defines a patentable process. In *Bilski v. Kappos*, the court overturned the Federal Circuit's "machine-or-transformation test," as noted above. The Court held that a method for hedging risks in commodities trading in the energy market may indeed be a "process," but it was an unpatentable, abstract idea. The Court explained that the "machine-or-transformation" test is not an absolute test for what constitutes a process; however, it remains a helpful, "investigative tool, for determining whether some claimed inventions are processes under § 101."[71]

This did not end the Supreme Court's inquiry on the matter of the machine-or-transformation test, nor its interest in a more precise analysis of what constitutes a patentable process. In *Prometheus Labs., Inc. v. Mayo Collaborative Serv.*,[72] the Federal Circuit held that a patent claiming a method for calibrating proper dosages of thiopurine drugs to treat autoimmune diseases was a patentable process, as it satisfied the machine-or-transformation test. Subject to its decision in *Bilski*, the Supreme Court granted certiorari to *Prometheus Labs.*, vacating the judgment and remanding the case for further consideration.[73] After further consideration, the Federal Circuit upheld their prior ruling, noting that the Supreme Court ruled only that the machine-or-transformation test was not the exclusive test for patentable processes and that it remained a useful tool in the determination of patent eligibility of method claims.[74] The Supreme Court again granted certiorari,[75] hopefully to clarify how useful the machine-or-transformation test remains and if there should be any difference between its application to include or exclude processes as patentable or un-patentable respectively, and to also clarify the analysis of claim limitations related to mental steps and their role in assessing eligible subject matter.

The theme in *Bilski* and its progeny is similar to that in *KSR*. As will be discussed later,[76] the Federal Circuit's revival of the "machine-or-transformation" test had an immediate and substantial impact on patent law. Nonetheless, like in *KSR*, the Supreme Court in *Bilski* was not daunted by the sweeping effect that their decision would have on a core issue of patent law. Also similar to *KSR*, the Court played a moderating role, calling for less rigidity in the application of judicially developed tests, when they are not supported by legislative texts. As with *KSR*, the Federal Circuit's test is not entirely scrapped; rather, the Supreme Court is merely interested in subduing the circuit from turning non-statutory slogans into absolute rules of decision.

In sum, *KSR Intel. Co. v. Teleflex Inc.* and *Bilski v. Kappos* illustrate the Court is not only comfortable with getting involved with difficult doctrinal issues but also willing to dramatically change the course of patent law itself. Indeed, by repeatedly granting certiorari on the same broad issue between *Bilski* and *Prometheus*, there can be no doubt that the Supreme Court is very comfortable with taking absolute control over the interpretation of patent issues, especially when the Court sees the need to enforce the integrity of the distinction between absolute statutory law and non-statutory tests and practices.

An illustration of the Supreme Court's willingness to grapple with difficult issues of patent law, especially for the sake of maintaining statutory integrity, is particularly pronounced in *Microsoft v. i4i*.[77] i4i sued Microsoft for willfully infringing its patent for an improved method for editing computer documents, which stores a document's contents separately from the metacodes associated with the document's structure. Microsoft defended that i4i's patent was invalid subject to the on-sale bar of § 102(b), claiming that i4i had sold the patented technology in a program called S4 more than a year prior to filing a patent application. Notably, when reviewing i4i's patent application, the PTO examiner had not been presented with evidence of S4 and its prior sale.

Microsoft argued that in such a circumstance, a preponderance of the evidence standard should be applied. They argued that a patent's presumption of validity is established by its passing review by the PTO. If the prior art issue relevant to the invalidity of the claim had not been reviewed by the PTO, it would seem that there is no logical ground to presume that the patent is valid. The Court noted the logic of the argument, but concluded, "[w]e find ourselves in no position to judge the comparative force of these policy arguments."[78] What is more, in spite of supporting case law, the Court declined to uphold Microsoft's position as, "[n]othing in § 282's text suggests that Congress meant . . . to enact a standard of proof that would rise and fall with the facts of each case."[79] The Court does, however, grant that, "new evidence supporting an invalidity defense may carry 'more weight' in and infringement action than evidence previously considered by the PTO."[80]

Like *KSR Intel.* and *Bilski v. Kappos*, the Court in *Microsoft v. i4i* has shown its willingness to take on difficult, fundamental issues of patent law. Furthermore, the Court continues to do so in an effort to maintain statutory integrity, noting the importance of "commonsense"[81] instrumental tools, practices and policies, but taking a strong position against their crystallization into black letter law.

Determination to Ensure that Patent Law is like any other Area of the Law

Patent law is not an island. Beyond being related to other intellectual property regimes, that is, copyright, trademark, and trade secrets, patent law interacts with many other areas of the law including antitrust law, administrative law, and federal courts jurisprudence. Under this view, patent law doctrine should not stray from main stream legal doctrines, otherwise patent law will not remain complementary to other areas of the law. *Ebay, Inc. v. MercExchange, L.L.C.*,[82] *MedImmune, Inc. v. Genentech, Inc.*,[83] and *Global-Tech Appliances, Inc. v. SEB S.A.*[84] illustrate that the U.S. Supreme Court is determined to ensure that patent law is like any other area of the law.

First, the U.S. Supreme Court was keenly focused on ensuring that permanent injunctions in patent law are like permanent injunctions in any other area of the law. In *Ebay, Inc. v. MercExchange*, the respondent owned a patent directed to an electronic market designed to facilitate the sale of goods between private individuals. The respondent – who neither produced products nor offered services that embodied the patent claims – sought to license the patent to the petitioner. The petitioner refused. In a patent infringement suit, the respondent prevailed on both validity and infringement. This was enough in the Federal Circuit's view to justify granting the respondent a permanent injunction, enjoining the petitioner from practicing the respondent's claimed invention. The U.S. Supreme Court disagreed.

In a 9–0 vote with a short majority opinion, the Court set aside long-standing Federal Circuit practice that, as a general rule, district courts should automatically issue permanent injunctions against infringers once infringement and validity have been determined. The Court noted that a district court's discretion to grant or deny injunctive relief in patent cases is no different than its discretion in any other area of the law. Indeed, a court's discretion lies in the traditional principles of equity which are embodied in a four-factor conjunctive test:

> A plaintiff must demonstrate . . . (1) that it has suffered an irreparable injury; (2) that remedies available at law, such as monetary damages, are inadequate to compensate for that injury; (3) that, considering the balance of hardships between the plaintiff and defendant, a remedy in equity is warranted; and (4) that the public interest would not be disserved by a permanent injunction. [85]

In sum, the *Ebay* Court calibrated the standard for obtaining permanent injunctions in patent law to the standard for obtaining permanent injunctions in any other area of the law. Effectively, this change raised the standard for obtaining permanent injunctions in district courts as a remedy for patent infringement. Indeed, *Ebay* illustrates the ripple effect caused by an across-the-board change in the patent system. This ripple effect will be discussed below.

As another example, the Supreme Court also ensured that declaratory judgment jurisdiction in patent law is treated in a manner consistent with declaratory judgment jurisdiction in any other area of the law. In *MedImmune v. Genentech*, the petitioner, a licensee to a patent claiming a drug for respiratory infections, sought a declaratory judgment that the patent was invalid or unenforceable against the respondent, the licensor-patentee. The Federal Circuit held the petitioner could not obtain a declaratory judgment because without breaking or terminating the licensee agreement there was no "case or controversy" for a court to adjudicate under the Declaratory Judgment Act.[86] The U.S. Supreme Court disagreed.

In an 8–1 vote, the Court held the petitioner did not have to break or terminate its license agreement with the respondent before seeking a declaratory judgment that the patent was invalid or unenforceable. In a footnote, the Court criticized the Federal Circuit's "reasonable apprehension of suit" test for declaratory judgment jurisdiction.[87] Reasonable apprehension of suit was only satisfied when the patentee expressly threatened to sue the putative declaratory judgment plaintiff.[88] The Supreme Court rejected this test, citing a number of non-patent cases in which declaratory relief was deemed appropriate under less imminent circumstances.[89] Subsequent to the *MedImmune* decision, the Federal Circuit has concluded that the Supreme Court's footnote set aside nearly all of its declaratory judgment jurisdiction jurisprudence.[90]

In sum, the *MedImmune* Court calibrated the standard for declaratory judgment jurisdiction in patent law to the standard for declaratory judgment jurisdiction in any other area of the law. Effectively, this change lowered the standard for declaratory judgment. While empirical data has not yet been collected on declaratory judgment filings post-*MedImmune*, the Federal Circuit suspects *MedImmune* and its progeny will create a race to the court house.[91]

Finally, the Supreme Court is determined to standardize the rule for culpable mental states between patents and other areas of the law. In *Global-Tech*, a patentee claimed infringement against a party who had copied and sold their design for a cool-touch deep fryer. The copied fryer was manufactured for sale outside of the United States, so it did not bear a patent label. The Federal Circuit ruled that "deliberate disregard" of a patent satisfies the statutory "knowledge" requirement for induced infringement.[92] The Supreme Court disagreed, holding the statute requires "knowledge of the existence of the patent . . ."[93] Nonetheless, they affirmed the circuit court based on the criminal law doctrine of "willful blindness," which treats "deliberately shielding" oneself from knowledge the same as having actual knowledge.[94]

Many of the themes discussed so far, both those that relate to the Federal Circuit's instrumentalism and to the Supreme Court's willingness to deal with difficult patent law issues, are apparent in *Global-Tech*. Nonetheless, the most important theme here is the Supreme Court's interest in bringing the workings of patent law closer to those of general law. In bringing the doctrine of "willful blindness" to bear on a statutorily mandated mental state in patent law, the Court makes very clear that patent law is not an island. Although in many details, patent law has a distinct and specialized quality to its jurisprudence, the Court has shown that such a distinction does not warrant separation from uniformity with the greater legal system and generally applicable legal principles.

Awareness of the Federal Circuit's National Appellate Jurisdiction

Just as commentators debate the propriety of the Federal Circuit's national appellate jurisdiction,[95] so do some Supreme Court Justices. For example, statements by both Justice Stevens and Justice Bryer in recent opinions illustrate that the U.S. Supreme Court is aware of the Federal Circuit's national appellate jurisdiction.

Justice Stevens suggested judicial competition may benefit patent law. In *Holmes Group, Inc. v. Vornado Air Circulation Systems, Inc.*, Justice Stevens emphasized, in a concurring opinion, that the Federal Circuit has exclusive appellate jurisdiction over patent law claims, not patent law issues.[96] Moreover, Justice Stevens pointedly noted that "occasional decisions by courts with broader jurisdiction will provide an antidote to the risk that the specialized court may develop institutional bias."[97]

Likewise, Justice Breyer also recently suggested that judicial competition may benefit patent law. In *Laboratory Corp. of America v. Metabolite Lab., Inc.*,[98] the U.S. Supreme Court dismissed a writ of certiorari in a case involving the validity of a patent claiming a process for diagnosing vitamin deficiencies. Justice Breyer stated, in a dissenting opinion, that "a decision from this generalist Court could contribute to the important ongoing debate, among both specialists and generalists, as to whether the patent system, as currently administered and enforced, adequately reflects a 'careful balance' that 'the federal patent laws . . . embod[y].'"[99]

Statements by both Justice Stevens and Justice Breyer illustrate that the U.S. Supreme Court is cognizant of and perhaps concerned by the Federal Circuit's national appellate jurisdiction. Furthermore, these statements also suggest that the U.S. Supreme Court may prefer judicial competition in any patent possibility in the future.

PATENT SYSTEM REFORM

Some commentators argue that the patent system is broken and legislative reform is needed to fix it.[100] With the resent passage of the Leahy-Smith America Invents Act (AIA),[101] this view is in many ways confirmed. This section reviews the recent efforts at both statutory and judicial reform and their ultimate outcome in Congress' sweeping reform of U.S. patent law. Recent reform efforts prior to the new legislation, illustrate that two clear stakeholders are coming to the fore: large pharmaceutical/biotechnology companies ("Pharma") and information technology companies ("IT"). Importantly, these two stakeholders rely on the patent system to different degrees and in a different manner as they attempt to appropriate benefits from the marketplace for their innovations. Any patent possibility that includes a unitary patent system will therefore need to reconcile these stakeholders' differential reliance. Furthermore, new legislation seems to reflect a strong inclination to bring American patent law more into line with internationally popular patent law regimes. The first section explains Pharma's and IT's differential reliance on patents. The following section shows how statutory reform illustrates the difference. The next section then summarizes the most groundbreaking changes to the patent system introduced by the AIA. The final sections analyze the changes as they relate to the interest in molding patent law to mirror more internationally popular patent standards and also to comport with Pharma's and IT's sometimes conflicting and sometimes unified interests and show how judicial reform also underlines this difference.

Pharma's and IT's Differential Reliance on the Patent System

Patents, like other property, are assets. Patents as assets facilitate, among other things, paying for the cost of creation, coordination of activities in the value chain, and financing/investing in technology creation and entrepreneurship. Pharma and IT represent two ends of the spectrum on how businesses rely on patents as assets.

At one end of the spectrum, Pharma relies heavily on patents as assets to benefit from innovation. Pharma spends millions of dollars in research and development to create drugs and other life science technology. Importantly, a small number of patents (frequently even one patent) are usually sufficient to protect drugs and other life science products. Accordingly, Pharma relies on patents as assets to provide clear, bright-line property rights to facilitate both paying for the cost of creation and for investing and profiting from technology development. On the other hand, Pharma relies less on patents as assets to facilitate coordination of the value chain because there is a limited value chain in Pharma technology – the ratio of patents to technology is low.

In contrast, IT is at the other end of the spectrum. IT relies less on patents as assets to benefit from innovation for two reasons. First, IT companies which operate in networked industries often rely alternatively on first mover advantage or reputational capital to benefit from innovation. Second, IT products or services are usually a bundle of functions and capabilities which cannot be sufficiently protected by a small number of patents.

First mover advantage – going into the market and grabbing market share – benefits the first mover in two ways. First, the first mover benefits from network effects, consumers derive more utility from a product or service when more consumers use the product or service. Second, the first mover benefits from switching costs, consumers are less willing to incur transaction costs to change to a second comer's product or service. Likewise, IT may benefit from innovation through the development of reputational capital by branding. Consumers often flock to companies that they perceive to be innovators.

Importantly, IT products or services are a bundle of functions. For example, a laptop computer may embody over 500 patents. Moreover, these patents do not necessarily contribute equal value to the bundle. Thus, IT companies are concerned with meticulously policing these individual contributions.

For these two reasons, IT takes a nuanced view to patents as assets. IT does not want patents to be clear, bright-line property rights that may perhaps facilitate payments for individual patented technologies. Moreover, clear, bright-line property rights frustrate IT's nuanced policing of contributions to the ultimate product or service. Indeed, clear property rights lead to royalty stacking where the licensee fees for all of the patents that go into a product or service could outweigh the revenue from the entire product or service. Thus, clear property rights in IT lead to a backward result: the sum of the parts is greater than the whole.

In sum, Pharma relies heavily on patents as assets to provide a clear, bright-line property right whereas IT takes a nuanced view of patents as assets. Interestingly, empirical work shows that by 1999 Pharma took in over six times more profits from its patents than it spent in patent litigation. On the other hand, by 1999, other industries including IT spent about four times the profits it took in from patents on patent litigation.[102]

Statutory Patent Reform

The patent laws had not received a legislative "overhaul" since the 1952 Patent Act was enacted. Putting it in context, prior to the AIA, the last overhaul occurred against a technological background far removed from contemporary technology. For example, the 1952 Act was enacted before James Watson and Francis Crick discovered DNA.[103] Further still, the 1952 Act was enacted before the transistor became the backbone of modern electronics. For the past few years, Congress has been interested in another overhaul. The 110th Congress failed to get legislative patent reform on President Bush's desk because only the House of Representatives passed a patent reform bill.[104]

The reform effort failed in 2007. The effort, nevertheless, sharply illustrates IT's and Pharma's differential reliance on the patent system and helps to understand and illuminate such reliance in the new context of the AIA. House Bill, H.R. 1908, which passed the House, reflects compromises between the IT and Pharma lobbies. This chapter does not offer a detailed analysis of H.R. 1908. Rather, this chapter seeks to demonstrate how the bill's provisions regarding apportionment of damages[105] and post-grant opposition[106] illustrate the compromise between IT and Pharma. First, this section explains how apportionment of damages illustrates this compromise. Next, it explains how post-grant opposition is another example of such compromise.

Apportionment of damages

H.R. 1908 § 5, which provided for apportionment of patent damages, illustrates a possible compromise between IT and Pharma. Section 5 purports to define 35 U.S.C. § 284 "damages adequate to compensate for infringement" as a reasonable royalty falling into essentially two categories. Section 5 provides that the court should apply the reasonable royalty to either "only that economic value properly attributable to the patent's specific contribution over the prior art" or the entire market value.[107] Section 5 also permits the court to consider "other factors," like nonexclusive licensing by third parties, when apportionment based on the prior art or the entire market value is inappropriate.[108]

Notwithstanding the fact that the Federal Circuit has expressed doubts on the workability of § 5,[109] this provision was written as a possible compromise between Pharma and IT. Again, § 5 illustrates IT's nuanced view of patents as assets. Even if an IT company infringed a patent claim not found to be invalid, the IT company could still argue that the patentee is only entitled to a small reasonable royalty. Thus, § 5 enables IT to effectively police marginal contributions and mitigate royalty stacking.

Similarly, § 5 illustrates Pharma's heavy reliance on patents as assets to provide clear, bright-line property rights. For example, because no more than a small number of patents usually protect a drug or other life science technology, a Pharma patentee could likely demonstrate that the § 5 reasonable royalty should be applied to the entire market value. Thus, § 5 enables Pharma to continue to use patents as assets to facilitate paying for the cost of creation and for investing in technology development. In addition, Pharma, in many circumstances, would be eligible to claim lost profits and bypass a reasonable royalty.

Post-grant opposition

H.R. 1908 § 6(f), which provided for a new post-grant opposition proceeding in the PTO, similarly illustrates the compromise between Pharma and IT. Section 6(f) purports to create a robust administrative proceeding to challenge the validity of issued patent claims, akin to the European and

Japanese opposition proceedings. The robust nature of the new proceeding is illustrated by four features.

First, anyone may file a cancellation petition up to one year raising any ground for invalidity under § 282(b) except failure to disclose that best mode under § 112 ¶ 1. Second, § 6(f) contemplates that the post-grant procedure may involve discovery and oral hearings. Third, the post-grant procedure's evidentiary standard to invalidate issued patent claims is preponderance of the evidence which is less than the district court's clear and convincing evidentiary standard in view of § 282's presumption of validity. Finally, § 6(f) contemplates that a completed, post-grant procedure which ends in a favorable ruling regarding the patentability of an issued claim estops the petitioner from raising any grounds for invalidity with respect to that claim in another post-grant opposition, a reexamination, a civil action, or before the International Trade Commission (ITC).

The specific details of the post-grant opposition procedure illustrates Pharma's reliance on patents as assets to provide clear, bright-line property rights. Indeed, the post-grant opposition proceeding is designed to provide a timely, thorough, and final challenge to an issued patent claim. Thus, the post-grant procedure is designed to forge clear, bright-line property rights. Accordingly, a patent claim that survives a post-grant opposition better facilitates investing in technology because the property right represented by the claim is more certain. Investing in technology is one of the reasons Pharma relies heavily on patents as assets. For example, a Pharma company would likely be interested in putting its newly issued patent directed to a new drug through opposition petitions in a 12–18-month time frame before investing additional millions of dollars in bringing the drug to the market.

Similarly, § 6(f) also illustrates IT's nuanced view of patents as assets. Currently, with concerns about patent litigations costs, a large IT company is probably willing to pay for several patent licenses even if the underlying patents are of questionable validity. Indeed, the alternatives – filing for an *inter partes* reexamination, filing a declaratory judgment action seeking a declaration of invalidity, or facing infringement litigation – are either limited or expensive. Thus, IT's current position on licensing of patented technologies is that it includes more questionable licensing payments than it would prefer.

Yet, the robust nature of this post-grant opposition procedure is potentially an attractive alternative to licensing patents of questionable validity. So long as the fees for post-grant opposition procedures are relatively low compared to litigation, a large IT company would probably choose to file oppositions rather than take licenses. Accordingly, the post-grant opposition provision facilitates IT's ability to police and weed-out marginal contributions and improvidently granted patents.

Summary of the Most Significant Changes to the Patent System Introduced by the AIA

First to file

Perhaps the most sweeping change to the American patent system affected by AIA is the transition from a First to Invent (FtI) system to a modified First to File (FtF) system.[110] Since the patent system was instituted in the United States, the first person to invent a new process, machine, manufacture or composition of matter was entitled to the patent for that invention.[111] Even if another inventor filed an application to patent that same invention first, the first to actually invent the subject matter had priority. The AIA changes this rule, basing priority in the granting of patents entirely on a modified first to FtF system. In other words, no matter who invented the subject matter first, the person who was first to file the patent application or the first to publicly disclose the invention is granted the patent.

The AIA both contemplates and makes an effort to correct possible unfairness that may result from the new rule. If two inventors work independently on a particular invention and one manages to apply for a patent first, it seems fair to grant the first inventor to file for the patent with the patent. If, however, a single inventor works on an invention and another inventor simply takes the idea for the invention and manages to apply for the patent first, the AIA provides a remedy for the inventor who actually developed the invention. In a "derivation action," if the first inventor can show that the first to file's invention is the same or substantially the same as the first inventor's invention, the patent will instead be granted to the first to invent from whom the first to file's invention was derived.[112]

More importantly, the AIA's FtF system does not necessarily create a race to the patent office. Indeed, the first inventors to invent subject matter may disclose their inventions and then have up to a year to file for a patent.[113] For inventors who subsequently seek to patent the same invention, the disclosure acts as prior art. Thus, in a way, rather than creating a strictly FtF system, the AIA really creates a modified FtF system with a first to disclose option.

Retroactive suites for patent infringement would also seem unfair under an FtF system. A party may have invented subject matter themselves and used it without patent protection. Then, a subsequent inventor might file for a patent on the subject matter and try to sue the prior user for infringement on a patent that the patent holder had not even yet invented. The

AIA thus grants an affirmative defense for uses that occurred one year to the prior of either the filing date of the patent or the date on which the claimed invention was disclosed.[114]

In many ways, this alteration to the patent system can be seen to unfairly favor larger firms and to discourage start-up firms. Firms that already have the available capital to expend on the patent process can capture the rights to innovations that startups may have invented first, but who still need time to gather resources to initiate the patent process. In turn, investors will turn away from investing in start-ups, fearing patent preemption by larger firms. So, the AIA also calls for a report on prior user rights and a small business study, to see if this change in the patent systems ultimately affects more of a positive change in the arena of conforming to international standards, or a negative one in the arena of eliminating funding for start-up firms and pricing patent protection outside of the grasp of small businesses.[115]

Filing by an assignee

Another related change to the patent system is the ability of non-inventors to file for a patent. Since patents are no longer granted on the basis of first to invent, but rather on the basis of first to file, even parties who are not themselves inventors of the subject matter may file for a patent if the inventor is obligated to assign the right to the patent to them. In this way, a patent must no longer pass through the hands of the inventor to the assignee. Instead, if the assignee is the real party in interest, the patent may be issued directly to them.[116]

Post-grant review

Post-grant review represents a wide expansion of the recently implemented *inter partes* patent reexamination process. Under the prior *inter partes* reexamination process, reexamination was limited to assertions of prior art and would only be granted if the petition was determined to raise a substantial new question of patentability.[117] The advantage, however, is that a party could prevail on a showing of invalidity by a mere preponderance of the evidence.

Under the new post-grant review, the petitioner also prevails by meeting a preponderance of the evidence standard and what is more, the petitioner may challenge the patent's validity on any grounds.[118] To merit post-grant review, the petition must be filed within nine months of the grant of the patent and must show that it is more likely than not that the petitioner will prevail to invalidate at least one claim in the patent. Furthermore, a ruling on patent invalidity cannot be reasserted in district court and can only be appealed to the Federal Circuit.

Inter partes review is also changed.[119] Although it is still limited to assertions of prior art, it is no longer limited to new questions of patentability. On the other hand, it is now limited to prior art consisting of patents or printed publications. As with post-grant review, petitioners must show that it is more likely than not that they will prevail in invalidating at least one claim in the patent. Parties are estopped from relitigating the issue in civil court or before the International Trade Commission and the ruling can only be appealed to the Federal Circuit.

Fee adjustment/non-appropriation

The AIA also responds to complaints that the PTO is underfunded and to concerns that underfunding results in the issue of patents that do not truly meet patentability requirements.[120] Traditionally, Congress has had the exclusive authority to set and adjust fees for patent materials and services. The AIA sets fees for patent materials and services; however, it places the authority to adjust those fees in the hands of the PTO itself.[121] Also, whereas Congress used to have the power to appropriate money collected by the PTO, AIA makes patent fees usable exclusively for expenses of the PTO.[122] This may curtail the incentive to grant patents in order to collect extra fees to pay for PTO expenses, while making it easier for the PTO to process more patents at a faster rate.

Best mode

Prior to the AIA, failure to disclose the best mode of practicing an invention was grounds for invalidating the patent, when it could be shown that the inventor had knowledge of the best mode and yet declined to disclose it.[123] The AIA expressly states that "failure to disclose the best mode shall not be a basis on which any claim of a patent may be canceled or held invalid or otherwise unenforceable."[124] It will be interesting to see if courts interpret this to mean that no matter what, an inventor's non-disclosure of best mode is never grounds for invalidating a patent or if some cases of failure to disclose the best mode may still be grounds for invalidation when the failure rises to the level of inequitable conduct.[125]

Interest in Harmonizing American Patent Law with Popular International Patent Law

Regularity with international patent law

Many of the most sweeping changes to the American patent system introduced in AIA can be traced to the interest of standardizing the American patent system with the laws common to the patent systems of other countries. There is no better example of this guideline than the transition for the FtI to the modified FtF rule. The U.S. has long been one of the only countries to stick to an FtI rule for the granting of patents; the AIA brings the U.S. into harmony with the patent laws of most other countries.

In the U.S., an inventor can only be the person who made the invention, while abroad financiers of inventions and corporations can be inventors. Allowing assignees to file for patents takes the U.S. one step closer towards broadening the standard for who or what can be an inventor. Under the AIA, the inventor remains the person who invented the subject matter; however, letting assignees file for the patent and receive it directly takes a large step toward cutting the human inventor out entirely.

Lastly, the institution of a post-grant review system brings the U.S. into line with a more international standard. As mentioned earlier, Europe and Japan both have patent opposition proceedings similar to the new post-grant review proceedings.[126]

The influence of Pharma and IT

Apportionment of damages Unlike H.R. 1908, the AIA does not have a section relating to changes in the law of damages for infringement. It is important to note, however, that the original bill introduced in the Senate, did include changes to the law of damages, stating "[t]he court shall identify the methodologies and factors that are relevant to the determination of damages, and the court or jury shall consider only those methodologies and factors relevant to making such determination."[127] In other words, the idea is to take the determination of damages out of the hands of the jury. This is similar to the driving point of H.R. 1908 that sought to legislate two discrete damage categories for judges to decide between ahead of time only then to give over to the jury to apply. Also, like H.R. 1908, S. 23 would have required a judge to designate a methodology for the determination of damages, for example "contribution over prior art" or "entire market value" depending on the circumstance and the jury would then be bound to decide within the given methodology.

This would appear to be substantially the same compromise to benefit both IT and Pharma as far as their differential interests are concerned. Very likely, however, the provision had to be removed, because of its substantial Seventh Amendment implications from both a legal and political standpoint.

Post-grant review The AIA's post-grant review process is virtually identical to H.R. 1908 § 6(f). Instead of a one year period to institute a post-grant review, the AIA makes post-grant review available only within nine months. Like H.R. 1908, however, the AIA's post-grant review mechanism may involve discovery and oral hearings. The evidentiary standard to invalidate is a preponderance of the evidence and the ruling in post-grant proceedings estop the issue from being reexamined in a civil action or before the International Trade Commission. So, as far as H.R. 1908 § 6(f) is illustrative of the common but differential reliance of Pharma and IT on the patent system, the AIA only serves to further illustrate the point.

First to file and fee adjustment Although the major push to change over to a modified FtF system was most likely a desire to conform with more popular international standards, it is also reflective of the differential reliance of Pharma and IT on patent law. The new FtF system represents a benefit to Pharma as it creates a bright-line standard for inventorship. Under an FtI standard, controversy and conflicting evidence can be raised over who was indeed the first inventor. Who was the first to conceive of the invention and did the first to conceive diligently work to reduce the invention to practice? If not who was the first to reduce the invention to practice? The first to file system establishes an absolute, non-controversial standard to designate to whom the patent should be awarded.

Such a bright-line rule, far from offending the interests of IT, works well to serve their interests in this context. An FtF system demands that a patentee make an initial investment to patent the subject matter, which means that a patentee must in many cases convince investors and managers ahead of time of the value of the patent. Inventors with limited funding must be certain ahead of time that their inventions will make a substantial return on the amount they will need to spend to go through the patent process. This means that incremental or slight improvements are more likely to go unpatented, saving IT firms from litigating numerous possible patent infringements on small IT related components.

True, start-ups and small businesses may disclose their inventions to protect them from subsequent filers for patents for the same invention, but the moment they do so the clock starts ticking on their window to find investors. Once the one-year grace period ends, their inventions enter the public domain absolutely, again saving large IT firms from costly litigation and increasing their bargaining power within the one year grace period for licensing terms.

Like the FtF rule, the fee adjustment provision of the AIA is not a primary indication of Pharma's and IT's influence; however, it is easy to see how it is beneficial to their purposes. Of course the drive to allow the PTO to adjust fees for its materials and services is a response to underfunding and its corresponding incentive to issue patents, even for subject matter that may not truly meet the standard for patentability. Indeed, given the precedent entrenched in *Molecular Pathology* granting strong deference to the PTO on matters of patentability, the importance of accuracy in the PTO's assessments of patentability cannot be overstated. Nonetheless, handing the reigns of control over patenting fees to an under-funded PTO makes it far more likely that they will raise patenting fees. Pharma is certainly not concerned with a fee hike and, on the contrary, would prefer to have its patents processed more quickly in exchange for higher patenting fees. Higher fees also mean less patents issued on slight or incremental improvements and more difficulty for startups to gain access to the patent system. That means less litigation and a stronger bargaining position for large IT firms.

Judicial Reform

Congress gave the Federal Circuit national appellate jurisdiction over patent law cases to promote uniformity at the appellate level. Yet, since 1993, commentators have called for uniformity at the next lower level, the trial courts.[128] For example, Judge James F. Holderman, Chief Judge of the United States District Court for the Northern District of Illinois, endorsed a proposal to give one existing district court uniform jurisdiction over patent infringement litigation.[129] Calls for patent law uniformity at the trial courts have not gone unheard by Congress. Nevertheless, judicial reform, like statutory reform, will occur in the context of Pharma's and IT's differential reliance on the patent system. This Part reviews recent federal legislation which seeks to encourage specialization among trial judges in patent cases.

Several legislative reforms have been proposed to create opportunities for specialization at the district court level in patent cases.[130] For instance, in 2007, the Senate Judiciary Committee considered House Resolution 34 that sought "to establish a pilot program in certain United States district courts to encourage enhancement of expertise in patent cases among district judges."[131] This Bill would permit district court judges to "request to hear cases under which one or more issues arising under any Act of Congress relating to patents or plant variety protection must be decided."[132] The assumption, of course, is that allowing judges to specialize in patent litigation will lead to better resolution of patent disputes. The House version of the same proposal, H.R. 628 from the 111th Congress, was passed by the House and Senate and signed into law by President Obama on January 4, 2011.[133] Under this law, a new pilot program will be implemented in certain U.S. District Courts to enhance the expertise of federal judges hearing patent disputes.[134] A minimum of six U.S. District Courts in at least three different judicial circuits will be designated as the initial trial courts for piloting this program.[135] These courts will be selected from among the 15 judicial districts with the most patent filings in 2010 or from judicial districts that have adopted local rules for patent cases.[136] Participation in this pilot program is optional; judges from the selected districts have the choice to opt in.[137] The pilot program is scheduled to run for a period of 10 years.[138] The objective of this pilot program is to steer patent cases to district court judges who have the interest and aptitude to hear more patent cases thereby increasing the level of judicial expertise in patent litigation. So far, 14 judicial districts have been chosen as designated districts under this pilot program.[139]

Nevertheless, some empirical work suggests that legislation to encourage trial judges to specialize in patent cases would not necessarily benefit the patent system.[140] Claim construction is the heart of patent litigation because it informs the parties' validity and infringement positions. One commentator has empirically shown that district court judges' reversal rate on claim construction by the Federal Circuit does not decrease as the judge handles more patent cases.[141]

Although there is no call for specialized patent trial courts in the AIA, the Act will put many more patent litigation issues directly before the PTO and will keep those issues out of federal district courts to some degree. Post-grant review opens a forum for petitioners to challenge patents on any grounds of unpatentability with some of the fixings of a civil trial (discovery/hearings) and with very desirable benefits to patent challengers. This will make the difficult issues of patentability far more likely to be tried by the PTO itself. Furthermore, the fact the post-grant and *inter partes* review estop parties from pursuing civil litigation will keep the issues out of civil trial courts. Also, the new derivation proceedings will be held exclusively in the PTO. In short, the AIA seems to guide many of the more complex issues of patent litigation into a forum that is specialized to deal with patent issues.

COMPREHENSIVE CHANGES HAVE RIPPLE EFFECTS ON THE PATENT SYSTEM

Because different legal and regulatory institutions in the patent system are closely interlinked, one change that is promulgated ripples through the entire system. Indeed, patent law doctrine is so intertwined that making one change to doctrine A often results in an unforeseen change in doctrine B, doctrine C, and so on. Thus, any patent possibility must account for the ripple effects of comprehensive across-the-board changes. This Part illustrates the ripple effect factor by briefly reviewing such effects from the *Bilski* and *Ebay* decisions and from *inter partes* reexamination.

The *Bilski* Court's purported revival of the "machine-or-transformation" test has had a ripple effect in the PTO. The Federal Circuit only handed down the *Bilski en banc* opinion in October 2008, but the Board of Patent Appeals and Interferences (BPAI) is now increasingly relying on *Bilski*. In fact, *Bilski* has emboldened the BPAI to raise subject matter eligibility *sua sponte*. For example, the BPAI has recently applied the machine-or-transformation test *sua sponte* to reject a "computerized method performed by a data processor,"[142] a method for "converting a unidirectional domain name to a bidirectional domain name,"[143] a seismic "fault identification method,"[144] and a "method for maintaining a user profile."[145] Thus, *Bilski* illustrates how a Federal Circuit change in patent doctrine regarding eligible subject matter may have ripple effects at the PTO and elsewhere.

As a second example, the U.S. Supreme Court's decision in *Ebay* which changed the standard to obtain permanent injunctions as a remedy for patent infringement in the district courts has had a ripple effect at the International Trade Commission (ITC). Effectively, the *Ebay* decision raised the standard for obtaining permanent injunctions in district courts. As a consequence, aggrieved patentees are now seeking injunctive relief elsewhere. Indeed, actions under § 337 of the Smoot-Hawlery Tariff Act of 1930[146] in the ITC have increased dramatically post-*Ebay*.[147] The ITC is a limited but powerful forum. Among other things, the ITC may issue general exclusion orders where the U.S. Customs Service destroys imported infringing articles. Today, after finding infringement, empirical work suggests that the ITC is three times as likely as a district court to grant injunctive relief.[148] In response, some commentators recommend limiting the ITC's jurisdiction.[149] *Ebay* illustrates how a U.S. Supreme Court decision changing patent remedies may have ripple effects and create incentives for strategic behavior at other patent litigation forums such as the ITC.

Finally, *inter partes* reexamination,[150] illustrates how statutory reform may have ripple effects that may perhaps be too strong. *Inter partes* reexamination was created to compliment *ex parte* reexamination.[151] Although some commentators argue *inter partes* reexamination is "the most strategically advantageous avenue for an accused infringer seeking to invalidate a patent,"[152] only a little over 300 *inter partes* reexaminations have been requested since the procedure was created in 1999.[153] Interestingly, patents directed to mechanical inventions comprise 56 percent of all *inter partes* reexaminations whereas patents directed to computers and communications only comprise 7 percent of all *inter partes* reexaminations.

Nevertheless, the elimination rate for patents in *inter partes* reexamination is high – maybe too high. For example, data through August 2008 shows 73 percent of all *inter partes* reexaminations lead to complete elimination of all claims for which reexamination was sought.[154] On the other hand, the complete elimination rate drops to 53 percent when the patentee responds to all the *inter partes* reexamination office actions. Still, this rate exceeds the 12 percent complete elimination rate in *ex parte* reexamination from 2000–2008. Moreover, the courts do not invalidate patents at such high rates. Given the AIA's substantial empowerment of the reexamination process with the introduction of post-grant review, the magnitude of the ripple effect from this far broader mode for challenging issued patents will doubtlessly result in strategic changes in behavior and counter responses by litigants in the years to come.

The ripple effect of the massive change in the patent system that the AIA represents is assuredly difficult to project. It is possible to see AIA as a bane to small businesses and to start-ups and a boon to incumbent businesses and corporations. The modified FtF system, post-grant review, and *inter partes* review may discourage investment in start-up companies and weaken patent protection for small businesses. On the other hand, the FtF system does not create a race to the patent office and start-ups and small businesses and universities may disclose their inventions, granting them a one year grace period to file for patents for inventions that are financially successful. Furthermore, although post-grant review may give larger firms more leverage to threaten small inventors with costly post-grant proceedings that they may find difficult to bear, this would only affect inventions that find themselves somehow on the margins of patentability. In addition, such challenges have to be made within a post-issuance, nine months period. Fee adjustment may possibly price some inventors out of the patent market, but a solution is necessary for underfunding to the PTO. One thing is clear. The AIA, with its emphasis on Patent Office practice, will have a massive ripple effect on many different areas of patent law. What the effects will be remains to be seen.

CONCLUSION

Reviewing recent developments in U.S. patent law and patent policy with an eye towards the future is no easy task – the temptation is too great to speculate on the entire future of patent law and the patent system. That said, there is no crystal ball or legal or empirical test that might predict the future of patent law and policy.

This chapter contends that recent developments in patent law and patent policy illustrate four trends which will bear on any patent possibility in the future: continued active shaping of patent law doctrine and patent policy by the Federal Circuit; the U.S. Supreme Court's significant, renewed interest in patent law; recent legislative changes to the patent law, including statutory reform and judicial reform with the passage of both the AIA and the pilot patent specialization program in designated judicial districts; and the ripple effects of these developments on the patent system as a whole.

Importantly, recent patent legislative reform illustrates that two clear stakeholders are coming to the fore – large pharmaceutical/biotechnology/life science companies and large information technology companies. Any patent possibility that includes a unitary patent system – the same patent law for all technology sectors – must account for these stakeholders' differential reliance on patent assets to appropriate benefits from the marketplace for their innovations lest the motivation for a continued unitary system may be lost. It is also clear that Congress is interested in bringing U.S. patent law into conformity with popular international law. In many ways, it is possible to see the AIA as a move towards that goal as well as a unitary solution for Pharma and IT, with the possible concern that it comes at the expense of discouraging innovation by start-ups and small business. These are indeed exciting times for patent aficionados.

NOTES

1. Commission on Revision of the Federal Court Appellate System, Structure, and Internal Procedures: Recommendations for Change 152, 67 F.R.D. 195, 370 (1975).
2. Federal Courts Improvement Act of 1982, Pub. L. No. 97-164, 96 Stat. 25–28 (codified as amended at 28 U.S.C. § 1295 (2006)).
3. Describing the next 25 years as a set of patent possibilities is motivated by Lawrence B. Solum, 'Constitutional Possibilities', Illinois Public Law Research Paper No. 06-15 (Jan. 7, 2007) *available at* http://papers.ssrn.com/sol3/papers.cfm?abstract_id=949052 (last visited April 26, 2012).
4. *See* 17 U.S.C. §§ 101–1332 (2006).
5. Pat., Trademark & Copyright J. (BNA) No. 430 at A-1 (May 24, 1979).
6. 383 U.S. 1 (1966).
7. Legal instrumentalism is policy-driven analysis where the decision maker applies legal rules only when the rules produce desired outcomes. Legal Theory Lexicon, available at http://lsolum.typepad.com/legal_theory_lexicon/ (last visited April 26, 2012).
8. 499 F.3d 1365 (Fed. Cir. 2007) *vacated*, 89 U.S.P.Q. 2d 1641(Fed. Cir., 2009) *remanded to*, 554 F.3d 967 (Fed. Cir. 2009).
9. 500 F.3d 1346 (Fed. Cir. 2007) *reh'g denied*, 515 F.3d 1361 (Fed. Cir. 2008) *cert. denied*, 129 S.Ct. 70 (2008).
10. 545 F.3d 943 (Fed. Cir. 2008) *overruled by* Bilski v. Kappos, 130 S. Ct. 3218 (2010) (rejecting the "machine-or-transformation test" as the sole test for what constitutes a "process" under 35 U.S.C. § 101 and affirming the judgment holding the subject matter to be an abstract process).
11. No. 2010-1406, 2011 WL 3211513 (Fed. Cir. July 29, 2011).
12. Sec. Exch. Comm'n. v. Chenery Corp., 318 U.S. 80 (1943).
13. *Comiskey*, 89 U.S.P.Q. 2d 1641, 1647 (Fed. Cir. 2009) (Moore, J., dissenting).
14. *Compare Comiskey*, 554 F.3d 967 (Fed. Cir. 2009) *with Comiskey*, 499 F.3d at 1380.

15. *Nuijten*, 500 F.3d. at 1351.
16. *Id.* at 1356 (citing Diamond v. Chakrabarty, 447 U.S. 303 (1980)).
17. *Bilski*, 545 F.3d at 958, 960 n.19.
18. *Id.* at 976 (Newman, J., dissenting).
19. *See* Ass'n for Molecular Pathol. v. United States Patent & Trademark Office, No. 2010-1406, 2011 WL 3211513, at *18 (Fed. Cir. July 29, 2011).
20. *Id.* at *23.
21. 35 U.S.C. § 101 (2006).
22. *Chakrabarty*, 447 U.S. at 308-09 (quoting S. Rep. No. 1979, at 5 (1952); H.R. Rep. No. 1923, at 6 (1952)).
23. *Bilski,* 545 F.3d at 955.
24. *Id.* at 966–76 (Dyk, J., concurring).
25. *Id.* at 966 (Dyk, J., concurring).
26. *Id.* at 997 (Newman, J., dissenting); *id.* at 1013 (Rader, J., dissenting).
27. *Id.* at 976 (Newman, J. dissenting).
28. *Id.* at 1006 (Mayer, J. dissenting).
29. Bilski v. Kappos, 130 S. Ct. 3218 (2010).
30. *Id.* at 3226.
31. *Id.* at 3229.
32. *See id.* at 3231.
33. This new approach to the machine-or-transformation test will be discussed later.
34. Ass'n for Molecular Pathol. v. United State Patent & Trademark Office, No. 2010-1406, 2011 WL 3211513, at *35 (Fed. Cir. July 29, 2011).
35. *Id.*
36. 149 F.3d 1368 (Fed. Cir. 1998).
37. *Bilski,* 545 F.3d at 1004 (Mayer, J., dissenting) (citing PTO statistics).
38. Class 705 has no more than a 20–30 percent claim allowance rate which is one of the lowest allowance rates among all the PTO art groups. Indeed, the PTO regularly rejects claimed business methods under § 102 or § 103. *See* Brief for 22 Law and Business Professors Supporting Appellants, *In re* Bilski, 545 F.3d 943 (Fed. Cir. 2008).
39. *See* above.
40. 498 F.3d 1373 (Fed. Cir. 2007) *reh'g denied.*
41. 532 F.3d 1318 (Fed. Cir. 2008), *reh'g denied* (Fed. Cir. Sept. 25, 2008), *cert. denied*, 129 S. Ct. 1585 (2009).
42. 35 U.S.C. § 271(a) (2006).
43. *Id. at* § 271(b), (c).
44. *Muniauction, Inc.*, 532 F.3d at 1330.
45. U.S. Const. art. I § 8 cl. 8.
46. *BMC Resources, Inc.*, 498 F.3d at 1381.
47. *Muniauction, Inc.*, 532 F.3d at 1330.
48. *BMC Resources, Inc.*, 498 F.3d at 1381.
49. *See* Uniloc USA, Inc. v. Microsoft Corp., 632 F.3d 1292.
50. *See* above.
51. 576 F.3d 1348 (Fed. Cir. 2009), *cert. denied*, 130 S. Ct. 1088 (2010).
52. *Id.* at 1362.
53. 35 U.S.C. § 271(f) (2006).
54. Deepsouth Packing Co. v. Laitram Corp., 406 U.S. 518 (1972).
55. 425 F.3d 1366 (Fed. Cir. 2005).
56. 576 F.3d at 1365.
57. *See, e.g.*, Mark D. Janis, *Patent Law in the Invisible Age of the Supreme Court*, 2001 U. ILL. L. Rev. 387.
58. Markman v. Westview, 517 U.S. 370 (1996).
59. Dickinson v. Zurko, 527 U.S. 150 (1999).
60. J.E.M. AG Supply, Inc. v. Pioneer Hi-Bred Int'l, Inc., 534 U.S. 124 (2001).
61. 550 U.S. 398 (2007).

62. 130 S. Ct. 3218 (2010).
63. 131 S. Ct. 2238 (2011).
64. 547 U.S. 388 (2006).
65. 549 U.S. 118 (2007).
66. 131 S. Ct. 2060 (2011).
67. Graham v. John Deere Co., 383 U.S. 1, 18 (1966).
68. *In re* Geiger, 815 F.2d 686 (Fed. Cir. 1987).
69. Abbott Laboratories v. Sandoz, Inc., 544 F.3d 1341, 1351 (Fed. Cir. 2008).
70. 35 U.S.C. § 101.
71. Bilski v. Kappos, 130 S. Ct. 3218, 3227 (2010).
72. 581 F.3d 1336 (Fed. Cir. 2009), *reh'g and reh'g en banc denied* (2010).
73. 130 S. Ct. 3543 (2010).
74. 628 F.3d 1347 (Fed. Cir. 2010).
75. No. 10-1150, 2011 WL 973139 (U.S. June 20, 2011).
76. *See* above.
77. 131 S. Ct. 2238 (2011).
78. *Id.* at 2252.
79. *Id.* at 2250.
80. *Id.* at 2251.
81. *Id.*
82. 547 U.S. 388 (2006).
83. 549 U.S. 118 (2007).
84. 131 S. Ct. 2060 (2011).
85. *Ebay*, 547 U.S. at 392.
86. 28 U.S.C. § 2201 (2006).
87. *MedImmune*, 549 U.S. at 132 n.11.
88. *See* Teva Pharm. USA v. Pfizer, Inc., 395 F.3d 1324, 1333 (Fed. Cir. 2005).
89. *MedImmune*, 549 U.S. at 132 n.11.
90. Micron Tech., Inc. v. Mosaid Tech., Inc. 518 F.3d 897, 902 (Fed. Cir. 2008) ("[T]he now more lenient legal standard facilitates or enhances the availability of declaratory judgment jurisdiction in patent cases.").
91. *Id.* ("[T]he ease of obtaining a declaratory judgment could occasion a forum seeking race to the courthouse between accused infringers and patent holders.").
92. Global-Tech Appliances, Inc. v. SEB S.A131 S. Ct. 2060, 2068 (2011).
93. *Id.* at *7.
94. *Id.* at *8.
95. *See, e.g.*, Craig Allen Nard & John F. Duffy, *Rethinking Patent Law's Uniformity Principle*, 101 Nw. U. L. Rev. 1619 (2007).
96. *Holmes Group, Inc.*, 535 U.S. at 837-38 n.3 (Stevens, J., concurring).
97. *Id.* at 839.
98. 548 U.S. 124 (2006).
99. *Id.* at 138 (Breyer, J., dissenting) (quoting Bonito Boats, Inc. v. Thunder Craft Boats, Inc., 489 U.S. 141, 146 (1989)).
100. *See, e.g.*, James Bessen & Michael J. Meurer, Patent Failure (2008).
101. H.R. 1249, 112th Cong. (2011).
102. *Id.* at 139 fig. 6.5.
103. J.D. Watson & F.H.C. Crick, *Molecular Structure of Nucleic Acids: A Structure for Deoxribose Nucleic Acid*, 171 Nature 737 (1953).
104. H.R. 1980, 110th Cong. (as passed by House, Sep. 7, 2007) *available at* http://frwebgate.access.gpo.gov/cgi-bin/getdoc.cgi?dbname=110_cong_bills&docid=f:h1908eh.txt.pdf; S. 1145, 110th Cong. (as placed on S. Legis. Calendar, Jan. 24, 2008) *available at* http://frwebgate.access.gpo.gov/cgi-bin/getdoc.cgi?dbname=110_cong_bills&docid=f:s1145rs.txt.pdf (last visited April 26, 2012).
105. H.R. 1980, 110th Cong. § 5 (as passed by House, Sep. 7, 2007).
106. *Id.* at § 6(f).

107. *Id.* at § 5(b)(2), (3).
108. *Id.* at § 5(b)(4).
109. Letter from Hon. Paul Michel, Chief Judge, Federal Circuit to Sen. Patrick Lahey & Sen. Orrin G. Hatch, S. Comm. on the Judiciary (May 3, 2007) *available at* http://www.patentlyo.com/patent/files/MichelLetter.pdf (last visited April 26, 2012).
110. Leahy-Smith America Invents Act, H.R. 1249, 112th Cong. § 3 (2011).
111. 35 U.S.C 102(a).
112. H.R. 1249 § 3(i).
113. *Id.* § 3(a).
114. *Id.* § 5.
115. *Id.* § 3(l)–3(m).
116. *Id.* § 4(b).
117. 35 U.S.C 311–312.
118. H.R. 1249 § 5(d).
119. *Id.* § 5(a).
120. *See e.g.* SUZANNE T. MICHAEL, CHIEF COUNCIL, INTELLECTUAL PROPERTY, FEDERAL TRADE COMMISSION, TO PROMOTE INNOVATION: THE PROPER BALANCE OF COMPETITION AND PATENT LAW AND POLICY – EXECUTIVE SUMMARY: A REPORT OF THE FEDERAL TRADE COMMISSION, OCTOBER 2003, *reprinted in* 867 PLI/Pat 429, 441 (2006), *available at* http://www.ftc.gov/os/2003/10/innovationrpt.pdf (last visited April 26, 2012).
121. *Id.* § 10–11.
122. *Id.* § 22.
123. U.S. Gypsum Co. v. Nat'l Gypsum Co., 74 F.3d 1209, 1215–1216 (Fed. Cir. 1996).
124. H.R. 1249 § 15(a).
125. *See* U.S. Gypsum, 74 F.3d at 1215 n.8.
126. *See* above.
127. S. 23, 112th Cong. § 4 (2011) (reported Feb.3d).
128. *See, e.g.*, Hon. James F. Holderman, *Judicial Patent Specialization: A View From the Trial Bench*, 2002 U. Ill. J.L. Tech. & Pol'y 425, 430–31 n.31–34.
129. *Id.* at 430–31.
130. *See, e.g.*, H.R. 5418, 109th Cong. (2006); S. 3923, 109th Cong. (2006).
131. H.R. 34, 110th Cong. (2007).
132. *Id.* § 1(a)(1)(A).
133. H.R. 628, 111th Cong. (2009).
134. *Id.*
135. *Id.*
136. *Id.*
137. *Id.*
138. *Id.*
139. *See* John Council, *Program Funnels Infringement Suits to Judges for Patent Expertise*, Tex. Law., Mar. 28, 2011, *available at* http://www.law.com/jsp/tx/PubArticleTX.jsp?id=1202487881711&slreturn=1 (last visited April 26, 2012).
140. David L. Schwartz, *Practice Makes Perfect? An Empirical Study of Claim Construction Reversal Rates in Patent Cases*, 107 MICH. L. REV. 223 (2008).
141. *Id.* at 256 (noting that the study did not include multivariate analysis).
142. Gutta, (BPAI Jan. 15, 2009) *available at* http://des.uspto.gov/Foia/BPAIReadingRoom.jsp (last visited April 26, 2012).
143. Atkin, (BPAI Jan. 20, 2009) *available at* http://des.uspto.gov/Foia/BPAIReadingRoom.jsp (last visited April 26, 2012).
144. Barnes, (BPAI Jan. 22, 2009) *available at* http://des.uspto.gov/Foia/BPAIReadingRoom.jsp (last visited April 26, 2012).
145. Becker, (BPAI Jan. 26, 2009) *available at* http://des.uspto.gov/Foia/BPAIReadingRoom.jsp (last visited April 26, 2012).
146. 15 U.S.C. § 1337 (2006).

147. *See, e.g.*, Robert W. Hahn & Hal J. Singer, *Assessing Bias in Patent Infringement Cases: A Review of International Trade Commission Decisions*, 21 HARV. J.L. & TECH. 457 (2008).
148. *Id.* at 490.
149. *Id.* at 488.
150. 35 U.S.C. §§ 311–18 (2006).
151. 35 U.S.C. §§ 301–307 (2006).
152. Tun-Jen Chiang, *The Advantages of Inter Partes Reexamination*, 90 J. PAT. & TRADEMARK OFF. SOC'Y 579 (2008).
153. Andrew S. Baluch & Stephen B. Maebius, *The Surprising Efficacy of* Inter Partes *Reexamination: An Analysis of the Factors Responsible for its 73% Patent Kill Rate and How to Properly Defend Against it* 1 (2008) *available at* http://www.patentlyo.com/patent/law/baluchmaebius.pdf (last visited April 26, 2012).
154. *Id.* at 11.

6. Issues and possible solutions in Japan: patent filing activities of Japanese companies, resulting backlog problem, and possible solutions

Futoshi Yasuda

INTRODUCTION[1]

The 16th U.S. President Abraham Lincoln once said, "The patent system added the fuel of interest to the fire of genius." As symbolically pointed out by this remark, the primary role of the patent system has always been to give an incentive for inventors to pursue innovation by granting exclusive rights to them and to develop industry by promoting technological development. In fact, there were many examples where the inventor of a significant invention obtained a patent on the invention and developed related business and provided society with further technological developments. These examples indicate that the patent system has played an important role in industrial development.

However, in addition to these merits, the patent system gradually has been spinning off demerits as well. In recent years, the patent system has not necessarily contributed to industrial development because it has caused new types of issues such as the proliferation of patent portfolios containing a great number of patents, the growth of patent thickets made of defensive patents, the growing patent backlog as a result of large-volume patent filing activity, and the emergence of patent trolls. These issues are attributable to the diversification of the functions of the patent system caused by such changes as the expansion of the scope of patent protection, an increase of patent players both in number and type, the changes in the environment surrounding inventors, and the reevaluation of patents in business activities.

In modern society, except for some cases involving pharmaceutical products, etc.,[2] a patent does not necessarily guarantee exclusive business opportunities. As exemplified by electric and electronic equipment, most products are the embodiment of accumulated innovations. It is said that each electric or electronic product incorporates as many as several hundreds to several thousands of patents. To make matters even more complicated, those patents are owned by many patentees.

In this situation, it is common for a company to obtain as many patents as possible in order to strengthen its position, even if only slightly, although those patents will not necessarily guarantee exclusive business opportunities. Patents are used as a business tool to conduct license negotiations, to secure freedom to operate future marketing, and to prevent other companies from entering the market.

The spread of the use of the patent system for these purposes has a strong relation to the causes of the backlog problem, which is one of the most serious issues that the Japan Patent Office currently faces.

The Japan Patent Office has long tried to solve the problem of this backlog. Nowadays, Japan is not the only country that is tackling this issue: most developed countries face the same situation and even some developing countries are beginning to find this a problem too.

While there are various problems with regard to the patent system, this chapter focuses on one of the most serious problems in Japan, that is, the issue of backlog. In this chapter, the first section outlines the changes in the functions of the patent system. The following sections and beyond focus on the current trend of Japanese companies in the practice of filing patent applications and examination requests in order to try to identify the causes and distinctive features of the backlog problem and to try to find a possible solution.

Changes in the Functions of the Patent System

As mentioned above, the patent system was established primarily to promote creative activities by granting exclusive rights to individual inventors. In modern society, however, the patent system is not necessarily used as a means of promoting individual inventors' creative activities. It has become more common for companies to use the patent system as a business tool in order to secure their market superiority and freedom to operate. While the patent system has long served these functions intrinsically since its introduction, these functions have become increasingly important in modern society.

The statistics show that the number of patent applications recently filed by individuals stands at 10,000 to 14,000 (13,000 applications filed in 2007, a ratio of 3 percent). This is almost the same as the level in 1953. In this early post-war period, the number of patent applications filed by individuals stood at 14,000 (ratio 58 percent; the ratio of utility model applications filed by individuals: 80 percent). In contrast, the number of patent applications filed by companies, mostly large corporations, has increased significantly to the point that patent applications are filed mostly by companies (380,000 applications filed in 2007: ratio 97 percent).[3] It is not an overstatement to say that this means that the current patent system almost serves as a business tool for companies. (According to some reports, even though the patent system is designed to promote individuals' creative activities, the patent system does not effectively encourage individuals to invent. In fact, in the case of an employee's invention, the employee is given reasonable compensation when he/she assigns the invention to the company by the patent system. However, such compensation is not the main motive for inventing. Instead of the motivation provided by patent system, the main motive is the employee's desire to contribute to scientific and technological development and to solve challenging problems.)[4]

Typically, a company uses the patent system as a business tool in the following ways. For example, to ensure its market superiority or to preserve its freedom to operate. It is common for a company to try to obtain as many patents as possible to strengthen its position, for example, in cross license negotiations and patent pool negotiations, even though those patents will not necessarily guarantee exclusive business opportunities. Furthermore, a company uses the patent system to build up patent portfolios by obtaining as many patents as possible for peripheral technologies in addition to a patent for the core technology of its product. Those patents on peripheral technologies are expected to help the company maintain its market superiority even after the expiration of the patent for the core technology by making it practically impossible for other companies to enter the market due to the existence of the patents for peripheral technologies. (The patent system was often used for this purpose by IT companies and electric equipment makers. It has been reported that such practice has spread throughout industries including the pharmaceutical industry.)[5]

A patent is a strong and exclusive right that enables the right holder to exclusively produce, use and sell the patented invention and to demand an injunction against any infringement. If a company that develops a product embodying many patented inventions infringes even one patent of another company, an injunction would be issued against the product of the company in an extreme case. In some cases, this function of a patent might be used by a company that enters the market at a later stage due to a delay in technological development. Such a company searches rival companies' deficiencies or lack of patent portfolios and obtains those patents which should have been included in the patent portfolios in order to discourage rival companies and prevent them from monopolizing the market. In this way, the patent system may be used to strengthen market superiority, even if only slightly. In other cases, a company may use the patent system to discourage rival companies by filing patent applications and leaving them unexamined, or by filing many divisional applications so that the scope of a patent right will remain undetermined for a long period of time.

Furthermore, when a company develops a technology, even if the company does not or will not commercialize it, the company may use the patent system to obtain a defensive patent on the technology in order to prevent other companies from patenting a similar technology and deter them from commercializing it.

Thus the patent system is used for many purposes. Companies, mostly large ones, devised intellectual property strategies in order to develop their businesses advantageously. The so-called intellectual strategy of a company means the tactical use of intellectual property systems including the patent system in each phase, for example, the filing, acquisition, and use of a patent.

In actual intellectual property negotiations, the more patents a negotiator possesses, the more advantage the negotiator has over the opposite party regardless of the type of patent (such as a patent obtained for a licensing purpose, a patent obtained to build up a patent portfolio, or a patent obtained for the purpose of defense). In this way, companies are motivated to file as many patent applications as possible. In recent years in particular, the increasing efforts of large companies to obtain many patents for these reasons have encouraged a situation whereby small and medium sized companies also have to obtain a large number of patents in order to compete with large companies. This is why Japanese companies have come to file so many patent applications.[6] (Another reason for companies to obtain a large number of patents could be the perception that the number of patents is an indicator of corporate value. In view of increasing public awareness of the importance of patents, companies have actively disclosed to shareholders and other parties that the number of patents is an indicator of corporate technological development capability.)

As described above, in modern society, the patent system functions as a business tool for companies to develop their business.[7] So currently companies are motivated to obtain as many patents as possible.

Background to the Backlog Problem of Unexamined Patent Applications

As mentioned above, many patent applications are filed because it is seen to be important for companies to obtain as many patents as possible (this is a worldwide phenomenon). The number of patent applications filed in Japan is especially high in comparison with other countries. This is attributable to the fact that Japanese companies are unique in the following respects. First, in a typical Japanese company, a wide range of employees participate in the effort to invent, from production-site employees, who tend to make improvement inventions, to basic-research employees. Second, a large number of companies compete with each other in the same industry unlike any other country. Third, Japanese companies share a corporate culture of preferring to keep pace with other companies. Fourth, Japan has many electrical and precision equipment manufacturers whose products comprise many parts, necessarily including many inventions. Thus, Japan leads the world in the number of patent applications and has faced a serious problem of backlog as a result.

The backlog causes a delay in patent examination and a lengthy patent pending period prevents the patent system from performing its function fully. The backlog prevents the patent system from granting necessary patents in a timely manner and could eventually prevent the patent system from serving its function altogether. Excessive filing of patent applications causes not only a backlog that leads to a lengthy patent pending period but also a patent thicket and an increase in the risk of litigation and transaction costs. Moreover, excessive filing of defensive patent applications ends up restricting the number of new technologies that can be used because they have been granted the right of exclusive use. Consequently, from the viewpoint of society as a whole, there is a possibility that the demerits of defensive patents outweigh their merits, such as enabling the company to hold a defensive patent to maintain its freedom to operate.

While it should be noted that active patent filing activity itself is a positive thing in general because it is an indicator of technological development, most patent applications filed in Japan are for improvement inventions, which reflects the corporate patent filing practice of putting priority on patent quantity over patent quality. But with the diversification of the functions of the patent system, the number of patent applications filed in Japan has increased dramatically, causing the backlog. It would be inappropriate to restrict corporate patent filing activity administratively in order to solve the backlog because companies are currently using the patent system in a law-abiding manner. It would be more appropriate to solve the problem by redesigning the patent system to meet the needs of modern society.

When redesigning the patent system in order to solve the issue of backlog, we need to take into consideration the unique patent filing practice of Japanese companies. Before jumping to the conclusion that the backlog problem can be solved by increasing the JPO's examination resources, we need to conduct a multi-perspective study on whether such large-volume patent filing activity has a positive effect on the Japanese economy as a whole.[8]

CURRENT PATENT FILING AND ACQUISITION ACTIVITY OF JAPANESE COMPANIES

The number of patent applications filed in Japan has increased in tandem with post-war economic development. For years Japan led the world in terms of the number of patent applications filed with the JPO until 2005 when the U.S. outpaced her.

Since 2003, the Japanese government has adopted a pro-patent policy and issued an annual Intellectual Property Strategic Program. However, even before such a policy was adopted, Japanese companies were actively filing patent applications. There is no statistical evidence that the pro-patent policy increased their patent filing activity. In recent years, the number of domestic patent applications filed by Japanese applicants has been leveling off and decreasing slightly. In the following sections, we will analyze the trend in patent filing activity of Japanese companies.

Patent Filing Activity in Japan

The trend in the filing of applications for patents and utility models

Figure 6.1 shows the number of applications for patents and utility models filed in Japan by Japanese and non-Japanese applicants. The number of patent applications filed in Japan, especially those filed by large companies, has increased dramatically in the post-war period. In recent years, the number of patent applications filed in each year has leveled off at around 400,000.

The number of utility model applications has also increased significantly during the post-war period. Until 1980, the number of utility model applications had always been greater than that of patent applications. The number of utility model applications peaked at slightly more than 200,000 and started to decline in 1986 and fell below 80,000 in 1993, when the system to examine utility model applications was abolished. Since the introduction of the non-examination utility model system in 1994, the number of utility model applications has plummeted to slightly less than 10,000 and leveled off in recent years.[9]

When patent applications filed with the JPO are broken down between those filed by Japanese applicants and those filed by non-Japanese applicants, the number of patent applications filed by Japanese applicants

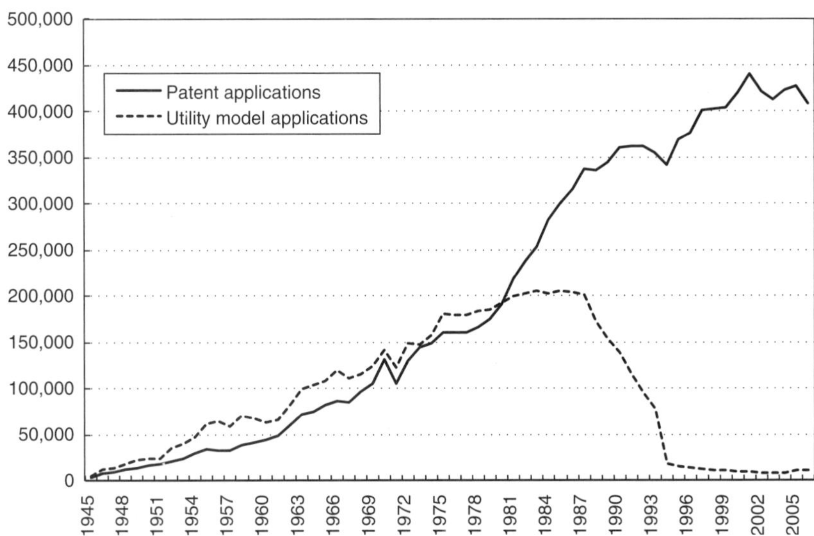

Source: This graph was created based on the JPO, "Japan Patent Office Annual Report" for each year.

Figure 6.1 Number of patent applications and utility model applications

can be seen to be on the decline in recent years. The number peaked at around 390,000 in 2000 and declined by about 60,000 to about 330,000 in 2007.[10]

The decrease in the number of patent applications filed by Japanese applicants is often attributed to the fact that patent filing activity has shifted from Japan to other countries;[11] that the number of companies that started to file domestic patent applications more selectively by adopting a stricter business selection and concentration policy and a quality-over-quantity policy has gradually increased since the collapse of the bubble economy; that the use of the improved multiple claim system has become widespread;[12] and that the patent examination procedure has recently been tightened.[13] While these changes are taking place, not all Japanese applicants are slowing down their patent filing activity. As described below, the main reason for the decrease is that the number of patent applications filed by some major applicants has just decreased.

Trends in the number of patent applications filed by large companies

Figure 6.2 shows trends in the number of patent applications filed by large companies (mostly electrical equipment makers) that filed more than 10,000 patent applications in 1990. The number of patent applications

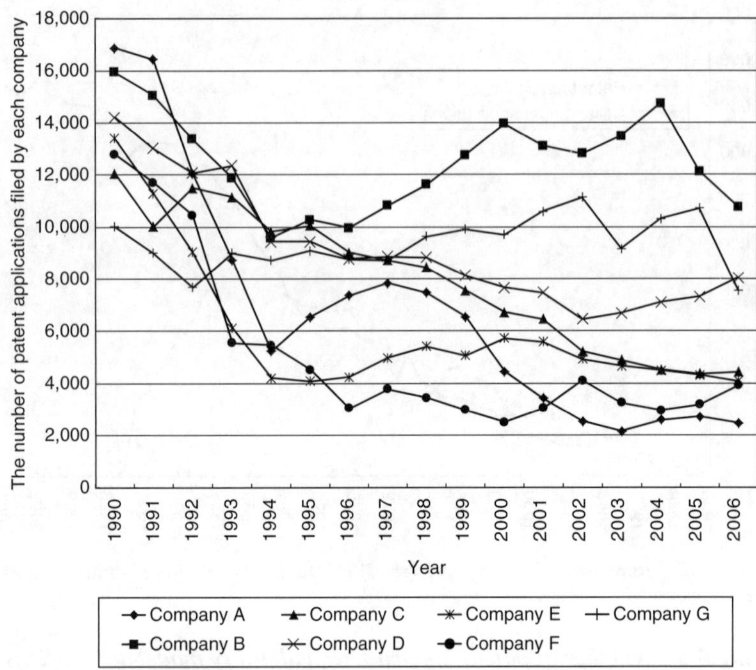

Source: These graphs were created based on the PATOLIS database. The companies covered by the graphs were selected from among those that filed more than 10,000 patent applications in 1990.

Figure 6.2 Trends in the number of patent applications filed by large companies

filed by Japanese applicants has been on the decline because large companies have slowed their domestic patent filing activity.[14]

On the other hand, during the period covered by Figure 6.2, the total number of domestic patent applications filed by Japanese applicants increased by about 14,000 from 333,000 in 1990 to 347,000 in 2006, while the number has been on the decline since 2000. This shows that, even though large companies decreased their patent filing activity during this period, many other applicants increased their patent filing activity so much that the total number of patent applications increased.[15]

This trend reflects the fact that small and medium sized companies have recently become more aware of the importance of intellectual property in their business operations and increased their patent filing activity to compete with larger companies.[16]

The future trend in the number of patent applications filed in Japan will be affected by a decrease in patent filing activity by large companies, an increase in patent filing activity by small and medium sized companies and non-Japanese applicants, a rise in the number of companies that keep inventions secret, and the recent economic changes. Close monitoring of the trend will be necessary for years to come.[17]

RELATION BETWEEN RESEARCH AND DEVELOPMENT COST AND PATENT FILING ACTIVITY (DOMESTIC PATENT FILING ACTIVITY)

Figure 6.3 shows the relation between the research and development cost and domestic patent filing activity of Japanese corporate users of the

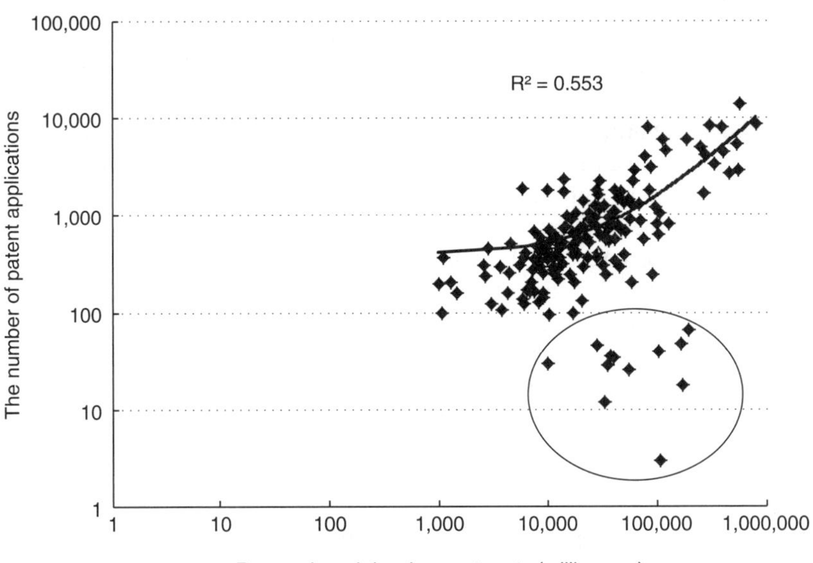

Source: This graph was created based on the data on the number of patent applications filed in 2006 by companies placed high on the list of frequent patent system users and the number of patent applications filed by major pharmaceutical companies (extracted by the author) presented in JPO, "Japan Patent Office Annual Report 2008," (Statistical Data), pp.50–59, and on the data on the research and development costs shown in their financial statements (it should be noted that some companies prepared the data on a calendar year basis, while others prepared it on a fiscal year basis).

Figure 6.3 Research and development costs and the number of patent applications

patent system (168 companies). (Those within the circle correspond to 12 pharmaceutical companies.)

This figure reveals a certain correlation between research and development costs and domestic patent filing activity. On average, the 156 companies subject to the study excluding the pharmaceutical companies filed 20.4 patent applications per ¥1 billion of research and development costs. (On the other hand, pharmaceutical companies on average filed 0.4 patent application per ¥1 billion of research and development costs.)

Difference Between Categories of Industries in Terms of Research and Development Costs and Domestic Patent Filing Activity

Table 6.1 shows the number of domestic patent applications filed by each industry per ¥1 billion of research and development costs. According to this table, 62.3 applications, which is the largest number for such research and development costs, were filed by "Other products (manufacturing industry)," followed by 48.2 applications filed by "Machinery," 44.3 applications by "Textile and Apparels," and by 41.3 applications by "Pulp and paper." On the other hand, "Electrical Appliances" and "Information and telecommunications" outnumber other industries in terms of the total number of patent applications, but with regard to the number of patent applications filed by each industry for research and development costs, 23.4 applications were filed by "Electrical Appliances," while 6.7 applications were filed by "Information and telecommunications." Therefore, the number of patent applications filed for such costs by these industries is not particularly high compared to other industries. This table indicates that, in Japan, a wide range of industries except for the pharmaceutical industry file a large number of patent applications for research and development costs.

RELATION BETWEEN RESEARCH AND DEVELOPMENT ACTIVITY AND PATENT FILING ACTIVITY (INTERNATIONAL COMPARISON)

International Comparison Between the Number of Patent Applications and the Cost of Research and Development

Figure 6.4 shows the relation between the number of patent applications and the cost of research and development and the relation between the number of patent applications and the number of researchers in major countries. It is particularly noticeable that the number of patent

Table 6.1 Industry-specific relation between the cost of research and development and the number of patent applications

Number of patent applications filed at research and development costs of ¥1 billion in 2006	
Construction	27.3
Textiles and Apparels	44.3
Pulp and Paper	41.3
Chemicals	24.8
Oil and Coal Products	37.2
Rubber products	28.0
Glass and Ceramics Products	40.0
Iron and Steel	31.4
Nonferrous Metals	30.8
Metal Products	25.1
Machinery	48.2
Electrical Appliances	23.4
Transportation Equipment	10.1
Precision Instruments	37.4
Other Products (Manufacturing industry)	62.3
Electric Power and Gas	22.0
Information and Communication	6.7
Pharmaceutical	0.4
Average (excluding Pharmaceutical)	20.4

Source: This table was created based on the data on the number of patent applications filed in 2006 by companies placed high on the list of frequent patent system users and the number of patent applications filed by major pharmaceutical companies (extracted by the author) presented in JPO, "Japan Patent Office Annual Report 2008," (Statistical Data), pp.50–59, and on the data on the research and development costs shown in their financial statements (it should be noted that some companies prepared the data on a calendar year basis, while others prepared it on a fiscal year basis).

applications filed for a given amount of research and development costs or by a given number of researchers in Japan is several times higher than Western countries (for example, Japan: 3.4 times more than the U.S. and 3.2 times more than Germany, while the number of patent applications filed by a given number of researchers in Japan is 2.6 times higher than the U.S. and 1.5 times higher than Germany).

In sum, the number of patent applications filed by Japanese applicants is larger than that of patent applications by applicants of Western countries despite the fact that the number of patent applications filed in Japan has been leveling off or rather decreasing in recent years. The reasons for this difference were discussed previously in Chapter 2.

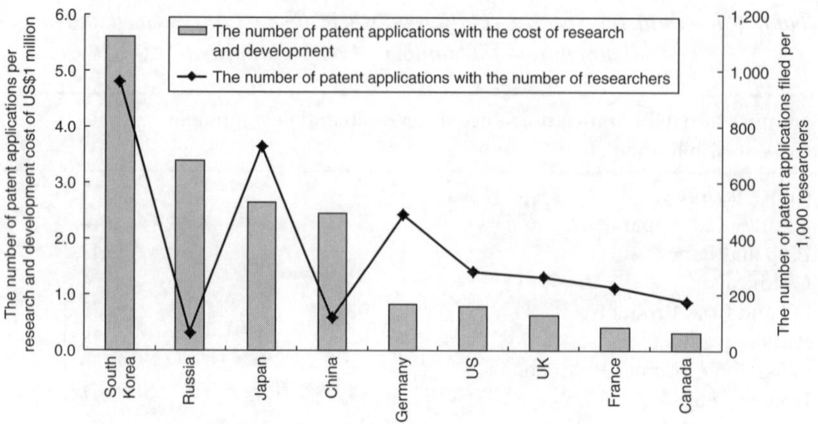

Source: These graphs were created based on the data on the number of applications filed at a given amount of research and development costs (WIPO, "WIPO PATENT REPORT 2008") and the data on the number of researchers (Statistics Bureau, the Ministry of Internal Affairs and Communications, "World Statistics 2008") (it should be noted that the year of data acquisition and the definition of data are different from one country to another).

Figure 6.4 Country-specific relation of the number of patent applications with the cost of research and development and with the number of researchers

Circumstances Surrounding Inventors in Japan and the West

As described above, Japan has several times more applications per researcher than Western countries. This is partly attributable to the difference in the range of employees involved in inventive activities. A report which compares Japan with Western countries with regard to important international applications filed by applicants in those countries ("important applications") reveals that the inventors in Western countries tend to be researchers who have higher levels of education and longer research and development experience than inventors in Japan.[18] This finding on the tendency of inventors cannot be directly applied to the inventions subject to purely domestic application. However, it may be speculated that a comparison between Japan and Western countries with regard to purely domestic patent applications filed in those countries could also have a similar tendency, that is that inventors in Western countries tend to be researchers who have higher levels of education and longer research and development experience than inventors in Japan. This tendency reflects the aforementioned fact that a relatively wide range of employees take

Table 6.2 The number of U.S. patents obtained by each industry per €1 million

Industry	Japanese companies	U.S. companies	European companies
Electric and Electronic Appliances	0.70	0.50	0.39
Information and Telecommunications	0.19	0.31	0.11
Transportation Equipment	0.17	0.16	0.12
Chemicals	0.33	0.48	–
Pharmaceutical	–	0.08	0.04
Average	0.46	0.31	0.17

Source: The data on the costs of research and development and the year of patent acquisition are based on statistics for 2007. The sources of the statistics are IPO, "Top 300 Organizations Granted U.S. Patents in 2007" and European Commission, "The 2008 EU industrial R&D investment SCOREBOARD" (2008). The industrial categories used in the table are a reclassified version of the categories used in "The 2008 EU industrial R&D investment SCOREBOARD." The categories are reclassified in such a way that allows comparison between the industries where each region is represented by at least two companies. The figures shown in the section "average" are the national averages of the companies ranked in the "Top 300 Organizations Granted U.S. Patents in 2007." The hyphen indicates that there are no companies ranked in the top 300 in the industry.

part in inventive activities in Japan. Those employees range from those working at production sites to those long engaged in research and development activities.

An international comparison shows that Japanese companies file a larger number of patent applications than Western companies for a given amount of research and development costs (or for a given number of researchers). As explained later, this is attributable, in part, to the fact that Japanese companies file a relatively large number of applications for improvement technologies.

The Number of Industry-specific Patents Obtained in the U.S. for a Given Amount of Research and Development

Table 6.2 shows the industry-specific data on the number of U.S. patents obtained by major Japanese, U.S., and European companies respectively for a given amount of research and development costs (€1 million) in 2007. First, it should be noted that Japanese companies (those that are placed within the top 300 companies in terms of the number of U.S. patents they obtained) are already very active in obtaining U.S. patents. The number of patents obtained by Japanese companies for the research and development costs was 0.46, which is much larger than 0.31 patents obtained by U.S.

companies in the United States. (This finding is not limited to the Japanese companies that are placed within the top 300 companies in terms of the number of U.S. patents they obtained. A comparison between Japanese companies as a whole and U.S. companies as a whole also reveals that the number of U.S. patents obtained by Japanese companies as a whole for a given amount of research and development costs (0.28 per US$1 million) was higher than that of U.S. companies as a whole (0.26 per US$1 million).[19])

According to the industry-specific data on the number of U.S. patents obtained by Japanese, U.S., and European companies respectively, the number of patents obtained for a given amount of research and development costs is higher in the electric or electronic industry than in other industries regardless of the nationality of the companies.

A simple comparison between Table 6.1 and Table 6.2 is inappropriate because Table 6.1 shows the number of patent applications filed in Japan, not in the U.S., and industrial categories are somewhat different between the tables. However, Table 6.2 reveals that the electric and electronic appliances industry obtains a large number of patents for a given amount of research and development costs. In light of this and because many industries in Japan file more patent applications than the electric and electronic appliances industry, this indicates that Japanese companies file many patent applications in a wide range of industries.

THE LEVEL OF TECHNOLOGY PATENTED BY JAPANESE COMPANIES AND THE USE OF THOSE PATENTS

The Level of Technology Patented by Japanese Companies

Figure 6.5 shows the results of an older survey on the self-evaluated level of technology patented by Japanese companies. According to the figure, slightly more than 75 percent of the total respondents evaluated the level as a "great improvement" or "small improvement to existing technology," whereas slightly more than 20 percent evaluated it as "highly innovative" or "highly creative."

While it is difficult to speculate on the level of technology currently subject to patent application, it would be fair to say that most of the inventions claimed in patent applications could be still evaluated as "great improvement" or "small improvement to existing technology." This is because, as mentioned earlier, many small and medium sized companies have intensified their patent filing activity in order to obtain as many

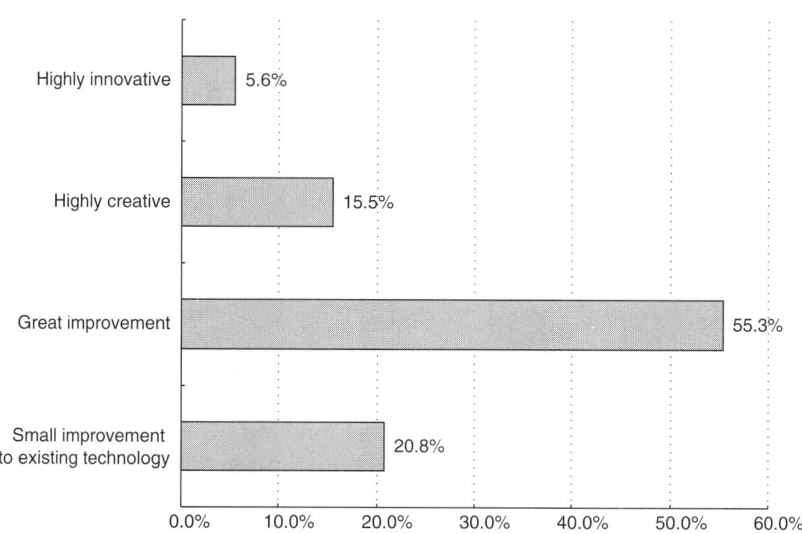

Source: Japan Techno Mart, "Miriyou tokkyo jouhou jittai chousa houkoku" (Report on the state of unused patent information), 1996.

Figure 6.5 Self-evaluated level of technology patented by Japanese companies

patents as possible (although some companies, especially large ones, have grown more selective in their domestic filing activity since this survey was conducted).

These facts might not be sufficient to support the speculation that the ratio of patent applications for inventions evaluated as "highly innovative" or "highly creative" is lower in Japan than the West. However, in view of the fact that researchers in the West who make inventions tend to have higher levels of education and longer research and development experience than inventors in Japan, and that the number of patent applications filed for a given amount of research and development costs is several times higher in Japan than in the West, it is likely that the ratio of applications for inventions evaluated as "highly innovative" or "highly creative" in Japan is lower than in the West.

Use of Patents

Figure 6.6 shows the situation regarding the use of patents in Japan. While about 1 million patents exist, only about half of them are in use. The patent use rate has been on the rise since 1995, when the patent use

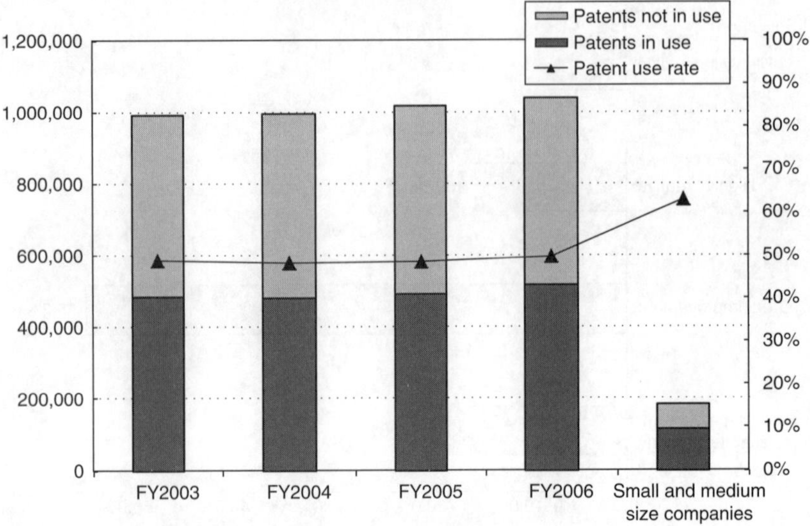

Source: These graphs were created based on data from JPO, "Results of the Survey of Intellectual Property-Related Activities 2007".

Figure 6.6 Use of domestic patents

Table 6.3 Use of domestic patents FY2006

	Patent use and purposes	Ratio
Patents in use	Ratio of patents used by the patent holders themselves	44%
	Ratio of patents licensed to other companies	8%
Patents not in use	Ratio of defensive patents	31%
	Ratio of patents that can be open to a third party	11%

Source: These graphs were created based on data from JPO, "Results of the Survey of Intellectual Property-Related Activities 2007".

rate was 33 percent[20] (the patent use rate among small and medium sized companies is higher than the average of all companies). The proportion of defensive patents to all unused patents is high (see Table 6.3). The table was created based on the data compiled on the use of registered patents. Such patent registration is made only after an examination has been conducted in response to an examination request, which tends to be made for a patent application for an invention with certain prospects for future use. Therefore, in the phase of application filing, the proportion of the applications for defensive patents is presumed to be even larger because the ratio of patent applications for inventions with uncertain prospects for future use is naturally higher than that in the phase of examination request.[21]

SUMMARY OF THE PATENT FILING AND ACQUISITION ACTIVITIES OF JAPANESE COMPANIES

The patent filing and acquisition activities of Japanese companies described above may be summarized as follows.

1. The number of patent applications filed by Japanese companies has significantly increased since the end of the war and remained the world's highest until 2005. However, in recent years, the number leveled off at around 400,000, reflecting the fact that the number of domestic applications filed by large companies has been on the decline whereas the number of applications filed by small and medium sized companies and foreign applicants has been on the rise.
2. There is a correlation between the costs of research and development and the number of patent applications. The number of domestic patent applications for a given amount of research and development costs and for a given number of researchers are several times higher in Japanese companies than in Western companies.

   This tendency is not limited to Japan. Even in the U.S., Japanese companies outnumber their U.S. and European counterparts in terms of the number of patents obtained for a given level of research and development costs.

   The industry-specific data on the number of patent applications (registrations) for a given amount of research and development costs shows that companies in all three regions, that is, Japan, U.S., Europe, tend to obtain the largest number of U.S. patents in the electrical appliance industry. On the other hand, with regard to the number of domestic patent applications filed by Japanese companies for a given amount of research and development costs, the electrical appliance industry tends to be outnumbered by other industries such as machinery and textiles.
3. With regard to the level of technology patented by Japanese companies, in view of the fact that Japanese companies have a relatively wide range of researchers participating in inventive activities and

> filing a comparatively large number of patent applications for a given amount of research and development costs, it is speculated that the ratio of patent applications for inventions that are "highly innovative" or "highly creative" in Japan is lower than in Western countries. Furthermore, regarding registered patents, 31 percent of unused patents are defensive patents, which might mean a higher ratio of patents for inventions of "small improvement to existing technologies". In the phase of application filing, it is speculated that defensive patent applications account for an even larger proportion.

These facts suggest that Japanese companies file an exceptionally large number of patent applications in comparison with their Western counterparts even when the unique domestic circumstances of Japan and the recently decreasing patent filing activity of some large companies are taken into consideration. As mentioned earlier, Japanese companies are strongly motivated to obtain as many patents as possible and the intensity of patent filing activity by Japanese companies exceeds such activity in the rest of the world. Such intensity cannot be explained simply by the necessity for Japanese companies to use the patent system to obtain defensive patents and build patent portfolios to maintain their freedom to operate.[22] What else could be the reason for the exceptionally high number of patent applications filed in Japan in comparison with developed countries in the West?

As mentioned earlier, various factors have contributed to the increasing number of patent applications. One of the factors noticeable particularly in Japan is the tendency of Japanese companies to do what other companies are doing. Namely, Japanese companies have a strong urge to keep pace with each other and consequently compete with rival companies in patent filing activity. For example, they try to defeat rival companies in terms of the comprehensiveness of patent portfolios and the number of patent applications. This unique tendency has brought about a peculiar situation whereby Japan leads the world in terms of the numbers of patent applications. Since this has become a norm among business activity, when two companies conduct license negotiations, both of them would be expected to have a certain number of patents and it would be difficult for a company to disregard this.

Another factor noticeable particularly in Japan, in contrast to Western companies' assumption that inventions should be made by highly educated and experienced engineers, is shown in Figure 6.1 which indicates that Japanese companies have long made active use of the utility model system and encouraged a wide range of employees to make improvement inventions even at production sites. This caused the current high level of patent filing activity by Japanese companies.

At the end of the war, Japanese companies did not have the current level of awareness about the importance of the relationship between intellectual property strategies and business strategies. However, they made active use of the patent system and the utility model system because those systems were in line with the Japanese corporate culture that encourages all employees, including those at production sites, to pursue improvement in the spirit of unity. Those systems have contributed to promoting improvement by giving an incentive for further increase in productivity and product quality. Subsequently, Japanese companies learned from the intellectual strategies adopted by rival or advanced companies and from their experience in licensing negotiations and disputes with domestic or foreign companies. With the renewed recognition of the importance of intellectual property in conducting business, Japanese companies sought to make more strategic use of the patents and utility model rights obtained through long-continued active filing practice. In the process, the current form of intellectual property strategy has become widely adopted by Japanese companies, which has resulted in more large-volume patent filing activity among Japanese companies to keep pace with other companies as mentioned earlier. (It should be noted that large companies are more experienced than small and medium sized companies in terms of intellectual property management. Such a gap in experience is reflected in the difference in their patent filing activity. Currently, medium sized companies are in the process of catching up with the intellectual property management of large companies.)

It is difficult to determine whether such an exceptionally large number of patent applications filed in Japan is good or bad for Japanese industrial development. Large-volume patent filing activity would not necessarily be undesirable if the Japanese corporate culture encourages the pursuit of improvement functions as an effective tool to manufacture high quality products with high-level productivity and if the patent system still plays a role in maintaining such corporate culture. However, if an excessive number of patent applications are being filed, the demerits could outweigh the merits.

In fact, most Japanese companies producing and selling the same products in Western countries would file a smaller number of patent applications in the Western countries than in Japan. In comparison with Japanese companies, most large Western companies file a much smaller number of patent applications. In view of this, it would be meaningful to examine whether it is appropriate for Japanese companies to file an exceptionally large number of domestic patent applications.

REQUESTS FOR EXAMINATION

The number of patent applications is affected mostly by the strategy of applicants' patent acquisition policy. On the other hand, the number of examination requests is affected not so much by the applicants' patent acquisition policy but rather by the structure of the system such as the limits on the length of the period between the filing of an application and the filing of a request for examination. Many countries have adopted the examination request system, which has a flexible examination request period in order to effectively handle patent applications filed in the respective countries. The examination request system helps applicants determine which application is subject to patent examination. In particular, Japan considers the system as an important tool to solve or alleviate the backlog problem caused by large-volume patent filing.

The Purpose of the Examination Request System

The Japanese patent system used to examine all of the applications filed by applicants. In order to alleviate the backlog, Japan revised this system in 1951 so that an application is subject to examination only if the applicant files an examination request. Under the new system, when filing an application, the applicant is given a certain period (three years for applications filed in October 2001 and thereafter) in order to determine whether the application needs to be examined.

Under this system of a prescribed examination period, an applicant would not file an examination request in the following cases: (1) where, even though the applicant did not necessarily need exclusive rights for the invention, the applicant filed an application for fear that another party might obtain exclusive rights for the invention and prevent the applicant from working the invention, (2) where the applicant filed an application, despite the applicant's belief that the invention was unpatentable, for the purpose of preventing another party from filing an application and obtaining a patent for the same invention so that an invalidation trial or other complicated procedures would be avoided, and (3) where the applicant filed an application for a technology that subsequently lost economic value as a result of the development of an alternative technology, discouraging the applicant from obtaining exclusive rights. Consequently, examination resources would be concentrated on the patent applications filed based on a strong desire to obtain a patent. In this way, the examination request system is expected to expedite examination of patent applications as a whole within a limited resource for examination.[23]

The examination request system has been adopted by many countries, and the system varies from one country to another in terms of the length of the examination request period. (For example, the U.S. doesn't have such a system; the request period is three years in China, five years in South Korea, and seven years in Germany. The EPO offers a six-month examination request period starting from when a European Search Report is prepared (about two years from the filing of an application).)

Shortening the Examination Request Period

In Japan, the examination request system was introduced in 1951. Initially, the examination request period was to be seven years from the filing of an application. From October 2001, the period was shortened to three years from the filing of an application for the following reasons: (1) if a company has already filed a patent application for an invention but has not made an examination request, a third party that plans to conduct certain business relating to the invention would be uncertain as to whether the company would seek exclusive rights and what kind of exclusive rights, if any, would be granted to the company. Due to such uncertainty, the third party would have to face the risk that its business might infringe a future patent of that company. The examination request period was shortened in order to minimize such uncertainty. (2) Furthermore, in spite of the fact that other countries find the results of the JPO's patent examination to be reliable, a long examination request period in Japan would cause corresponding foreign applications to be first examined in foreign countries. As a result, the JPO's patent prosecution history and examination results would not be taken into effective consideration by foreign patent offices.

A Trend in the Number of Examination Requests and the Influence of the Shortening of the Examination Request Period

Figure 6.7 shows a trend in the number of examination requests when examination requests subject to a seven-year examination request period and those subject to a three-year examination request period coexisted (from 2001 to 2008). The number of examination requests peaked in 2005, reaching 397,000.

This increase in the number of examination requests may be attributable, in large part, to the following two factors. First, the former examination request system overlapped with the new system for a certain period. This overlap caused a temporary coexistence of examination requests subject to a seven-year examination request period and those subject to a three-year examination request period. (The solid line in Figure 6.7

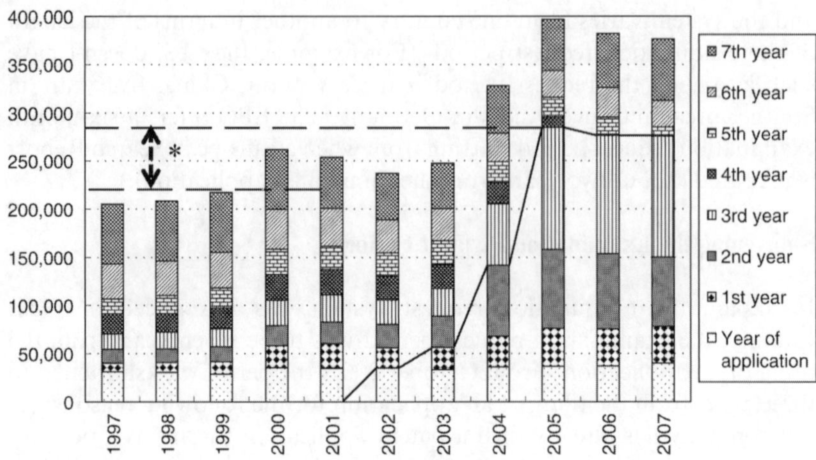

Source: These graphs were created based on the JPO, "Japan Patent Office Annual Report" for each year. It should be noted that "Year of application" does not mean that a request for examination was filed within one year from the application date. It means that an examination request was filed within the year of patent filing. For instance, in a case where an application is filed in December 2000, if a request for examination is made in January 2001, the examination request would be considered to be made not in the year of application but in the first year.

Figure 6.7 A trend in the number of examination requests

divides each bar graph into the upper part and the lower part. The upper part shows the number of examination requests subject to a seven-year examination request period, while the lower part shows the number of examination requests subject to a three-year examination request period. Since 2001, these two types of examination requests have coexisted.) Second, the shortening of the examination request period to three years caused most applicants to make more examination requests although those applicants would not have made such requests if the examination request period had remained at seven years (the portion marked * in Figure 6.7).

When shortening the examination request period, the JPO predicted that, although the waiting period could temporarily become longer, it would gradually be shortened to a manageable level and that the problem of backlog would be eventually solved. However, the recent increase in the number of examination requests is much larger than expected. The resulting increase in the amount of backlog and in the length of the waiting period is also much larger than predicted.[24]

The shorter examination request period increases the number of examination requests for the following reason. Under the first-to-file system, applicants file applications not only for inventions for which they have already established a commercialization plan but also for inventions for which they only have vague prospects for commercialization. It is common for an applicant to file an application for an invention and to take time to determine whether to commercialize the invention and, even if there is no solid plan for commercialization, whether to seek a patent in order to gain leverage in license negotiations with rival companies, etc. Under these circumstances, in the case of an application for which the applicant has not determined whether to seek a patent, one of the motives for the applicant to file a request for examination is to avoid the disadvantage that the applicant would have to suffer as a result of not seeking a patent for the invention claimed in the application in the future. The ratio of applications for which the applicants have not determined whether to seek patents is higher at the time of the third year from the application date than at the time of the seventh year from the application date. This discrepancy caused an increase in the number of examination requests. Usually, the shorter the examination request period, the higher the ratio of applications for which examination requests are filed for the purpose of avoiding such disadvantage.

A Trend in the Eventual Examination Request Ratio

Figure 6.8 shows a trend in the ratio of filing examination requests for patent applications before the examination request period expired. The ratio was around 70 percent when the examination request system was introduced. The ratio gradually decreased to 45 percent in 1988. This decrease is attributable largely to the JPO's effort to expedite patent examination through the implementation of measures to prevent the filing of unnecessary applications and examination requests. Those measures were gradually strengthened until 1988 (the JPO implemented the Selective Examination Request Program (AP80) on the top 100 major corporate applicants to ask them to file examination requests more selectively; when the JPO withdrew this request, the eventual examination request ratio started to increase). Since the shortening of the examination request period to three years, the ratio surged by around 10 percent and has been leveling off at around slightly over 66 percent. While the appropriateness of the JPO's decision to make such a request is questionable, the fact that the request caused a decline in the eventual examination request ratio suggests that it has been a customary filing practice for applicants to file a certain number of applications and examination requests although applicants have little need for patent protection.

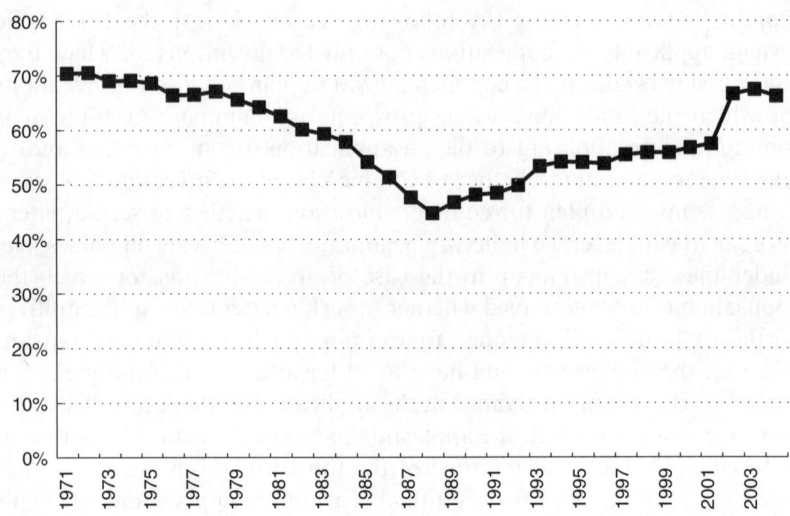

Source: This graph was created based on the JPO, "Japan Patent Office Annual Report" for each year.

Figure 6.8 A trend in the eventual examination request ratio

A Trend in the Length of the Period Between the Application Date and the Examination Request Date

Figure 6.9 shows a trend in the length of the period between the application date and the examination request date. A comparison is made between applications subject to a seven-year examination request period and those subject to a three-year examination request period to reveal a pattern in the length of the period between the application date and the examination request date. Regardless of whether an application is subject to a seven-year examination request period (filed between 1998 and 2000) or a three-year examination request period (filed between 2002 and 2004), the applicant is most likely to file an examination request in the final year of the examination request period. In the case of applications subject to a three-year examination request period, the proportion of applications for which an examination request is filed in the final year of the examination request period is more than 40 percent. This is much higher than the corresponding ratio in the case of applications subject to a seven-year examination request period. This indicates that, when uncertain of the need for patent protection, applicants tend to file examination requests in the final year of the examination request period in the hope of avoiding

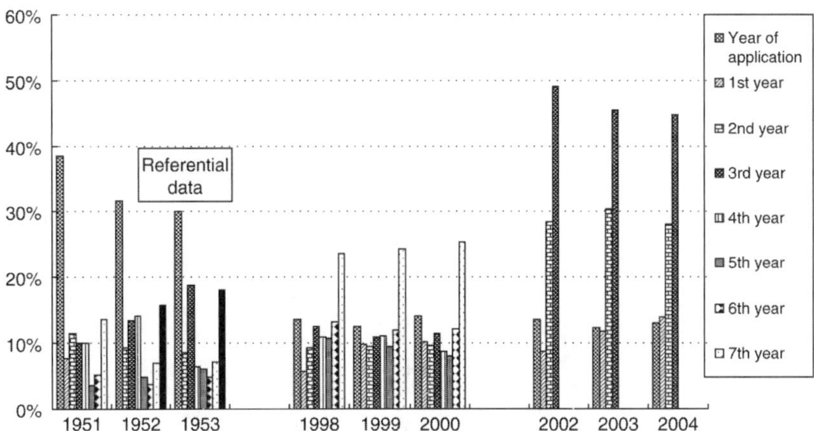

Source: These graphs were created based on the JPO, "Japan Patent Office Annual Report" for each year.

Figure 6.9 Length of the period between the application date and the examination request date

the disadvantage that would come from a decision not to seek a patent. (A comparison between the applications filed between 1998 and 2000 and those filed between 2002 and 2004 reveals that, regardless of the difference in the length of the examination request period, these two groups of applications are almost the same in terms of the proportion of applications for which examination requests were filed within one year. This similarity suggests that the two groups of applications are almost the same in terms of the ratio of applications for inventions that have already been commercialized or that are scheduled to be commercialized.)

Figure 6.9 divides all the applications filed in Japan into different groups according to the length of the period between the application date and the examination request date. Similarly, Figure 6.10 shows a breakdown of the applications filed in Japan by U.S. applicants. According to Figure 6.10, the ratio of applications for which examination requests are filed in the final year of the examination request period is even higher than that shown in Figure 6.9. The same tendency can be seen in the breakdown of the applications filed in Japan by German applicants according to the length of the period between the application date and the examination request date.[25] This shows that the tendency to file an examination request in the final year of the examination request period is not limited to Japanese companies.[26]

As mentioned above, an examination request is most likely to be filed

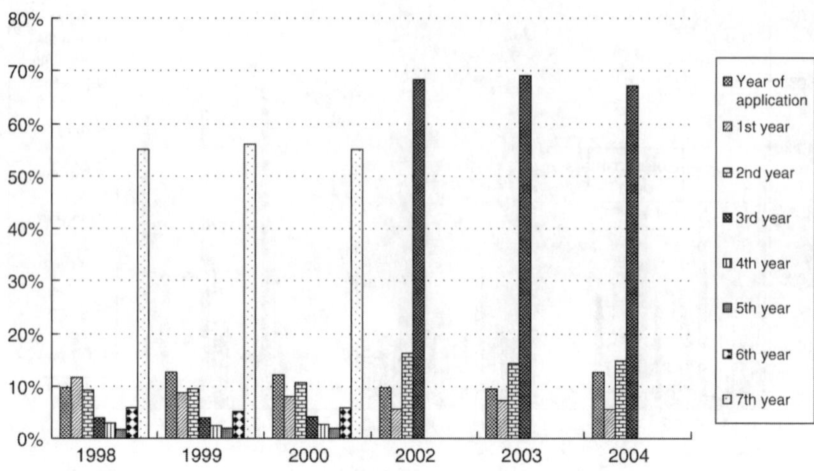

Source: Author.

Figure 6.10 Length of the period between the application date and the examination request date for U.S. applicants

in the final year of the examination request period. This tendency was not observed during the first few years after the introduction of the examination request system (see Figure 6.9 for the referential data on the applications filed between 1951 and 1953). During those years, applicants were most likely to request examination in the year of application. Since then, the length of time before the filing of an examination request has been increasing. Today, applicants are most likely to request examination in the final year. This is probably attributable to the fact that the examination request system has become well-established among applicants' and that, since the introduction of the examination system, there has been an increase in the ratio of defensive applications and other applications for which patent protection is not immediately necessary.[27]

The Effect of a Rise of an Examination Request Fee on the Eventual Examination Request Ratio

The JPO revised fees in the hope that applicants would file examination requests only for high-quality applications. With this revision, the JPO almost doubled the examination request fee for any application filed in April 2004 and thereafter. At the same time, the JPO decreased the patent fee.[28] Table 6.4 shows a trend in the eventual examination request ratio. It should be noted that all the applications covered by Table 6.4 were subject

Table 6.4 A trend in the eventual examination request ratio in the case of applications subject to a three-year examination request period

Year of application	Oct–Dec 2001	2002	2003	2004
Final year	Oct–Dec 2004	2005	2006	2007
Eventual examination request ratio	66.4%	66.6%	67.4%	66.2%

Source: This table was created based on the JPO, "Japan Patent Office Annual Report" for each year.

to a three-year examination request period.[29] According to Table 6.4, while the examination request fee was revised in 2004, the eventual examination request ratio in 2004 was only slightly lower than the preceding years. The effect of the revision may thus be considered to be negligible. So far, the effect of the revision of the examination request fee has been much smaller than expected.

This may be attributable to the following facts. First, the effect of the revision was limited because the examination request fee was only a small part of the total application costs including the patent application fee, patent fee, and agency fee. Second, the revision of the fees was beneficial only to the applicants whose grant rate was 50 percent or higher from the view of total costs calculation (according to the author's calculation). In view of the recent grant rate, which has been around 50 percent on average, the revision of the fees would function as an incentive for applicants to file examination requests more selectively only if their grant rate is much lower than 50 percent. For other applicants, however, the revision of the fees would not function as a strong incentive. On the contrary, for applicants whose grant rate is high, the reduction in the patent fee decreased the total costs, which might have ironically motivated them to increase the number of examination requests. (In the revision of the Patent Act in 2008, the patent fee was further reduced. This would also affect the eventual examination request ratio.)

Relation Between the Grant Rate and the Number of Years to the Examination Request from the Filing Date

Figure 6.11 shows the relation between the grant rate and the length of the period between the application date and the examination request date. In general, it is assumed that the grant rate tends to be high in the case of an application filed with a relatively strong determination to seek a patent. When an examination request is filed soon after the application date, it would be the reflection of the fact that an applicant has a strong

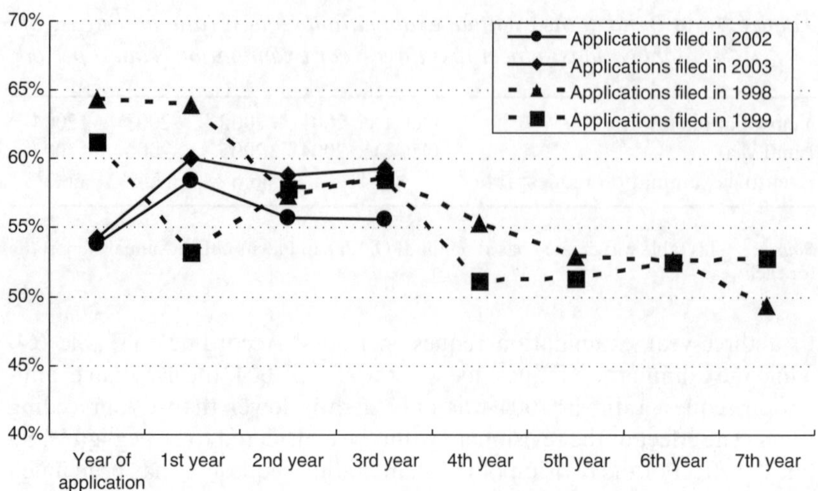

Source: Author. (It should be noted that this graph covers only the applications for which examination results were determined.)

Figure 6.11 Relation between the grant rate and the length of the period between the application date and the examination request date

determination to seek a patent. In fact, in the case of applications subject to a seven-year examination request period, the shorter the period between the application date and the examination request date is, the higher the grant rate (dashed line). This tendency is not observable among applications subject to a three-year examination request period (solid line). Although further analysis would be necessary to identify the cause of this difference, the difference is probably attributable, in part, to the fact that the shortened examination request period increased the remaining patent protection period after patent registration. Consequently, it has become more difficult for applicants to predict whether patent protection will become necessary in the future. As a result, applicants find it necessary to seek a patent (even if for a narrower scope of claims) from the perspective of risk management. (The remaining patent protection period would be longer in the case where an examination request is filed in the final year of a three-year examination request period than in the case where an examination request is filed in the final year of a seven-year examination request period. The longer the remaining patent protection period is, the more uncertain the patent will be used. This could increase the likelihood that applicants obtain patents just in case.)

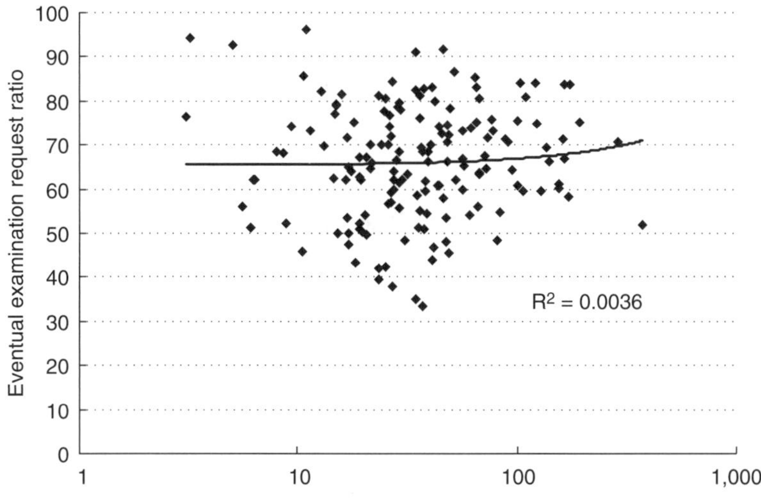

Source: This graph was created based on the data on the number of patent applications filed by each company placed high on the list of frequent patent system users and its examination request ratio presented in the JPO, "Japan Patent Office Annual Report 2008," (Statistical Data), pp.50–59 and also on the data from the research and development costs shown in its financial statements (it should be noted that some companies prepared the data on a calendar year basis, while others prepared it on a fiscal year basis). The research and development costs per application are calculated based on statistics for 2006, while the eventual examination request ratio is calculated with regard to the applications filed in 2004.

Figure 6.12 The research and development costs per application and the eventual examination request ratio

Relation of the Research and Development Costs with the Examination Request Ratio and with the Grant Rate

This section will examine the relation of the research and development costs per application with the examination request ratio and the grant rate. Generally speaking, the larger the research and development costs, the higher the invention will be in terms of significance and quality. Therefore, a company that spends a relatively large amount of research and development costs per application tends to seek patents and consequently have a higher examination request ratio and a higher grant rate.

Figure 6.12 shows the relation between the research and development costs and the examination request ratio. According to this figure, in the case of a company whose research and development costs per application

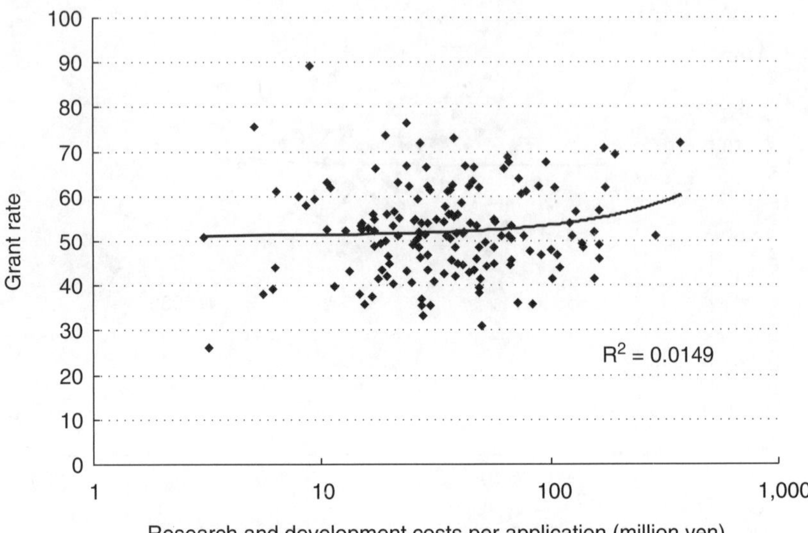

Source: This graph was created based on the data on the number of patent applications filed by each company placed high on the list of frequent patent system users and its grant rate presented in the JPO, "Japan Patent Office Annual Report 2008," (Statistical Data), pp.50–59 and also on the data from the research and development costs shown in its financial statements (it should be noted that some companies prepared the data on a calendar year basis, while others prepared it on a fiscal year basis). The research and development costs per application are calculated based on statistics for 2006, while the grant rate is calculated with regard to the applications filed in 2007.

Figure 6.13 The research and development costs per application and the grant rate

are high, its examination request ratio tends to be relatively high as well. However, a large amount of research and development costs are not necessarily linked with a high examination request ratio.

Similarly, the relation between the research and development costs and the grant rate shown in Figure 6.13 shows that, in the case of a company whose research and development costs per application are high, its grant rate also tends to be relatively high. However, this does not necessarily mean that the larger the research and development costs are, the higher the grant rate will be.[30]

This is attributable to the fact that, even if the same amount is spent on research and development to make a core invention, the patent acquisition policy for peripheral technology related to the core invention (patent portfolio policy) differs from one company or industry to another and that the patent acquisition policy for defensive patents and patents for improvement inventions made at production sites also differs from one company or industry to another. Although there is a certain correlation between the number of patent applications and research and development costs, it is difficult to find an overall causal relation between the research and development costs and the examination request ratio or with the grant rate because companies differ in terms of patent acquisition policy. (For example, despite a tight budget for research and development, some companies adopt a patent acquisition policy that prioritizes the number of patents rather than the quality in order to strengthen their market superiority, even if only slightly, and to actively seek patents including not only core patents but also peripheral patents and improvement patents. On the other hand, other companies adopt a policy of not actively obtaining peripheral patents and improvement patents related to core patents.)

Consequently, the quality of patent applications subject to examination request greatly varies from one company to another. Similarly, the quality of patents also varies greatly.

Summary of the Examination Request System

In the preceding sections, we have been analyzing the situation in the examination requests filed in Japan. The findings may be summarized as follows:

1. The examination request period was shortened from seven years to three years in 2001. The former examination request system overlapped with the new system for a certain length of time. This overlap caused a temporary coexistence of examination requests subject to a seven-year examination request period and those subject to a three-year examination request period. Consequently, the number of examination requests filed in Japan increased. Furthermore, in the case of an application for which the applicant has not determined whether to seek a patent, the applicant is more likely to file an examination request under the current system. As a result, the eventual examination request ratio has jumped from around 50 percent to 66 percent. This has caused a continuous increase in the number of examination requests.
2. With regard to the timings of examination request, an applicant is most likely to file an examination request in the final year of the examination request period regardless of whether the application is subject to a seven-year or a three-year examination request period. In the case of applications subject to a three-year examination request period, the

proportion of applications for which examination requests are filed in the final year is more than 40 percent. This indicates that applicants tend to file examination requests in the final year even though they are still uncertain about the need for patent protection. This tendency is observable not only among Japanese applicants but also among foreign applicants.

3. The increase in the examination request fee and the decrease in the patent fee had only a limited effect on the examination request ratio of companies. In order to motivate companies to file examination requests more selectively, it would be necessary to increase the examination request fee to such an extent that it will account for a much larger proportion of the total patent acquisition fees.
4. With regard to the relation between the grant rate and the length of the period between the application date and the examination request date, in the case of applications subject to a seven-year examination request period, the longer the period between the application date and the examination request date is, the lower the grant rate will be. However, in the case of applications subject to a three-year examination request period, such a relation is not seen.
5. With regard to the relation between the research and development costs and the examination request ratio, neither company-specific nor industry-specific analysis found a clear correlation between the research and development costs and the examination request ratio. Similarly, with regard to the relation between the research and development costs and the grant rate, no clear correlation was found. This suggests that the patent acquisition policy differs from one company to another. Consequently, the quality of patent applications for which examination requests are filed as well as the quality of patented inventions vary from one company to another.

The introduction of a shorter examination request period has greatly motivated companies to avoid disadvantages that they would have to suffer as a consequence of not seeking patents. As a result, the number of examination requests has increased significantly despite an increase in the examination request fee and other measures taken to encourage companies to file examination requests more selectively. This corporate behavior is natural in view of the fact that it was common for corporate users of the patent system to file many defensive applications and file examination requests for them in the final year of the examination request periods. While we need to keep monitoring the effect of the measures to encourage companies to file examination requests more selectively, the number of examination requests is expected to remain high.

Japan is different from Western countries in terms of the corporate patent filing practice. Therefore, it is necessary to establish an examination request system that best suits Japan's unique situation. The applicants' behavior discussed above suggests that policies to make the examination request period more flexible would be more effective than charging fee policies.

As mentioned earlier, the diversification of the examination request period would not necessarily have a clear-cut effect on the relationship between the quality of applications for which examination requests are filed and the quality of resulting patents. Such quality improvement would need a different approach with further measures. However, the diversification of the examination request period would at least alleviate or solve the problem of backlog.

As discussed earlier, it would be meaningful to examine the possibility of solving the backlog problem by encouraging companies to file patent applications more selectively. However, in view of the fact that the patent system has contributed to industrial development in Japan by promoting improvement inventions, it would be more appropriate to devise measures to encourage companies to file examination requests more selectively.

POSSIBLE WAYS TO SOLVE THE BACKLOG PROBLEM

Current State of Patent Examination

Before discussing the possibility of solving the backlog problem, this section will outline the current state of patent examination. Figure 6.14 shows trends in patent examination in Japan. With an increase in the number of examination requests in recent years as shown in Figure 6.7, the number of applications waiting for examination and the length of the examination waiting period have been on the rise. As of the end of 2007, the number of applications waiting for examination stood at slightly less than 900,000, while the length of the examination waiting period reached 26 months.[31]

In response, the JPO increased the number of first office actions to slightly more than 300,000 in 2007 by employing more fixed-term examiners and outsourcing a greater number of prior-art searches. However, if the number of examination requests were to keep rising, it would be difficult to reduce the increase in the number of applications waiting for examination and in the length of the examination waiting period.

Under the current situation, it will be necessary for the JPO to invest

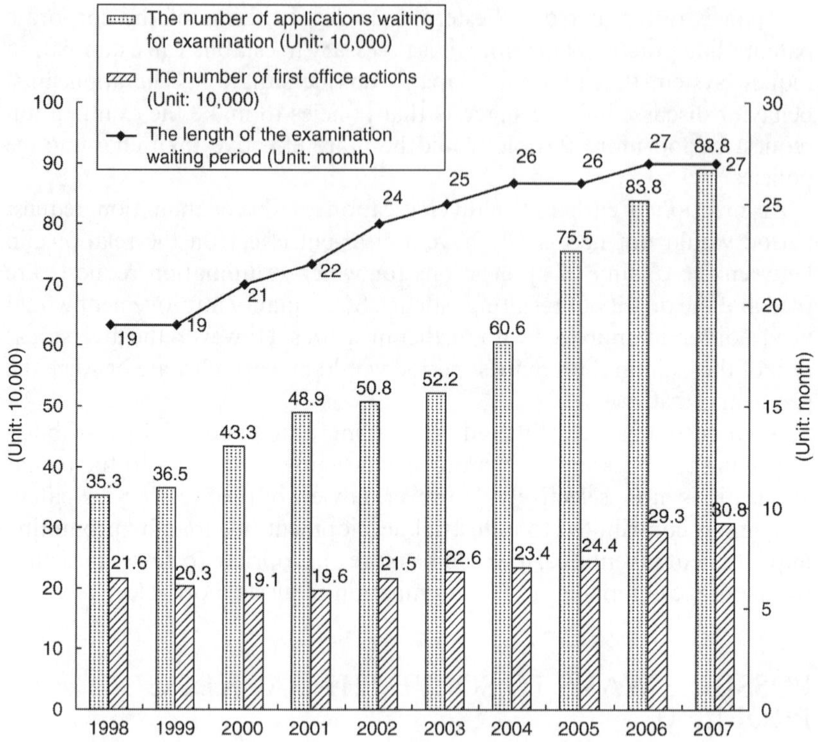

Source: These graphs were created based on the JPO, "Japan Patent Office Annual Report" for each year.

Figure 6.14 The number of applications waiting for examination, the number of first office actions, the length of the examination waiting period

an ever-increasing amount of examination resources in each application because of the continuous increase in the complexity of patent applications, the number of claims, and the volume of prior-art documents.[32] This means that, if the level of examination resources remains unchanged, the number of applications subject to examination will continue to decline. The workload related to international patent applications (PCT applications) has also been on the rise, exacerbating the backlog problem even further.[33]

For instance, on the hypothesis that the burdens on examiners will remain unchanged at the current levels with the number of patent applications at 400,000 and the examination request ratio at 66 percent (this means that 264,000 examination requests will be filed every year), the number of PCT applications being 26,000 (as of 2007), on the condition that each examiner examines 219 applications,[34] the minimum number of patent examiners necessary to handle those applications is slightly more than 1,300. This is higher than the level in 2003, that is, 1,126 examiners. Since 2003, the JPO has increased the number of fixed-term examiners.[35] In view of the fact that the contracts of those fixed-term examiners will eventually expire, there will be a constant shortage of patent examiners.

Assumption of Backlog Discussions

As described earlier, the patent system has functioned as a tool for companies to ensure their business superiority. This has led to the current situation where companies file a large number of patent applications in Japan. It is difficult to imagine that Japanese companies will quickly become comparable to their Western counterparts any time soon in terms of the number of applications for a given amount of research and development costs. In this respect, Japanese companies are expected to maintain the current level, which is higher than that of Western companies, while it is probable that Japanese companies, especially large ones, will slightly reduce the number of domestic applications as a result of a shift from domestic applications to foreign applications and more selective filing of domestic applications.

However, at this stage, in view of the positive role played by the patent system in promoting industrial development in Japan by encouraging improvement inventions, it would be inappropriate to conclude that the patent system should be promptly revised in such a way that will restrain patent filing activity. Therefore, in this chapter, we suggest the following approach. First, while it is not necessary to drastically change the current patent filing practice, companies should refrain from excessive patent filing activity by filing applications to some extent. Second, companies should focus on selecting a request for examination that is truly necessary in order to maintain early global information dissemination of examination results from the JPO. Based on these approaches, specific measures against the backlog problem are discussed below. It should be noted that the following measures are presented as examples with the hope of sparking further debate. Needless to say, further study would be necessary on the effect of each measure presented below.

Specific Measures to Resolve the Backlog Problem

Diversification of the examination request period[36]

It would be ideal for an applicant to file an examination request when patent protection becomes necessary and to smoothly obtain a patent.

Therefore, a single fixed patent examination period would be inconvenient in some cases.

The length of time between the filing of an application and the commercialization of the invention varies from one product to another. It is usually desirable to decide when to obtain a patent in view of the commercialization schedule. In the case of an application for a product with a short life cycle or for an invention that has been subject to a dispute over possible infringement of application filed, early patent protection would be desirable. However, this does not apply to all applications.

In light of the unique patent filing practice in Japan as described earlier, it would be meaningful to give applicants sufficient time to evaluate the necessity to seek patents in order to encourage them to file examination requests more selectively. Such selective filing of examination requests would allow the JPO to concentrate examination resources on applications that are truly necessary. Consequently, the backlog problem would be alleviated or solved. Other positive effects would be a reduction in the number of technologies that are not available for public use because they are protected by unused patents ensuing from excessive filing of defensive applications. As a result, the number of technologies placed in the public domain would increase.

It is important to discuss the diversification of the examination request period from the perspective of global information dissemination of the examination result of the JPO. In order to allow the JPO to fulfill its international role and promote the entry of Japanese companies into overseas markets amid the increasingly globalized economy, when an international application is filed with the JPO as the office of first filing, it is important for the JPO to become the first office to examine the application and disseminate information on the prosecution history and examination results.

Possible measures to achieve these goals include diversification of the examination period. For instance, in the case of an international application filed with the JPO, the examination request period should be the same as or shorter than the currently stipulated period of three years. In the case of a purely domestic application, the examination request period should be longer than three years.

However, the introduction of a longer examination request period for applications other than international applications could cause a negative effect such as an increase in the number of unexamined patent applications, which will present impediments to the business of third parties, and a rise in the number of patent applications filed for the purpose of preventing other companies from conducting similar business.

In this respect, since the revision of the Patent Act in 2006, the Act has prohibited an amendment to change the "special technical feature of an invention" (shift amendment). The resulting increase in the foreseeability of the scope of patents has removed the impediments to the business of third parties to a certain extent.[37] Other possible measures include the placement of tighter restrictions on amendment after the lapse of a certain period and modification of the examination request system in such a way that increases its usability for third parties.

Restrictions on the right to demand an injunction

A patent gives the patentee exclusive rights including the right to demand an injunction, which gives strong protection to the patentee. In an extreme case, for example, when a company develops a product embodying numerous patented inventions, if the product infringes even one patent owned by another company, the commercialization of the product could become impossible. In order to avoid such a situation, it is common for companies to make it their intellectual property policy to file as many patent applications as possible for technologies that could be commercialized in the future. This practice is one of the reasons why companies file a large number of patent applications.

Under the current system, in the case of a product embodying many patented inventions, if even a single peripheral technology related to the core technology used in the product infringes a patent contained in another company's patent portfolio, an injunction will be issued against the product as a whole. It is necessary to reconsider the appropriateness of such a system. In today's world where so many patent applications and patent rights exist, it has become increasingly difficult to check all patents for possible infringement or to conduct business without using any patented inventions of third parties.

Currently, it has become more common for companies engaged in the business of making products embodying many patented inventions to conclude cross-license agreements. Some companies use patent pools as a solution. However, companies still face the risk of another company filing a petition for an injunction. This risk increases with the rise in the number of patents.

In order to mitigate this problem, it is worth considering restricting the exercise of the right to demand an injunction under certain circumstances[38] in the case of a product incorporating many patented inventions as mentioned above, unless the infringed patented invention constitutes the core technology of the product.[39] Since the wide use of patented inventions will contribute to industrial development, it might be appropriate in some cases to restrict the exercise of the right to demand an injunction even if the infringed patented invention constitutes the core technology as long as the right holder has no intention of commercializing the invention.

If the right to demand an injunction is restricted, companies would stop excessive efforts to build patent portfolio and file defensive patents which is a defensive measure against another company's use of the right to demand an injunction. Furthermore, the activity of patent trolls would also slow down.

However, it would be undesirable for a patent infringer to benefit from such restrictions on the right to demand an injunction because it is unfair to a patentee if the damages arising out of the infringement are equivalent to the license fee for the patent. Therefore, the right to demand an injunction should be restricted in such a way that best suits each case of infringement.

Closer collaboration with foreign patent offices

A global consensus has been reached that close collaboration among patent offices in many countries is indispensable for solving the backlog problem. Patent examination has been expedited through various international collaborative efforts such as the shared use of information on examination results and the results of searches conducted in the course of examination. However, the positive effects of international collaboration has been rather limited in terms of the number of applications that benefit from international collaboration. Further efforts need to be made to enhance global collaboration.

If work sharing in patent examination is promoted, each patent office should act as follows in the spirit of international collaboration. When an application is filed with a certain patent office as the office of first filing, it is important for that office to become the first patent office to examine the application and actively disseminate information on the prosecution history and examination results. Such work sharing would be desirable because it would allow each patent office to fulfill its international role and promote domestic companies to enter overseas markets.

In order to ensure early information dissemination despite the backlog delay in the examination procedure as a whole, it would be necessary in some cases to introduce a system that places a higher examination priority on international applications. The necessity for the introduction of such a system should be determined by consideration of the progress in the implementation of the measures already adopted.

One way of creating such a prioritization system is to diversify the examination request period as mentioned above. For instance, in the case of an international application designating the JPO as the office of first filing, the examination request period should be shorter than in the case of a purely domestic application.

The efficiency and reliability of examination results and search results differ from one country or technical field to another. It is relatively easy for patent offices to share information on search results and examination results in the case of an application related to the field of biotechnology or chemistry because such an application is examined based on the same database regardless of which country examines the application. On the other hand, in the case of an application related to the field of electrical and electronic technology, in which Japan overwhelms other countries by the volume of patent documents, the JPO often needs to conduct additional searches because it is likely that it will find prior-art documents that are more appropriate than those found by foreign patent offices. In view of this, it might be meaningful to discuss the possibility of applying a different style of work sharing depending on the technical field in question or in consideration of the characteristics of the database of each patent office.

Before promoting early information dissemination from Japan, we need to improve the situation where it is sometimes disadvantageous for an applicant to have his/her application examined in Japan. Since the JPO's prior art search is very thorough, it is proper that the JPO could disseminate information on a prior-art document that would not have been found in other countries. Even if the prior-art document denies the patentability of the invention claimed in the application, the detection of such a document is desirable for patent stability. However, applicants would be discouraged from choosing the JPO as the office of first filing for international applications if Japan imposes support requirements and description requirements more strictly than Western countries[40] or disseminates examination results with a narrower scope of claims because of the stricter requirement in Japan. Applicants would be further discouraged if the scope of a patent determined by the JPO is narrower than the scope that would have been determined if examination had been conducted in Western countries.[41]

In order to seek closer collaboration with foreign patent offices, further international harmonization needs to be achieved so that the aforementioned differences in information dissemination practice can be overcome.[42]

Introduction of stricter examination guidelines (raising inventive step hurdle)

As described earlier, due to the great difference in patent filing practice between Japan and the West, the inventions claimed in many of the large number of patents filed in Japan are improvement inventions that do not involve high technology.

The excessive patent filing activity is attributable not only to applicants' business practice but also to the level of the JPO's patent administration standard. For instance, the number of applications tends to increase if the inventive step hurdle used to determine patentability is too low or if the examination guidelines are unclear or unstable.[43] In other words, if the inventive step hurdle is too low, trivial patents would be issued. In such a situation, companies would have to file an even larger number of patent applications in order to prevent other companies from obtaining many trivial patents. In fact, it has been pointed out that the inventive step hurdle is too low and should be made more difficult. The low inventive step hurdle might induce a large number of patent filing.[44]

As mentioned earlier, patent protection for improvement inventions has improved and maintains the morale of employees working at production sites and other sites. Their relentless pursuit of technical development has boosted the level of production technology of Japanese companies. In view of these positive effects of patent protection for improvement inventions, some would oppose making it harder to pass the inventive step hurdle. If the inventive step hurdle becomes too high, it would have negative effects which would discourage inventors from patent filing activity and invention disclosure.

On the other hand, as mentioned above, some have requested that the inventive step hurdle should be higher. Opinions are divided over the appropriateness of the height of the current inventive step hurdle.

Since the circumstances surrounding improvement inventions differ from one industry or technical field to another, the appropriate height of the inventive step hurdle might vary from one industry to another depending on whether the technology in question is advanced technology or mature technology. The height of the inventive step hurdle should be determined in consideration of these factors. Furthermore, international harmonization needs to be taken into account because it would be inappropriate for Japan to adopt a much higher hurdle than that of other countries and cause the level of patent foreseeability to vary from one country to another.

Some oppose making any changes to the inventive step hurdle arguing that if such change is made, it would be difficult to conduct examination under the new inventive step hurdle in a stable manner for some time after the introduction of the new hurdle. However, in consideration of the current situation where the existence of many trivial patents on improvement inventions is causing impediments to corporate business activities, it would be meaningful to consider the introduction of a raised inventive step hurdle.

CONCLUSION

The center of invention has shifted from individuals to companies. As a result, companies started to use the patent system as a business tool in order to maintain their freedom to operate. Their efforts to build patent portfolios and to obtain defensive patents for the purpose of preserving their freedom to operate have led to the phenomenon of large-volume patent filing. In most business situations, the number of patents has become essential for companies to ensure their business superiority. A continuous increase in the number of patent applications is a global trend, although each country has somewhat different domestic situations. As a result, Japan and many other countries have faced the problem of a growing backlog.

If such large-volume patent filing promotes industrial development, the backlog problem should be solved through the efforts of the examination authorities. However, in order to solve the inconveniences in addition to the backlog problem caused by large-volume patent filing, it would be necessary to consider modifying the patent system to deal with the changing environment.

In this chapter, we have discussed the Japanese patent system with emphasis on the patent filing activity of Japanese companies and the resulting backlog problem. Many other problems have ensued from the changes in the environment surrounding the patent system. Those problems have intensified discussion on the current patent system.

In any event, the change of business environment and the speed of technological development will be accelerated. In such an environment, in order for companies to contribute to industrial development through sound competition, it is important to constantly review the patent system. Further discussion would be necessary to determine the future direction of the patent system.

NOTES

1. A part of this chapter was written with reference to the discussion conducted at the "Atarashii jidai no tokkyoseido ni kansuru kenkyukai" (Seminar on the Patent System of the New Era) held by the Institute of Intellectual Property. I would like to express my gratitude to those concerned.
2. Even in the pharmaceutical industry, there has been a growing trend that companies obtain many patents in order to build patent portfolios for the purpose of preventing generic drug companies from entering the market. See http://www.jetro.de/j/IP/News/20081201_EC_Competitive_Preliminary_Report_Pharmceutical_Sector_Inquiry.pdf (last accessed April 23, 2012).
3. In particular, Japan has a much higher ratio of applications filed by large companies than Western countries. The following table makes a comparison among Japan, the U.S., and Europe. It should be noted that the data concerning Japan and the U.S were calculated based on the number of applications filed with the JPO, the USPTO, or the EPO, while the data concerning Europe were calculated based on the number of applications filed in any of six countries, namely, Germany, France, the U.K., Italy, Spain,

or the Netherlands. The table shows that Japan has a higher number of applications filed by large companies than Western countries. This tendency is also observable in the domestic applications filed in each country.

	Japan	U.S.	Europe
Large companies (with more than 250 employees)	87.8%	81.1%	70.6%
Small and midsize companies	8.7%	14.0%	22.5%
Universities and other higher education institutions	2.3%	2.2%	3.2%
Public research institutions and other governmental institutions	0.7%	0.1%	2.2%
Judicial foundations and other organizations	0.5%	2.1%	–

Nagaoka and Tsukada, "Hatsumeisha kara mita nihon no inobeishon katei: RIETI hatsumeisha sabei no kekka gaiyou" (Innovation Process in Japan: Findings from the RIETI Inventors Survey), REITI Discussion Paper Series 07-J-046, Sadao Nagaoka and John P. Walsh, "Inventions and the innovation process in Japan and the US: Highlights from the US-Japan Inventor Survey," 2008.

4. Nagaoka and Tsukada, "Hatsumeisha kara mita nihon no inobeishon katei: RIETI hatsumeisha sabei no kekka gaiyou" (Innovation Process in Japan: Findings from the RIETI Inventors Survey), REITI Discussion Paper Series 07-J-046.
5. See note 2 for information on cases where a company builds patent portfolios in order to prevent generic drug companies from entering the market. This report contains such quotes as "We identify options to obtain or acquire patents for the sole purpose of limiting the freedom of operation of our competitors[. . .]Rights covering competitive alternatives are maintained in major markets until risk of competing products appearing is minimal" and "I suppose we have all had conversations around 'how can we block generic manufacturers.' [. . .]Get claims on key intermediates that cover a number of routes. Process patents are not the biggest block but can put generics off if a superior chemistry job is done." These quotes illustrate one aspect of the current corporate patent strategy.
6. Such patent filing activity is called an "arms race" in *The Economist*, "Survey: Patents and Technology" Oct 20, 2005. This expression reflects the competitive nature of patent filing activity.
7. A patent is a tool to ensure exclusive use of a technology. However, companies do not necessarily consider a patent as the only means to ensure exclusive use rather seeing a patent as merely one of many means of achieve exclusivity. According to a survey on "Technological opportunities and appropriating the returns from innovation" (1997) carried out by the Goto & Nagata group of the National Institute of Science and Technology Policy (NISTEP) (a summary is available at http://www.nistep.go.jp/achiev/abs/jpn/rep048j/rep048aj.html (last accessed April 23, 2012)), respondents mentioned the following measures as the means to ensure exclusivity: early commercialization (40.7 percent), patent protection (37.8 percent), ownership and maintenance of production facilities and know-how (33.1 percent), ownership and maintenance of sales and service networks (30 percent), and confidentiality of technological information (25.6 percent). The results of a similar survey were presented in Nagaoka and Tsukada, "Hatsumeisha kara mita nihon no inobeishon katei: RIETI hatsumeisha sabei no kekka gaiyou" (Innovation Process in Japan: Findings from the RIETI Inventors Survey), REITI Discussion Paper Series 07-J-046.
8. According to the results of a U.S. survey presented in *Patent Failure*, J. Bessen and M. Meurer (2008, Princeton University Press), a comparison between the profits earned by public firms from their patents and the total patent litigation costs shouldered by defendant companies reveals that the pharmaceutical and chemical industries enjoy benefits from the patent system, while other industries gain no benefits.

   According to a study on the contribution of the patent system to the success or failure of the commercialization of products and the success or failure of development projects, such contribution varies from one industry to another. For instance, the patent system plays a relatively important role in the pharmaceutical and chemical industries, while it does not play such a significant role in other industries. According to Edwin Mansfield (1986), "Patents and innovation: an empirical study," in response to the question, "Did a development project succeed without patents?," 60 percent of the pharmaceutical companies answered yes, while 65 percent of their projects failed to commercialize products. To the same question, 38 percent of the chemical companies answered yes, while 30 percent of their projects failed to commercialize products. In the case of other industries, i.e., machinery, metal, electrical appliance, apparatus, office equipment, automobile, rubber, and textile, 0–18 percent of the companies answered yes, while 0–25 percent of their projects failed to commercialize products.

9. In 1994, the utility model system was changed from a conventional examination system into a non-examination system. Since the implementation of the non-examination utility model system, the number of utility model applications decreased from 17,000 in 1994 to around 10,000 in recent years. When the non-examination utility model system was introduced in 1994, the number of utility model applications plummeted by slightly less than 70,000 from the previous year, in which the former examination system was still in place. However, the number of patent applications in 1994 was smaller than in the previous year. It is interesting that an expected rise in the number of patent applications did not occur.

   The sharp decline caused by the introduction of the non-examination utility model system is attributable to such factors as the lack of stability of the rights granted without examination, the need to show the technological evaluation certificate provided by the JPO before exercising a utility model right, the short protection period, and the less variety of technical objects of protection in comparison with patents. On the other hand, it is speculated that the reason the decline did not cause an increase in the number of patent applications was because companies, which used to file many utility model applications although there was little need, have started to file applications more selectively since the legal revision.

10. JPO, "Japan Patent Office Annual Report 2007".

11. The number of domestic patent applications filed by Japanese companies peaked at 387,000 in 2000 and declined by 40,000 to 347,000 in 2006. In contrast, the number of foreign applications increased by 62,000 from 105,000 in 2000 to 167,000 in 2006. This phenomenon is attributable to companies' growing awareness of the importance of active patent filing activity in foreign countries with the globalization of their business. Furthermore, patent infringement disputes in other countries have made them increasingly aware of the importance of patent filing activity in foreign countries. In addition to such growing awareness, the increasing losses caused by counterfeits and pirated goods in Southeast Asia prompted Japanese companies to decrease the number of domestic applications and increase the number of foreign applications. The following table shows a breakdown of application-related costs between domestic applications and foreign applications. This cost analysis also reflected the fact that patent filing activity has shifted from Japan to other countries.

	FY2004	FY2005	FY2006
Ratio of the application and examination costs for domestic applications	43%	42%	39%
Ratio of the application and examination costs for foreign applications	57%	58%	61%

Source: This table was created based on the statistical tables presented in the JPO, "Intellectual Property Activity Survey" for each year.

Furthermore, according to the following table listing major countries for a country-specific comparison between the number of domestic applications and the number of foreign applications, the country-specific proportion of foreign applications reveals Japan's strong tendency of domestic patent filing activity in comparison with other developed countries. However, Japanese companies are second only to U.S. companies in terms of the number of foreign applications, indicating that Japanese companies are active in filing foreign applications as well.

Nationality of applicants	Number of domestic applications	Number of foreign applications
Japan	347,060	166,987
U.S.	221,784	169,031
Germany	48,012	82,794
South Korea	125,476	47,233
France	14,529	30,148
U.K.	17,484	23,601
Canada	5,522	16,033

Source: Country-specific data on domestic and foreign patent applications in 2006 (created based on the WIPO, "WIPO PATENT REPORT 2008").

Such an increase in the number of foreign applications may be attributable to the experience of some major Japanese companies who were involved in a series of patent infringement *lawsuits filed by patentees seeking and forced to pay large damages around 1990 in the U.S. Since then, intellectual property management has been recognized as a part of corporate management. Such a renewed recognition seems to have given great momentum to* Japanese companies' strategic patent filing activity in foreign countries.

12. Introduced by the legal revision in 1982.
13. The patent grant ratio decreased from 63.8 percent in 1999 to 48.5 percent in 2006 (JPO, "Japan Patent Office Annual Report 2008").
14. It took only those large companies subject to Figure 6.2 to achieve a reduction of more than 50,000 applications over the period from 1990 to 2006. This reduction is attributable not only to the shift to foreign applications and the adoption of a stricter business selection and concentration policy but also to the JPO's implementation of the Selective Examination Request Program (AP80) from 1988 on the top 100 major corporate applicants in order to ask them to file examination requests more selectively.
15. For more information on the recent situation, please refer to the JPO, "Japan Patent Office Annual Report 2008," p. 131.
16. As has often been mentioned in recent years, the patent system is designed to grant a patent on an invention in exchange for its publication. If a company files a patent application but does not obtain a patent, the company is simply publicizing technological information to third parties. Unlike the good old days of paper publication, in today's world of advanced IT technology, an invention will be publicized to the whole world instantly, which will lead to the wide use of the invention by third parties immediately after the publication. In light of this situation, companies need to assess the merits of filing a patent application for an invention and choose to protect the invention as know-how in some cases. Protection of an invention as know-how would be appropriate for inventions related to production methods or processes. If the name of the invention claimed in a patent application includes the term, "production method" or "process," such an application may be speculated as an application concerning a production method or process. A search for this type of application by use of the IPDL shows that the number of patent applications concerning production methods or processes accounts for 9.3 percent of the total number of patent applications filed in 1995

and 11.0 percent of the total number of patent applications filed in 2006. This indicates an overall increase in the ratio of patent applications concerning production methods or processes despite the increasing need for protecting such inventions as know-how.

It is reported that the number of inventions which were not subject to patent application but were protected as trade secrets accounted for 10 percent of the total number of inventions reported in companies as shown in the following table.

Results of the Survey of Intellectual Property-*Related Activities (the JPO, 2007)*

Ratio of the internally-reported inventions for which patent applications were not filed			Ratio of the internally-reported inventions for which patent applications were filed
	Ratio of the inventions protected as know-how	Ratio of the inventions publicized	
26%	10%	2%	62%

17. According to the JPO, "Results of the Survey of *Intellectual Property*-Related Activities 2007," the number of patent applications is expected to increase by 0.1 percent over the period from 2006 to 2008. However, due to the ongoing global recession and other factors, the number of applications is likely to be lower than this expectation.
18. Nagaoka and Tsukada, "Hatsumeisha kara mita nihon no inobeishon katei: RIETI hatsumeisha sabei no kekka gaiyou" (Innovation Process in Japan: Findings from the RIETI Inventors Survey), REITI Discussion Paper Series 07-J-046, Sadao Nagaoka and John P. Walsh, "Inventions and the innovation process in Japan and the US: Highlights from the US-Japan Inventor Survey," 2008. Regarding this survey, it should be noted that the data concerning Japan and the U.S were calculated based on the number of applications filed with the JPO, the USPTO, or the EPO, while the data concerning Europe were calculated based on the number of applications filed in the following six countries: Germany, France, the U.K., Italy, Spain, and the Netherlands. The average age of the inventors was 39.5 in Japan, 52.7 in the U.S., and 45.4 in Europe. This data shows that relatively young inventors file important applications in Japan in comparison with Western countries. The proportion of important applications filed by those with a doctorate is 12.4 percent in Japan, 44.9 percent in the U.S., and 26 percent in Europe, indicating that inventors in Western countries are more highly educated than their counterparts in Japan. According to the "Kyouiku shihyo no kokusai hikaku 2008" (International comparison of educational indexes) published by the Ministry of Education, Culture, Sports, Science and Technology, the number of doctors of Science, Engineering, or Agriculture stood at 7,149 in Japan in 2005, 19,943 in the U.S. in 2004, 8,700 in the U.K. in 2005, 5,707 in France in 2005, and 10,242 in Germany in 2002.
19. Calculated based on the number of patents obtained in the U.S. presented in the JPO, "Japan Patent Office Annual Report 2008" and on the domestic research and development costs presented in the Statistics Bureau, Ministry of Internal Affairs and Communications, "World Statistics 2008."
20. JPO, "Japan Patent Office Annual Report 2007."
21. Regarding studies on the purposes of patent application, refer to Nagaoka and Tsukada, "Hatsumeisha kara mita nihon no inobeishon katei: RIETI hatsumeisha sabei no kekka gaiyou" (Innovation Process in Japan: Findings from the RIETI Inventors Survey), REITI Discussion Paper Series 07-J-046, Sadao Nagaoka and John P. Walsh, "Inventions and the innovation process in Japan and the US: Highlights from the US-Japan Inventor Survey," 2008, Fig. 22 (the following table was created based on these sources). The following table shows a list of purposes for filing of patent applications that are rated as extremely important inventions. The important applications are

broken into international applications and non-trilateral office applications (purely domestic applications, i.e., applications filed with neither the USPTO nor the EPO). Between those types of important applications, a comparison is made for each of the listed purposes for patent acquisition. The important applications filed in Japan and those filed in the U.S. are mostly similar in terms of the ratio listed for each purpose. However, a close analysis reveals that the ratio of internal exclusive use in Japan is lower than in the U.S. In the case of non-trilateral office applications, the ratio of internal exclusive use is even lower. This suggests that it is more common in Japan than in the U.S. to see a patent application filed for a purpose other than internal exclusive use. According to the PATVAL survey, as far as important patents are concerned, the patent utilization rate in Europe (patent applications filed in any of the six countries, namely, Germany, France, the U.K., Italy, Spain, and the Netherlands) is 63.9 percent.

	Important applications filed in Japan	Non-trilateral office applications filed in Japan	Important applications filed in the U.S.
Internal exclusive use of the invention	44%	35%	60%
Blocking patent	20%	21%	22%
Prevention of circumvention	8%	8%	9%
One-way licensing	16%	15%	16%
Cross licensing	14%	12%	11%
Pure defense	20%	21%	22%
Reputation of the company	7%	5%	11%
Reputation of the inventor	2%	2%	6%

22. The table presented in the preceding footnote shows that Japan and the U.S. are similar in terms of the ratio of so-called important international applications filed for the purpose of defense. The ratio of defensive patents would be even higher for purely domestic applications because of Japan's strong tendency of domestic patent filing activity in comparison with Western countries. (The ratio of purely domestic applications is 77 percent for Japanese companies, 54 percent for U.S. companies, and 40 percent for European companies according to the "Japan Patent Office Annual Report 2008," p. 134.)
23. "Kougyo shoyuken seido ni kansuru toushin" (Policy report concerning the industrial property system) (November 1968).
24. According to the JPO, "Patent Strategic Plan," the eventual examination request ratio was expected to be around 49 percent for the applications subject to a 3-year examination request period. However, the ratio was actually more than 66 percent (JPO, "Japan Patent Office Annual Report 2008," p. 4).

    In anticipation of an increase in the number of examination requests, the JPO has taken the following measures to encourage applicants not to file examination requests for unpatentable applications in the first place: the creation of the Industrial Property Digital Library, which allows users to conduct online prior-art searches easily, the revision of the examination request fee and the patent fee in such a way that is beneficial for those who file examination requests for patentable applications, and the introduction of a system to return half of the examination request fee if an application is withdrawn even after the filing of an examination request. However, these measures have turned out to be less effective than expected.
25. In the case of applications filed by German applicants in 2000, the breakdown of the applications according to the length of the period between the application date and the examination request date is as follows: examination requested in the application year (10 percent), the first year (9 percent), second year (9 percent), third year (2 percent), fourth year (2 percent), fifth year (1 percent), sixth year (10 percent), and seventh year

(57 percent). In the case of applications filed in 2004, examination requested in the application year (8 percent), the first year (9 percent), second year (25 percent), and third year (59 percent). However, it has been reported that, in the case of German domestic applications, the proportion of the applications for which examination requests are filed in the application year is 67 percent. This indicates that, in the case of applications filed by German applicants, the length of the period between the application date and the examination request date greatly varies depending on whether the application in question is filed with the German patent office or filed with the JPO. Further analysis would be necessary to determine the reasons for this distinction. See http://www.jpo.go.jp/shiryou/toushin/toushintou/ki6_2.htm (last accessed April 23, 2012).

26. Both U.S. and German applicants eventually requested examination for 90 percent of the total number of applications filed in 2004. This suggests that they have grown more selective in their patent filing activity since the early days of filing activity in Japan.
27. Some argue that the introduction of the examination request system itself has promoted the filing of unnecessary patent applications. Figure 6.1 shows that the number of patent applications has been constantly increasing since before the introduction of the examination request system which justifies the aforementioned argument to some extent. However, the correlation between the introduction of the system and the increase in the number of patent applications is unclear.
28. The purpose of the revision of the fees was to stop the practice of supplementing the examination costs of low-grant rate applicants with the patent fees of high-grant rate applicants. Such a mechanism was necessary because the examination request fee was too low to cover actual examination costs. The revised fees were set in such a way that the total of the examination request fee and the patent fee would be lower only if an applicant filed an examination request for a patentable application. On the other hand, if an applicant filed an examination request for an application that would eventually be denied, the costs would be about twice as high. The revised fees were expected to encourage applicants to file examination requests for patentable applications.

	Application fee	Examination request fee	Patent fee	Total
Current fee (former fee)	¥21,000	¥99,500	¥356,200	¥476,700
Revised fee (new fee)	¥16,000	¥199,000	¥166,600	¥381,600

A comparison between the new fee and the former fee charged on an average application (number of claims: 7.6, maintenance period: 9 years) ("Patent Strategic Plan," JPO, from July 8, 2003). On the assumption that an applicant files the same number of examination requests as before and pays the patent fee after the grant of a patent, if calculated based on the table above, the revision of the fees would cause an increase in the total cost if the applicant's grant rate is 50 percent or lower and a decrease in the total cost if the applicant's grant rate is higher than 50 percent.

29. JPO, "Japan Patent Office Annual Report," p. 4.
30. Although details are not described in this chapter, an industry-specific detailed analysis shows the same tendency.
31. The examination waiting period is an index (measured value) showing the length of the average period from the date of examination request to first office action actually conducted. This is different from an index showing how long an applicant who files an examination request will have to wait before first office action (predicted value). Therefore, a decline in the number of examination requests in 2006 and thereafter would not immediately shorten the examination waiting period. The length of the examination waiting period is expected to increase until 2009. According to the Intellectual Property Strategic Program, which is published on an annual basis, the numerical target of the examination waiting period is set at less than 30 months for 2008 and 11 months for 2013.

32. The average number of claims contained in a patent application increased by 1.7 from 8.1 for an application filed in 2000 to 9.8 for an application filed in 2007 (JPO, "Japan Patent Office Annual Report 2008," p. 6).
33. The number of PCT International Search Reports more than tripled from 8,468 in 2000 to 26,033 in 2007 (JPO, "Japan Patent Office Annual Report 2008," p. 7).
34. The number of cases examined per examiner is 219 (JPO, "Japan Patent Office Annual Report 2008," p. 151).
35. JPO, "Japan Patent Office Annual Report 2008" (Statistical Data), p. 161.
36. The Patent Act (Article 48-6) specifies the prioritized examination system designed to satisfy the demand for patent protection with a varying degree of urgency. Furthermore, the JPO introduced the accelerated examination systems (including the Patent Prosecution Highway program) from 1986 and a pilot project called the *Super* Accelerated Examination from 2008.
37. The examination request period is not the only impediment to the business of third parties. The fundamental resolution of this problem would be impossible as long as the divisional application system exists.
38. In the eBay v. MercExchange Case (May 15, 2006), which is a patent infringement lawsuit concerning the "Buy-It-Now function" of eBay, a major online auction company in the U.S. The Supreme Court rejected conventional automatic injunctive relief and held that the following four-factor test must be applied to a patent infringement case in order to determine whether to grant injunctive relief or not.
    A plaintiff seeking a permanent injunction is required to demonstrate:

    1. that it has suffered an irreparable injury;
    2. that remedies available at law, such as monetary damages, are inadequate to compensate for that injury;
    3. that, considering the balance of hardships between the plaintiff and the defendant, a remedy in equity is warranted; and
    4. that the public interest would not be disserved by a permanent injunction.

39. According to JPO, "New Intellectual Property Policy for Pro-Innovation" (2008), a committee will be established to discuss legal theories concerning patent abuse to clarify the principles adopted by those theories.
40. For example, in the case where the plaintiff demanded the revocation of the JPO's decision to cancel a patent, 2005 (Gyo-Ke) No.10042, while a patent application for a production method for polarizing film was filed with the JPO, the USPTO, and the EPO, only the JPO found it to be violating the description requirement. Also, in comparison with the USPTO and the EPO, the JPO is more likely to find the invention claimed in a gene patent application as not involving an inventive step. (Intellectual Property Management, vol. 57, no. 4, April 2007, Japan Intellectual Property Association.)
41. Another issue related to the U.S. system is that, if an application is examined by the JPO first, it would make the U.S. procedure more expensive. This is because the U.S. has a system called Information Disclosure Statement (IDS). Under this system, any applicant who has chosen the JPO as the first office to examine his/her application is required to translate and submit to the USPTO various documents including prior art documents used in the JPO's examination procedure. This means that, the JPO's effort for early information dissemination about examination results ends up causing applicants to pay more for the USPTO's examination procedure. This suggests that the IDS may also discourage applicants from choosing the JPO as the office of first filing.
42. It is rather ironic that, in the case of Japan, international work sharing would not contribute to solving the backlog problem in the short term for the following reasons. First, international work sharing would prevent the JPO from using the results of patent examination already conducted by another country. Second, in light of the current balance of patent filing activity between Japan and other countries, the number of patent applications filed by Japan in other countries is much higher than the patent applications filed by other countries to Japan. If these applications are to be

preferentially examined by the JPO, applications for examination requests which would not have been filed with the JPO under the former system would be newly subject to patent examination, increasing the number of applications that need to be examined.

43. The clearer examination guidelines greatly affected the number of applications for business-related inventions which was about 19,600 in 2000. The clarity of the examination guidelines was enhanced in 2000. In 2001, the JPO publicized the "Tokkyo ni naranai bijinesu kanren hatsumei no jireishu" (Examples of unpatentable business-related inventions). Thanks to these efforts, the number of applications for business-related inventions decreased to about 7,000 in 2006, see http://www.jpo.go.jp/tetuzuki/t_tokkyo/bijinesu/biz_pat.htm (last accessed April 23, 2012) and http://www.jpo.go.jp/tetuzuki/t_tokkyo/bijinesu/tt1303-090_jirei.htm (last accessed April 23, 2012).
44. According to the Ministry of Economy, Trade and Industry, Manufacturing Industries Bureau, "Seizougyou ni kakaru chiteki zaisanken no genjo to kigyou no torikumitou ni tsuite" (Current situation of intellectual property rights in the manufacturing industries and corporate initiatives) (October 2001), many companies in various industries have pointed out that, since examination was accelerated, inventions that would have been found unpatentable before such acceleration are now found to be patentable. These companies are calling for the introduction of stricter inventive step criteria.

PART III

Developing countries and the future of their patent systems

7. The Indian patent system: the road ahead

N.S. Gopalakrishnan and T.G. Agitha

INTRODUCTION

The patent law of a nation often reflects the industrial and scientific policies adopted by that nation. The development of scientific and technological capabilities and growth of domestic industries are the major objectives based on which countries mould their patent laws. However, the modern patent system appears to be the result of international politics aimed at protecting trade interests rather than developmental interests.[1] The "one-size-fits all" approach of the TRIPS, therefore, is considered by many as problematic, as they feel that "[i]t is far from self-evident that protecting IPRs is an effective development policy at all levels (or perhaps 'stages') of economic development".[2]

The modern patent system is the result of the strong conviction, shared by many, including economists, and lawyers that strong and broad patents are conducive to economic progress.[3] Rich dividends paid by the patent system to the developed countries are projected as examples for forcing the developing nations to follow a similar patent system so as to boost their industrial and scientific growth.[4] The historical contexts in which the patent system developed and the space availed of by these countries to set standards so as to use the system to their advantage were often ignored in this process.[5] While it is true that there are many positive elements in the modern patent system, the experience of the developed countries in the last three decades also reflects the limitation of the modern patent system in promoting uniform economic growth.[6] The experiences of emerging economies from Asia, particularly Japan and China, also suggest that the patent system has to be intelligently used to promote the economic and industrial growth of the nation.[7] The Indian experience in the field of pharmaceutical sector points to this.[8] Before the introduction of the Patents Act, 1970 that came into force in 1972, TNCs dominated the industry in India and the 1911 Patents and Designs Act was used by them to prevent indigenous firms from manufacturing patented drugs invented abroad.[9] The Act of 1970, by de-recognizing product patents in pharmaceuticals and providing for shorter terms of protection for pharmaceutical process patents, etc., provided the indigenous firms with the opportunity to realize their potential and in the process further enhance their capabilities.[10] The technical skills developed indigenously, enabled the Indian Pharmaceutical industry not only to successfully check the domination of MNCs in India but also to start exporting to the regulated markets of the developing countries.[11]

However, since the establishment of the World Trade Organization and the adoption of the Trade Related Aspects of Intellectual Property Rights (TRIPS) Agreement, there is an increasing tendency to advocate for a more uniform/standardized patent system to promote global trade under the guise of ensuring economic stability of nations, particularly of developing countries. Though there are many academic critiques to this approach,[12] it can be seen that during the last decade governments of many developing countries have shown a tendency to believe this and they have made considerable efforts to change their patent laws, blindly following models from developed countries. These countries seem to be ignorant of the problems that have been emerging in the developed countries from the liberal use of the modern patent system and the efforts they themselves are making to reform the system to make it useful and efficient.[13] The Report of the European Patent Office, *Scenarios for the Future*, for example, expresses the concern of the EPO over the erosion of patentability standards resulting in the patenting of trivial "inventions," the growing use of patents leading to blocking of further technological advancements, etc. Similarly, the FTC reports share the same concern.[14]

Thus any attempt to examine the future of the patent system in developing countries needs to address many critical issues. These include not only domestic concerns of economic growth and providing access to patented products at an affordable cost to majority of the population, but also facilitating international trade and its impact on domestic economy. Some rightly hold the view that how the "developing countries implement the TRIPS standards through their domestic laws will determine the balance between private incentives to innovate and the public interest in free competition."[15] And this balancing process will necessarily have global implications.

INDIAN PATENT SYSTEM: POLICY CONCERNS

Although the patent system was introduced in India by the British administration about a century before independence, it could not ensure the desired result of industrialization and elimination of unemployment and poverty. On the other hand, as the experiences from the Indian pharmaceutical industry clearly indicate, it only promoted the Trans National Corporations, which were only interested in exporting their products to India rather than setting up manufacturing plants in India.[16] Even after Independence, the same law continued for more than two decades. The review committees[17] set up after independence to examine the then existing patent system revealed that the majority of patents were owned by foreigners.[18] The patent monopoly was used to exploit the Indian market and prevent Indian industrial growth.[19] It also resulted in the patented products becoming unaffordable to the majority of the Indian population. In fact India was facing the problem of providing basic needs like food, health, housing, education etc. to her population. Being primarily an underdeveloped agrarian economy, independent India's various policies on areas like education, health, agriculture, science, technology and industry were aimed at promoting economic growth and facilitating access at affordable cost.

A mixed economy based on public and private participation was followed for a considerable period of time to build the modern India.[20] This motivation is also reflected in the policy adopted by the government in the patent system. The Patent Act 1970 is the result of much deliberation and was oriented to ensure that patent monopoly is used to encourage economic growth of the nation and facilitate access to products at affordable cost.[21] This is reflected in various provisions of the Act dealing with patentable subject matter, exceptions and limitations, compulsory license, government use etc. Even after India refocused her economic and industrial policies and joined the WTO and amended her Patent Act in 1999, 2002 and 2005, the desire to provide access to patented products at affordable cost while promoting industrial and scientific growth remains the basic objective of the Indian patent system.[22] It is true that the obligations imposed on India based on the TRIPS Agreement put considerable restraint on India's approach to create a balanced patent law keeping in mind the above objectives. But considerable efforts are being made to find the available gaps in the TRIPS Agreement and to calibrate the revised patent law to project these policy objectives. In this chapter we examine some of the major provisions in the Patent Act reflecting the above objectives and suggest suitable changes so that the Indian patent system becomes a model not only for developing countries but also for the developed countries faced with the challenge of their patent systems being "the victim of its own success."[23]

PATENTABLE SUBJECT MATTER

The Patent Act 1970 has followed a unique approach in identifying the patentable subject matter, which remains even after its last/recent amendment in 2005. While the important definitions are given in section 2 of the Act, sections 3, 4 and 5 collectively contribute in identifying inventions that are not eligible for patent protection. The objective seems to be the protection of public interest involved in identifying and limiting the areas that require monopoly protection. The most important aspect of public interest is in preserving the much needed open space for the progress of science and technology while rewarding the inventive genius by laying down the standards of patentability like novelty, inventive step and industrial applicability. Public interest is said to be effectively protected when, along with rewarding inventive genius, enough open space is kept unprotected by patent to ensure scientific and technological progress. This could be achieved by laying down the correct standards of novelty, inventive step and industrial application. These standards could be set so as to ensure that monopoly is not created if it goes against the interest of facilitating competition by providing competing products in the market. It is commonly accepted that a patent monopoly is justified only when it acts as a genuine incentive to research and brings in new products to market. Therefore, "patents should be granted only for inventions that are really novel, that are really non-obvious or really have a substantial inventive step, that are really useful or really technological, and that are really enabled."[24]

It is worth noting that since there were no international norms to determine the level of creativity necessary to satisfy these conditions, countries followed different standards to maintain this balance. In the initial stages of development of the patent system many countries insisted on higher levels of inventiveness to grant patent.[25] The standard followed was the evidence of an intellectual leap of inventive genius by the individual researcher.[26] But with the development of science and technology and a shift in the approach towards research, based on investment and market needs, the test slowly got diluted enabling even protection of incremental innovations with minimal inventive faculty.[27] This resulted in lowering the standard of patentability in many developed countries.[28] This is evident from the standards used to find out "obviousness" or "inventive step" in the U.S.[29] and England.[30] The term "person skilled in the art" is also interpreted liberally to encourage investment in incremental research rather than to use the patent system to encourage a substantial leap in technology, especially in areas like biotech and pharmaceutical research.[31] The reason seems to be the way in which inventive research progressed in some important fields of technology like chemicals and pharmaceuticals.[32] This also seems to be the reason for the problem faced by the patent system today in the context of the grant of patents in the fields of biotechnology and computer software.[33] Liberal patenting standards resulted in large numbers of patent being granted to derivative inventions with very minimal creativity leading to patent thicket and trolls.[34] The net result is the demand for revisiting the standards of patentability in many developed countries to solve the present crisis.[35] This is clearly reflected in the recent observation of the U.S. Supreme Court in *KSR International v. Teleflex*:[36]

> We build and create by bringing to the tangible and palpable reality around us new works based on instinct, simple logic, ordinary inferences, extraordinary ideas, and sometimes even genius. *These advances, once part of our shared knowledge, define a new threshold from which innovation starts once more.* And as progress beginning from higher levels of achievements is expected in the normal course, the results of ordinary innovation are not the subject of exclusive rights under the patent laws. Where it otherwise patents might stifle, rather promote, the progress of useful arts. [37] (authors' emphasis).

It is interesting to note that internationally there is no specific standard stipulated for finding out "obviousness" or "person skilled in the art" and the Paris Convention has not prescribed any patentability standards. It was the TRIPS Agreement in Article 27[38] that introduced these standards for the first time. The important obligation under Article 27 is to make available product or process patent for any inventions provided they are "new, involve an inventive step and capable of industrial application." The mandate is not to discriminate the invention based on a particular filed of technology. This means that the Member States cannot deny patent to an invention in a particular field of technology if it satisfies the three tests. Since no definition is laid down by the TRIPS Agreement for these terms, a Member State is free to lay down its own standards of patentability.

Thus the TRIPS Agreement leaves the member countries with enough space to follow different approaches to ensure that the application of the three tests facilitate the progress of science and technology on the one side and the developmental needs of those countries on the other, maintaining a competitive industrial environment to protect the larger public interest of the nation. The fact that the Indian Parliament also follows the same approach is evident from the amendments introduced into the Patents Act, 1970. These amendments were introduced with a view to protecting Indian public interest while conforming with Article 27 of the TRIPS Agreement.

Before the recent amendments, the definition for invention in section 2(j)[39] in the Patent Act 1970 resembled more the U.S. wording[40] and used only the terms "new" and "useful," although without definition. The amendment introduced in 2002 to the definition of invention in section 2(j)[41] of the Patents Act specifically included the three tests – novelty, inventive step, capable of industrial application – and brought it into line with Article 27. All these terms are further defined making the legislative intent clear as to the standard of inventiveness to be followed in India. The introduction of the definitions of new invention,[42] inventive step[43] and capable of industrial application[44] are indicative of this. It is the definition of inventive step that is crucial in determining the level of inventiveness. The definition insists on "technical advance" or "economic significance" or both in the features of the invention and demands that it is "not obvious to a person skilled in the art." The requirement for "technical advancement" could be construed to exclude incremental innovations. However, some are of the opinion that the inclusion of mere "economic significance" sufficient to constitute "inventive step" may lead to "erroneous outcomes" arising from "exaggerated claims regarding economic value of the invention that the patent applicant would be tempted to make to take advantage of this provision."[45] Though these terms are not defined, one could locate legislative guidelines to find the scope and content of these terms from some of the provisions in section 3 of the Act which declares that certain inventions are not patentable. The exclusion of inventions that are frivolous,[46] discoveries,[47] new use of a known substance,[48] admixture resulting only in aggregation of properties of the components,[49] mere arrangement or re-arrangement,[50] traditional knowledge[51] etc., from patent protection is indicative of the guidelines. An examination of these provisions makes it clear that these inventions are linked to the requirement of novelty or an inventive step. None of these provisions is confined to any specific field of technology. Irrespective of the field of technology, if an invention falls within the scope of these provisions, it is not treated as invention for grant of patent because it lacks novelty or inventive step or both. Thus if one read the definitions in section 2 together with provisions in section 3, it clearly reflects the legislative intent to insist on a higher standard for an invention to qualify for patent protection. It is interesting to note that though the definitions of novelty and inventive step are recent entries into the Indian law, these concepts were evolved by judicial interpretation even before the amendments. Thus it could be seen that the latest amendments are influenced by the standard laid down by the Supreme Court in *Bishwanath Prasad Radhey Shyam v. Hindustan Metal Industries*[52] based on the provisions of the Act before amendment. The Supreme Court laid down strict standards for patenting a new invention, even if the invention is an improvement of existing technology. The observation of the Court is quite pertinent:

> It is important to bear in mind that in order to be patentable an improvement on something known before or a combination of different matters already known, should be something more than a mere workshop improvement; and must independently satisfy the test of invention or an "inventive step". *To be patentable the improvement or the combination must produce a new result, or a new article or a better or cheaper article than before.*[53]

The observation of the Court on the standard of inventive step quoting from the Encyclopedia Britannica is worth quoting:

> A patentable invention, therefore, must involve something which is outside the probable capacity of a craftsman – which is expressed by saying it must have "subject-matter" or involve an "inventive step".
> The expression "does not involve any inventive step" used in Section 26(1) (*e*) of the Act and its equivalent word "obvious," have acquired special significance in the terminology of patent law. The *"obviousness" has to be strictly and objectively judged.*[54]

This makes it clear that the amendments introduced in the Act set the standards of patentable subject matter in India exercising the flexibility available in Article 27 of TRIPS. There is no discrimination based on field of technology. The standard is uniformly applicable to all inventions. Hence there is no discrimination on recognition of the right to patent based on different field of technology. It is also clear that the standard is not based on minimal creativity but on higher standards. This also seems to be in line with the recent trend set by the U.S. Supreme Court and the demand to follow higher standards to preserve the credibility of the patent system. It is important that the Indian Patent Office while granting patents must keep this in mind. This will prevent the Indian patent system from repeating the mistake committed by the developed countries and also ensure that India does not fall into the same trap of the modern patent system in developed countries.

However, the amended provisions are not free from charges of TRIPS non-compatibility, arising from various quarters: a widely discussed and very controversial provision in the amended Act is Section 3(d). The main criticisms against it relate to TRIPS compatibility and potential negative impact on indigenous innovation.[55] This provision excludes mere discovery of new forms[56] (derivatives)[57] of known substances from patentability unless they result in the enhancement of known efficacy of the substance. This "efficacy" provision is further explained to mean differing "significantly in properties with regard to efficacy." This restriction is aimed at circumventing ever-greening of patents. Section 3(d) also excludes from patentability new methods of using known substances. This makes the Indian law different from the U.S.[58] and the European systems.[59] There is much criticism with respect to the term "efficacy." In the *Novartis case*,[60] the criticism that this term is not properly defined and no sufficient guidelines are provided for its interpretation was levelled against this legal provision.[61] Some academics share this criticism.[62] The petitioner also criticized the explanation to the provision in the same lines. However, rejecting this argument, the Court held:

> The argument that the amended section must be held to be bad in Law since for want of guidelines it gives scope to the Statutory Authority to exercise it's power arbitrarily, has to be necessarily rejected since, we find that there are in-built materials in the amended section and the Explanation itself, which would control / guide the discretion to be exercised by the Statutory Authority.[63]

The Court concluded the issue by holding that the amended section has in-built measures to guide the Statutory Authority in exercising its power under the Act and therefore it does not suffer from the vice of vagueness, ambiguity and arbitrariness. For holding thus the court interpreted "efficacy" to mean "the ability of a drug to produce the desired therapeutic effect" relying on Darland's Medical Dictionary. Then the Court went on interpreting "therapeutic" thus:

> Darland's Medical Dictionary defines the expression "efficacy" in the field of Pharmacology as "the ability of a drug to produce the desired therapeutic effect" and "efficacy" is independent of potency of the drug. Dictionary meaning of "Therapeutic", is healing of disease – having a good effect on the body. Going by the meaning for the words "efficacy" and "therapeutic" extracted above, what the patent applicant is expected to show is, how effective the new discovery made would be in healing a disease / having a good effect on the body? In other words, the patent applicant is definitely aware as to what is the "therapeutic effect" of the drug for which he had already got a patent and what is the difference between the therapeutic effect of the patented drug and the drug in respect of which patent is asked for. Therefore it is a simple exercise of, though preceded by research, – we state – for any Patent applicant to place on record what is the therapeutic effect / efficacy of a known substance and what is the enhancement in that known efficacy. The amended section not only covers the field of pharmacology but also the other fields. As we could see from the amended section, it is made applicable to even machine, apparatus or known process with a rider that mere use of a known process is not an invention unless such a known process results in a new product or employs at least one new reactant. Therefore the amended Section is a comprehensive provision covering all fields of technology, including the field of pharmacology. In our opinion, the explanation would come in aid only to understand what is meant by the expression "resulting in the enhancement of a known efficacy" in the amended section and therefore we have no doubt at all that the Explanation would operate only when discovery is made in the pharmacology field.[64]

The Court finally concluded:

> Scientifically it is possible to show with certainty what are the properties of a "substance". Therefore when the Explanation to the amended section says that any derivatives must differ significantly in properties with regard to efficacy, it only means that the derivatives should contain such properties which are significantly different with regard to efficacy to the substance from which the derivative is made. Therefore in sum and substance what the amended section with the Explanation prescribes is the test to decide whether the discovery is an invention or not is that the Patent applicant should show the discovery has resulted in the enhancement of the known efficacy of that substance and if the discovery is nothing other than the derivative of a known substance, then, it must be shown that the properties in the derivatives differ significantly with regard to efficacy.[65]

The Draft Manual of Patent Procedure and Practice 2008 also quote from the Madras High Court decision in *Novartis case* to explain the term "efficacy."[66]

However, some query whether the provision is intended to cover only "therapeutic efficacy" or if it could be widely defined to encompass non-therapeutic advantages like heat stability, manufacturing efficiencies etc.[67] We feel that the expansion of efficacy to non-therapeutic efficacy may bring back what the provision has attempted to keep out. It is also interesting to note that in *Pfizer Inc. v. Apotex Inc.*,[68] a post-KSR decision from the U.S. Federal Circuit, discounting the physical properties of improved stability and tablet processing, the court focused only on whether there was any therapeutic effect.[69] It would seem that the post-KSR decisions tend to set the non-obviousness standards for inventions relating to pharmaceuticals and biotechnology high, in the U.S.[70] and Abbott and Reichman, citing the example of the USPTO applying an efficacy test to pharmaceutical inventions, say that the efficacy requirement "is hardly a startling proposition."[71]

It is interesting to note that although the Indian pharmaceutical industry, including both research-based and generic companies, is unanimous in opposing patent extension through ever-greening, and are insisting on a narrow definition of patentability, the MNCs insist that patenting of incremental improvements such as derivatives of known substances of the type listed in section 3(d) would directly benefit the type of innovation for which the majority of the Indian drug makers (generic firms) are best equipped.[72] It is already admitted and accepted that developmental interests, which include the physical well-being and health of its people, is an equally strong concern of every nation along with the concern for its industrial development, while adopting patentability standards. And this is well recognized under the TRIPS provisions. Therefore allowing patent protection to incrementally modified drugs (IMDs) even for the sake of helping out indigenous industry may weigh low when compared to the urgent need for providing access to drugs and pharmaceuticals at an affordable cost. Moreover, the provision covers not only the pharmaceutical sector but all fields of technology including biotechnology, computer hardware and software etc., and in many of these fields, questionable patents for incremental innovation are creating problems. Therefore the U.S. and European studies also support the approach of avoiding incremental innovation from the purview of patentability at least in these fields and suggest high patentability standards as desirable.[73]

Another criticism raised against section 3(d) is that it discriminates on the basis of technology and thus violates the TRIPS mandate under Article 27, because it allows differential treatment for pharmaceuticals.[74] However, this criticism is quite unfounded in that, as already noted, section 3(d) covers not only the pharmaceutical field but all fields of technology. It is also interesting to note that now there is a widespread belief that the one-size-fits-all approach of the TRIPS to all fields of technology is damaging to the patent system itself.[75] In high-tech fields it is desirable to have high standards of patentability when faced with the situation of patent thickets and patent trolls stifling/blocking technological development.[76] If discrimination among technologies is permissible in the name of competition it should also be available for the sake of public interest.

A major flaw in the Act appears to be in relation with the definition of "pharmaceutical substance"[77] which reads as follows: "any new entity involving one or more inventive steps." This provision is confusing because it is very wide in scope and capable of covering even non-pharmaceutical substances. Some suggest that any new "chemical entity" would have been more appropriate.[78] It is felt that adding a qualification to the term "any new entity" making it apt for a pharmaceutical substance would have been more appropriate. One more disturbing fact in connection with this provision is that the term "pharmaceutical substance" finds no place anywhere else in the statute and this renders the inclusion of its definition in the Act meaningless.

Other important areas of invention that limit patent protection to ensure access to products and also facilitate competition are inventions relating to life and computer programming. In the area of life patenting it is made clear that "discovery of any living thing or non-living things occurring in nature"[79] are not inventions. In addition to this there is also the exclusion of patenting of "plants and animals in whole or in any part thereof other than micro-organisms but including seeds, varieties and species and essentially biological processes for production or propagation of the plants and animals."[80] It is interesting to note that seeds, varieties and species are included in the exception. If the standards of patentability are interpreted strictly along with these express exclusions, it is strongly felt that this will enable India to avoid the problems faced by the developed countries in the field of inventions relating to biotechnology. But one needs to find out how the patent office and the courts are going to interpret these provisions. In the light of the difficulties faced in the developed countries due to the liberal interpretation of obviousness and persons skilled in the art, it is strongly advocated that the legislative intent in India is to avoid this by following strict standards of inventive step as laid down by the Supreme Court.

Another area is the patent protection for computer programming. John H. Barton has raised serious doubts as to the capability of software patents in promoting innovation.[81] He suggests a narrow definition of patentable subject matter globally, excluding patentability areas like computer software, algorithms, business methods etc., and raises the concern that patents in some of these areas may complicate or even deter subsequent research.[82] The Indian Act expressly excludes patenting of "mathematical or business method or a computer programme *per se* or algorithm."[83] Apart from this, "a mere scheme or rule or method of performing mental act or method of playing game" and "topography of integrated circuits"[84] are also excluded.[85] This is also intended to address the problem faced by the developed countries in this area. In the context of the strong demand for the limited use of patent law in this field these provisions need to be interpreted strictly. There is a warning against imitating other jurisdictions which have substantially diluted the patent law standards in protecting computer programmes due to their focus on "investments worth protecting" rather than "inventions worth protecting."[86] The words "*per se*" it is argued signifies those computer programmes that, although possessing practical utility of a minimal degree, lack inventive step and novelty as understood under patent law.[87] Though business methods have no technical character in themselves, can possess some technical character if directed to a data system. Even then, they are excluded from patentability as they possess only a low level of inventive step.

Another major exclusion from patentability is "an invention which, in effect, is traditional knowledge or an aggregation or duplication of traditionally known component or components."[88] The requirement under the new amendment to disclose the source and geographical origin of biological material in the specification when it is used in an invention[89] could be considered as a first step towards implementing the access and benefit sharing (ABS) requirement under the CBD for protecting genetic resources and associated traditional knowledge. The Act also included provisions for pre-grant[90] and post-grant[91] opposition on the grounds that the complete specification does not disclose or wrongly mentions the source or geographical origin of biological material used for the invention or that the invention is anticipated as having regard to the knowledge, oral or otherwise, available within any local or indigenous community in India or elsewhere.[92] A non-disclosure or wrong disclosure of the source or geographical origin of biological material used in the invention may lead to the revocation of patent.[93] Anticipation of the invention owing to the knowledge, oral or otherwise, available within any local or indigenous community in India or elsewhere also can lead to the revocation of patents.[94] These provisions, though inadequate, could be used to control access to biological material and associated traditional knowledge of indigenous communities by countries of source and countries of origin.

The other areas excluded from patentability are works protected under copyright,[95] presentation of information[96] and inventions relating to atomic energy.[97]

The above discussion makes it clear that an attempt has been made in the amended patent law in India to confine patent protection only to those inventions that maintain a high quality and also to ensure that many areas of public interest remain outside the purview of patent monopoly. One area that requires reconsideration is the standard of "capable of industrial application." The traditional understanding of a patent grant is that it should facilitate the industrial working of the invention. Since a patent is revoked if the invention is not worked in the nation, little attention was paid to this requirement. This condition is liberally interpreted to mean the capacity to apply the invention in industrial field rather than its actual use. In the context of liberal grant of patent and the problem of many patents never being brought into commercial market, there is a need to reconsider the scope of this test. It is true that at the time of patent application filing or at the time of grant of patent it may be difficult for anyone to assess the commercial viability of the invention. But it is important to evaluate the same a reasonable time after the grant of patent. Hence it is worth considering the automatic cancellation of a patent if the invention is not commercially exploited. Even if the product is not a success, for example if it is only used for commercial exploitation, then it is worth continuing with the protection if required by the patentee. But if it remained only on paper, it must be legally revoked and the existing option for the patentee to keep such invention live on payment of the prescribed fee must be restricted. It must be insisted that at the time of renewal of patent after a period of 10 years, the patentee must show that the invention was commercially exploited to keep the patent live in the register. This use does not have to be within the country. Commercial exploitation in any other jurisdiction could be considered sufficient to continue the renewal.

DISCLOSURE OF INVENTION

Another area that needs specific attention is the disclosure requirement. The *quid pro quo* for the grant of patent is the adequate disclosure of the invention to the public. This also enables the determination of the exact nature of the invention and its limit. The objective being to make the boundaries of the patent right clear to the public and the users so that they avoid violation of the rights and can freely develop new technology. Increasingly this has not been satisfied at the time of grant of patent. The speed with which patent is granted, the pressure of work in the patent office and the demand to grant the patents at the earliest possible time, prevent the patent office from ensuring that disclosure is adequate and full. Though it is possible to revoke the patent on the grounds of insufficient disclosure, because of the cost involved many patents may remain unchallenged. The Indian Patent Act insists on different kinds of disclosure before the patent is granted. In addition to the full and complete disclosure of the invention in the specification,[98] there is also the requirement to provide technical information including the deposit of the invention in case of biological materials[99] and the origin of the materials.[100] It is essential that these conditions are insisted on and strictly monitored to ensure the quality of the invention and to delineate the boundary of the patent as far as possible.

PRE-GRANT AND POST-GRANT OPPOSITION

The right to oppose the patent application before granting – pre-grant opposition – is a provision peculiar to Indian law.[101] It allows "any person" to file an opposition to an application for patent after its publication, but before grant of patent on various grounds such as the applicant wrongfully obtaining the invention, prior publication of the claims in India or elsewhere, the invention having already been claimed in another application, public knowledge about the invention prior to the application, obviousness, non-fulfilment of patentability standards, insufficient disclosure, non-disclosure or wrongful disclosure of source or geographical origin of biological material used for the invention, non-disclosure or wrongful disclosure of traditional knowledge. The idea is to provide an opportunity to interested groups to prevent invalid and illegal inventions being granted patent and also to ensure that only good quality inventions are patented. It is interesting that rival industries as well as vigilant consumer groups are making use of this pre-grant opposition procedure.[102] The Madras High Court in *Indian Network for People living with HIV/*

AIDS v. Union of India[103] held that the person filing the pre-grant opposition should be heard by the Controller before disposing the application and deciding to grant the patent. The Court stressed the importance of the public interest involved in the pre-grant opposition procedure and held:

> The petitioners in this writ petition are asserting their rights and voicing their concern on a broad public interest angle. So it cannot be said if their right is denied they will not suffer any prejudice by denial of an opportunity of hearing them to establish their rights. A right is a legally protected interest. Therefore when law consciously confers a right on a person to object at a pre-grant stage that right must be protected in the way it has been granted, namely the right to object with a right of hearing. For a Court to dilute the said right on the basis of an interpretative process and by looking at it from a narrow angle, would, in our judgment, be a travesty of justice. [104]

Though post-grant opposition is based on the same grounds, only the "person interested"[105] is allowed to file it. It has to be filed within one year of publication of grant of patent. *The Supreme Court in J. Mitra v. Asst. Controller of Patent and Design,*[106] examined the scope of these provisions while examining the sections dealing with appeal from the orders of the Controller and observed thus:

> There is, however, a radical shift due to the incorporation of Section 25(2) where an interested party is granted a right to challenge the patent after its grant. The ground of challenge under Section 25(1) is identical to Section 25(2) of the said 1970 Act. However, Section 25(1) is wider than Section 25(2) as the later is available only to a "person aggrieved". The main difference between Section 25(1) and Section 25(2), as brought out by Patent (Amendment) Act, 2005, is that even after a patent is granted, a "post-grant opposition" can be filed under Section 25(2) for a period of one year. The reason is obvious. In relation to patent that are of recent origin, a higher scrutiny is necessary. This is the main rational underlying Section 25(2) of the said 1970 Act . . .[107]

These judgments are indicative of the judicial approval of the legislative intent to protect the public interest while granting patent.

LIMITATIONS AND EXCEPTIONS

Though the nomenclature "property" is attached to IP generally, it is an accepted fact that IP, more often, does not match the traditional property concepts and hence the balancing of public and private rights is very important when dealing with different forms of IP. It is felt that the origin of limitations and exceptions could be traced back to its origin as a monopoly/privilege.[108] It is well accepted that patent is not an absolute monopoly right. Traditionally it was a privilege granted by the State based on many limitations. The main objectives were the promotion of science and technology, access to information and patented products at affordable cost. This compelled the patent system to develop suitable exceptions and limitations to achieve these objectives. In the initial stages of the growth of the patent system the authorities insisted on training local people in the art of making the product.[109] This was achieved because there was also a strict obligation after this to ensure the industry was started.

The growth of industries and the increase in the number of inventions led to the demand for express provisions to facilitate future research and development. The exception made for teaching and research using the patented technology is the outcome of this process. Irrespective of the objectives of the research (whether commercial or non-commercial), exception was granted in the case of research. The liberal approach followed in many developed countries appears to have been tightened in the context of the competitive research taking place not only within the industry but also in universities.[110] Thus, today, if any element of commercial activity is involved in the research output, developed countries require that permission should be granted by the patent holder.[111] Decisions made by developed countries, particularly the U.S. and England, are testimony to this. The decisions made by the U.S. Court in *Madey v. Duke University*[112] and *Integra Lifesciences I, Ltd. v. Merck KGaA*[113] reflect the limited interpretation given by the court. The observation of the Federal Circuit in *Madey* is worth quoting:

> In short, regardless of whether a particular institution or entity is engaged in an endeavour for commercial gain, so long as the act is in furtherance of the alleged infringer's legitimate business and is not solely for amusement, to satisfy idle curiosity, or for strictly philosophical inquiry, the act does not qualify for the very narrow and strictly limited experimental use defence. Moreover, the profit or non-profit status of the use is not determinative.[114]

The example given by the court for acting for "commercial gain" renders almost all cases of research and experimental use as infringement. The court has stated:

> For example, major research universities, such as Duke, often sanction and fund research projects with arguably no commercial application whatsoever. However, these projects unmistakably further the institution's legitimate business objectives, including educating and enlightening students and faculty participating in these projects. These projects also serve, for example, to increase the status of the institution and lure lucrative research grants, students and faculty.[115]

Some rightly hold the view that the logical result of *Madey* allows the courts to find some commercial application or purpose behind every use of the patented technology by the defendant and thus renders the research exemption a sham.[116]

In *Integra Lifesciences I, Ltd. v. Merck KGaA*,[117] again, the Federal Circuit court took a restrictive interpretation. However, in the dissenting judgement Judge Newman stated:

> the subject matter of patents should be studied in order to understand it, or to improve upon it, or to find a new use for it, or to modify or "design around" it. Were such research subject to prohibition by the patentee the advancement of technology would stop, for the first patentee in the field could bar not only patent-protected competition, but all research that might lead to such competition, as well as barring improvement or challenge or avoidance of patented technology.

The U.S. Supreme Court, in *Merck KgaA, Petitioner v. Integra Lifesciences*[118] resorted to an expanded interpretation of research exemption. In that case use of patented inventions for pre-clinical research was held not to constitute infringement even when the result is not submitted to the Food and Drug Administration for regulatory approval. However, as neither the Federal Circuit nor the Supreme Court in *Merck* opined on the common law experimental use exemption, the law laid down in *Madey v. Duke*, at least for the time being, states the current rule of the law, enunciating an extremely narrow scope of the common law exception.[119] Thus the U.S. standard of exception now seems to be very much limited only to research for curiosity and self-satisfaction. Many jurists have criticized this saying that it will have serious implications for achieving the main objectives of promoting the progress of science and creating space for freedom to carry out research.[120]

It is interesting to note that the TRIPS Agreement, for the first time, expressly laid down the norms for granting limited exceptions. It also included the principles of exhaustion in Article 6 as a limitation to the rights of the patent owner. The broad wordings of Article 30[121] provide adequate freedom for countries to structure limited exceptions although the interpretation given by the WTO Dispute Settlement Body puts limitations on the countries for its use.[122] It is in this context that one has to examine the provisions of the Indian Law. The exceptions given under the Patent Act can be divided into the following four headings: (1) teaching and research, (2) government use in some cases, (3) parallel import and (4) use for generating data for approval by authorities. While the first two are treated as conditions for the basis of the granting of the patent introduced in the Act from 1970 onwards, the last two are not considered to be infringements of the patent and were added in the 2002 Amendment to satisfy the TRIPS obligations. The obligation to introduce product patent in the pharmaceutical, chemicals, biotechnology fields etc., and the liberalization of the economy, seem to be the reasons for this addition. These exemptions will be discussed in detail below.

The research exception in the Indian Patent Act is worded very broadly in section 47(3).[123] The words "for the purpose merely for experimental or research including the imparting of instructions to pupils" include three types of activities; experiment, research and imparting instructions. The exemption permits the "making or using" of the patented invention for these purposes. The word "merely" qualifying the three types of activities exempted under this exception needs careful examination. The literal meaning of "merely" is "just," "only," "simply," "purely" etc. makes clear the intention for which the patented invention is made or used. It is evident that this is not related to the impact these activities are going to have on the owner of the patent. As long as the intention of making or using the patented invention is for experiment, research or teaching it is permitted and no permission is needed from the owner of the patent. Hence the activities of the user for furthering his economic interest from experiment, research or teaching are covered under this exception. This also conforms with the test laid down in Article 30 of the TRIPS Agreement. These activities in fact do not unreasonably conflict with a normal exploitation of the patent since the making or using is not for commercial exploitation of the patented invention. It also does not unreasonably prejudice the legitimate interests of the patent owner since the making or using is not directly affecting his economic return. Needless to say, permission is required if the competitor uses the patent to commercially exploit the results of his research. In fact it promotes the legitimate interest of the users since it facilitates the progress of science, learning and maintaining competition by innovating the existing products or processes. It is true that there are no judicial pronouncements in this area. It is expected that the Indian courts will not follow the restricted interpretations of this exception based on U.S. and English precedents which result in the limiting of progress in science and competition.

One of the unique exceptions in Indian law is the limited government use of the patented invention without any authorization from the owner of patent. This includes importing or making of the patented invention by or on behalf of the government for government use;[124] use of process patent by or on behalf of government for government use[125] and import of patented drugs for the use of the government and distribution through government hospitals and dispensaries for the general public.[126] The use by government for domestic reasons without permission or payments of royalties is controversial in many countries. Although this exception has been in the statute book for a long time there are no instances where this provision is misused or used against the legitimate interest of the owners of patent. As long as the activities of the government remain not for profit and public purpose oriented this exception can be used in limited special cases and will not be against the mandate of the obligations under the TRIPS Agreement.

The introduction of product patent in certain fields like pharmaceuticals, agricultural chemicals, biotech products etc., to satisfy the TRIPS obligations forced policymakers to consider steps to be taken to facilitate access to these products at affordable cost. The first measure is to ensure the import of products from other markets to maintain a market condition to reduce the price using the principles of exhaustion available in the TRIPS Agreement. As per Article 6[127] of the TRIPS Agreement countries have the freedom to introduce provisions to facilitate the import of genuine goods from other countries. The use of the phrase "nothing in this Agreement shall be used to address the issue of the exhaustion of intellectual property rights" makes it clear that this exhaustion principle can affect the importation right granted to the holder of patent in Article 28. Taking advantage of this provision and also to ensure that patented products are not priced beyond the purchasing capacity of Indian consumers, Section 107A(b)[128] was included in the Act to facilitate the import of products patented in India from other countries. This provision puts limitations on the rights of the patent owner to restrict the movement of the products from one country to another once it is sold in the market. There are interesting issues regarding the scope of this provision. The idea of parallel import is to facilitate products that are not infringing products manufactured in some other country to enter the Indian market while the patent is in force in India through distributors not authorized by the owner of patent. That means the owner of patent might have ensured the availability of the products in the Indian market either by way of manufacture in India or import of the products from another country. Section 107A(b) authorizes an independent distributor who has no license from the owner of patent to import the products into India, by enjoying the legal right of parallel import, to purchase the same product distributed by a licensed manufacturer of another country, where there is a valid patent for the product, and bring it to India and sell it in the Indian market. This is irrespective of the territorial limit for the sale of products included in the conditions of license by the owner of patent to the manufacturer in that country. The product can also be purchased from a manufacturer from a country where patent is not in force because it is not an infringed product.

Initially the Indian legal provision, introduced in 2002, only authorized parallel importation of a patented product "from a person who is duly authorized by the patentee to sell or distribute the product." This provision was incapable of covering all forms of parallel import. Hence the section was further amended in 2005 to replace theses words with "who is duly authorized under the law to produce and sell or distribute the product."[129] This is much broader in scope. It permits importation of patented products even from countries not recognizing patent for that invention because in such cases the importer or the person from whom he buys it is acting legally. The word "patented product," used in this section, only means the product patented in India, and not in the country from where the product is imported, as the exclusion from infringement is evidently of the patent granted in India. Similarly the word "law" used in this section is the law applicable in the county from where the product is imported and not Indian law.[130] This is in tune with the objectives of the principles of exhaustion given in Article 6 of the TRIPS Agreement. Since this is an express exclusion from the rights given under Article 28 of the TRIPS, this cannot be read into Article 30 to find out whether this exception is a limited exception. The use of principles of exhaustion is a freedom given to the WTO member countries and is not a limited exception as per Article 30. If that was the case there would not have been a separate Article, also in Part 1 of the TRIPS Agreement dealing with "General Provisions and Basic Principles." The principles of exhaustion need to be interpreted from the point of view of public interest rather than from the angle of protecting the interest of the owner of patent. Public interest would include not only the availability of the product but also the transfer of technology to countries that lack manufacturing capacity. It is clear that the Indian provision is structured to take full advantage of the flexibility available under the TRIPS Agreement to make the patented products available to the Indian public at the cheapest possible price through market mechanisms. This will not only facilitate the import of the product from countries where there is a patent for the product but also from a country where the owner has not received a patent. This will compel the owner of a patent to seek patents in all countries and also ensure that there is not much price difference. This will also ensure that the patent owner invests money in the manufacture of the patent products even in the least developed countries to ensure that his rights are not misused by his competitor. A restricted interpretation of exhaustion would also go against the interest of least developed countries that are given more time in the transitional period to move towards a TRIPS compliant patent system.[131]

Use of patented invention for generating data for manufacturing and marketing approval by regulatory authorities is another exception introduced in the Patent Act in 2002 and 2005 in the context of introducing product patent for pharmaceutical products. According to Section 107A(a)[132] the act of making, constructing, using, selling or importing a patented invention for the sole purpose of generating information is not considered as an infringement of the patent rights. This is substantially similar to the exception permitted by the Dispute Settlement Body of the WTO in the *Canadian case.*[133] This is also to ensure that a manufacturer who is interested in producing the product as soon as the patent period is over has the freedom to use the patented invention without fear of infringement to generate the necessary information to get market approval well in advance. This will enable the off-patented product entering the market at the earliest possible time so that the price of the product will automatically come down.

It is evident that all the above exceptions are introduced in the Act to facilitate access to the patented product at affordable cost and also to promote the progress of science and technology. It is important to note that India used the flexibilities available in this area in the TRIPS Agreement to the maximum extent to protect Indian public interest. It is to be noted that there are no judicial pronouncements in these areas and it is expected that given the trend shown by the Indian judiciary, it will continue to recognise the public interest involved in these provisions and interpret them in such a way that the owners of patents cannot enjoy monopoly to the detriment of public interest.

COMPULSORY LICENSE

Traditionally compulsory licensing provisions have been used to prevent the owner of an intellectual property right from refusing to exploit his right in a country where intellectual property protection is granted, or from enjoying an absolute monopoly by forcing him to permit competition from other producers, subject only to reasonable payment of royalties or license fees.[134] It is a well established fact that the maximum benefit of the patent system will be enjoyed by a country granting patent if the invention is manufactured and distributed in that country. This will ensure not only industrial development and employment generation but also progress in science through research and development. It was also a concern that in cases where the invention is not worked in the country where a patent has been granted, the patent owner would use the patent monopoly to expand his market for selling the patented products manufactured in some other country. In the early stages of the development of the patent system the patent used to be revoked on the grounds that the patented invention was not worked in the country to satisfy the obligations of grant of patent.

The demand for recognizing importation of a patented product as the right of the patent owner was resisted at the international level to retain the freedom of the countries to introduce appropriate measures to prevent the abuse of patent monopoly detrimental to the industrialization of the country. Countries used different strategies to ensure actual manufacture of the invention locally. Grant of compulsory license was considered as one effective method for ensuring this. The Paris Convention recognizes right of countries to impose compulsory licenses "to prevent abuses of the exclusive rights conferred by the patent, for example, for failure to work."[135]

Before the TRIPS Agreement, countries had considerable freedom in determining the grounds and conditions of issue of compulsory licenses. However, now the WTO member states are required to follow the mandate under Article 31 of the TRIPS agreement. Article 31 of TRIPS lists detailed conditions which must be complied with when a WTO member chooses to use compulsory licensing. These include the need to grant licenses on a case-by-case basis, evidence of unsuccessful prior request for a voluntary license, non-exclusivity of the license and the requirement for compensation. There are also conditions governing the termination of licenses and restrictions on export and on assignment of licenses to third parties. In spite of all this, many are of the view that there is still flexibility for the WTO member countries in legislating on compulsory licenses, especially in the context of the Doha Declaration and the proposed amendment based on it.[136]

There are two main justifications for granting compulsory licenses: safeguarding public interest by providing access to the public and encouraging technology transfer, and the promotion of local industrial development by allowing competition. There is considerable debate regarding the limitations of Article 31 of the TRIPS Agreement in preventing the abuse of patent monopoly.[137] Resistance by foreign patent holders in South Africa to the measures adopted by the government to ensure the availability of patented AIDS medicine in the country is a clear example of this.[138] The clarification and changes introduced to this provision in the Doha Declaration now enable countries to introduce different types of compulsory licenses to prevent abuse of patent monopoly. In the context of strong opposition to implement compulsory license in some fields like the pharmaceutical industry, it is interesting to note that the need for compulsory licensing and even licenses of right[139] for the sake of competition and commercial working of patents are being pressed for by the developed countries themselves, at least in the high-tech research areas / cumulative innovation fields such as innovation and the communication technology sector.[140]

India is one country who has made use not only of the flexibility available in the TRIPS agreement, but also the changes accepted by the WTO Ministerial Conference in its Doha Declaration and the consequential amendment proposed to the TRIPS agreement,[141] and has created different types of compulsory licenses. But there are those who still hold the view that India did not fully exploit the range of flexibility available.[142] India's compulsory licensing provisions are considered by others as the "broadest and most comprehensive of all the world's patent systems."[143] Nonetheless, the provisions have very rarely been made use of in India. The reason for this could be attributed to the lack of necessity of the only competent industry in India at that time that could make use of the provision, viz., the pharmaceutical industry.[144] The refusal of product patent for inventions pertaining to this field and the comparatively short period of protection etc., allowed the manufacture of these products using indigenous processes enabling them to effectively compete with the patent owner. Thus it was not necessary for them to undergo the laborious process of obtaining a compulsory license. However, the situation has undergone a sea change since 2005, that is, after introducing product patent for pharmaceutical substances in India. Hence the same sluggishness could no longer be expected in utilizing these provisions.

It is important to note that the general principles of working of patent in India are well articulated in the chapter dealing with compulsory license. Section 83 (of the Patents Act 1970) makes it clear that the patent must be worked in India on a commercial scale; can only enjoy monopoly by importation of the patented product; protection and enforcement of patent right must contribute to the promotion and dissemination of technology; should not act as an impediment to public health and nutrition; the use of patent should not unreasonably restrain trade or adversely affect international transfer of technology and must make the patented invention available at affordable price to the public. Based on these principles the compulsory licensing provisions available under the Indian Patent Act could be broadly classified into three categories: (a) general compulsory licensing provisions, (b) provision relating to pharmaceuticals patents in case of emergency, and (c) license to export pharmaceuticals to countries with insufficient manufacturing capabilities.

The general compulsory license provisions are largely based on the Paris Convention and hence conform with TRIPS obligations. The grounds on which compulsory license can be requested three years after granting the patent by a person interested are: (a) reasonable requirements of the public have not been satisfied; (b) patented invention not available to the public at a reasonably affordable price, and (c) the patent has not been worked in India.[145] Section 84 also explained the circumstances that result in not satisfying the reasonable requirements of the public.[146] This is largely based on the general principles of working of the patent in Section 83 of the Act. Protection of existing trade and industry, development of new industrial activities, promotion of export, availability of the product at an affordable price, prevention of unreasonable terms in voluntary license like grant back, packaging, prevention on challenge etc.,[147] exploitation of the market based only on import etc. are the circumstances covered in this provision.

It is evident that these grounds will help to ensure the patent is used for the economic and industrial development of India. However, some have expressed concern as to the TRIPS compatibility of section 84(1)(a) as explained by section 84(7).[148] As per the deeming provision, "the reasonable requirements of the public with respect to the patented invention" is not satisfied if by reason of the refusal of the patentee to grant license on reasonable terms, "a market for export of the patented article manufactured in India is not being supplied or developed." The apprehension raised by Jancie Mueller is that this provision violates Article 31(f) of the TRIPS agreement which requires that compulsory licenses are to be granted "predominantly for the supply of the domestic market." Though section 90 adds that in settling the terms and conditions of a license under section 84, the controller "shall endeavour to secure that the licence is granted with a predominant purpose of supply in the Indian market" while allowing the licensee to export the patented product, if needed, in accordance with the provisions of section 84(7)(a)(iii),[149] she feels that only after observing the method of implementation of the provision, could one ensure that there is no conflict with TRIPS Article 31(f).[150]

Another general compulsory licensing provision which is criticized for being inconsistent with TRIPS is the granting of compulsory license on the grounds that the invention is not worked in India.[151] However, we feel that this criticism is unfounded because this provision is in tune with Article 5A of the Paris Convention, which is being incorporated in to the TRIPS agreement. Article 27.1 of the TRIPS agreement only states that "*patents shall be available and patent rights enjoyable* without discrimination as to the place of invention, the field of technology and *whether products are imported or locally produced.*" The provision granting compulsory licenses on the ground of non-working of the patent in the territory of India is in no way interfering with the right under Article 27.1 as it does not affect the availability of patent or enjoyment of patent rights. As Article 31 keeps open the grounds under which authorization to use the subject matter of a patent by the governments and third parties without permission from the patent right holder, it cannot be said that the Indian provision allowing granting of compulsory license on the grounds of not working it locally is also violative of Article 31.

It is to be noted that the ability of the applicant to work the invention in India is a pre-requisite for the grant of compulsory license.[152] This presupposes that compulsory license will make a difference only in sectors where India has existing industries with manufacturing capabilities. The provision can be used by existing industries to negotiate for a reasonable voluntary license from the owner of patent since this is also a pre-requisite for applying for compulsory license. It also envisages a fair procedure for granting compulsory license by the Controller of Patent.[153] There are also guidelines regarding the fixing of the terms and conditions of the license[154] and these conform with Article 31 of the TRIPS agreement. It is also stipulated that the decision on the application shall be taken ordinarily within one year.

The second category of compulsory license relates to situations of national emergency.[155] The provision states that where, in circumstances of national emergency or in circumstances of extreme urgency or in case of public non-commercial use, the government is satisfied that in respect of any patent it is necessary that compulsory license should be granted at any time after the sealing of the patent, it may make a declaration to that effect by notification in the official gazette. In such cases the license can be granted without waiting for the lapse of three years after the sealing of patent.[156] However, there is confusion when one attempts to interpret subsections 2 and 3. According to subsection 2, all the provisions under sections 87–90 are to be applicable while granting compulsory licenses under this provision. But subsection 3, which is a *non obstante* clause, authorizes the controller, if he is satisfied that it is necessary, to exempt the application from the procedural requirements contained under section 87, relating to notice to the patentee and giving the patentee a chance to be heard, in cases including public health crises relating to AIDS, HIV, tuberculosis, malaria or other epidemics. The confusion relates to the reason for such differentiation in cases of emergency, the extent to which the differentiation is applicable and the reason for giving discretionary power to the Controller in determining whether it is a fit case to be exempted from the procedural requirements under section 87. With regard to the purpose behind incorporating such a special provision, the ideal situation would be to exempt entire applications under this provision from the procedural requirement under section 87 to expedite the granting of compulsory license. Therefore, we feel that, at the least, section 92 needs to be amended, deleting subsection 3 altogether and deleting from subsection 2 the reference to section 87. Thus all the above-mentioned confusion could be removed. Taking into consideration the gravity of the situation which section 92 intends to cover, there is no justification for insisting for compliance with section 87 requirements. Moreover, there is also no justification for conferring any discretionary power on the Controller in determining whether a patent is to be exempted from the procedural requirements under section 87. But a better option would be to follow a different procedure in these cases. A statutory form of license with safeguards to protect the interest of the owner of patent would be preferable. The license could be automatic so that the interested parties could use the patent immediately after notification to meet the urgency. There could be provisions for negotiations of the terms and conditions after the working of the patent if the parties have difficulty in reaching reasonable agreement. The possibility of the owner of patent seeking injunction from the Court in such cases also needs regulation. In the absence of these modifications it would be easy for the owner of the patent to defeat the purpose of the notification. India is yet to see a notification based on this provision and only when it is put into practice can one clearly articulate the need for change in this section.

The third type of compulsory license was introduced in 2005 by inserting section 92A to facilitate the manufacture and export of patented pharmaceutical products to countries having insufficient or no manufacturing capabilities.[157] This provision is based on para 6 of the Doha Declaration.[158] In line with the requirement under para 6 of the Doha Declaration the TRIPS General Council decided on August 30, 2003[159] to waive the obligations of an exporting member under Article 31(f) of the TRIPS Agreement for the purpose of production and export of a pharmaceutical product to an eligible importing member.[160] Later in 2005 the General Council again decided to adopt the protocol amending the TRIPS agreement to insert Article 31 bis[161] after Article 73.[162]

Issue of compulsory license from the importing country or a notification permitting import from India is mandatory before issue of compulsory license by the Controller of Patent permitting manufacture and import of the patented pharmaceutical products from India. It is also clarified that "pharmaceutical product" would include not only patented products and processes but also ingredients necessary for their manufacture and the diagnostic kits required for their use. It may be noted that the agreement reached on Para 6 and the proposed Article 31 bis mandate exporting countries also to take precautionary measures such as notification to the WTO, labelling standards etc., to ensure that the product will not enter the normal market. There is no statutory provision regarding this in the Indian Act. The Controller is permitted to issue a license based on such terms and conditions specified and published by him. It is also clear that the Controller in this case is not mandated to follow the normal procedures that are followed in issue of compulsory license. There are not many instances of use of this provision and only the future will show how this is going to work in India considering her strength in manufacturing generic drugs. In a recent development Natco Pharma Ltd., a Hyderabad-based cancer drug maker, announced withdrawal of its application under section 92A[163] to export cancer drugs to Nepal, as the company had not yet received an import requisition from the Nepal government for the drugs.[164] However, an interesting issue came up for consideration in connection with this application. The Controller of Patents gave the holders of patent (Roche and Pfizer) an opportunity to be heard while making a decision on Natco's application and Natco's petition questioning the legality of the Controller hearing the patent holder was dismissed by the patent office.[165]

The effectiveness of a compulsory license in preventing abuse of monopoly and safeguarding the public interest such as access to affordable patented product, transfer of technology, improvement of existing industry etc., is not well established. It is evident that the system will work only if there are interested parties – industrialists with adequate capital and technology – to manufacture the product in the country. The procedure for the issue of compulsory license must also be time-bound and less cumbersome so that there is adequate incentive for parties to apply for it. These procedures must also induce the owner of patent to grant a license voluntarily, on reasonable terms, rather than trying to delay it by using procedural benefits/loopholes/ambiguities and litigation strategies. Indian law needs further amendment to ensure this so that these provisions act as a real stimulus for industrialization either through direct investment by the patent owner or through reasonable licensing agreements with local industries.

ENFORCEMENT OF RIGHTS: JUDICIAL TRENDS

Enforcement of rights of patent owners only assumed prominence in recent years. There was hardly any serious patent infringement litigation before the economy became competitive. The recent judicial trend shows the emergence of a complex set of problems of infringement and enforcement of right. Since India is in the early stages of industrial development, the judicial trend in fixing the norms for infringement and enforcement of rights is giving emphasis to public interest. This is evident from the principles followed by the courts in granting temporary injunction in cases of alleged infringements. The role of injunction in balancing the conflicting interests involved in a patent litigation is decisive, since in most cases, if injunction is granted against the alleged infringer, he has to close down and the case virtually ends there. There is no specific mention in the Indian Patent Act on the principles to be followed in finding the infringement of rights, especially in cases where the validity of the patent is challenged on the basic grounds of lack of novelty and inventive step. The same is true with the principles to be followed in granting temporary reliefs such as injunction, when the patent has only recently been acquired. While applying the general norms in the Civil Procedure Code, the courts are trying to evolve new norms based on the experiences from other jurisdictions. An analysis of some of the important judgments will bring out the new trends adopted by the courts for maintaining a balance of competing interests in patent litigation.

One of the important and interesting issues regards the norms to be followed while granting temporary injunction in cases where the allegation is an infringement of a recently granted patent. This issue was addressed by the Gujarat High Court in *Cadila Pharmaceuticals Ltd., v. Instacare Laboratouries Pvt. Ltd.*[166] In this case the plaintiff invented a new process for the manufacture of penicillin and lactobacilli and started selling the product using the name "LMX". The new process is of coating lactobacilli, thereby isolating the dose of lactobacilli from the antibiotic substance with a thin protective film. The benefit of this process is that when such combination medicine is consumed orally, the lactobacilli remain effective for a long time, successfully counteracting the side effects caused by the antibiotic. Patent was granted to the plaintiff in India in March 2000. In a suit for infringement of patent, the defendants opposed the grant of temporary injunction and challenged the validity of the patent on the ground of lack of novelty. It was argued by the defendant, *inter alia,* that since the patent was of recent origin and the defendant entered the market in 2000, there was considerable doubt as to the validity of patent and the request for the injunction should be rejected. Accepting this and following the principles laid down by the English court in *American Cynamid case*[167] and the Supreme Court of India in the *Wander* case,[168] the Court observed:

> If, *prima facie*, the process evolved by the appellant is not found to be patentable, the defendant cannot be restrained from using the said process for its products and for marketing them. In the present case, as referred to herein above, the defendants have already entered the market with their products "Hipen LB & Hipenox LB" sometime in the month of December 2000. It should, therefore, also not be proper to restrain them from continuing to market its products which have already entered the market for quite a few months.[169]

The Court did not accept the argument of the plaintiff that the Patent Certificate is *prima facie* evidence of the validity of patent on the basis of which temporary injunction could be granted. Arguably, the Court stresses that the appearance of the defendant in the market with the product immediately after the grant of patent to the plaintiff is a clear indication that the information regarding the product and process are already in the public domain and that helped the defendant to design the product quickly. Also if the defendant designs the product a long time after grant of patent it may give credence to the conclusion that the product may be a violation of the patent. In such a situation the court may be justified in granting a temporary injunction. A challenge of the validity of the patent may not help the defendant in that event.

The issue of grant of temporary injunction for the violation of the Exclusive Marketing Right came up for consideration before the Bombay High Court in *Novartis AG v. Mehar Pharma*.[170] In this case the plaintiff, a Swiss pharmaceutical company, invented "Beta Crystalline form of Imatinib Mesylate" and filed a patent application in Australia on July 16, 1998 and another one in India on July 17, 1998. Patent was granted in Australia and the company also received market approval for sale of the drug in Australia on August 13, 2001. The Indian subsidiary applied for market approval in India, which was granted on December 5, 2002. The Indian subsidiary filed an EMR application in the Kolkata Patent Office on March 27, 2003 and it was granted on November 10, 2003. Meanwhile the defendant started manufacturing and selling the same drug. The plaintiff, after obtaining EMR, filed a suit to restrain the defendant from manufacturing and selling the same drug. It was contended by the defendant that the plaintiff's invention was not new since the same company patented the same invention in the U.S. in 1992 and in Canada in 1993 and since the invention was disclosed in India before the filing of the patent application, the plaintiff was not entitled to EMR. So there was no novelty to the invention to claim EMR. It was argued by the plaintiff that once any right is granted by an appropriate authority after examining the application, any violation of the right must be stopped by the court by grant of injunction. After referring to the principles laid down in previous cases dealing with design infringement[171] on grant of temporary injunctions, the Court rejected this argument and observed:

> Thus, the settled law appears to be that in relation to a patent, the Court will not grant an interlocutory injunction unless satisfied that (a) there is a real probability of the plaintiffs succeeding on the trial of the suit, and (b) where the patent is of a recent date, no interim injunction should be granted. More so, when there is a serious question as to validity of the patent raised by the defendants to be tried in the suit.[172]

The Court applied these principles to the facts of the case and the evidence advanced by the parties. The reasoning of the Court denying the temporary injunction is worth quoting:

> In so far as the present case is concerned, it is an admitted position that the EMR has been granted only in the month of November 2003. Therefore, it has been granted recently. Therefore, in order that the plaintiff become entitled to the grant of temporary injunction, I have to consider whether in this suit, the defendants have raised a serious question as to the validity of the EMR that have been granted in favour of the plaintiff.
>
> Perusal of various grounds that have been raised by the defendants to indicate that the grant of EMR in favour of the plaintiff is not valid, appears to my mind, to raise serious questions as to the validity of the EMR granted in favour of the plaintiffs. For example, it is clear from the application filed in Canada for patent by the plaintiff on 1st April 1993 that the salt form of the said compound is disclosed in that application . . . A comparison of what is stated in the application submitted in Canada for the patent in 1993 and the contents of paragraph 10, in my opinion, definitely raises a serious question as to whether the product in relation to which EMR has been granted is really a new product or not. In paragraph 8 of the plaint, the plaintiff describes the invention as B crystalline form of Imatinib Mesylate. In paragraph 10, the plaintiffs admit that Imatinib Mesylate crystals were found to be in two forms – Alpha (a) and Beta (B). Alpha was needle shaped. Beta was found to be thermodynamically stable and was prepared for use in pharmaceutical preparations. Perusal of the application submitted by the plaintiffs in 1993 for patent in Canada shows that the plaintiffs have disclosed the compound as well as its salt. Beta crystals are clearly disclosed in the application. Therefore, in my opinion, apart from other challenges, this challenge can definitely be said to be serious insofar as the validity of EMR granted is concerned and if that be so, in terms of the law that appears to be settled referred to above, the EMR being of recent origin, the plaintiff would not be entitled to the temporary injunction sought. It is further to be seen here that in the present case, it cannot be said that even if the plaintiffs ultimately succeed, the loss or injury that may be caused to the plaintiffs is not incapable of being compensated in terms of money.[173]

The significant contribution of the Court in this case is the seriousness given to the public interest in accessing life-saving medicines, while deciding the issue of balance of convenience. The need to produce and supply a life-saving drug at affordable cost was considered as an important element in deciding the issue of temporary injunctions in such cases. The observation of the Court is quite pertinent to note:

> In my opinion, the aspect of balance of convenience has also to be answered in favour of the defendants especially because the drug in relation to which EMR is granted is a anti-cancer drug, is a life saving drug and the plaintiffs do not manufacture the drug in India but import it from foreign country. The defendants have stated that the demand of capsule is over 3,000,000 per month.

> This does not appear to have been disputed by the plaintiffs. It is clear that the demand of this drug in India is very large, it is life saving drug. The defendants manufacture the drug in India. The plaintiffs do not manufacture the drug in India. They stated that they will import required quantity of the drug from a foreign country. Therefore, the plaintiffs will rely entirely on the international transport system for making the drug available in India in the required quantity. In case interim injunction is granted in favour of the plaintiffs, the manufacturing and marketing network of the defendants so far as the drug is concerned would be dismantled. If due to any problem, the plaintiff cannot make available the drug in required quantity in India, it obviously will be disastrous for the patients. This consequence is foreseeable, therefore in my opinion, the court should not pass any interim order which may possibly lead to such a situation. In my opinion, the aspect of the difference in price of the product of the plaintiffs and the defendants also cannot be ignored, especially at the stage of considering the question whether the plaintiffs are entitled to any interim relief.[174]

The precedent value of this judgment is clear: it addressed the important factors to be considered while granting temporary injunction, especially in cases of high public concern, like the violation of product patent on life-saving drugs. It is interesting to note that the Madras High Court had earlier taken a contrary view and granted temporary injunction to the same plaintiff against another defendant.[175] The Bombay High Court refused to follow this precedent since it was of the view that the Madras High Court had failed to follow settled principles in granting temporary injunctions in the case before it.[176] It is an undisputable fact that the Courts are duty bound to give due attention to issues of public interest, like the question of access to medicine at affordable cost, before granting interim relief.[177]

The above trend was further strengthened by the Delhi High Court recently in *F. Hoffman-la Roch Ltd., v. Cipla Ltd.*[178] In this case the plaintiff was granted a patent in India on February 23, 2007 for the cancer drug "Erlotinib." After approval from the Drug Controller, it was marketed with the trade name "Tarceva." The plaintiff discovered that the defendant was planning to launch the same drug and sought an injunction. The defendant argued that they obtained approval for marketing the drug in October 2007 and started marketing it from December 2007 under the brand name "Erlocip." It was also contented that the invention of the plaintiff lacked novelty and it was not an invention as per section 3(d) of the Patent Act. But while rejecting the application for injunction the Court found that the plaintiff had an arguable case because it impacted on the large number of cancer patients who were not parties to the suit. The observation of the Court is refreshing:

> Therefore, this Court is of the opinion that as between the two competing public interests, that is, the public interest in granting injunction to affirm a patent during the pendency of an infringement action, as opposed to the public interest in access for the people to a life saving drug, the balance has to be tilted in favour of the latter. The damage or injury that would occur to the plaintiff in such case is capable of assessment in monetary terms. However, the injury to the public which would be deprived of the defendant's product which may lead to shortening of lives of several unknown persons, who are not parties to the suit, and which damage cannot be restituted in monetary terms, is not only uncompensatable, it is irreparable. Thus irreparable injury would be caused if the injunction sought for is granted.[179]

It is worth noting that at least in the area of health care, the courts show willingness to depart from the conventional norms of granting an injunction to address public interest. This is also in tune with the sprit in which the amendments to the Patent Act were introduced. It is expected that the trend of giving predominance to public interest while protecting the patent monopoly will continue in India until the players in the market adequately address the reasonable requirements of the public.

Another area that needs careful judicial scrutiny is the interpretation of claims in the case of infringement suits. Since the claims in a patent specification are the principal determinants of the scope of the monopoly, interpretation of claims is the main issue in an action for infringement. A strict literal interpretation of the claims may at times defeat the purpose for which patent is granted as it is often hard to define the claims accurately due to the nature of the technology and the inability of words to achieve precision. However, public interest necessitates that the limits of the inventor's rights has to be clearly demarcated enabling others to formulate and build within the public domain beyond the patentee's rights. Reconciling these conflicting purposes is the essence of claim construction.[180] We have yet to witness serious judicial exercise of claim interpretation under Indian law, understandably, due to lack of serious infringement litigation. However, we hope that the Indian judiciary may keep in mind the need for balancing the conflicting interests and safeguarding the national interest and evolve its own jurisprudence without blindly following the U.S or the European model.[181]

THE ROAD AHEAD

It is often said that patent system is not the perfect means to promote the progress of science and technology and the industrialization of a nation whether developed or not. Since no other effective mechanism has been proved worth following, and the patent system has survived for a long time, it is now globally a well-accepted legal tool to promote industrial growth in a market-based economy. The long history of the patent system teaches us that this double-edged sword needs to be carefully calibrated again and again to ensure maximum efficiency. A balanced patent system, it has been proved, is one that promotes maximum public welfare with optimal market incentive to accelerate innovation through public-private participation. This delicate balancing requires the constant monitoring of the patent system by various players. Of the different functionaries involved in the working of the patent system, the patent office and the judiciary play critical roles. Patent being a statutory grant, the patent office assumes the role of a watch dog ensuring that limited monopoly is granted only to inventions that actually promote technological progress.[182] This is achieved by making sure before the grant of patent that there is high quality in the invention, adequate disclosure of the technological advancement and the boundaries of the monopoly right are properly and adequately defined. There is an increasing tendency world over, on the part of the patent offices, to shirk this responsibility owing to various practical reasons. The tendency to assess the efficiency of the patent office based on statistics rather than the quality of the work they do is a major contributor to the erosion of the values essential to the patent office. The dilution of the standards of patentability, non-insistence on adequate and effective compliance of the disclosure requirement and the liberal interpretation of the claims by the judiciary would seem to be another reason for this shift in attitude. The responsibility to maintain the balance of the patent system now appears to be left to market forces rather than the patent office and judiciary making a concerted effort to this effect. Only by re-assuming this role effectively, can the credibility of the patent system be sustained, given the problems that have surfaced in developed economies. The patent offices need to be more vigilant in scrutinizing inventions and ensuring that only quality inventions attract patent protection. Thanks to modern technology, it is much easier to maintain the efficiency of the patent offices to meet the increasing work load. Sacrificing quality in the name of efficiency (which is now being assessed based on the number of patents granted rather than the quality of them), particularly by the patent office of countries like India, will be suicidal.

It is an accepted fact that the market has a role to play in fostering the industrial development of a nation. Maintaining competition is the key to the success of a market-based economic development. Keeping the patent law as one of the effective instruments to achieve this seems to be the major challenge. This will only be possible if efforts are taken to ensure that the patent claims are carefully structured to provide monopoly for what the inventor actually invented and to preserve adequate space for further developments. The law must also ensure adequate exceptions to facilitate follow on invention and prevent abuse of monopoly by the players in the market.

From the analysis of the major features of the post TRIPS patent law of India, it is evident that the Indian parliament made considerable, although inadequate, efforts to safeguard the interest of the large population of India, while maintaining her international obligations. Though there are a few gaps in the law, it is possible to overcome these if they are creatively interpreted by the agencies implementing it. What is important for India is the way in which the Indian Patent Office is going to implement the provisions, particularly in granting patents. There has been considerable pressure on the Indian Patent Offices, particularly in the last few years, because of the increased filing of patent applications, especially from foreign corporations. Modernization of all four Patent Offices (Delhi, Mumbai, Kolkata and Chennai) is in progress and it is expected that the Offices will maintain their credibility by granting quality patents. There is a concerted effort to develop a Manual of Patent Procedure and Practice[183] to narrow down the disparity in the application of standards by different offices in India. It is expected that with the help of modern technology the Indian Patent Offices will be equipped to handle the additional pressure effectively without sacrificing the quality of the patent.

It is heartening to note that the Indian judiciary is also catching up with the challenges of handling complex patent litigation. The trend, though moderate, is to evaluate and appreciate the legislative policy from the perspective of public interest. Recent judicial decisions reflect the caution with which the courts handle patent litigation, showing an eagerness to prevent abuse of monopoly. The courts are also taking adequate measures to protect the interest of the patent owners, without sacrificing public interest. It is true that the largest number of judicial interventions in the last decade has been in the field of public health. But the general expectation is that the same trend will be followed in other fields as well, given the general constitutional jurisprudence developed by the courts in the area of protection of private property.

If one looks at the patent law of India in theory and practice as it stands today it may be possible to infer that it will act as an effective tool to promote domestic research and development and slow but steady industrialization. It is expected that the Patent Office and judiciary will learn from developed countries to implement the positive aspects of the patent system and to take adequate measures to prevent the negative effects that are now being witnessed in those countries. A balanced patent system, giving primacy to the interest of the larger population of India, is expected to make India one of the emerging economic powers of the world.

NOTES

1. Cristopher May, "The hypocrisy of forgetfulness: The contemporary significance of early innovations in intellectual property" 14 *Review of International Political Economy* 1 (February 2007) 1–25, at p. 19. He says, "Certainly nowadays, the discourse privileging trade interests in IPR protection has almost completely drowned out the development aspects, to the extent that the development issues have often been folded into an account of IPRs which suggests that productivity and efficiency must be maximized through the commodification of knowledge for trade. For many developing countries these issues are secondary to the more pressing need to access information and knowledge that will support their further economic development."
2. *Ibid.*, p. 18. The European Patent Office Report, *Scenarios for the Future*, while pointing out that the problems of the modern patent systems (like patent thickets and trolls) are not applicable to all technologies equally, suggests that the one-size-fits-all paradigm of patent law is broken. Also see Susan K. Sell *Private Power, Public Law – The Globalization of Intellectual Property Rights*, Cambridge University Press, 2003, at p. 13. See also J.H.Reichman, "The TRIPs Component of the GATT's Uruguay Round: Competitive Prospects for Intellectual Property Owners in an Integrated World Market" 4 *Fordham Intell. Prop. Media & Ent. L.J.* 171 (1993–1994), available at http://eprints.law.duke.edu/archive/00000464/01/4_Fordham_Intell._Prop._Media_%26_Ent._L.J._171 (1993-1994).pdf, pp. 188–192 and Prof. Paul A. David, "Economic Fundamentals of the Knowledge Society" available at http://www-econ.stanford.edu/faculty/workp/swp02003.pdf (last accessed December 12, 2008).
3. Roberto Mazzoleni and Richard R. Nelson, "The benefits and costs of strong patent protection: a contribution to the current debate" *Research Policy* 27 (1998), at pp. 273–284.
4. For example, Machulp and Penrose say that Continental writers were prone to take the rapid industrialization of England and the U.S. along with the presence of patent system there as sufficient grounds for inferring a causal relation between patents and progress. Fritz Machulp and Edith Penrose, "The Patent Controversy in the Nineteenth Century" X *Journal of Economic History* 1 (1950), at p. 21. See also William M. Landes and Richard A. Posner, "The Political Economy of Intellectual Property Law" available at http://www.aei.org/docLib/20040608_Landes.pdf (last accessed December 30, 2008). William M. Landes and Richard A. Posner state that the political factor behind the sharp increase in the scope of intellectual property protection in the U.S. dating from 1976 was the belief that one of either the causes or consequences of the economic malaise of the 1970s was a decline in the competitiveness of U.S. industry attributable to a loss of technological momentum to competing nations, notably Japan. According to them, the expansion of intellectual property rights was also propelled by a desire to alleviate the chronic trade deficits in the U.S., by increasing the income of owners of copyrights and other intellectual property, most of those owners being American (p. 24). However, whether the increases in the legal protection of intellectual property since 1976 have conferred net benefits on the U.S. economy is uncertain. (p. 25).
5. See for example the history of patents in the US, UK and other major developed economies. Christopher May and Susan K. Sell, "Forgetting History is Not an Option! Intellectual Property, Public Policy and Economic Development in Context" presented at Intellectual Property Rights for Business and Society Birkbeck College, University of London, September 15, 2006, available at http://www.dime-eu.org/files/active/0/MaySell.pdf (last accessed May, 1, 2012). Christopher May and Susan K. Sell, *Intellectual Property Rights – A Critical History*, Lynne Rienner Publishers, 2006. Also see Ha-Joon Chang "Intellectual Property Rights and Economic Development: historical lessons and emerging issues" 2 *Journal of Human Development* 287 (2001), at pp. 288–293. See Adam Mossoff, "Rethinking the Development of Patents: An Intellectual History, 1550–1800" 52 *Hastings Law Journal* 1255. A historical analysis

reveals that the patent system originated as a monopoly rather than as a form of private property. Fritz Machulp and Edith Penrose, "The Patent Controversy in the Nineteenth Century" X *Journal of Economic History* 1 (1950), at pp. 9, 16, discuss how the strong movements in nineteenth-century Europe, against patent privilege and monopoly, made it strategically essential for the defenders of patent system to separate the idea of patent protection from the monopoly issue and from the free trade issue. According to the authors, "(t)his was attempted by presenting the case of patent protection as one of natural law and private property, of man's right to live by his work and society's duty to secure him his fair share, and of society's interest in achieving swift industrial progress at the smallest possible cost." See also Christopher May, *A Global Political Economy of Intellectual Property Rights: The New Enclosures?* Routledge, 2000, at p. 206.

6. See *Scenarios for the Future*, European Patent Office, 2007 and the FTC Report 2003, *To Promote Innovation: The Proper Balance of Competition and Patent Law and Policy*.
7. Graham Dutfield and Uma Suthersan, "Innovation and Development" in Uma Suthersan, Graham Dutfield and Kit Boey Chow (eds), *Innovation Without Patents*, Edward Elgar Publishing Inc., 2007 at p. 10 cite the example of the Japanese Patent Office taking 29 years to grant patent for an Integrated Circuit, which was one of the most important inventions of the second half of the twentieth century. This enabled Japanese companies to acquire the technology from the patent specification published 18 months after filing of patent application and they could control 80 percent of the U.S. market for computer semiconductors by improving upon the technology. See also Christopher May, "The hypocrisy of forgetfulness: The contemporary significance of early innovations in intellectual property" 14 *Review of International Political Economy* 1 (February 2007) 1–25, at p. 19. He says "When the experience of the Newly Industrialised Countries (NICs) of East Asia is examined, the tension between trade and development issues becomes clearer. The reliance on weak (or non-existent) IPR protection in earlier stages of development benefited the NICs quite extensively." Surveying a number of studies, Nagesh Kumar concludes that "[T]he east Asian countries, viz., Japan, Korea and Taiwan have absorbed substantial amount[s] of technological learning under weak IPR protection regime[s] during the early phases [of economic development]. These patent regimes facilitated the absorption of innovation and knowledge generated abroad by their indigenous firms. They have also encouraged minor adaptations and incremental innovations on the foreign inventions by domestic enterprises." Nagesh Kumar "Intellectual Property Rights, Technology and Economic Development" 38(3) *Economic and Political Weekly* (2003) 209–225, at p. 216.
   As these local industries started to innovate themselves, then a stronger regime of protection was established, *but only then*.
8. Sudip Choudhury, "The Pharmaceutical Industry" in Subir Gokarn, Anindya Sen and Rajendra R. Vaidya (eds), *The Structure of Indian Industry*, Oxford: Oxford University Press, 2004. See also Biswajit Dhar and K.M.Gopakumar, *Post-2005 TRIPS scenario in patent protection in the pharmaceutical sector: The case of the generic pharmaceutical industry in India,* UNCTAD, IDRC and ICSTD, November, 2006.
9. Sudip Caudhuri, *The WTO and India's Pharmaceuticals Industry: Patent Protection, TRIPS, and Developing Countries*, Oxford University Press, 2005, at pp. 39, 128–132. Also see Jancie Mueller, "The Tiger Awakens: The Tumultuous Transformation of India's Patent System and the Rise of Indian Pharmaceutical Innovation" 68 *University of Pittsburgh Law Review* 491 (2007), at p. 508. Sudip Choudhury, "The Pharmaceutical Industry" in Subir Gokarn, Anindya Sen and Rajendra R. Vaidya (eds), *The Structure of Indian Industry*, Oxford: Oxford University Press, 2004, at p. 154; Sudip Chaudhuri, "TRIPS Agreement and Amendment of Patents Act in India" *EPW Special Article*, August 10, 2002 and Sudip Chaudhuri, "TRIPS and Changes in Pharmaceutical Patent Regime in India," Working Paper No. 535, January, 2005, Indian Institute of Management, Calcutta.

10. *Ibid.* However, in Rajiv Dhavan, Lindsay Harris and Gopal Jain, "Whose Interest? Independent India's Patent Law and Policy," 32 *Journal of Indian Law Institute* 429 (1990), the authors criticize the Act and the Tek Chand and Ayyangar Committee Reports for not following the Japanese or German model of excluding food, medicine and chemicals from the purview of patentability (at pp. 433, 434). They also criticize the Ayyangar Committee for not seriously considering whether the patent system was actually suited to India and recommending a patent system just because such a system had been working for over a century (at pp. 445, 474).
11. Sudip Choudhury, "The Pharmaceutical Industry" in Subir Gokarn, Anindya Sen and Rajendra R. Vaidya (eds), *The Structure of Indian Industry*, Oxford University Press, 2004, at pp. 159–163, 168 examines how the Patents Act of 1970 has enabled the Indian pharmaceutical companies not only to successfully compete with the MNCs in the domestic market but also to make their presence felt in the international markets. See also Biswajit Dhar and K.M.Gopakumar, *Post-2005 TRIPS scenario in patent protection in the pharmaceutical sector: The case of the generic pharmaceutical industry in India,* UNCTAD, IDRC and ICSTD, November, 2006. The authors are of the view that even in the post-TRIPS context the Indian pharmaceuticals are faring well in the global markets. See also Sudip Caudhuri, *The WTO and India's Pharmaceuticals Industry: Patent Protection, TRIPS, and Developing Countries*, Oxford University Press, 2005, at pp. 46–53.
12. See generally, John H. Barton, "Issues Posed by a World Patent System" in Keith E. Maskus and Jerome H. Reichman (eds), *International Public Goods and the Transfer of Technology: Under a Globalized Intellectual Property Regime*, Cambridge University Press, 2005. He endorses the view that such a system is not as valuable to the developing world as it is to the developed world, and, in some situations it can positively harm developing nations (at p. 622). Frederick M. Abbott and Jerome H. Reichman, "The Doha Round's Public Health Policy: Strategies for the Production and Diffusion of Patented Medicines under the Amended TRIPS Provisions" *10 J. Int'l Econ. L.* 921 (2007) at p. 925.
13. See *Scenarios for the Future*, European Patent Office, 2007, at p. 37. The EPO Report quotes Dr. Ronald Grossenbacher, Chairman of the EPO, stating that too high a level of patent and too low a threshold is hindering spontaneous innovation. Also see the interview with Francis Ahner, available at http://documents.epo.org/projects/babylon/eponet.nsf/0/599C2F1A3C1C346EC12572D800376DD7/$File/Interview_Ahner.pdf (last accessed May 1, 2012) at p. 14, and the FTC Report 2003, *To Promote Innovation: The Proper Balance of Competition and Patent Law and Policy*. In Chapter 3 of the report the effect of strong patent protection on different types of industries such as pharmaceutical, biotech, internet, computer software and hardware industry are analyzed in detail and it was reported that whereas pharmaceutical and biotech industries testified that strong patent protection is essential to innovation in their fields, by contrast, computer hardware and software industry representatives are concerned about the increasing tendency in their field to create patent thickets which adversely affect both commercialization of the technology and R&D activities.
14. FTC Report 2003, *To Promote Innovation: The Proper Balance of Competition and Patent Law and Policy*, FTC Report 2007, *Antitrust Enforcement and Intellectual Property Rights: Promoting Innovation and Competition*.
15. Frederick M. Abbott and Jerome H. Reichman, "The Doha Round's Public Health Policy: Strategies for the Production and Diffusion of Patented Medicines under the Amended TRIPS Provisions" *10 J. Int'l Econ. L.* 921 (2007) at p. 960.
16. Sudip Choudhury, "The Pharmaceutical Industry" in Subir Gokarn, Anindya Sen and Rajendra R. Vaidya (eds), *The Structure of Indian Industry*, Oxford University Press, 2004, at p. 146.
17. See Bakshi Tek Chand Committee (The Patents Enquiry Committee 1948–50) and Rajagopala Iyyagar Committee on the Revision of Patent Law (1959).
18. Rajagopala Iyyagar Committee on the Revision of Patent Law (1959) states at p. 12,

quoting from the interim report of the Patents Enquiry Committee, that the proportion of grants of patents to Indians and foreigners during the period 1930–37 was roughly 1:9.

19. The experience in the Indian pharmaceutical industry is discussed in detail in Sudip Caudhuri, *The WTO and India's Pharmaceuticals Industry: Patent Protection, TRIPS, and Developing Countries*, Oxford University Press, 2005, at pp. 39, 128–132.
20. For example, in the case of pharmaceutical industry, the private sector has greatly benefited from the support from the plants set up in the public sector like Hindustan Antibiotic Ltd. (HAL) and Indian Drugs and Pharmaceuticals Ltd. (IDPL) and the assistance received from CSIR laboratories in developing drugs. See Sudip Chaudhury, "Pharmaceutical industry" in Subir Gokarn, Anindya Sen and Rajendra R. Vaidya (eds), *The Structure of Indian Industry*, Oxford University Press, 2004, at pp. 161–163.
21. The Objects and Reasons of the Act states that in view of the substantial change in the political and economic conditions of the country, the Act aims at ensuring that "patent rights are not worked to the detriment of the consumer or to the prejudice of trade or the industrial development of the country . . .". However, there is criticism that India did not opt for a patent free state even in the case of pharmaceuticals as did Japan and Germany. See Rajeev Dhavan, Lindsay Harris and Gopal Jain, "Whose Interest? Independent India's Patent Law and Policy" 32 *Journal of Indian Law Institute* 429 at pp. 433, 434, 445, 451. The authors criticize the Ayyangar Committee for its conclusion that patent system is the most desirable method of encouraging inventions and rewarding them (at p. 451).
22. See section 83 of the Act as amended.
23. See *Scenarios for the Future*, European Patent Office, 2007, at p. 36.
24. John H. Barton, "Issues Posed by a World Patent System" in Keith E. Maskus and Jerome H. Reichman (eds) *International Public Goods and Transfer Technology under a Globalized Intellectual Property Regime*, Cambridge University Press, 2005, at p. 346.
25. For example, the view shared by many is that it is the change in the U.S. patent system owes its origin to the setting up of the Federal Circuit Courts of Appeal in 1982, which has brought in three major changes affecting innovation, namely, lowered standards for patentability, increased uncertainty and unpredictability as to the outcome of patent litigation, and excessive damages for patent infringement. See generally, Cecil D. Quillen, Jr., "Innovation and the U.S. Patent System" 1 *Virginia Law & Business Review* 207 (2006). She says that it started with *Graham v. John Deere Co. of Kan. City*, 383 U.S. 1 (1966), who felt it necessary to have a change in the concept of "person of ordinary skill in the Art," in view of the widening of "[t]he ambit of applicable art in given fields of science" by disciplines unheard of a half century ago. See also Adam B. Jaffe and Josh Lerner, *Innovation and its Discontents: How Our Broken Patent System is Endangering Innovation and Progress, and What To Do About It*, Princeton University Press, 2004, at p. 10.
26. In the U.S., for example, in *Cuno Engineering Corp. v. Automatic Devices Corp.* 314 U.S. 84, 51 U.S.P.Q. 272 (1941), it was held that the invention "must reveal the flash of creative genius, not merely the skill of the calling" (at p. 91). See also Jeanne C. Fromer, "The Layers of Obviousness in Patent Law" 22 *Harvard Journal of Law & Technology* (forthcoming 2008) at pp. 4, 5, available at http://ssrn.com/abstract=1119723 (last accessed December 28, 2008).
27. For example, the chemical and biotechnological inventions necessitated a lowering of patentability standards. In these fields, most often the pre-existing information fell "only a little short of what is claimed to be inventive" and in such cases it was thought that the standard of inventive step could not be the same as that required for other inventions. See Cornish, *Intellectual Property Law*, Fifth Edition, Sweet and Maxwell, p. 203. He cites the example of Lord Diplock's willingness to accord patents for the purpose of giving "some security to the investment involved" in *American Cyanamid (Dann's) Patent* [1971] R P C 147 at 241, Robert M. Hunt, "Nonobviousness and

the Incentive to Innovate: An Economic Analysis of Intellectual Property Reform" March 1999, Working paper No. 99-3, at p. 3.
28. Jay P. Kesan, "Carrots and Sticks to Create a Better Patent System" 17 *Berkeley Technology Law Journal* 763 (2002), Robert P. Merges, "Uncertainty and the Standard of Patentability" 7 *High Tech. L.J.* 1 (1992), *Scenarios for the Future*, European Patent Office, at pp. 11, 18.
29. Jay P. Kesan, "Carrots and Sticks to Create a Better Patent System" 17 *Berkeley Technology Law Journal* 763 (2002), Mark Schankerman, "The Economics of Patent Reform: Improving the Design of Incentives and Mechanisms for Enforcement" Beesley Lecture on Regulation, November 15, 2007, at p. 3, Cecil D. Quillen, Jr. "Innovation and the U.S. Patent System" 1 *Virginia Law & Business Review* 208, (2006), at pp. 210, 212.
30. *Scenarios for the Future*, European Patent Office, at pp. 11, 18.
31. See Philippe Ducor, "In Re Deuel: Biotechnology Industry v. Patent Law?" [1996] 18 *EIPR* 35, John M. Golden, "Biotechnology, Technology Policy, and Patentability: Natural Products and Inventions in the American System" 50 *Emory Law Journal*, 101 (2001).
32. Edmund J. Sease, "Chemical Properties: Are they a Sensible Yardstick of Patentability" 9 *Patent L. Rev.* 161 (1977), "Standards of Obviousness and the Patentability of Chemical Compounds" 87 *Harv. L. Review* 607 (1974): 6 *Patent L. Review* 151 (1974), Harold C. Wegner, "Chemical and Biotechnology Obviousness in a State of Flux" 26 *Biotechnology Law Report* 437 (October 2007).
33. Peter E. Montague, "Biotechnology Patents and the Problem of Obviousness" 4 *AIPJ* 3 (1993), p. 8.
34. *Scenarios for the Future*, European Patent Office, p. 37.
35. See, *Scenarios for the Future*, European Patent Office, FTC Report of US, *To Promote Innovation: The Proper Balance of Competition and Patent Law and Policy*, 2003, Gustavo Ghidini, *Intellectual Property and Competition Law: The Innovation Nexus*, Edward Elgar, 2006.
36. 550 US 398 (2007).
37. *Ibid.*
38. "Article 27(1) reads: 'Subject to the provisions of paragraphs 2 and 3, patents shall be available for any inventions, whether products or processes, in all fields of technology, provided that they are new, involve an inventive step and are capable of industrial application. Subject to paragraph 4 of Article 65, paragraph 8 of Article 70 and paragraph 3 of this Article, patents shall be available and patent rights enjoyable without discrimination as to the place of invention, the field of technology and whether products are imported or locally produced.'"
39. Section 2(j) before amendment reads: "'invention' means any new and useful (i) art, process, method or manner of manufacture; (ii) machine, apparatus or other article; (iii) substance produced by manufacture and includes any new and useful improvement of any of them, and an alleged invention."
40. Jancie Mueller, "The Tiger Awakens: The Tumultuous Transformation of India's Patent System and the Rise of Indian Pharmaceutical Innovation" 68 *University of Pittsburgh Law Review* 491 (2007) at p. 549.
41. Section 2(j) reads: "invention means a new product or process involving an inventive step and capable of industrial application" (amended in 2002).
42. Section 2(l).
43. Section 2(j(a)) reads: "'inventive step' means a feature of an invention that involves technical advance as compared to the existing knowledge or having economic significance or both and that makes the invention not obvious to a person skilled in the art" (introduced in 2005).
44. Section 2(a(c)) reads: "capable of industrial application in relation to an invention means that the invention is capable of being made or used in an industry" (introduced in 2002).

45. Biswajit Dhar and K.M.Gopakumar, *Post-2005 TRIPS scenario in patent protection in the pharmaceutical sector: The case of the generic pharmaceutical industry in India,* UNCTAD, IDRC and ICSTD, November, 2006 at p. 16.
46. Section 2(a) reads: "an invention which is frivolous or which claims anything obvious contrary to well established natural laws."
47. Section 3(c) reads: "the mere discovery of a scientific principle or the formulation of an abstract theory or discovery of any living thing or non-living substance occurring in nature."
48. Section 3(d) reads: "The mere discovery of a new form of a known substance which does not result in the enhancement of the known efficacy of that substance or the mere discovery of any new property or new use for a known substance or of the mere use of a known process, machine or apparatus unless such known process results in a new product or employs at least one new reactant.

    For the purposes of this clause, salts, esters, ethers, polymorphs, metabolites, pure form, particle size isomers, mixtures of isomers, complexes, combinations and other derivatives of known substance shall be considered to be the same substance, unless they differ significantly in properties with regard to efficacy."
49. Section 3(e) reads: "a substance obtained by a mere admixture resulting only in the aggregation of the properties of the components thereof or a process for producing such substance."
50. Section 3(f) reads: "the mere arrangement or re-arrangement or duplication of known devices each functioning independently of one another in a known way."
51. Section 3(p) reads: "an invention which in effect is traditional knowledge or which is an aggregation or duplication of known properties of traditionally known component or components."
52. (1979) 2 SCC 511.
53. *Ibid.* at p. 518 (author's emphasis).
54. *Ibid.* at p. 519 (author's emphasis).
55. Jancie M. Mueller, "The Tiger Awakens: The Tumultuous Transformation of India's Patent System and the Rise of Indian Pharmaceutical Innovation" 68 *University of Pittsburgh Law Review* 491 at p. 558. The author cites the example of ayurvedic therapies and states that in its zeal to prevent pharmaceutical product patent holders from extending their monopolies through follow on process patents, India may have suppressed an important means of stimulating indigenous innovation (see pp. 558–559).
56. Another criticism is with regard to the use of the term "discovery". See D. Christopher Ohly, "What's 'New'? – Isn't it Obvious?" 13 *Journal of Intellectual Property Rights*, 498 (2008), at p. 501. The author says that it is the least complicated but the most critical term in the Act and it could only cover instances where there is no human intervention and only mere observation which led to the finding of the new form of known substance. This interpretation tends to limit the application of the provision to unexpected extents.
57. Where Jancie Mueller uses the term derivatives for "new form of known substance" Shamnad Basheer expresses doubts as to whether they could actually be considered as derivatives.
58. 35 U.S.C. § 100 (b).
59. The Swiss-type patent claims first got judicial recognition in *Re Eisai Co Ltd* (*"Eisai"*) [1985] OJ EPO 64, Case GR 05/83.
60. *Novartis AG v. Union of India*, W.P. Nos.24759 and 24760 of 2006 decided on August 6, 2007.
61. It was argued by the petitioner that: "Under the amended section, the patent applicant is required to show that the invention has enhanced efficacy of the known substance. Though the efficacy of a known substance may be well known, yet, unless there are some guidelines in the amended section itself to understand the expression 'enhancement of the known efficacy' namely, what would be treated as 'enhanced efficacy', an uncontrolled discretion is given to the Patent Controller to apply his own standards,

which may not be uniform, in deciding whether there is enhancement of the known efficacy of that substance. Such wide discretion vested with a Statutory Authority without any guidelines to follow, would result in arbitrary exercise of power. In other words, the Patent Controller may be in a position to decide any case, based on his whims and fancies, namely, whether there is enhancement in the known efficacy or not. On this short ground, the section must be held to be violative of Article 14 of the Constitution of India." *Ibid.*, Para 3.

62. See Jancie Mueller, "The Tiger Awakens: The Tumultuous Transformation of India's Patent System and the Rise of Indian Pharmaceutical Innovation" 68 *University of Pittsburgh Law Review* 491 (2007), at pp. 551–556; Shamnad Basheer and T. Prasanth Reddy, "The 'Efficacy' of Indian Patent Law: Ironing out the Creases in Section 3 (d)" 2008 5: 2 *SCRIPT – ed* 232 at p. 234.
63. *Novartis AG v. Union of India*, W.P. Nos.24759 and 24760 of 2006 decided on 06.08.2007, Para 16. The court also quotes from AIR 1961 SC 1602 (*Jyoti Pershad v. Union Territory of Delhi*) where the Supreme Court held: "So long as the Legislature indicates, in the operative provisions of the statute with certainty, the policy and purpose of the enactment, the mere fact that the legislation is skeletal, or the fact that a discretion is left to those entrusted with administering the law, affords no basis either for the contention that there has been an excessive delegation of legislative power as to amount to an abdication of its functions, or that the discretion vested is uncanalised and unguided as to amount to a carte blanche to discriminate. If the power or discretion has been conferred in a manner which is legal and constitutional, the fact that Parliament could possibly have made more detailed provisions, could obviously not be a ground for invalidating the law."
64. *Ibid.*, para 13.
65. *Ibid.*, para 13.
66. See the *Draft Manual of Patent Procedure and Practice* (2008) para 4.5.6.
67. Shamnad Basheer and T. Prasanth Reddy, "The 'Efficacy' of Indian Patent Law: Ironing out the Creases in Section 3 (d)" 2008 5: 2 *SCRIPT – ed* 232, at pp. 243–244. The authors express the view that if efficacy is restricted to only "therapeutic efficacy, new drug delivery mechanisms, a category of inventions in which Indian companies are particularly proficient, will fall out of the scope of protection."
68. *Pfizer Inc. v. Apotex Inc.* 480 F. 3d 1348 (Fed. Cir. 2007), *PharmaStem Therapeutics Inc. v. ViaCell Inc.* 491 F.3d 1342 (Fed. Cir. 2007).
69. Jancie Mueller, "Chemicals, Combinations and 'Common Sense': How the Supreme Court's KSR decision is Changing Federal Circuit Obviousness Determinations in Pharmaceutical and Biotechnology Cases" University of Pittsburgh School of Law, Legal Studies, Research Paper Series, Working Paper No. 2008-07, December 2007, available at http://ssrn.com/abstract=1079118, at p. 16.
70. *Ibid.*
71. Frederick M. Abbott and Jerome H. Reichman, "The Doha Round's Public Health Policy: Strategies for the Production and Diffusion of Patented Medicines under the Amended TRIPS Provisions" *10 J. Int'l Econ. L.* 921 (2007) at p. 959 (see n. 170). They add that since India remains the largest supplier of generic drugs to the developing world market at the present time, the results of its legislative balancing act at home could affect the availability and affordability of essential medicines in all developing countries for a considerable time.
72. Jancie Mueller, "The Tiger Awakens: The Tumultuous Transformation of India's Patent System and the Rise of Indian Pharmaceutical Innovation" 68 *University of Pittsburgh Law Review* 491 (2007), at p. 551, 556. The author quotes from an interview with the Director of Corporate Affairs, Pfizer India, New Delhi on November 15, 2005.
73. See FTC Report 2003, Chapter III, EPO Report. See also *Scenarios for the Future*, European Patent Office, at p. 89. In fields like computer software, desirability of patent protection is a hotly debated issue. See John H. Barton, "Issues Posed by a

World Patent System" in Keith E. Maskus and Jerome Reichman, *International Public Goods and Transfer of Technology under a Globalized Intellectual Property Regime*, Cambridge University Press, 2004, at p. 347.
74. Shamnad Basheer, *Limiting the Patentability of Pharmaceutical Inventions and Micro-organisms: A TRIPS Compatibility Review*, IP Institute, 2005 at pp. 6 (short summary), 35 and 49 (conclusion).
75. *Scenarios for the Future*, European Patent Office, at pp. 94–96.
76. *Ibid.*, Also see Report of the FTC, *To Promote Innovation: The Proper Balance of Competition and Patent Law and Policy* , Ch. III.
77. Section 2 (ta).
78. Biswajit Dhar and K.M.Gopakumar, *Post-2005 TRIPS scenario in patent protection in the pharmaceutical sector: The case of the generic pharmaceutical industry in India,* UNCTAD, IDRC and ICSTD, November, 2006 at p. 16. Shamnad Basheer, "India's Tryst with TRIPS: The Patents (Amendment) Act, 2005" 1 *Indian Journal of Law and Technology* 15 (2005), at p. 23 is very sardonic about the broad definition.
79. Section 3(c) reads: "the mere discovery of a scientific principle or the formulation of an abstract theory or discovery of any living thing or non-living substance occurring in nature."
80. Section 3(j) reads: "plants and animals in the whole or any part thereof other than micro-organism but including seeds varieties and species and essentially biological process for the production or propagation of plants and animals." Jancie Mueller apprehends that since "micro-organism" is not defined under TRIPS, the Mashelkar Committee, which was also asked to look into whether it would be TRIPS complaint to exclude micro-organisms from patentability, might come up with a narrow definition of "micro-organism" so as to minimize the scope of allowable subject matter (see pp. 559–560). However, at present, the Draft Manual of Patent Procedure and Practice (2008) suggests that any discovered micro-organism from the nature is not patentable (see para 4.10.1).
81. John H. Barton, "Issues Posed by a World Patent System" in Keith E. Maskus and Jerome H. Reichman (eds) *International Public Goods and Transfer Technology under a Globalized Intellectual Property Regime*, Cambridge University Press, 2005, at p. 347.
82. *Ibid.*
83. See section 3(k).
84. Section 3(o) reads: "topography of integrated circuits."
85. See section 3(m).
86. Yogesh Anand Pai, "Patent Protection for Computer Programmes in India: Need for a Coherent Approach" *The Journal of World Intellectual Property* (2007) 1, at p. 18.
87. *Ibid.*, at p. 19.
88. Section 3(p).
89. Section 10(4) proviso (ii)(D).
90. Section 25(1)(j).
91. Section 25(2)(j).
92. Section 25(1)(k) and 25(2)(k).
93. Section 64(p).
94. Section 64(q).
95. Section 3(l) reads: "a literary, dramatic, musical or artistic work or any other aesthetic creation whatsoever including cinematograph works and television productions."
96. Section 3(n) reads: "a presentation of information."
97. Section 4 reads: "No patent shall be granted to an invention relating to atomic energy falling subsection (1) of Section 20 of Atomic Energy Act 1962."
98. Section 10 (4) reads: "Every complete specification shall: (a) fully and particularly describe the invention and its operation or use and the method by which it is to be performed; (b) disclose the best method of performing the invention which is known to the applicant and for which he is entitled to claim protection; and (c) end with a claim or claims defining the scope of the invention for which protection is claimed."

99. Section 10(4)(d)(ii) reads: "if the applicant mentions a biological material in the specification which may not be described in such a way to satisfy clause (a) and (b), and if such material is not available to the public, the application shall be completed by depositing the material to an international depository authority under the Budapest Treaty."
100. Section 10(4)(d)(D) reads: "disclose the source and geographical origin of the biological material in the material when used in an invention."
101. Section 25: pre-grant opposition provision was introduced into Indian law for the first time in the 1911 Act. This provision was modelled after the then English patent law. Jancie Mueller says that today India is one of only a handful of countries like Brazil and Jordan that still permits pre-grant opposition. See Jancie Mueller, "The Tiger Awakens: The Tumultuous Transformation of India's Patent System and the Rise of Indian Pharmaceutical Innovation" 68 *University of Pittsburgh Law Review* 491 (2007), at p. 568.
102. For a detailed analysis of the practical working of the pre-grant opposition provision in Indian patent law, see *ibid.* at pp. 570–572 where it is stated that between January and November 2005, 30 pre-grant oppositions were filed with the Indian Patent Office's Delhi Branch alone and as of February 2006, Indian pharmaceutical companies including Cipla, Ranbaxy and Cadila had filed around 45 pre-grant oppositions in the form of representations with the Controller of Patents (quoting from Gladys Mirandah, "War on Pharmaceuticla Patents Begins" *Managing Intellectual Property*, February 2006 at p. 135). See also Jancie Mueller, "Taking TRIPS to India – Novartis, Patent Law, and Access to Medicines" *The New England Journal of Medicines* 541, February 8, 2007, at p. 542 where she states that generic firms and patient-advocacy groups are already making use of "robust opposition provisions" in Indian law. She cites the example of a group of cancer patients who opposed the Geevec application resulting in the rejection of the application.
103. MANU/TN/1217/2008.
104. *Ibid.*, at para 33.
105. "Person interested" is defined under section 2 (1) (t) to include "a person engaged in, or in promoting, research in the same field as that to which the invention relates."
106. MANU/SC/3435/2008.
107. *Ibid.*, at p. 3448.
108. See Adam Mossoff, "Rethinking the Development of Patents: An Intellectual History, 1550–1800" 52 *Hastings Law Journal* 1255, at p. 1260.
109. *Ibid.* The first letters patent in the nature of manufacturing monopoly was granted to Henry Smith by Edward VI in 1552. The main purpose behind granting such a monopoly was to benefit the subjects by making Normandy glass available to them for a reasonable price and to train them in making it themselves. Thus the main reason for granting a monopoly was to bring a trade to England and the conditions attached were to train the English in a new trade and make another commodity available in England for trade at a cheaper price, thus promoting competition.
110. See Benjamin G. Jackson, "*Merck v. Integra*: Bailing Water Without Plugging the Holes" 20 *BYU J. Pub. L.* 579 (Notes and comments).
111. See Kevin Iles, "A Comparative Analysis of the Impact of Experimental Use Exemptions in Patent Law on Incentives to Innovate" 4 *Nw. J. of Tech. & Intell. Prop.* 61 (Fall 2005) and Norman Siebrasse and Keith Culver, "The Experimental Use Defence to Patent Infringement: A Comparative Assessment" 56 *University of Toronto Law Journal* (2006) 333.
112. 307 F.3d 1351 (2002).
113. *Integra Lifesciences I, Ltd. v. Merck KGaA*, 331 F.3d 860, 2003 U.S. App. LEXIS 11335 (Fed. Cir., 2003).
114. 307 F.3d 1351 (2002) at p. 1362.
115. *Ibid.*
116. Benjamin G. Jackson, "*Merck v. Integra*: Bailing Water Without Plugging the Holes" 20 *BYU J. Pub. L.* 579 (Notes and comments) at p. 582.

117. *Integra Lifesciences I, Ltd. v. Merck KGaA*, 331 F.3d 860, 2003 U.S. App. LEXIS 11335 (Fed. Cir., 2003). However, the dissenting view of Judge Newman is worth quoting:

> The purpose of a patent system is not only to provide a financial incentive to create new knowledge and bring it to public benefit through new products; it also serves to add to the body of published scientific/technologic knowledge. The requirement of disclosure of the details of patented inventions facilitates further knowledge and understanding of what was done by the patentee, and may lead to further technologic advance. The right to conduct research to achieve such knowledge need not, and should not, await expiration of the patent. That is not the law, and it would be a practice impossible to administer. Yet today the court disapproves and essentially eliminates the common law research exemption. This change of law is ill-suited to today's research-founded, technology-based economy. I must, respectfully, dissent.

118. *Merck* KGaA, *Petitioner v. Integra Lifesciences I, Ltd., et al.*, 545 U.S. 193 (2005).
119. Wolrad Prinz zu Waldeck und Pyrmont, "Research Tool Patents After *Integra v. Merck* – Have They Reached a Safe Harbor?" 14 *Michigan Telecommunications and Technology Law Review* 367 (2008) at p. 392, *available at* http://www.mttlr.org/vol fourteen/waldeck.pdf (last accessed December 13, 2008).
120. John H. Barton, "Patents and Antitrust: A rethinking in the light of Patent Breadth and Sequential Innovation" 65 *Antitrust Law Review*, 449 (1997); John F. Duffy, "Harmony and Diversity in Global Patent Law" 17 *Berkeley Technology Law Journal* 685 (2002) (where he says that a strict interpretation of experimental use exemption may provide incentive for certain industries to locate their research operations outside of the United States), at p. 719. This view is shared by Jancie Mueller, "The Evanescent Experimental Use Exemption from United States Patent Infringement Liability: Implications for University and Nonprofit Research and Development" 56 *Baylor Law Review,* 917 (2004) at p. 920. She cites the example of software industry and states that software development firms are "motivated to outsource their programming research and development to foreign countries that recognize an experimental use exemption, which could potentially immunize the research activity" such as India (p. 921, f.n. 10.), Michelle Cai, "*Madey v. Duke University*: Shattering the Myth of Universities Experimental Use Defense" 19 *Berkeley Technology Law Journal* 175 (2004).
121. Article 30 reads: "Members may provide limited exceptions to the exclusive rights conferred by a patent, provided that such exceptions do not unreasonably conflict with a normal exploitation of the patent and do not unreasonably prejudice the legitimate interests of the patent owner, taking account of the legitimate interests of third parties."
122. WT/DS114/R dated 17 March 2000 Decision of DSB in EU v. Canada case (Canada – Patent Protection of Pharmaceutical Products).
123. Section 47(3) reads: "any machine, apparatus or other article in respect of which the patent is granted or any article made by the use of the process in respect of which the patent is granted, may be made or used, and any process in respect of which the patent is granted may be used, by any person, for the purpose merely of experiment or research including the imparting of instructions to pupils."
124. Section 47(1) reads: "any machine, apparatus or other article in respect of which the patent is granted or any article made by using a process in respect of which the patent is granted, may be imported or made by or on behalf of the Government for the purpose merely of its own use."
125. Section 47(2) reads: "any process in respect of which the patent is granted may be used by or on behalf of the Government for the purpose merely of its own use."
126. Section 47(4) reads: "in the case of a patent in respect of any medicine or drug, the medicine or drug may be imported by the Government for the purpose merely of its

own use or for distribution in any dispensary, hospital or other medical institution maintained by or on behalf of the Government or any other dispensary, hospital or other medical institution which the Central Government may, having regard to the public service that such dispensary, hospital or medical institution renders, specify in this behalf by notification in the Official Gazette."

127. Article 6 reads: "For the purposes of dispute settlement under this Agreement, subject to the provisions of Articles 3 and 4 nothing in this Agreement shall be used to address the issue of the exhaustion of intellectual property rights."
128. Section 107A (b) reads: "importation of patented products by any person from a person who is duly authorized by under the law to sell or distribute the product shall not be considered as an infringement of patent rights." This clearly indicates that India has opted for the international exhaustion principle.
129. Section 107A (b) reads: "importation of patented products by any person from a person who is duly authorized under the law to produce and sell or distribute the product shall not be considered as an infringement of patent rights."
130. Thus it enables the Indian generic drug manufacturers to "capitalize on the breadth of this provision by shifting their manufacturing base to neighbouring LDCs such as Bengladesh (which have time till 2015 to shift to a pharmaceutical product patent regime) and importing the same to India." Jancie Mueller, "The Tiger Awakens: The Tumultuous Transformation of India's Patent System and the Rise of Indian Pharmaceutical Innovation" 68 *University of Pittsburgh Law Review* 491 (2007), p. 610. She feels that India may respond to Shamnad Basheer's view that such an act is not "exhaustion" and therefore not exempted by TRIPS, by stating that India is "making the most of the flexibilities provided by TRIPS, particularly in view of the explicit recognition in the Doha Ministerial Declaration that the effect of the provisions in the TRIPS Agreement that are relevant to the exhaustion of intellectual property rights is to leave each member free to establish its own regime for such exhaustion without challenge, subject to the MFN and National Treatment provisions of Articles 3 and 4" (p. 612).
131. For a contrary view see Shamnad Bhasher and Mrinalini Kochupillai, "Exhausting Patent Rights in India: Parallel Import and TRIPS Compliance," 13 *Journal of Intellectual Property Rights* (September 2008), pp. 486–497.
132. Section 107A (a) reads: "any act of making, constructing, using, selling or importing a patented invention solely for uses reasonably relating to the development and submission of information required under any law for the time being in force, in India, or in a country other than India, that regulates the manufacture, construction, use, sale or import of any product shall not be considered as an infringement of patent rights."
133. See Report of the Panel, WT/DS114/R dated March 17, 2000.
134. Michael D. Scott, "Compulsory Licensing of Intellectual Property in International Transactions" 10 *EIPR* (1998) p. 319.
135. Article 5A (2).
136. Sisule I. Musungu, Susan Villanueva and Roxana Blasetti, *Utilizing TRIPS Flexibilities for Public Health Protection Through South-South Regional Frameworks*, South Centre, 2004, pp. 12–13. See also Carlos Correa, *Implications of The Doha Declaration on The TRIPS Agreement And Public Health*, WHO, 2002, p. 15.
137. Sisule I. Musungu, Susan Villanueva and Roxana Blasetti, *Utilizing TRIPS Flexibilities for Public Health Protection Through South-South Regional Frameworks,* South Centre, 2004, pp. 12–13.
138. When South Africa, with more than 5 billion of its population affected by AIDS, introduced the Medicines and Related Substances Control Amendment Act in 1997 in order to ensure availability of affordability of HIV/AIDS related drugs using parallel importation and compulsory licensing methods, the U.S. Government and 41 pharmaceutical companies challenged the Act in the African High Court as unconstitutional and TRIPS non-compatible. See Haochen Sun, "The Road to Doha and Beyond: Some Reflections on TRIPS Agreement and Public Health" 15 *EJIL* 123

(2004) at p. 131. Also see Divya Murthy, "The Future of Compulsory Licensing: Deciphering the Doha Declaration on the TRIPS Agreement and Public Health" 17 *Am. U. Int'l L. Rev.* 1299 at pp. 1312–1316.

139. The reason for suggesting license of right is that it could stop court injunctions against alleged inventors and thereby force the patentee to give a license to anyone.
140. *Scenarios for the Future*, European Patent Office, pp. 95, 96. However, it suggests strong patent protection in areas like the pharmaceutical sector, as demanded by the industry.
141. Article 31 bis.
142. Biswajit Dhar and K.M.Gopakumar, *Post-2005 TRIPS scenario in patent protection in the pharmaceutical sector: The case of the generic pharmaceutical industry in India,* UNCTAD, IDRC and ICSTD, November, 2006, at pp. 21–24.
143. Jancie Mueller, "The Tiger Awakens: The Tumultuous Transformation of India's Patent System and the Rise of Indian Pharmaceutical Innovation" 68 *University of Pittsburgh Law Review* 491 (2007), at p. 580. However, others hold the view that the Indian provisions "may not fully meet the requirements of the domestic pharmaceutical industry" as there is a requirement under Section 84 for waiting three years before granting compulsory licence. See Biswajit Dhar and K.M. Gopakumar, *Post-2005 TRIPS scenario in patent protection in the pharmaceutical sector: The case of the generic pharmaceutical industry in India,* UNCTAD, IDRC and ICSTD, November, 2006, at p. 21.
144. The complex set of procedures before grant of licence, the possibility of prolonged litigation even after the licence is granted, the changing nature of the existing industry in terms of joint ventures and equity participation, reasonable voluntary licence etc. could also be the reason for the low number of compulsory licenses. Systematic study is lacking in this area.
145. See section 84(1).
146. See section 84(7).
147. This makes use of the flexibility available in Articles 31 (k) and 40.
148. Jancie Mueller, "The Tiger Awakens: The Tumultuous Transformation of India's Patent System and the Rise of Indian Pharmaceutical Innovation" 68 *University of Pittsburgh Law Review* 491 (2007), at p. 590. She apprehends that this provision violates Article 31(f) of the TRIPS which requires that compulsory licenses are to be granted "predominantly for the supply of the domestic market."
149. Section 90(1)(vii).
150. Jancie Mueller, "The Tiger Awakens: The Tumultuous Transformation of India's Patent System and the Rise of Indian Pharmaceutical Innovation" 68 *University of Pittsburgh Law Review* 491 (2007), at p. 591.
151. Section 84(1)(c). *Ibid.*, p. 593.
152. See section 84(6).
153. See sections 85, 86, 87, 88 and 89.
154. See section 90. Another form of compulsory license under Indian law is the one authorized by Section 91 which enables the holder of a patent of a related invention if he is prevented or hindered from working his patent efficiently without such a license from another patentee to apply for a compulsory licence for such patent. This provision is in line with Article 31(l) of the TRIPS.
155. Section 92.
156. See section 92(1).
157. Section 92A reads:

    "(1) Compulsory licence shall be available for manufacture and export of patented pharmaceutical products to any country having insufficient or no manufacturing capacity in the pharmaceutical sector for the concerned product to address public health problems, provided compulsory licence has been granted by such country or such country has, by notification or otherwise, allowed importation of the patented pharmaceutical products from India.

> (2) The Controller shall, on receipt of an application in the prescribed manner, grant a compulsory licence solely for manufacture and export of the concerned pharmaceutical product to such country under such terms and conditions as may be specified and published by him.
> (3) the provisions of sub-sections (1) and (2) shall be without prejudice to the extent to which pharmaceutical products produced under a compulsory license can be exported under any other provision of this Act."

For the purpose of this section, "pharmaceutical products" means any patented product manufactured through a patented process of the pharmaceutical sector needed to address public health problems and shall be inclusive of ingredients necessary for their manufacture and diagnostic kits required for their use.

158. WT/MIN(01)/DEC/2.
159. WT/L/540. This is commonly known as "the waiver decision."
160. Para 2 of the decision of the TRIPS General Council of August 30, 2003.
161. See Annex to the Protocol amending the TRIPS Agreement.
162. WT/L/641, Decision of December 6, 2005. The Members were given time to accept the protocol until December 1, 2007. This was later on extended to December 31, 2009.
163. India's first compulsory licensing application under section 92A.
164. C.H. Unnikrishnan, "Natco withdraws plea on making patented cancer drugs" Corporate News livemint.com *The WallStreet Journal*, posted September 28, 2008, available at http://www.livemint.com/2008/09/28214903/Natco-withdraws-plea-on-making.html (last accessed December 23, 2008).
165. Natco's Doha CL Application: 'Patent Office Rules in Favour of Pfizer', July 5, 2008, available at http://spicyipindia.blogspot.com/2008/07/natcos-doha-cl-application-patent.html.
166. 2001 PTC 472 (Guj).
167. *American Cynamid Co. v. Ethicon Ltd.*, [1975] 1 All. ER 504.
168. *Wander Ltd., v. Antox India Pvt. Ltd.*, [1999] Supp. SCC 727.
169. 2001 PTC 472 at p. 479.
170. 2005 (30) PTC 160 (Bom.).
171. *M/s. Niky Tasha India Pvt. Ltd., v. M/s/ Faridabad Gas Gadgets Pvt. Ltd.*, 1984 PTC 87; *Mohd. Abdul Karim v. Mohd. Yasin*, AIR 1934 All. 789.
172. 2005 (30) PTC 160 at p. 172.
173. *Ibid.* at p. 173 (*per* D.K. Deshmukh, J).
174. *Ibid.* at p. 174.
175. See *Novaris AG v. Adarsh Pharma*, 2004 (29) PTC 108 (Mad.). For a critical analysis of the case see N.S. Gopalakrishnan, "Intellectual Property Laws" XL *ASIL* (2004) 389 at pp. 392–396. See also *Wockhardt Ltd., v. Hetero Drugs Ltd.*, 2006 (32) PTC 65 (Mad) (DB). For a critical view see N.S. Gopalakrishnan, "Intellectual Property Laws" XLII *ASIL* (2006) 467 at p. 474.
176. 2005 (30) PTC 160 at p. 174.
177. It is also pertinent to note the judgement was delivered with the backdrop that the patent office had rejected the patent on the grounds of lack of novelty and inventive step based on section 3 of the Act and an appeal in that matter was pending before the Appellate Tribunal. For details see C.R. Sukumar, "Novartis loses patent claim on cancer drug – Patent Controller upholds Natco contention" *The Hindu Business Line*, Internet Edition, January 26, 2006, available at www.thehindubusinessline.com/2006/01/26/stories (last accessed December 28, 2008).
178. 2008 (37) PTC 71 (Del.).
179. *Ibid.* at p. 108, *per* Justice S. Ravindra Bhat.
180. Robert C. Kahrl. *Patent Claim Construction*, 1–8. See also Simon Thorley, Richard Miller, Guy Burkill, Colin Birss and Douglas Campbell, *Terrill on the Law of Patents*, 16th ed., Sweet and Maxwell, at p. 122.

181. Karen C. Mitch, "Comment, Pondering a 'Baffling' Situation: The 'Reconstruction of Claim Construction,'" 4 *J. Marshall Rev. Intell. Prop. L.* 623 (2005).
182. As rightly stated by Adam B. Jaffe and Josh Lerner the standard of "novelty" and "non-obviousness" adopted by a nation depends on the patent office examiners who apply them. See Adam B. Jaffe and Josh Lerner, *Innovation and Its Discontents: How Our Broken Patent System is Endangering Innovation and Progress, and What To Do About It*, Princeton University Press, 2004, at p. 8. He says that "how carefully they ensure that only true innovators are awarded patents depends on the incentives they face, the rules under which they operate, and their training and ability." He cites the example of the impact of the changes brought in to the administrative set up of the USPTO, whereby it was converted from an agency funded by tax revenues, which collected nominal fees for patent applications, into one funded by the fees it collects. This, he feels, has led to a substantial change in the attitude of the PTO, which started thinking of itself as an "organization whose mission is to serve patent applicants" and this, in turn, encouraged more people to apply for dubious patents (at p. 11). He adds that the patent officials were "chronically strained for resources," especially in the "new" areas of software, financial methods, and biotechnology where it had not previously had much expertise and this added to the gravity of situation which led to the "patent explosion."
183. See *Manual of Patent Office Practice and Procedure*: Version 01.11 As modified on March 22, 2011, available at http://www.ipindia.nic.in/ipr/patent/manual/HTML%20AND%20PDF/Manual%20of%20Patent%20Office%20Practice%20and%20Procedure%20-%20pdf/Manual%20of%20Patent%20Office%20Practice%20and%20Procedure.pdf (last accessed May 1, 2012).

8. The Brazilian patent system: challenges for the future

Viviane Yumy Mitsuuchi Kunisawa

INTRODUCTION

Globalization has led not only to a change in trade and cultural relationships among countries, but it has also created a friendly environment towards innovation worldwide. The world has recently witnessed fast-growing innovation in many areas: the fields of information technology and biotechnology being a representative example. In this globalized era, economic development is closely related to technological development. In a society where wealth creation is no longer based solely on real estate, but rather on the magnitude of digital and genetic information, intellectual assets have become a major source of economic growth. Along with the development of industrial, commercial and cultural business, the advancement of high technology founded on information and knowledge, that is Research and Development (R&D), is vital to a country's economic growth.

In this regard, a country's technological development is closely linked to its patent system. The patent system is a mechanism to protect pioneer industrialists and investors against the spillover of innovative information and, thus, competition by those who have not taken the initial financial risks. By assuring the exclusive use of the patented innovation for a limited time, the patent system facilitates the disclosure of such techniques and the possibility for the public to benefit thereof within a relatively short term.

Nevertheless, to receive patent protection, inventions must meet eligibility requirements. Otherwise, they would represent an unfair monopoly and improperly prevent free competition, rather than fostering technological progress. In addition, national laws provide for the exclusion of certain subject matter from patentability for reasons such as public order and morality.[1]

In this connection, the establishment of harmonized and sound patent systems in each country was the object of governments' concerns in the World Trade Organization's (WTO) negotiation rounds. Different standards of intellectual property protection, including patent rights, were amounting to trade barriers and harmonization needed to be sought. On the other hand, because of its own sovereignty, each country would establish specific requirements to afford exclusivity rights to the inventor. Accordingly, recognizing the importance of harmonious patent systems in its Member States, the WTO established minimum standards of protection in the Agreement on Trade Related Aspects of Intellectual Property Rights (TRIPS). Moreover, TRIPS determined obligations for the member countries to assure the enforcement of patent rights, such as the adoption of border seizure measures and legal action available to prevent infringement.

In Brazil, the current Industrial Property Law, Law N. 9279, of May 14, 1996 was enacted to comply with the obligations assumed by the Brazilian government when signing TRIPS.[2] Brazilian technological development, however, has been striving against decades of import substitution policies, which has hindered technology innovation in general instead of fostering R&D. In addition, a combination of 70 years without patents in the chemical and pharmaceutical industries – until the implementation of TRIPS in 1996[3] – with the absence of patent enforcement in other technological fields created a legal scenario of breach in patent-related knowledge, jurisprudence and case law.

This chapter analyzes the Brazilian patent system, including the patentability requirements and enforcement measures. The chapter will also consider some standards of patent protection that could be pursued by the Brazilian patent system in order to attract investments in R&D, allow technology transfer and, afterwards, increase production of the Brazil's own technology. A special section regarding patent protection in the biotechnology field was included due to the importance of this area of technology for the country, taking into consideration the country's expansive biodiversity and the agribusiness share of the economy.

THE FOUNDATIONS OF THE PATENT SYSTEM

Patent rights have been the subject of many studies from legal and economical perspectives. As summarized by Machlup, the justification of the patent system can be classified under four categories: "natural-law," "reward-by-monopoly," "monopoly-profit-incentive" and "exchange-for-secrets" theories.[4]

Some scholars justify the existence of intellectual property rights on the "natural-law" theory of John Locke according to which man has a natural property right when he employs his own labor to cultivate land.[5]

Under the "reward-by-monopoly" thesis, inventions are useful to society and, thus, justice requires that inventors be rewarded for their services to society. Patent rights on the inventions represent such a reward because they amount to temporary monopolies.

The "monopoly-profit-incentive" theory argues that industrial progress and technological development is a very risky task that would be undertaken by private persons and companies only if they could receive return and profits for their investments. This model establishes that property rights promotes saving and investing, as well as the internalization of externalities.[6] It provides incentives for innovators to invest their efforts and money into the creation of inventions under the circumstances of the "appropriability problem" associated with intangible assets.[7] Inventing and developing products are a time-consuming and costly activity, which would not be performed without the possibility of recouping the investment.

The fourth theory of "exchange-for-secrets" assumes that patent rights stimulate innovation and industrial development, because they promote dissemination of technical knowledge that would, otherwise, be kept secret. It presumes a bargain between the inventor and the society, the former revealing his knowledge and information in exchange for a temporary monopoly to be secured by the latter. The monopoly aims to protect the inventor against the spillover effects concerning the invention once it is disclosed by preventing competitors from entering the market. In some areas where the product can reach the market without the information being revealed to the society or competitors (i.e. without the possibility of reverse-engineer technology), this theory plays an important role.

The volume of technological knowledge incorporated in patent documents is certainly one of the largest databases for consultation by industry. The largest part of income growth in developed countries results from the increase of technical knowledge and of the human ability to use accumulated technical information. The transfer of technology operates by means of direct investments and agreements on the delivery of technology and associated knowledge. Frequently, the amount of investment and the technical complexity of the enterprise may lead to the creation of a subsidiary or the development of an existing one. On other occasions, an association between a foreign investor and a local entrepreneur and/or the state may be the result.[8]

Basing a country's industrial development on the imitation of foreign technology may harm its economic development in the long term. Because of the complexity of certain technologies, a simple copy is not possible without the related knowledge. By not allowing intellectual property protection in certain fields of technology, the country prevents itself from conducting local research, from creating incentives for foreign and national investment, from improving local infrastructure, as well as from training local researchers and technicians.[9]

At this point, it is worth remembering the Japanese model of technological development according to which technology imported from the Occident, after being "digested" by local industry, led to the development of Japan's own technology. According to Saotome's analysis, Japan had the pre-requisites indispensable for the development of Japanese industry: i) an educational system and research organization; ii) important infrastructure of transportation, distribution, communication and energy; iii) the capacity to furnish parts, raw materials, repairs etc.; and iv) the general culture necessary for technology and market management.[10] In fact, the ability to invent or create new technology results directly from a country's social, cultural and economic development. In order to achieve the goal of innovation, a deep and wide background is mandatory. For this reason, the international patent system works as a system of communicative knowledge database with easy access. The Japanese government representative, Mr. Takahashi, when visiting the United States Patent Office (USPTO), declared:

> We have looked around us to see which nations are the greatest, so that we can be like them. We said, "What is that make the United States such a great nation?" and we investigated and found that it was patents, and we will have patents.[11]

For a country like Brazil, it is important to observe and study the technology of more developed countries and to store all the technical information available, in order to benefit from the transfer of technology. Therefore, the insertion of the country in the stream of development of R&D in the international arena, and effective participation in the international industrial property system may be a valuable instrument for incorporating knowledge obtained of the productive system. Facilitating the access to foreign technology is an important step to stimulate the internal development of technology.

THE RESEARCH & DEVELOPMENT PANORAMA IN BRAZIL

Brazil's development as a nation should be grounded on the capacity to accumulate human intelligence and apply it in industry, commerce, and economy, so that it can be transformed into new technologies.

According to data from the Brazilian Ministry of Science and Technology, about US$ 24.3 million was spent in R&D in Brazil in 2009.[12] In contrast to the developed countries, where R&D is concentrated in private companies, from a total of a 231,910 persons engaged in R&D activities in Brazil in 2010, 79.8 percent were in universities and only 17.8 percent in the private sector (the remaining belonging to governmental institutions).[13]

Even considering the lack of resources of Brazilian institutions and researchers, the country's scientific research is relatively developed and has been growing during the last years. It is responsible for 2.69 percent of science produced in the world in 2009. In 1981, 1,949 articles were published in international scientific journals, while in 2009 this number increased to 32,100. It is not a discrepant number in relation to the effort and money invested.[14]

Most of the research activities concentrated in universities are performed with an academic focus. Nevertheless, a few universities, such as the University of Campinas (Unicamp), the University of São Paulo (USP) and the Federal University of Minas Gerais (UFGM), were able to introduce policies and internal proceedings concerning technological management and patenting.[15]

Although Brazilian scientific research might be within acceptable parameters, the country's technological production is still small. The low number of patent applications at the Instituto Nacional da Propriedade Industrial (INPI), the Brazilian patent office, statistically corroborates this.[16] When considering the United States Patent and Trademark Office (USPTO), Brazil obtained 24 patents in 1980 and 175 in 2010. For South Korea, on the other hand, the number of patents increased from nine to 11,671 in the same period.[17]

The high level of South Korea's technological development is always thought of as the most efficient among countries with late industrialization. Until the mid-1970s, South Korea had a profile of expenses in science and technology similar to Brazil's at that time, with only 15 percent of the investments made by companies. The South Korean government progressively increased investment of public resources in R&D, directing it to the private sector, as well as introducing tax incentives.[18] As a result, private investment in R&D multiplied, creating a virtuous cycle: more innovation, more competitiveness, more exports, more employment, higher demand for qualified professionals and an improvement in the educational system.

As opposed to the South Korean model, Brazil's research finance was directed towards post-graduate courses in federal universities. Governmental policies were focused on the education of highly qualified researchers who it was believed would create a scientific basis in order to further stimulate private investment in technological innovation. However, the low quantity of researchers in the companies led to the low technological competitiveness of Brazilian industry and to the lack of ability of the country to transform science in technology.

The issue of risk underlies the Brazilian technological development. Until the beginning of the 1990s, Brazilian economic growth was based on a policy whereby national industry was protected from international competition, since importation was not allowed. Without the need to undertake risky tasks to improve their products and services to supplant competition, an efficient patent system was never thought of as essential to the development of national industry.

This is clear in the chemical and pharmaceutical fields, where research demands a very high and risky investment. In Brazil, until the enactment of Law N. 9279/1996, in order to promote national industry, patents on pharmaceuticals were not allowed. However, governmental studies reveal that the highest rate of denationalization in the sector occurred after 1969, when there was no longer any patent protection for pharmaceuticals.[19] The existing economic model did not encourage taking the risk of developing national technological research. Even if the results of the research were positive, they would not afford protection against competition in such a way to provide returns on the investments. National industry continued to base its production on existing drugs and, although scientific research progressed, technological development was rare.

After the enactment of Law N. 9279/1996, which introduced a stronger patent protection in the country, foreign investment, which fluctuated between US$ 1 billion and US$ 3 billion from 1987 to 1994, rose in 1996 to US$ 11.2 billion and was more than US$ 30 billion in 1998 and 1999.[20] This data shows that there is a correlation between foreign investments and the protection of intellectual property assets, guaranteed after the integration of Brazil into the WTO system.

In this context, it is worth citing the words of Straus:

> [. . .]technology transfer alone is certainly not sufficient to enable the developing and emerging markets to catch up in terms of technology. The decisive factors for entrepreneurial decisions are amongst others the commercial and political conditions of a country such as fiscal legislation, competition law, trade policy and generally the investment climate. [. . .] Pioneering industrial structures will only emerge in the developing countries if local enterprises develop technological skills locally and become innovative themselves.

Conscious of this, the Brazilian government has been implementing a program to encourage technological development in Brazilian enterprises and an innovative business environment to increase investment in R&D,

as well as a legal framework to foster research. In 2004 the government launched its industrial, technological and international trade policies,[21] in order to promote tax incentives for R&D activities and collaboration between the public and private sector. In the same year, Law N. 10973, of December 2, 2004, was enacted seeking to foster innovation and science and technology activities. The State would share the risk of investments with national companies, improving public-private linkages. Subsequently, Law N. 11196, of November 21, 2005 was enacted to provide tax incentives for companies performing technological research and innovation. In the biotechnology field, Decree N. 6041, of February 8, 2007 regulates the policies towards the developments in this area.

The criticism raised by Brazilian companies of the patent system concerns especially the huge backlog and the long time taken by the INPI to examine applications and the lack of protection available in the country for several of the inventions.[22]

BRIEF HISTORICAL OVERVIEW

The idea of promoting incentives to a person to disclose new information useful to society may date back to ancient Greece, where there was a system to reward cooks for new excellent recipes.[23] Nevertheless, the Venetian legislation of 1474 is considered a historical landmark as the first patent statute. Followed by similar laws in different European territories, the most significant of its successors was the Statute of Monopolies in the 17th century attempting to attract foreign know-how to the English territory and to cultivate domestic industry.

The introduction of patents into the Brazilian legal system occurred with the enactment of the Alvará in April 28, 1809, by the Portuguese Regent Prince D. João VI, which granted a temporary privilege for exclusive exploitation to their creators of new machines and inventions useful in industry.[24] Far from being a totally new field of law, patent law is one of the oldest in the Brazilian legal system. The first Constitution of 1824 safeguarded the property of inventions to their inventors, and the Law of August 28, 1830 was enacted to regulate this right.

From the end of the 19th century until the Second World War, Brazil maintained a level of protection of patents (and other intellectual property rights) which was established in international agreements. Brazil was a founding contracting state of the Paris Union for the protection of industrial property, which entered in force on March 20, 1883.[25]

The economic policies adopted by the Brazilian government (protecting national industry against competition from imported products), for the period from the Second World War until the beginning of 1990s, led to a discredit of the patent system and a breach of patent legal knowledge (with little scholarly production and few judicial decisions). According to these policies, the country tried to profit from the technologies created in developed countries (in the public domain or not) in order to benefit national industry.[26] This created a culture of despising patents as an important component of industrial development.

After the end of the previous economic model and the accession of Brazil into the WTO, intellectual property rights (especially patents) have been seen as a bargaining instrument. The Brazilian government used them as an exchanging tool to enhance foreign private investments and further export national products.

THE PATENTABILITY REQUIREMENTS

The Brazilian Federal Constitution of 1988 establishes in article 5, item XXIX, that the law shall provide for the protection of industrial creations and temporary privileges on the use of industrial inventions by their creators. Implementing this constitutional guarantee in accordance with TRIPS, Law N. 9279, of May 14, 1996, was enacted to regulate rights relating to industrial property.

According to article 8 of the patent statute, patentable inventions must meet the requirements of novelty, inventive step and industrial application.

Novelty is a basic requirement specified in article 11 of the patent statute as the non-disclosure of an invention in the state of the art. It is to be analyzed objectively, independent of prior knowledge by the inventor of the state of the art, and according to what is disclosed in a single prior art reference. In this connection, the state of the art comprises everything made accessible to the public before the date of the filing of the patent application or the priority claimed (as per article 4 of the Paris Convention).[27] For the purposes of determining novelty, the content of pending applications filed in Brazil, but not yet published, will be considered as part of the state of the art from the date of filing or priority, provided that such application is subsequently published.[28]

Furthermore, the patent statute provides for a 12-month grace period.[29] It establishes that the disclosure of the invention which occurs within 12 months preceding the date of filing or priority of the patent application will not bar its novelty. Such disclosure has to be made by the inventor, by the INPI in an official publication without the inventor's consent, or by third parties on the basis of information obtained from him.

The inventive step requirement is foreseen in article 13 of the patent statute, which establishes that an invention will involve inventive step when it does not derive in an evident or obvious manner from the state of the art for a person skilled in the art. It is a requirement of subjective nature, since it is linked to the obviousness of the invention's subject matter to a person skilled in the art. The knowledge of this person skilled in the art will serve as the parameter on the analysis of the inventive step requirement. Thus, he must be a professional with a general education in the field who dominates the general principles of analogue industries and is no longer a beginner.[30] In some fields of very advanced technology, such as biotechnology, the person skilled in the art may be someone with a high level of knowledge and education, frequently with doctoral titles.

It must be noted that the statute is silent on considering non-published pending patent applications as part of the state of the art for the purposes of analyzing the inventive step requirement.

The inventive step is a new requirement, only expressly introduced in the legislation by Law 9279/1996. Nevertheless, its notion has always underlined the Brazilian patent system as an essential element contained in the invention's concept.[31] In addition to novelty, inventive step is an important factor in the relationship between the inventor and the State: the latter grants an exclusive right to the former in exchange for the disclosure of the invention. Where the invention is not new, already exists in the state of the art, or derives obviously therefrom, such an exclusive right will constitute an unfair monopoly.[32]

With regard to industrial application, article 15 of the patent statute establishes that an invention meets such a requirement when it can be made or used in any kind of industry. The term industry shall be interpreted in a broad sense as any branch of production activity, including agriculture, and it represents, thus, a low hurdle to overcome. This concept was already present in the Paris Convention, in article 1(3).[33] Bodenhausen, the most famous commentator of this international convention, affirmed that Member States are not obliged to grant patents on wines, animals or fruits. This provision has the sole goal of avoiding exclusion from the protection afforded by industrial property of activities and products which could otherwise suffer the risk of not being assimilated by the industry itself.[34]

The disclosure should also be considered a requirement for the granting of a patent. More related to formality aspects, it demands that the applicant describe the subject matter of the invention clearly and sufficiently, so as to enable a person skilled in the art to carry it out and to indicate, when applicable, the best mode of its execution, as per article 24 of the patent statute. In addition, article 25 establishes that the claims must be based on the specification, characterizing the particularities of the application and defining clearly and precisely the subject matter to be protected. This provision mandates that the boundaries of the claimed invention be accurately determined.

The reasoning behind this disclosure requirement lies on the fact that the patent description should have the objective of assuring the public that the invention can be actually performed, that is that it can be understood and reproduced by someone skilled in the art. This is the benefit society receives for granting the inventor an exclusive right of exploitation. Furthermore, it also aims at guaranteeing that the monopoly generated by the claims does not extend beyond the actual contribution of the invention to the state of the art, as described in the specification.

The inventions are, therefore, patentable provided they meet the novelty, inventive step, industrial application and disclosure requirements, set forth in articles 8, 24 and 25 of Law 9279/1996. Furthermore, the generic classification is adopted and the eligible categories of inventions are not enumerated. Subject matters entitled to patent protection are defined by exclusion in the law, meaning that they should not belong to the statutory bars of articles 10 (subject matter not eligible for lack of a patentability requirement) and 18 (subject matter expressly excluded, despite fulfilling the patentability requirements).[35]

Under article 10, the following are excluded from the concept of invention: discoveries, scientific theories and mathematical methods, purely abstract concepts, schemes, plans, principles or methods of a commercial, accounting, financial, educational, publishing, lottery or fiscal nature, literary, architectural, artistic and scientific works or any aesthetic creation, computer programs per se, the presentation of information, rules of games, operating or surgical techniques and therapeutic or diagnostic methods, for use on the human or animal body and natural living beings, in whole or in part, and biological material, including the genome or germ-plasma of any natural living being, when found in nature or isolated therefrom, as well as natural biological processes.

Article 18 determines that those that are not patentable are those contrary to morals, good customs and public security, order and health, substances, matter, mixtures, elements or products of any kind, as well as the modification of their physical-chemical properties and the respective processes of obtaining or modifying them, when they result from the transformation of the atomic nucleus and living beings, in whole or in part, except transgenic micro-organisms fulfilling the three patentability requirements – novelty, inventive activity and industrial application, that is which are not mere discoveries. Transgenic micro-organisms are defined as organisms, except the whole or part of plants or animals, which display features that cannot be usually achieved by such specie under natural conditions, resulting from direct human intervention in their genetic composition.

One should bear these general provisions on patentability requirements in mind whenever one analyzes issues specifically concerning a particular field of technology.

SOME COMMENTS ON PATENTS IN THE BIOTECHNOLOGY FIELD

Brazilian potential in the biotechnology field can be seen in the impact of agribusiness on the Brazilian economy. Agribusiness is based on exportation of primary products, such as soybean and meat, which are apparently low technology-added goods. However, it also relates to the use of new processes and equipment to increase production, such as the creation of genetically modified organisms (GMOs) and new pesticides. These new processes, on the other hand, are high technology-added goods and result from R&D.

In Brazil, the Federal Constitution did not restrict the protection by patents on inventions in the field of biotechnology, since it does not establish to which technological areas the privileges can be granted. It left this decision to the legislator when enacting the patent statutes.

The former patent statute, Law N. 5772, of December 21, 1971, did not prohibit specifically biotech-patents, requiring that all inventions fulfill the requisites of morality, novelty, industrial application and publication of the description. The only related provision was article 9, letter f), establishing that "the uses or employment related to discoveries, including varieties or species of microorganisms, for a determined end" are not patentable.

In this connection, patents of discoveries regarding living matter were not allowed. It shall be noted that discoveries are distinct from inventions and are not subject to patent protection. Inventions regarding living matters were, however, prohibited on essentially moral grounds. In addition, the ban of patenting chemical-pharmaceutical products and processes, medicaments and foodstuff generally prevented most of biotech-inventions from being patented, since these fields of science frequently intercommunicate.

The lack of legal provision expressly prohibiting patenting plants, animals and living beings is due to the incipient development of the science of biotechnology as it is conceived today. However, already in the 1970s, only two years from the enactment of the former statute, the first gene was cloned in bacteria, the origin of modern biotechnology.

The current patent statute, Law N. 9279/1996, was enacted to adapt Brazilian industrial property legislation to more advanced technology standards in light of TRIPS. As already mentioned, it divides the subject matter not subject to patent protection into two groups: those which are not patentable for lack of a patentability requirement, not being defined as an invention as such (article 10); and those which are excluded by a legal bar, although consisting in an invention (article 18).

Article 10, item I, of the patent statute expressly excludes from the concept of inventions discoveries, scientific theories and mathematical methods. Article 10, item IX, of the patent statute states that "natural living beings, in whole or in part, and biological material, including the genome or germ-plasma of any natural living being, when found in nature or isolated therefrom, and natural biological processes" are not considered to be inventions or utility models.

This is the distinction between the concepts of invention and discovery. Discovery is usually considered as not being the result of the creation of mankind. Man, through observation and analysis, only notices the existence of something to which he was not sensitive before. On the other hand, invention involves human creativity. Discovery, thus, consists of revealing what already existed, resulting from the speculative human spirit, the investigation of phenomena and laws of nature. It enhances human understanding of the physical world, but it does not satisfy any practical need or solve any technical problem. The separation of the concepts of discovery and invention is based on the non-existence of the latter before the human intervention and on the pre-existence of the former, which was previously hidden and is, then, revealed.

The text of item IX of article 10 of the patent statute, when it uses the adjective "natural" to qualify living beings and biological processes, establishes that these are elements produced by nature, in which there is no human activity or intervention. It considers that there is no novelty and/or inventive step and, thus, it relates to a discovery. The reference to biological material found in nature is interpreted in the same way. The genome and the germ-plasma, because they represent the genetic material of animals and plants, are also included in the statutory prohibition. Except when differentiated from their state in nature, they are understood to be naturally occurring part of living beings, consisting of discovery and lacking inventiveness.

Furthermore, the patent statute, influenced by ethical, moral, religious, environmental and political considerations – not due to the lack of a patentability requirement – sets an express statutory prohibition on the patentability of the subject matter of article 18. Among those prohibited matters, item I reads that it is not patentable if it "is contrary to morals, good customs and public security, order and health." In item III, article 18 of the patent statute further establishes that "living beings, in whole or in part, except transgenic micro-organisms meeting the three patentability requirements (novelty, inventive step and industrial application) provided for in article 8 and which are not mere discoveries, are not patentable."

This legal provision bars patenting living beings and their parts, which includes cells. It differs from article 10, once these living beings are subject to modifications, through human intervention, not being found likewise in nature. Transgenic plants and animals are, thus, not patentable.

Nevertheless, the Brazilian prohibition does not cover *transgenic micro-organisms* and the non-natural processes for obtaining and modifying living beings, even superior ones. It allows, for example, processes for cloning animals (except human beings).[36]

With regard to patentable subject matter, TRIPS establishes that Member States shall not discriminate against any field of technology, allowing the exclusion from patentability of plants and animals *other than microorganisms*, and essentially biological processes for the production of plants or animals other than non-biological and microbiological processes.[37]

When compared to TRIPS, the Brazilian patent statute is stricter towards the patentability of biotechnological inventions. TRIPS does not provide for the exclusion of parts of plants and animals, or microorganisms in general. The Brazilian patent statute only admits as patentable subject matter *transgenic* microorganisms having novelty, inventive step and industrial application. A sole paragraph of article 18 defines transgenic microorganisms as "organisms, except the whole or part of plants or animals that exhibit, due to direct human intervention in their genetic composition, a characteristic that cannot normally be attained by the species under natural conditions."

The requirement that a microorganism be transgenic in order to be patentable is a restriction not found in the text of article 27 of TRIPS. This more stringent rule might be considered a violation of the international obligations assumed by Brazil when accessed the WTO.

In addition, TRIPS obliges Member States to protect plant varieties either by patents or by a *sui generis* system, admitting the exclusion of plants from patentability. Brazil has opted for the *sui generis* system, implemented by Law N. 9456, of April 25, 1997.[38]

The issue of the disclosure requirement regarding the patentability of transgenic microorganisms must also be analyzed. Very often in the biotechnology field, it is not possible to describe living matters in a sufficient and clear way. Under these conditions, it is admitted that the description of the patent application be supplemented by the deposit of a sample of the microorganism in depositary institutions.

At the international level, the Budapest Treaty on the International Recognition of the Deposit of Microorganisms for the Purposes of Patent Procedure, concluded in 1977, plays an important role in patent application procedures.[39] A Contracting State must recognize the deposit of a microorganism with any "international depositary authority," irrespective of whether such authority is in or outside the territory of the said state.

In addition to microorganisms *per se*, it is possible to deposit plant and animal cells, or any matter that is auto-reproducible or can be reproduced via replication of its host-organism. The term "microorganism" is, thus, interpreted in a broad sense, covering biological material whose deposit is necessary for the purposes of disclosure, especially for inventions relating to the food and pharmaceutical fields.

The Budapest Treaty system establishes the requirements for a depositary institution to be recognized as an international depositary authority, the proceedings and the conditions for depositing the biological material and for furnishing it to third parties.

Considering that the deposit of the biological material supplements the description of the patent application, the material should be made accessible to the public from the date of publication of the patent application. However, due to the nature of the material, acquiring samples may be subject to certain requirements, such as notification and/or authorization of the patent applicant, assurance regarding safe manipulation and compromise of non-dissemination of the material.

Brazil is not a Contracting State to the Budapest Treaty. In spite of that, the INPI recognizes the deposit with one of the international depository authorities of the Budapest Treaty system, when interpreting article 24, sole paragraph of the patent statute – which provides for the deposit of the biological material in order to supplement the description of the patent application for the purposes of fulfilling the disclosure requirement.[40]

Resolution N. 82, of November 22, 2001, enacted by the INPI, establishes the requirements for Brazilian institutions to habilitate as depositary authorities. Until that date, no national institution was recognized as a depositary authority for the purposes of the sole paragraph of article 24 of the patent statute. On April 3, 2006, the Commissioner of the INPI announced the creation of an institution to serve as a national depositary authority, in the city of Xerém in the State of Rio de Janeiro.[41] However, this depositary center has not yet started operating.

With the national depositary center, the question remains whether the deposit made by applicants in an international depositary authority of the Budapest Treaty system will still be recognized. As an alternative, as already implied by the Commissioner, the INPI may demand applicants to also deposit samples in Brazil since the country is not a member of the Budapest Treaty and is not obliged to recognize such international deposits.

Moreover, Provisional Measure N. 2186-16, of August 23, 2001, establishes in its article 31 that the granting of industrial property rights on processes and products obtained from samples of genetic heritage components are conditioned to the compliance with this piece of legislation.[42] Applicants for property rights are then required to indicate the origin of the genetic material and the associated traditional knowledge as appropriate.

Finally, because one of the biggest areas of the application of biotechnological inventions is the pharmaceutical field, it is necessary to mention the requirement of prior approval by the Agência Nacional de Vigilância Sanitária (ANVISA), the authority primarily responsible for the marketing approval of drugs.[43] According to article 229-C of the patent statute, after being examined by the INPI, any patent claiming pharmaceutical invention has to be submitted to the ANVISA for prior approval before issuance. Nevertheless, there are no legal guidelines on the requirements for prior approval, and the ANVISA has decided on its own discretion to re-examine the patent applications, analyzing novelty, inventive step and industrial application requirements. The limitations of the ANVISA's activities are currently under judicial analysis and are the object of discussion among policymakers.

As discussed previously, patenting products isolated from the nature is currently not allowed in Brazil. Article 10, item IX, of the Brazilian patent statute establishes that natural living beings, in whole or in part, when found in nature or isolated therefrom, and natural biological processes are not considered inventions. In addition, article 18, item III, prohibits the patentability of living beings (in whole or in part), even non-natural ones, except transgenic microorganisms. So, even if animals, plants or parts thereof result from human manipulation, they are not patentable due to this bar.

With the interpretation of articles 10, item IX, and 18, item III, of the patent statute, the INPI issued the Guidelines for Examination of Patent Applications in the field of biotechnology, which consubstantiate their practice when examining patent applications. In this respect, some issues are of interest, as follows.

Claimed Inventions Consisting of Microorganisms

In order to be patentable microorganisms must be transgenic and present novelty, inventive step and industrial application, not representing mere discoveries.[44] For the purposes of the patent law, transgenic microorganisms are those which have genetic characteristics not occurring under natural conditions and exist due to direct human intervention in the genetic material, according to the sole paragraph of article 18 of the patent statute.

For the INPI, only leaven, bacteria and fungi may be included within the meaning of microorganisms. They will, thus, be patentable only where they are transgenic (according to the definition of the sole paragraph of article 18 of the patent statute).

Animal and plant cells, even genetically modified, are not considered as microorganisms. Host cells are also not comprised by the concept of microorganisms.

The INPI interprets that only where the cell loses its fundamental characteristics (i.e. one of the organelles is substantially changed or eliminated), such a cell will be comprised by the concept of microorganisms. This is the case of hybridomas and monoclonal antibodies.

Although hybridomas result from the fusion of cells (which are in themselves considered part of living beings), the INPI do not consider them as "whole or part of plants or animals", because they represent an autonomous unit due to the fusion process. As to the monoclonal antibodies, the INPI understands that they are simply the proteins produced by a hybridoma and, thus, they must be analyzed as such (i.e. as proteins – which will be analyzed below).

Viruses are regarded as chemical products and they should be analyzed as such. With due care to article 10, item IX, they may be patentable where they are differentiated from naturally occurring ones.

The guidelines also state that "mutant microorganisms are patentable provided that they are stable and able to be reproduced".

Claimed Inventions Related to Genes

The INPI analyzes polynucleotides and synthetic polypeptides and proteins as chemical compounds for patentability purposes. It considers that products expressed by cultures transformed by expression vectors can be considered chemical products. DNA sequences, vectors, plasmids, cosmids, virus, viroids are treated as chemical products, since chemical products are all organic and inorganic products, including those extracted from living beings, independent from their obtaining process, chemical or biological.

As chemical compounds, the INPI does not allow claims towards DNA sequences solely characterized by their encoding protein or sequence of amino acids, or by exhibiting a certain activity, under the argument that these claims would not fulfill the determination of article 25, lacking clarity and precision in the determination of the object to be protected.[45]

It is, however, necessary to describe the application of the DNA sequence (i.e. the activity it exhibits or the codifying protein) in the specification under the penalty of non-compliance of the industrial application requirement.

The meaning of "application of the DNA sequence" as understood by the INPI in order to meet the industrial application requirement has not been clarified by the examiners. Questions concerning which kind of activity (biological or technical) needs to be disclosed in the patent application were still not raised. As a consequence of the INPI's practice to require applicants to claim their inventions in the two-part claim format, the examiner may also demand that the application of the DNA sequence is described in the first part of the claim (the preamble).[46]

According to the INPI's interpretation of the law, any substance isolated from nature, even if it has a pharmacological activity or industrial interest, cannot be patented, because of lack of novelty and/or inventive step, falling either under the prohibition of article 10, item I (if they are not biological, being classified as mere discoveries), or item IX (if they are biological). Only synthetic substances, compositions containing the natural occurring substances in a combination not found in nature, or the processes to isolate them may be patentable – but the natural occurring substance itself is not.

In this connection, patents on proteins obtained by using recombinant DNA technology may not be allowed where they have an identical natural occurring correspondent. They would be deemed to lack novelty irrespective of the process of its production. In this case, only the process of obtaining such proteins may be patentable or a homologous protein (which will not, thus, be identical to the one found in nature).

Where the DNA sequence is already known, but a new encoded protein or activity is found, because DNA sequences are considered chemical compounds, the second or further use format claims may be available.[47] The same applies to proteins for which a new activity is identified.

Claimed Inventions Related to Processes in the Biotechnology Field

Patents on most inventions consisting of processes in the biotechnology area are allowed, provided that they present novelty, inventive step and industrial application, and are not "natural biological processes." The INPI understands that the following can be regarded without any further problems: synthetic processes for preparation of chemical compounds; biological or enzymatic processes for provision of chemical compounds;

processes of extraction and isolation; processes for genetic modification of microorganisms; process of using a superior living organism to obtain a product; processes for obtaining plants; processes involving stem cells; processes for obtaining hybridoma; and monoclonal antibodies.

With regard to processes for obtaining animals, the INPI allows patents only when such processes of modification of the genetic identity of animals do not entail any suffering by those animals. It also permits those that, although involving some kind of suffering of the animal, result in some substantial medical benefit to human beings or animals. Furthermore, the INPI deems unpatentable processes of cloning human beings, processes of modification of the human genome and the uses of human embryos for industrial or commercial purposes. The same criterion is adopted by the INPI when analyzing the patentability of processes for obtaining a product wherein one step involves obtaining an animal.[48] This approach takes into consideration article 18, item I, of the patent statute.

Finally, with relation to processes for obtaining antibodies, the INPI considers that, in general, the main step in such processes occurs in the organism of a living being that was inoculated with the corresponding antigen. This step consists of a natural biological process. Thus, a process claim related to obtaining antibodies defined exclusively by such a step is not allowed under article 10, item IX, of the patent statute. The INPI will only allow claims that contain additional steps, sufficiently defined, in order to comply with the accuracy requirement for the object of the protection.

Due to the huge backlog in the examination of patent applications, there are not many biotechnology related applications granted or rejected with a final decision. In spite of that and as an example, two patents were granted claiming: i) a DNA molecule and a method for control of weeds in a field containing a crop of plants which are glyphosate resistant as a result of a chimeric gene; and ii) a chimeric plant gene, vectors, plasmid and a method for producing a plant.[49] Moreover, the INPI has already issued several Official Actions applying its understanding of the law as contained in the guidelines and described above. Nonetheless, discussions on patentability issues of biotechnology inventions still need to be developed.

THE RIGHTS CONFERRED BY A PATENT AND ENFORCEMENT UNDER TRIPS CONTEXT

Keeping in mind the small number of patents enforced in the country, the present analysis regarding the rights conferred will take into consideration the compliance by Brazilian legislation with the TRIPS provisions.[50]

Within the minimum standards of patent protection, TRIPS provides not only for patentable subject matter, but also for the content of the rights conferred and for enforcement measures. As reminded by Straus,[51] the implementation of the TRIPS provisions into Member States' national legislations should always take into account the objectives of the agreement as laid down in article 7:

> The protection and enforcement of intellectual property rights should contribute to the promotion of technological innovation and to the transfer and dissemination of technology, to the mutual advantage of producers and users of technological knowledge and in a manner conducive to social and economic welfare, and to a balance of rights and obligations.

As a developing country, Brazil enacted Law N. 9279/1996 in order to equate its legal framework to TRIPS. Enforcement measures, however, are also regulated by other pieces of legislation, such as the Civil Procedure Code.

Harmonious with article 33 of TRIPS, the patent term in Brazil is 20 years as of the filing date (or priority date). However, taking into consideration the extensive backlog at the INPI, the statute safeguards a minimum period of 10 years of protection.

The extension of protection awarded by a patent to its right holder, as per article 41 of the patent statute, is determined by the content of the claims, interpreted in light of the specification and drawings. Combined with article 25, the two provisions clearly set the important role of the claims in defining the scope of protection given to a patentee.

It is important to mention that article 186 of the patent statute determines that infringement of patent rights still occurs even if the violation does not affect all the claims of the patent or if it is restricted to the use of means equivalent to the subject matter of the patent. This provision establishes a statutory ground for infringement by equivalence in the Brazilian Law.

The patent statute grants the patent owner the right to exclude others from using any valid claim without the patentee's prior consent. It specifies in article 42 that a patentee can prevent third parties without consent from manufacturing, using, offering for sale, selling or importing for such purposes a product that it is the subject matter of a patent, or a process, or a product directly obtained by a patented process. This provision confers a large scope of rights to the patentee in perfect compliance with what article 20 of TRIPS provides for.

Article 42 of the patent statute further stipulates in paragraph 1 that the patentee can also prevent third parties from contributing to the unauthorized acts (enumerated above) performed by other parties. This provision expressly introduces into Brazilian statutory law what is generally called indirect infringement by scholars. In addition, article 185 of the patent statute establishes that it is a crime to supply a component of a patented product, or material or equipment for carrying out a patented process, when the final application of such component, material or equipment necessarily leads to an unauthorized exploitation of the patent.[52]

As a result of deeming infringement those unauthorized acts related to products directly obtained by a patented process, paragraph 2 of article 42, establishes that "the rights in a process patent will be violated [. . .] when the holder or owner of a product fails to prove, through specific judicial ruling, that it was obtained by a manufacturing process different from that protected by the patent." It establishes a reversal of the burden of proof. The defendant holds the burden to prove that his product was not manufactured by the process patented.

In implementing article 34 of TRIPS, the Brazilian legislative opted for the second alternative provided in paragraph 1 of this article.[53] Brazilian law does not require that the product obtained by the patented process is new in order to reverse the burden of proof of infringement. Such reversal will be obtained through specific judicial ruling, which will analyze whether there is a substantial likelihood that the product was made by the patented process and that the patentee has been unable to determine the process used. The judicial authority will also analyze whether the defendant has legitimate interests in protecting their manufacturing and business secrets.

Under the three-step test of article 30 of TRIPS, article 43 of the patent statute establishes exceptions to the rights conferred to the patentee. In this regard, those exempted from infringement liabilities are:

a) acts practiced by unauthorized parties privately and without commercial ends, provided they do not result in prejudice to the economic interests of the patentee;
b) acts practiced by unauthorized parties for experimental purposes, related to studies or to scientific or technological research;
c) the preparation of a medicine according to a medical prescription for individual cases, executed by a qualified professional (i.e., pharmacist), as well as the medicine thus prepared;
d) a product manufactured in accordance with a process or product patent that has been placed on the internal market directly by the patentee or with his consent;[54]
e) third parties who, in the case of patents related to living matter, use, without economic ends, the patented product as the initial source of variation or propagation for obtaining other products;

f) third parties who, in the case of patents related to living matter, use, place in circulation or commercialize a patented product that has been introduced lawfully onto the market by the patentee or his licensee, provided that the patented product is not used for commercial multiplication or propagation of the living matter in question; and
g) acts performed by unauthorized third parties with the patented invention done exclusively to produce information, data and test results seeking market approval in Brazil or abroad, in order to exploit or commercialize the patented product after the patent term has expired.

In addition, a prior user, that is a person who in good faith exploited the patented subject matter in Brazil prior to the filing (or priority) of the patent application, is also exempted of infringement, being allowed to continue such exploitation in the previous form and conditions.[55]

Article 44 of the patent statute assures the patentee of obtaining compensation for the unauthorized exploitation of the subject matter of the patent, including one which occurred between the date of publication of the application and the grant of the patent. It aims to protect the patentee to a certain extent against competitors who might take advantage of the delay in the granting of a patent. It intends to be a counter-measure for the early publication of the content of the application before the patent is granted.[56] With regard to biological material deposited in an institution for the purposes of the disclosure requirement, the right of compensation will be only conferred if such material has been made available to the public, as determined by paragraph 2 of this article. Additionally, paragraph 3 affirms once more that the rights of the patentee are limited to the contents of the subject matter of the patent as defined by the claims.

Compulsory licenses, as per article 31 of TRIPS, are dealt in Brazilian legislation by articles 68 to 74 of the patent statute, which will be analyzed below.

Finally, making use of the option provided in article 61 of TRIPS, the Brazilian legislative established that infringement of a patent shall be deemed a statutory felony, independently of willfulness and commercial scale. Articles 183, 184 and 185 of the patent statute provides for criminal penalties for the acts of infringements there established.[57] Criminal proceedings will follow the rules on Criminal Procedure Law.

THE COMPULSORY LICENSES PROVISIONS

As a limitation to patent rights under article 31 of TRIPS, compulsory licenses may be granted in the following cases: (i) exercise of the patent rights in an abusive manner or abuse of economic power by means of rights; (ii) non-exploitation in the Brazilian territory by lack or incomplete manufacture of the product or by lack of complete use of a patented process; (iii) insufficient commercialization; (iv) dependency of one patent upon another; and (v) national emergency or public interest.

Because of the nature of exception to patent rights, compulsory licenses are always granted on a non-exclusive basis and sublicensing is not allowed pursuant to article 72 of the patent statute. Assignment of the license is only possible together with the related business undertaking. In the absence of legitimate reasons, as per article 74 of the patent statute, the licensee has a one-year term as of the license grant to begin exploitation of the licensed patent subject matter, admitted an interruption for an equal period. Where the licensee does not comply with such a term, the patentee may request revocation of the license. This is different from voluntary non-exclusive license cases, where the licensee will be vested with the power to act in defense of the patent.

The requirement that a patent be exploited in the Brazilian territory by complete manufacture of the product or complete use of a patented process under the penalty of being subject of a compulsory license has been argued to be against the non-discrimination principle established in article 27, paragraph 1, of TRIPS. Such a Brazilian local working requirement has triggered a panel request by the U.S. before the WTO's Dispute Settlement Body.[58] The Brazilian government started press campaigns alleging that the U.S. complaint at the WTO would jeopardize its program of free-distribution of medicines for the treatment of AIDS and gained favorable public opinion which led to a mutual agreement, with the U.S. withdrawing the panel request.

Except for the cases of compulsory licenses granted based on national emergency and public interest, article 73 of the patent statute determines that an interested party must file an application for a compulsory license indicating the conditions offered to the patentee, who must answer within a 60-day term. Upon the patentee's silence, the license under the proposed conditions will be deemed accepted. The allegation of abuse of patent rights or economic power must be documentary evidenced. The burden of proof of lack of exploitation lies on the patentee. Upon the patentee's contest, the INPI will take the necessary steps to analyze and decide the case and may establish a committee for arbitrating the remuneration. Appeals against decisions concerning the granting or rejection of a compulsory license may be filed to the INPI's Commissioner and will not suspend the effects of the first decision. As any decision of the public administration, the decision on the grant or denial of compulsory licenses is subject to judicial review.

Article 71 of the patent statute provides for the *ex officio* grant by the Brazilian government of compulsory licenses in national emergency and public interest cases, which will be declared in an act of the executive government. Decree N. 3201, of October 6, 1999, regulates the statute, determining the procedure for the grant and covers all kinds of patents, including pharmaceuticals. It defines a national emergency as imminent public danger covering the whole or part of the country's territory. Public interest, on the other hand, is defined through a non-exhaustive list of examples such as issues related to public health, nutrition, defense of the environment and those important for the technological or social-economic development of the country.

The Brazilian Ministry of Health enacted on June 24, 2005, Ordinance 985/2005 declaring of public interest medicines containing active ingredients lopinavir and ritonavir, used in the cocktail for the treatment of AIDS. Following this first ordinance, Resolution 352/2005 declared the granting of a compulsory license of the patent covering Abbott's Kaletra. After intensive negotiations, Resolution 352/2005 was suspended and an agreement between the government and Abbott was reached on the drug price.

In May 2007, the Brazilian government granted a compulsory license of Merck's Efavirenz patent. Efavirenz was also part of the drug cocktail for the treatment of AIDS and the license was granted aiming at a cost reduction of the program. The grant of this compulsory license was the result of unsuccessful negotiations between the government and Merck on the drug price. After being compulsory licensed, the generic drug was initially imported from India, purchased by the Brazilian government from Rambaxy and Aurobindo. Brazilian manufacture of the drug only started in 2009 and part of it is still imported from India.

FURTHER ENFORCEMENT PROVISIONS IN THE BRAZILIAN LAW AND GENERAL PATENT LITIGATION RELATED ISSUES

One of TRIPS major achievements in the harmonization of intellectual property rights is the provisions on enforcement, contained in Part III of the agreement.[59] Accordingly, Member States shall ensure not only that patent rights are available to inventors, but also that such rights are effectively enforced against infringers.[60] Articles 41.2 and 42 of TRIPS state that the enforcement procedures shall be fair and equitable.

In Brazil, enforcement of patent rights against infringers follows the general rules of Civil Procedure Law. Under the Brazilian legal framework, the Federal Constitution establishes some general principles to be observed in civil procedures. As to any right holder, access to the Judiciary system is guaranteed to the patentee in order to defend his rights against violation or threat of violation.[61]

Furthermore, according to article 5, LIV and LV, the Federal Constitution provides for the principles of due process and full defense, aimed at ensuring that equity principles will be respected in judicial and administrative proceedings. Any defendant in infringement actions has the right to defend himself fully, under the penalty of invalidity of the action. The due process and right of full defense principles comprise the right of both parties of the proceedings, plaintiff and defendant, to be given the opportunity to substantiate their claims and to present all relevant evidence. Accordingly, article 42 of TRIPS concerning fair and equitable procedures is reflected in the highest legal instrument of Brazilian Law.

With regard to the production of evidence provided by article 43 (and article 50.1.b) of TRIPS – in addition to the specific provision on the reversal of the burden of proof related to allegedly infringing products obtained by patented process (foreseen in article 42 paragraph 2 of the patent statute) – the general provisions of the Brazilian Civil Procedure Code are applicable. Specifically, preliminary injunctions for: i) search and seizure of goods, ii) judicial exhibition of documents, and iii) anticipated production of evidence (consisting of parties and witness testimonials and expert examination) are available to the parties in the proceedings.[62]

Prevention of infringing acts from occurring or being continued is of paramount importance to an effective patent protection system. Because of that, article 50 of TRIPS obliges Member States to grant judicial authorities the power "to order prompt and effective provisional measures to prevent an infringement of any intellectual property right from occurring, and in particular to prevent the entry into the channels of commerce in their jurisdiction of goods, including imported goods immediately after customs clearance."

The provisional measures referred in article 50 of TRIPS may correspond to the interlocutory injunctions under the Brazilian system, which are regulated in articles 273 and 796 to 812 of the Civil Procedure Code. In the context of effectively protecting patent right holders against infringers, interlocutory injunctions play an important role in Brazil, especially considering the long period of time usually needed to obtain a trial court final decision on the merits of the case.

In this regard, a patentee may request the courts to grant an interlocutory injunction to stop the activities of the infringer provided that he can meet the requirements of the likelihood of success and urgency of the measure (i.e., the delay is likely to cause irreparable harm to the right holder).[63] The court may render the decision *inaudita altera parte* where there is a risk that the defendant, once summoned, may cause the measure to be ineffective.[64]

Moreover, taking into consideration the principle of fair and equitable proceedings, the interlocutory injunction will not be granted where there is a danger of irreversibility of the measure.[65] Another procedural guarantee for the defendant, allegedly an infringer, is that the interlocutory injunction can be revoked or modified at any time by courts in a grounded decision.[66]

Any decision of the trial court, interlocutory or final, shall be legally grounded and is subject to appeal.

Enforcement of patent rights is only possible after the patent is granted by the INPI. However, as previously discussed, article 44 of the patent statute guarantees the patentee the right to obtain compensation for the unauthorized exploitation of the subject matter of the patent, including one that occurrs between the date of publication of the application and the grant of the patent.

Brazil has two independent systems of courts: a Federal Court system and a State Court system. According to article 57 of the patent statute, patent invalidity lawsuits are only tried before the Federal Courts and the INPI when the plaintiff will not necessarily participate in the action. Some Federal Courts, such as the Trial and Appellate Courts located in Rio de Janeiro, with jurisdiction over the States of Rio de Janeiro and Espírito Santo, have created specialized courts for industrial property cases.

According to paragraph 2 of article 56 of the patent statute, an interlocutory decision may be granted determining the suspension of the effects of a patent, provided that the relevant procedural requirements are met. Namely, such requirements are the likelihood of success (in the invalidity of the patent) and urgency of the measure, as established by Civil Procedure Law for interlocutory measures in general.[67]

Patent infringement trials are only brought before State Courts, even if one of the parties is a foreigner. Foreign plaintiffs with no assets in Brazil are required to post a bond, usually in the form of a bank guarantee. Each State Court has its own organization, and some have been restructured in order to create specialized courts in intellectual property rights. For example, the State Court of Rio de Janeiro has created specialized trial courts to hear matters regarding intellectual property.[68]

Furthermore, invalidity is a statutory defense provided by paragraph 1 of article 56 of the patent statute. If this defense is raised, the State Court hearing the infringement case will have to decide whether the patent is enforceable against the defendant before deciding on any infringement issue. However, a decision from a State Court on any validity issues only affects the parties of the case (i.e. the decision has *inter partes* effect).[69] It does not render the patent invalid with *erga omnes* effect (which is the case of decisions from the Federal Courts in invalidity actions).

Finally, it is worth noting that Brazilian judges very rarely have technical background, being only legally trained. Therefore, due to the technical complexity of patent cases, especially in the field of biotechnology, trial judges rely heavily on the analysis rendered by a non-biased expert appointed by the court. This can be burdensome when obtaining interlocutory decisions which are usually requested in the early stage of the proceedings.[70]

CONCLUSION

The basic belief governing the patent systems is that the possibility of protection for a limited period provides an incentive for people to innovate and invest. For novel therapies and diagnostics based on specific DNA sequences, for example, the possibility of having patents granted for achievements in the field of biotechnology promotes industrial competitiveness. The social return from this incentive to innovate created by patent possibilities is an increase in the general knowledge and the creation of useful products from which ultimately the public benefits.

In the international scenario, where the globalized economy led to the need to establish a multilateral trading-system, intellectual property rights in general, and patents specially, were also the object of specific debates. Under the WTO structure, TRIPS endeavors to establish harmony among the Member States' patent systems by requiring minimum standards of protection.

TRIPS expressly determined in article 27 that any invention that presents novelty, inventive step and industrial application would be patentable subject matter. WTO Member States cannot discriminate against any kind of art, except those considered contrary to public order and morals, human, animal or plant health and life, in addition to surgical, therapeutic and diagnostics methods, as well as plants and animals, except microorganisms. Additionally, Member States are obliged to provide means for patent right holders to enforce their rights.

In Brazil, the new patent statute (Law N. 9279/1996) was enacted to comply with the TRIPS provisions. It states that microorganisms modified by human intervention and biotechnological processes not occurring in nature are patent subject matter, once they meet the novelty, inventive step and industrial application requirements. Microorganisms found in nature and other living beings (such as plants and animals) modified or not by genetic engineering, as well as natural products and biological materials (including the genome of living beings when found in nature) are excluded from protection. The Brazilian legislation is, thus, restrictive towards the patentability of many biotechnological inventions, allowing only the minimum required by TRIPS.

Considering the country's expansive territory and biodiversity, the prospective exploitation of genetic resources with possible applications in the pharmaceutical industry, the policy decision to deny patent protection to many biotechnological inventions may be criticized. The interpretation of the explicit exclusions from patentability, the extent of the invention concept and the actual content of the patent might need clarification. The patent-scope repercussion of patenting living organisms remains confusing because of the qualities of a living organism, such as the capacity to make copies of itself and the multiple uses of the components of the organism.

For instance, the debate on the notion of industrial application or function of a gene sequence to be disclosed in the patent specification is still under development. Such disclosure of the industrial application of a gene sequence aims to require from the inventor that the useful function that makes such sequence patentable is disclosed. Otherwise, granting patents on DNA sequences without any limitation to the function could confer to the patentee a scope of rights comprising any application (or useful function) of the gene sequence independently of whether he was responsible for such invention.

The example of biotechnology serves to evidence that Brazilian Patent Law is still in the early stages of maturity and the pathway of related legal knowledge is still driving the first steps towards a sounded system.

NOTES

1. For the purposes of this chapter, the terms "subject matter excluded from patentability" and "non-patentable subject matter" will be used synonymously, i.e. meaning that patents are not allowed for such subject matter.
2. Law N. 9279, of May 14, 1996, was published in the Official Gazette on May 15, 1996. It regulates rights and obligations related to the industrial property, dealing with patents, industrial designs, trademarks, geographical indications, unfair competition, transfer of technology and franchising contracts. For the purposes of this work, Law N. 9279/1996 will also be referred as the current industrial property law or patent statute.
3. TRIPS was enacted in Brazil by Decree N. 1355, of December 30, 1994 (published in the Official Gazette of December 31, 2004).
4. Fritz Machlup, "An Economic Review of the Patent System" (U.S. Senate, Committee on the Judiciary Study No. 15, 1958) in Robert P. Merges and Jane Ginsburg, *Foundations of Intellectual Property*, Foundation Press, 2004, pp. 51–61.
5. John Locke, "Second Treatise on Government (1690)" in *ibid.*, pp. 1–5.
6. Harold Demsetz, "Toward a Theory of Property Rights" in *ibid.*, pp. 6–12.

7. Richard C. Levin et al., "Appropriating the Returns from Industrial Research and Development" in *ibid.*, pp. 61–68.
8. Luiz Leonardos and Viviane Yumy Mitsuuchi Kunisawa, "O sistema de propriedade intelectual como fomentador da inovação tecnológica" Revista da ABPI 76[Q2], 2005, p. 20.
9. Robert Sherwood, "Why a uniform intellectual property system makes sense for the World" in Mitchell B. Wallerstein, Mary E. Mogee and Robin A. Schoen, *Global Dimensions of Intellectual Property Rights in Science and Technology*, The National Academies Press, 1993, pp. 75–76.
10. Shozo Saotome, "Driving forces for technology transfer and development" *AIPPI Journal*, September 1980, p. 111.
11. Guntram Rahn, "The role of industrial property in economic development: the Japanese experience" *International Review of Industrial Property and Copyright Law* 14, 1983, p. 450 (quoting Korekiyo Takahashi).
12. Ministério da Ciência e Tecnologia, 2.1.7 Brasil: Comparação dos dispêndios em P&D (em valores de 2009) com o produto interno bruto (PIB), 2000–2009, available at http://www.mct.gov.br/index.php/content/view/9138.html (last visited July 31, 2011).
13. *Ibid.*, 3.1.2 Brasil: Pesquisadores, em número de pessoas, por setor institucional e nível de escolaridade, 2000–2010, available at http://www.mct.gov.br/index.php/content/view/5860.html (last visited July 31, 2011).
14. *Ibid.*, 5.5.a Número de artigos brasileiros publicados em periódicos científicos indexados pela Thomson/ISI e participação percentual em relação ao mundo, 1981–2009, available at http://www.mct.gov.br/index.php/content/view/5711.html (last visited July 31, 2011).
15. Leonardos, *supra* note 17, p. 16.
16. The INPI is the Brazilian governmental authority responsible for the examination and granting of patents.
17. United States Patent Office, Historic Patents By Country, State, and Year – Utility Patents (December 2007), available at http://www.uspto.gov/web/offices/ac/ido/oeip/taf/cst_utl.htm (last visited December 27, 2008).
18. Simone Biehler Mateos, "Aposta na Inovação" *Indústria Brasileira*, August 2003, p. 23.
19. FINEP, "Tecnologia e Competição na Indústria Farmacêutica Brasileira" *FINEP*, 1978, p. 78.
20. T. Samuel, "The Value of Protection" *Managing Intellectual Property*, November, 2000, p. 47.
21. Política Industrial, Tecnológica e de Comércio Exterior (PITCE).
22. As announced by Alellyx' scientific director during the Seminar "Intellectual Property as a Strategy to Technological Development," which took place in Campinas on August 2, 2006, Brazil's strict rules on patentability of biotech inventions led to the situation where the company seeks patent protection for its inventions at the USPTO without being able to afford a similar protection in Brazil. See Renata Costa, *Registrar para Garantir*, Universia, August 17, 2006.
23. Donald Chisum et al., *Principles of Patent Law*, Foundation Press, 3rd ed., 2004, pp. 7–15.
24. João da Gama Cerqueira, *Tratado da propriedade industrial*, Revista dos Tribunais, 2nd ed., 1982, pp. 1–48.
25. World Intellectual Property Organization, Contracting parties: Paris Convention, available at http://www.wipo.int/treaties/en/ShowResults.jsp?lang=en&treaty_id=2 (last visited December 27, 2008). The last revision in Stockholm of the Paris Convention was enacted in Brazil by Decree N. 635, of August 21, 1992 (published in the Official Gazette of August 24, 1992), and Decree N. 1263, of October 10, 1994 (published in the Official Gazette of October 13, 1994).
26. Otto Licks, "Direito de patentes: material de classe" Seminário de Direito Comparado de Patentes, SBDI e EMARF 2ª Região, 2001, pp. 9–10.
27. Article 11, paragraph 1, of the patent statute.

28. Article 11, paragraph 2, of the patent statute.
29. Article 12 of the patent statute.
30. Maria Thereza Wolff, "Matéria óbvia e suficiência descritiva em invenções de biotecnologia" Revista da ABPI 26, 1997, pp. 25–26.
31. Pontes de Miranda, Tratado de Direito Privado 16, Revistas dos Tribunais, 4th ed., 1983, p. 274.
32. Cerqueira, *supra* note 46, pp. 305–306.
33. "Article 1(3). Industrial property shall be understood in the broadest sense and shall apply not only to industry and commerce proper, but likewise to agricultural and extractive industries and to all manufactured or natural products, for example, wines, grain, tobacco leaf, fruit, cattle, minerals, mineral waters, beer, flowers, and flour."
34. G.H.C. Bodenhausen, *Guide d'application de la Convention de Paris pour la protection de la propriété industrielle*, BIRPI, 1969, p. 26.
35. "Article 10. The following are not considered to be inventions or utility models: I – discoveries, scientific theories and mathematical methods; II – purely abstract concepts; III – schemes, plans, principles or methods of a commercial, accounting, financial, educational, publishing, lottery or fiscal nature; IV – literary, architectural, artistic and scientific works or any aesthetic creation; V – computer programs per se; VI – the presentation of information; VII – rules of games; VIII – operating or surgical techniques and therapeutic or diagnostic methods, for use on the human or animal body; and IX – natural living beings, in whole or in part, and biological material, including the genome or germ-plasma of any natural living being, when found in nature or isolated therefrom, and natural biological processes."

    "Article 18. The following are not patentable: I – that which is contrary to morals, good customs and public security, order and health; II – substances, matter, mixtures, elements or products of any kind, as well as the modification of their physical-chemical properties and the respective processes of obtaining or modifying them, when they result from the transformation of the atomic nucleus; and III – living beings, in whole or in part, except transgenic micro-organisms meeting the three patentability requirements – novelty, inventive activity and industrial application – provided for in Article 8 and which are not mere discoveries. Sole Paragraph – For the purposes of this law, transgenic micro-organisms are organisms, except the whole or part of plants or animals, which exhibit, due to direct human intervention in their genetic composition, a characteristic that can not normally be attained by the species under natural conditions."
36. The Guidelines for Examination of Patent Applications in the Fields of Biotechnology and Pharmacy expressly forbids the granting of patents for processes of cloning human beings. In spite of that, allowing patents for such processes would also strive against the statutory prohibition under item I of article 18 of the patent statute that excludes from patentability matters contrary to morality.

37. Article 27. Patentable Subject Matter.

    1. Subject to the provisions of paragraphs 2 and 3, patents shall be available for any inventions, whether products or processes, in all fields of technology, provided that they are new, involve an inventive step and are capable of industrial application. Subject to paragraph 4 of Article 65, paragraph 8 of Article 70 and paragraph 3 of this Article, patents shall be available and patent rights enjoyable without discrimination as to the place of invention, the field of technology and whether products are imported or locally produced.
    2. Members may exclude from patentability inventions, the prevention within their territory of the commercial exploitation of which is necessary to protect ordre public or morality, including to protect human, animal or plant life or health or to avoid serious prejudice to the environment, provided that such exclusion is not made merely because the exploitation is prohibited by their law.
    3. Members may also exclude from patentability:

(a) diagnostic, therapeutic and surgical methods for the treatment of humans or animals;
(b) plants and animals other than micro-organisms, and essentially biological processes for the production of plants or animals other than non-biological and microbiological processes. However, Members shall provide for the protection of plant varieties either by patents or by an effective *sui generis* system or by any combination thereof. The provisions of this subparagraph shall be reviewed four years after the date of entry into force of the WTO Agreement.

38. Brazil is a Member State of the International Union for the Protection of New Varieties of Plants (UPOV), having accessed the 1978 revision of the UPOV Convention on May 23, 1999. The UPOV Convention was enacted in Brazil by Decree N. 3109, of June 30, 1999 (published in the Official Gazette of July 1, 1999). The protection of biotechnological developments by other intellectual property rights (such as the *sui generis* protection of plant varieties) is not the object of this chapter.
39. World Intellectual Property Organization, Budapest Treaty on the International Recognition of the Deposit of Microorganisms for the Purposes of Patent Procedure, available at http://www.wipo.int/treaties/en/registration/budapest/index.html (last visited December 27, 2008).
40. It is worth noting that there is no legal act supporting such an interpretation by the INPI.
41. Adriana Brendler, Centro de armazenamento de material biológico deve ser criado no Rio até outubro, April 3, 2006, available at http://ultimosegundo.ig.com.br/materias/brasil/2328501-2329000/2328566/2328566_1.xml (last visited December 27, 2008).
42. Article 62 of the Brazilian Federal Constitution empowers the President to legislate in cases of relevance and urgency by enacting Provisional Measures. The Provisional Measures afford the same legal hierarchy as the statutes enacted by the Congress, meaning that Provisional Measure N. 2186-16/2001 and Law N. 9279/1996 have the same hierarchy.
43. The ANVISA is the Brazilian sanitary administration agency similar to the U.S. Food and Drug Administration (FDA) and comes under the umbrella of the Ministry of Health.
44. Article 18, III, of the patent statute.
45. The admitted claim wording is, for example: "DNA sequence characterized by exhibiting: (sequence)"; "DNA sequence characterized by being Seq. ID no. (x)"; or "Recombinant protein characterized by being Seq. ID no. (y)."
46. The INPI's Normative Act No. 127, of March 5, 1997, establishes that:

   1.3.3 – Formulation of claims:
   The claims shall:
   [. . .]
   c) contain, when necessary, a preamble – between the title and the expression ". . . characterized in that . . ." – specifying the characteristics already absorbed by the state of the art, indispensable to the definition of the claimed subject-matter;
   d) exhibit, therefrom, in a concise, clear and objective way, the technical characteristics of the claimed protection, related to the genuine particularities of the invention, which establish and delimit the rights of the inventor.

47. The Swiss-type of wording for claims may be used.
48. Issues related to ethics and morality of patenting animals and other living beings, or related processes, are not the subject of this chapter.
49. The patents are the PI1100006-6 and PI1100007-4, both granted to Monsanto Technology LLC on August 17, 1999.

50. As previously mentioned, there is a large backlog in the examination of patent applications by the INPI, not only in the biotechnology field. Moreover, the policies adopted by the Brazilian government in the past led to a breach in the patent legal knowledge, and few judicial decisions on patent related matters.
51. Joseph Straus, Reversal of the Burden of Proof, the Principle of "Fair and Equitable Procedures" and Preliminary Injunctions under the TRIPS Agreement. Journal of World Intellectual Property 3(6), 2000, p. 808.
52. In contrast to the U.S. patent statute, this provision does not distinguish active inducement and contributory infringement, aiming at covering both activities of indirect infringement. For comments in this regard, see Danneman, Siemsen, Bigler and Ipanema Moreira, "Comentários à Lei da Propriedade Industrial e correlatos" *Renovar*, 2001, pp. 104, 335–339.

53. Article 34. Process Patents: Burden of Proof.

    1. For the purposes of civil proceedings in respect of the infringement of the rights of the owner referred to in paragraph 1(b) of Article 28, if the subject matter of a patent is a process for obtaining a product, the judicial authorities shall have the authority to order the defendant to prove that the process to obtain an identical product is different from the patented process. Therefore, Members shall provide, in at least one of the following circumstances, that any identical product when produced without the consent of the patent owner shall, in the absence of proof to the contrary, be deemed to have been obtained by the patented process:
       (a) if the product obtained by the patented process is new;
       (b) if there is a substantial likelihood that the identical product was made by the process and the owner of the patent has been unable through reasonable efforts to determine the process actually used.
    2. Any Member shall be free to provide that the burden of proof indicated in paragraph 1 shall be on the alleged infringer only if the condition referred to in subparagraph.
       (a) is fulfilled or only if the condition referred to in subparagraph
       (b) is fulfilled.
    3. In the adduction of proof to the contrary, the legitimate interests of defendants in protecting their manufacturing and business secrets shall be taken into account.

54. This is the legal ground for the rule of the national exhaustion of patents in Brazil. It is generally understood that parallel importation is considered patent infringement.
55. Article 45 of the patent statute.
56. The early publication of the content of a patent application would be contradictory to the theory that a patent is granted as an incentive for the inventor to disclose his invention to society. By the time of early publication, the inventor would have already disclosed his invention, without having the guarantee that a patent would be granted for it. However, early publication is considered necessary in order to keep competitors in a given industry aware that a patent might be granted for a certain technology and that they should be careful in making investments on the exploitation of such technology. In order to balance this, this provision would guarantee to the patentee the right for compensation against unauthorized use of the content of the patent between the publication of the application and the granting.

57. Article 183 – A crime is committed against a patent of invention or a utility model patent by who: I – manufactures a product that is the subject matter of a patent of invention or a utility model patent, without authorization of the patentee; or II – uses a means or process that is the subject matter of a patent of invention, without

authorization of the patentee. Penalty – detention of 3 (three) months to 1 (one) year, or a fine.

Article 184 – A crime is committed against a patent of invention or a utility model patent by he who: I – exports, sells, exhibits or offers for sale, maintains in stock, hides or receives, with a view to use for economic purposes, a product manufactured in violation of a patent of invention or of a utility model patent, or that is obtained by a patented means or process; or II – imports a product that is the subject matter of a patent of invention or of a utility model patent or is obtained by a means or process patented in this country, for the purposes mentioned in the previous item, and that has not been placed on the external market directly by the proprietor or with his consent. Penalty – detention of 1 (one) to 3 (three) months, or a fine.

Article 185 – Supplying a component of a patented product, or material or equipment for carrying out a patented process, provided that the final application of the component, material or equipment necessarily leads to the exploitation of the subject matter of the patent. Penalty – detention of 1 (one) to 3 (three) months or a fine.

58. Brazil – Measures Affecting Patent Protection. Request for Consultations by the United States, June 8, 2000 (WT/DS199/1). Request for Establishment of a Panel by the United States, January 9, 2001 (WT/DS199/3). Notification of Mutually Agreed Solution, January 9, 2001 (WT/DS199/4).
59. Straus, *supra* note 73, p. 810.
60. Article 41.1 of TRIPS.
61. Article 5, XXXV, of the Brazilian Federal Constitution.
62. Preliminary injunctions proceedings for search and seizure of the goods are regulated in articles 839 to 843 of the Civil Procedure Code; for judicial exhibition of documents in articles 844 and 845 of the Civil Procedure Code; and for anticipated production of evidence (consisting of parties and witness testimonial and expert examination) in articles 846 to 851 of the Civil Procedure Code.
63. Articles 273 and 798 of the Civil Procedure Code.
64. Article 804 of the Civil Procedure Code.
65. Paragraph 2 of article 273 of the Civil Procedure Code.
66. Paragraph 4 of article 273 of the Civil Procedure Code.
67. As per article 273 and 798 of the Brazilian Civil Procedure Code.
68. Tribunal de Justiça do Estado do Rio de Janeiro, available at http://www.tj.rj.gov.br.
69. Where an invalidity action is pending before a Federal Court, it may be up to the Trial State Court to stay the infringement action until a final decision on the validity of the patent is issued. An interlocutory decision suspending the effects of the patent may lead to the stay of the infringement proceedings.
70. On these occasions, parties' experts may play an important role.

9. Review and perspective of the Chinese patent system

Zhang Ping

INTRODUCTION

A patent system does not necessarily promise the active promotion of social development; not all the countries that have established a patent system can realize the rapid development of scientific technology. Patent legislation happened earlier in Malaysia than it did in Japan, but Malaysia lags significantly behind Japan in the field of scientific technology. In China, it is over 20 years since the legislation of a patent law, but it is not clear whether businesses have actively benefited. In most cases, companies became aware of the importance of the patent passively through litigation. Meanwhile, Korea has achieved an increase in innovation by adopting a patent system in the last 20 years and has become a strong international patent power. A patent system conforming to international standards does not always produce economic benefits which also reflect international standards. Besides the economic infrastructure and technical basis, the effective use of a patent system is also a key factor.

The patent system has two faces, and may not simply have the function of promoting national economy and science and technology developments. Its positive effects have already been demonstrated through the experiences of developed countries. However, the system also has negative effects such as hampering innovation and restricting competition in countries with a weak technical base. Particularly, in recent years, issues involving the quality of patent applications, "patent trolls," and the abuse of lawsuits have become an international concern. The "alienation" of the patent system leads to malicious industrial competition.

China, with a less than perfect market economy, is a "late-developing" country in terms of a patent system, and has limited awareness and operational capability. In more than 20 years of patent practice, China has learned most of its lessons from being passively involved in lawsuits. Nowadays, in the age of information and patent reforms, there are boundless opportunities in China's massive and open market. If patent applications can be accurately handled and an effective patent strategy can be properly established, the patent system will certainly greatly promote development in science and technology and China's economy.

HISTORICAL DEVELOPMENT AND CHARACTERISTICS OF CHINESE PATENT LAW

From a historical point of view, the word "patent" appears in the book "Guo Yu" which dates back to more than 2,000 years ago, but it did not carry a legal meaning then.[1] From the viewpoint of technical innovation, ancient China can certainly be deemed as a "nation of great innovation" and the "four great inventions" resulted from this, namely, papermaking, gunpowder, the compass and woodblock printing. In ancient China, neither patent law nor a patent strategy existed. If there had been a patent law, China could have developed as a prosperous nation based on collecting patent fees to the benefit of its citizens. In 1859, during the period of the Taiping Heavenly Kingdom, the establishment of a patent system was proposed, and in 1898, the Guangxu Emperor published the "Regulations on Rewards for the Promotion of Technology" during "the Hundred Days Reform." In 1912, during the Xinhai Revolution, the "Interim Charter on Rewarding Industrial and Artistic Producers" was enacted, and in 1944, the Chinese Nationalist Government promulgated the patent law. However, they were not implemented because of consecutive wars. In 1950, after the foundation of the People's Republic of China, only four patents were issued, which all passed into obscurity in a series of political movements. The patent system in China substantively came into force in 1985 after the reform and opening-up.

Characteristics of the Patent Law of 1985

The patent law enacted in 1985 was called for as a result of the reform of the economic system and the liberalization of the market. The most basic function of the patent system is to encourage innovative activities in the market by granting a monopolistic right, to promote the development of science and technology, and strengthen the nation's economy. However, the Chinese economy at the time was based on a planned economy, and the patent system was required by the reform and opening-up and to invite foreign investment, rather than keeping pace with the development of society. The patent law of 1985 took note of the experience of other countries that had had a patent system for hundreds of years and also gave consideration to the domestic situation (China had just moved from a planned economy to a market economy). The law complied with the basic principles of international treaties but with Chinese characteristics.

The characteristics of the patent law of 1985 are briefly summarized as follows.

Implementation of a single patent protection system

The former Soviet Union and the former Eastern European socialist countries mostly adopted a dual patent system including an inventor certificates system and a patent certificates system, which was different from the traditional Western patent system. The dual patent system takes into account both the socialist public economy and a market economy, but is not beneficial for international communication. China adopted a single patent protection system in compliance with international practice, without employing an inventor certificates system, in order to strengthen the relationship between the patent system and the Paris Convention. In addition, a service invention and a non-service invention were separately defined, with consideration equally given to all the interests of the nation, collectives, and individuals.

Protection provided for patents in three different forms

The patent law of 1985 defines three forms of invention-creations including patent for invention, patent for a utility model, and patent for industrial design. Not many countries protect those three forms of innovative achievement as a single patent. In general, a patent law usually only deals with patent for invention, whereas utility models which are called "small inventions" are protected by a separate law, or not regarded as a patent. The industrial design or a new pattern of industrial product may be included in patent law in some countries, or may be protected by another separate law in other countries. In China, when the patent law was first established, science and technology was generally underdeveloped and there would be a large number of small inventions and small innovations for quite some time. In view of this, three forms of patents were defined by the patent law in order to promote and protect motivation for invention-creation, which is one of the characteristics of the Chinese patent law.

Coexistence of early publication, delayed examination, and patent registration system

In order to make patented technologies available to society quickly so that information related to patent applications could be available to the public as soon as possible, and to provide the applicant with time to determine whether or not to request substantive examination during the process of patent application (to alleviate the burden of carrying out the substantive examination, which is borne by the China Patent Office (the China Patent Office was renamed the State Intellectual Property Office in 1998)), Chinese patent law adopted the German patent law system, which employs an early publication and delayed examination system for invention patent applications. Specifically, the application is published 18 months after the date of filing, and then the procedure enters a phase of substantive examination under the request of the applicant. Further, Chinese patent law adopts a registration system without substantive examination for utility-model and industrial design patent applications, in which patent rights are granted simply based on a formal examination. As described above, the Chinese patent law is convenient for making small inventions available to society as soon as possible, which is beneficial for the dissemination of patented technology.

Coexistence of planned and compulsory license

When different forms of public economy, such as a state-owned economy and a collective owned economy, coexisted, if a significant service invention was made the relevant office in charge could permit other companies to use the invention. If a company which is qualified to implement the patent has made requests for authorization from the patentee to implement his patent on reasonable terms and conditions and such efforts have not been successful, the China Patent Office may award a compulsory license based on a request made by the company wanting to implement the invention. The planned license has Chinese characteristics, while the compulsory license follows international rules. The coexistence of planned licenses and compulsory licenses is in the national interest, avoids the violation of international treaties, prevents abuses of patent rights as well as taking the interests of the public into account.

Patent disputes are dealt jointly by administrative and judicial authorities

The patent law of 1985 defines the position and the official responsibilities of the patent administrative authorities so as to clarify its quasi-judicial role, in view of the fact that in China a patent dispute may be settled more effectively by the administrative authority than by the court. In a patent infringement dispute, a patentee or an interested party may directly file a lawsuit with the people's court, or may make a request to the administrative authority for dispute settlement. Patent law regulations include an independent chapter specifying the responsibilities of patent administrative authorities, which is one of the characteristics of Chinese patent law. Such provision is seldom found in other countries.

The law has international features while being in harmony with China's economy

Chinese patent law follows the German patent law system, which is appropriate for the scientific and technical development levels in developing countries while absorbing advantages of the patent systems in other countries. The patent system protects the interests of inventors and patentees in order to promote the motivation to make invention-creations, as well as giving consideration to national and social interests. The basic principles of the Chinese patent protection conform to the Paris Convention as well as the trend towards internationalization of the patent system.

First Amendment of the Patent Law (Patent Law of 1993)

In 1988, along with the U.S.–China negotiations on intellectual property rights, China began preparations for the first amendment of the patent law. The amended patent law entered into force on January 1, 1993. The details of the amended patent law and related Articles are as follows:

1. Definitions of a right of import were added. Specifically, a patentee shall have the right to prevent a third party from importing the patented product for the purpose of production and sales or from importing the product directly by using the patented process, without authorization of the patentee. In many countries, the right of import is defined as part of the patent right by the patent law. However, the Chinese patent law of 1985 defined only a right of manufacture, a right of use, and a right of sales as patent rights, which was insufficient as patent protection. With the enhanced right of import, the level of patent protection is thus raised.
2. The protection of a process patent was extended to a product obtained directly by using the process patent. The Chinese patent law of 1985 only defined a right of use of a process patent, whereas the amended patent law defines the use and sales of a product directly obtained by a process patent as a right of the patentee of the process patent.
3. The technical field subjected to patent protection was expanded. In Article 25 of the patent law of 1985 seven technical fields were excluded from patent protection. In the amended patent law, items 4 and 5, namely, foods, beverages, condiments, chemicals, and a product obtained by a chemical method, were deleted. As a result, the Chinese patent law was upgraded to a level closer to international standards in terms of protection scope.

4. A national priority right was added. The patent law of 1985 provided that a foreign applicant shall be given priority when applying for a patent in China after first filing an application for the patent or a utility model in a foreign country. The amended patent law additionally provides that an applicant shall enjoy priority when filing an application for a patent with the Patent Administration Department under the State Council within 12 months from the date of the application for the patent or a utility model on the same subject was first filed in China.
5. The scope of amendment in patent application was expanded from description, as originally provided in the Patent Law of 1985, to both the description and the specification.
6. The timescale for publishing a patent application was clarified. Specifically, the patent application must be published 18 months from the filing date of an application. An applicant may find it inconvenient if the application were published before being granted a patent. While the law provides that the application should be published in 18 months, the ideal time to publish the application is the last day of the 18-month period. Although the amended patent law adopts the laid-open period of 18 months, if the publication cycle of patent documents is taken into consideration, a maximum one-week delay may be allowed. Of course the application may be published earlier as requested by the applicant.
7. The grant of a patent at an earlier stage has been achieved. Under the amended patent law, the gazetting of examination has been eliminated, and where no reason for rejection is found after the substantive examination, the Patent Administration Department under the State Council will grant a patent for invention, issue a certificate and register and gazette the invention.
8. The pre-grant opposition procedure was revised to a post-grant revocation procedure. Abolishing the pre-grant opposition procedure may significantly accelerate the examination procedure and promote clerical efficiency within the patent office. The revocation procedure provides the public with a greater right to question the validity of the patent.
9. The scope of patent re-examination was expanded. A patentee dissatisfied with the decision of revocation of the patent right or the decision of maintenance of the patent made by the patent office may file a request for re-examination.
10. The duration of a patent right was prolonged. Protection for a patent for invention was extended from the original 15 years to 20 years, and the term of protection for a utility model and an industrial

design was extended to 10 years from the original five-year term with a three-year extension.

11. The timescale to request a declaration of invalidation was further restricted. The patent law of 1985 provided that the declaration of invalidation of a patent right for invention may be requested any time after the gazetting of the patent. The amended patent law provides that the declaration of invalidation of a patent right may be requested only after six months from the date of gazetting. This is because the revocation procedure was introduced in the amended law and the six-month post-grant period is considered sufficient for application for revocation.
12. The requirements for compulsory license have been revised. The patent law of 1985 was relatively clear with respect to the time and specific requirements for granting compulsory license. However, the amended patent law does not specify the time for granting a compulsory license with due regard to international practice.
13. The shift of burden of proof in patent infringement dispute was revised. The patent law of 1985 provided that, where an act of infringement was committed on a patent for a process of manufacturing a product, the infringer should furnish proof to show the process of manufacturing the product. Under the amended patent law, the product is specifically defined as "new" product, that is, the infringer shall furnish proof to show the process of manufacturing the new product where an act of infringement was committed on a process patent. This provision narrows the scope of burden of proof on a process patent, thereby increasing protection on a process patent.
14. A punishment provision for the act of passing any non-patented product off as a patented product or passing any non-patented process off as patented process was added. The patent law of 1985 defined a punishment provision only for the act of passing off the patent of another person as his own. However, there are many cases where unimplementable technologies and counterfeit or defective products are claimed as patented technologies or products. Stiff sanctions should be imposed for deceiving the public, stealing credit, and causing harm to society.

The first amendment of the patent law was carried out quickly under the intense pressure of U.S.–Chinese negotiations on intellectual property rights; therefore, the amended law still leaves some issues unsolved. China had already started preparations for the second amendment of the patent law for the re-entry in GATT soon after the first amendment, and later, for accession to the World Trade Organization (WTO), both of which require patent law to conform to the agreement on trade-related aspects of intellectual property rights (TRIPS agreement).

Second Amendment of the Patent Law (Patent Law of 2001)

The patent law was amended with the aim of achieving compliance with the demands of the TRIPS agreement of the WTO, and the amended law entered into force on July 1, 2001. The main contents of the second amendment are as follows:

1. The objective of the patent law to promote progress in science and technology and encourage innovation was clarified.
2. The contract-first principle was introduced, which allows a technical designer and a company/individual to enter into an agreement regarding the ownership of an invention-creation. It also clarified that the inventor of a service invention is entitled to remuneration rather than simply a reward.
3. The provision "unique" for state-owned businesses was deleted, and state-owned businesses and businesses may assign a patent or the right to apply for a patent without seeking approval from the competent authority at a higher level.
4. Patent protection was reinforced. Provisions pertaining to a right of offer to sale were added as part of the patent right.
5. The act of use or sale of an infringing product in good faith was revised from not being deemed as infringement to being exempted from liabilities for compensation.
6. Interim measures prior to litigation were added.
7. Provisions on the assessment of the amount of damage caused by an infringement and statutory damage were provided.
8. Procedures for patent examination and patent protection were simplified and improved.
9. It provided that the People's Court should make the final judicial determination on re-examination of a patent application and invalidation of a patent, thereby abolishing the final discretion which had been assigned to the Patent Re-examination Board.
10. The procedures for revocation of the three forms of patent rights were abolished.
11. Procedures for assigning a patent and filing a foreign application for a patent were simplified.
12. A clear legal basis was established for filing international patent applications (PCT) to comply with international treaties.

The amendments described above mainly originate from ensuring that the patent law conforms to the TRIPS agreement. The issues that arose in the course of the 15 years after the implementation of the patent system still needed further study. Due to such issues, Chinese businesses, especially after the accession to the WTO, were still in a disadvantageous position, because of unreasonable patent barriers, a lack of legal-level regulation, and the existence of systematic problems in Chinese patent law, which needed further improvements. As a result, the third amendment of the patent law was launched.

Third Amendment of the Patent Law (Patent Law of 2009)

The third amendment of the Chinese patent law was initiated to satisfy the demands of the development of the economy and the science and technology of China, rather than yielding to external pressure. The law was amended based mainly on the concepts described below:

1. Patent protection had already become one of the key factors in international competition. However, developed countries were actively driving further reformation of international regulations pertaining to intellectual property rights, based on the overall strengthening of intellectual property protection under the TRIPS agreement, in order to maintain and expand their advantages with respect to intellectual property protection. On the other hand, a large number of developing countries had felt more keenly the asymmetric nature of intellectual property protection and their disadvantageous position compared to developed countries. In recent years, the contradiction and conflict of interest between developing countries and developed countries concerning the reformation of international intellectual property rules have been becoming much more obvious and much more severe. In order to prevent China from standing in isolation in the formulation of international regulations on patent protection, China not only needed to take an active part in formulating and enforcing international regulations pertaining to intellectual property rights, but also needed to improve its domestic patent system in order to establish an efficient patent system which would be of a high quality, efficient, simple and convenient, low in cost, provide proper protection, be capable of adapting to the development of global changes, and possess vitality, and competitiveness.
2. In order to protect developing countries' rights in the public health field, to overcome epidemic diseases and save the lives of their citizens, as well as to carry through the Doha Declaration and the presidential statement issued in the declaration, Chinese patent law and the

implementing of regulations needed to reflect the principles and contents of the declaration. At the same time, in order to apply the legal regulations in the fields of genetic resources, traditional knowledge, and folklore, related provisions needed to be provided in Chinese patent law and the implementing regulations.

3. Article 7 of The TRIPS agreement provides as its objectives:

   > The protection and enforcement of intellectual property rights should contribute to the promotion of technological innovation and to the transfer and dissemination of technology, to the mutual advantage of producers and users of technological knowledge and in a manner conducive to social and economic welfare, and to a balance of rights and obligations.

   Article 8 provides that:

   > Members may, in formulating or amending their laws and regulations, adopt measures necessary to protect public health and nutrition, and to promote the public interest in sectors of vital importance to their socio-economic and technological development, provided that such measures are consistent with the provisions of this Agreement.

   Those issues are closely related to the national interests of China, and therefore China must reconsider its interests and supplement relevant provisions to its patent law and its implementing regulations.

4. Chinese businesses frequently encounter intellectual property right disputes, and have become acutely aware of the importance of and difficulty in protecting intellectual property rights. Chinese businesses currently depend on the priority of low price of products and apparently lag behind in new product development, particularly lacking innovations with advanced technology. In order to promote growth and sustainable development in China, the ability to create self-reliant intellectual property rights should be enhanced, particularly the ability concerning self-reliant intellectual property in the high-tech field. Comprehensive improvement encompassing intellectual property creation, implementation, protection, and administration in China should be made in all directions.

   Accordingly, the State Intellectual Property Office commenced work on several research projects from 2005 prior to the third amendment of the patent law. The third amendment of the patent law was promulgated on December 27, 2008, and entered into force on October 1, 2009.

The 2009 amendments were chiefly as follows:

1. Article 1 further emphasized the legislative objective of promoting applications of invention-creations and enhancing innovative abilities.
2. The substantive patent right requirements were revised from the original "combined standard" to an absolute novelty standard to conform to the international trend.
3. An explicit provision on double patenting was provided. The provision aims to solve the problem of granting double patents, namely, a patent for an invention and a patent for a utility model, by clarifying that only one kind of patent shall be granted for one technology or one technical solution.
4. Provisions on restriction and disclosure of information concerning patent applications for biological and genetic resources were added.
5. The compulsory license system was improved; a compulsory license shall be granted under such circumstances as pharmaceutical patents regarding public health, not implementing patents, having influence on public interest and hampering competition.
6. Criteria for patent infringement were improved to clarify acts which will not be deemed as patent infringement.
7. A patent search report system for patents for industrial designs was introduced for industrial design, revised as the patent evaluation report.
8. The function of patent administrative enforcement and the degree of judicial protection were reinforced.
9. Circumstances that are not to be deemed as patent infringement were introduced in the amended patent law, which provides that where for the purpose of providing information needed for regulatory examination and approval, any person makes, uses or imports a patented medicine or a patented medical apparatus, and where any person makes or imports a patented medicine or a patented medical apparatus exclusively for that person, it will not be deemed as patent infringement (specifically known as the "BOLAR exception").

The third amendment to the patent law has two important characteristics, namely encouraging the promotion of innovative capacities and reinforcing patent protection.

Evaluation on Implementation of Chinese Patent System

Evaluation on legislation

The Chinese patent system now conforms to the basic requirements of the TRIPS agreement, and patent protection has also reached a level that complies with international standards. However, under the patent legislation which was passively accepted at first, the advanced aspects of promoting innovation were much more focused, whereas the anticompetitive effect likely to result from patent monopoly was underestimated. For this reason, China did not have a related antimonopoly law or a patent abuse prevention law at the time. Free competition is a basic principle of a market economy, which essentially excludes monopolies. All monopolies including market monopolies and technology monopolies are regarded as being contradictory to free competition, and patent protection is an exception to antimonopoly law, which lies with the nation acknowledging a legitimate technology monopoly. However, the concept of patents involves exclusiveness by nature, which contradicts the principle of free competition in a market economy, and therefore should be put under strict supervision in order to prevent restriction on competition. Therefore, in most countries which have established a patent system, an antimonopoly law has been legislated in coordination with the legislation of the patent law. However, in China, an antimonopoly law was not legislated early enough. The antimonopoly law eventually entered into force on August 1, 2008, but the development of subordinate laws relating to the antimonopoly law has not been enacted yet. In the future, implementing regulations other than the patent law should be enhanced to prevent the abuse of intellectual property rights and eliminate the restriction of competition imposed by intellectual property rights.

Evaluation on implementation

The number of patent applications received by the Chinese patent office (the State Intellectual Property Office, SIPO) is increasing at a great rate, which ranks China among the major powers in terms of patent applications. The number of patents granted is also growing year by year. However, when analyzing those figures for patent applications and patents granted in detail, many problems can be seen. In China, there is an imbalance between the increasing numbers of patent applications and patents granted among three types of patents: the numbers of patents for utility models and patents for industrial designs are high whereas the number of patents for inventions is low. Furthermore, quite a large number of patents for inventions belong to foreign companies and foreign-invested companies, leaving a very small number of patents for inventions for domestic patents, which are, for the most part, non-service inventions. Since 1985, the number of non-service inventions has been larger than that of service inventions, which implies that the implementation of the patent system has not been motivating Chinese companies to play an active role in the patent system. From 2007, along with the implementation of a national intellectual property strategy and a series of policies for promoting innovation (such as a revision to the Regulation of High-tech Enterprise Recognition, policies on corporate bidders participating in national research projects, and increased subsidies for patent applications) the number of patent applications filed by companies has started to increase.

Evaluation on enforcement of the law

Chinese patent law has been implemented at a relatively high level since its entry into force. Judicially, the Intermediate People's Courts in major cities established intellectual property rights tribunals at an early stage. The introduction of such a specialized court is advanced from a global point of view. Meanwhile, the Patent Administration Department has also established an efficient patent dispute settlement system, which is also rare in the international forum.

Countries at an early stage of economic development have seen, in most cases, the enforcement of the patent law evolving in stages from a lower level to a higher level. China, on the other hand, early in the development of the patent system, already provided patent administration and judicial protection at a relatively high level, which is not simply ascribable to trade pressure from developed countries but also stems from awareness. The author holds that the reinforcement of patent enforcement, especially administrative enforcement, should be mainly focused on those acts of infringement which adversely affect the competitive order and public interest, causing harm to society. Not all patent infringement disputes require interference for protection. The reinforcement of enforcement leads to an increase in cost, and therefore further discussion on whether or not such reinforcement is compatible with legal theory and the situation of China is required. It is considered that patent protection should be pursued mainly in respect of the judiciary, while the administrative protection should be limited to border measures and examination of intellectual property in important economic activities. The current U.S. patent system may be a good example to follow. Also, China should gradually weaken the current administrative protection system and reinforce the function of antimonopoly examination.

Evaluation on application

It is not until market subjects are capable of effectively using the patent system that the patent system can be implemented properly. In the past 20 years of implementation of patent law, universities and science research institutions, as the main Chinese innovative bodies, have not collaborated with companies. The government distributed a considerable amount of research funds to universities and public research institutions, but this did not lead to competitive patented technologies matching the input or having an effect in industry. A large number of Chinese companies made primitive accumulation of capital, paying more attention to short-term profit and less attention to investment in research and development (R&D). As a result, those companies have been faced with repeated set-backs in the international competitive market. Lacking also is the capacity for the application of patent strategy. Those implementing the patent system, namely, companies, universities, and research institutes, have a lower capability in patent protection and patent application, which will lead to a passive position in participating in international trade competition over a long period of time time.

SOCIAL FUNCTION OF THE PATENT SYSTEM

Reflecting on the past 100 years of world history, the following conclusion may be drawn: the most advanced countries in the world are all nations with great technical prowess, which, without exception, provide strong protection and encouragement for innovative activities through the patent system.

International Discussions on Evaluation of the Patent System

Despite the world now widely recognizing that the patent system has significantly promoted national development, there have been various milestones in the history of the development of the patent system. Britain has seen a retrogressive movement to "abandon the patent system."[2] In the Netherlands, moving in a different direction entirely, the patent system was once abolished.[3] Russia has implemented its own unique patent system, which treats domestic and overseas patents differently. Many distinguished jurists have challenged a proposition that the patent system promotes national development, while economists have cast a critical eye on patents, most of which take transaction costs into account. Described below are the positions of five scholars from different periods of history, which are representative examples of the international arguments described above.

In her book *The Economics of the International Patent System* published in 1951, Professor Edith Penrose stated:

> Any country must lose if it grants monopoly privileges in the domestic market which neither improve nor cheapen the goods available, develop its own productive capacity nor obtain for its producers at least equivalent privileges in other markets. No amount of talk about the "economic unity of the world" can hide the fact that some countries with little export trade in industrial goods

and few, if any, inventions for sale have nothing to gain from granting patents on inventions worked and patented abroad except the avoidance of unpleasant foreign retaliation in other directions. In this category are agricultural countries and countries striving to industrialize but exporting primarily raw materials . . . whatever advantages may exist for these countries . . . they do not include advantages related to their own economic gain from granting or obtaining patents on invention.[4]

Fritz Machlup, a scholar at Princeton University in the United States, after studying the U.S. patent system concluded in his 1958 report *An Economic Review of the Patent System*:

> If one does not know whether a system "as a whole" (in contrast to certain features of it) is good or bad, the safest "policy conclusion" is to "muddle through" – either with it, if one has long lived with it, or without it, if one has lived without it. If we did not have a patent system, it would be irresponsible, on the basis of our present knowledge of its economic consequences, to recommend instituting one. But since we have had a patent system for a long time, it would be irresponsible, on the basis of our present knowledge, to recommend abolishing it. This last statement refers to a country such as the United States of America – not to a small country and not a predominantly nonindustrial country.[5]

Lester Thurow, economist, wrote in "Needed: A New System of Intellectual Property Rights" in 1997:

> In a global economy, a global system of intellectual property rights is needed. This system must reflect the needs both of countries that are developing and of those that have developed. The problem is similar to the one concerning which types of knowledge should be in the public domain in the developed world. But the Third World's need to get low-cost pharmaceuticals is not equivalent to its need for low-cost CDs. Any system that treats such needs equally, as our current system does, is neither a good nor a viable system.[6]

Larry Lessig, a prominent academic lawyer, said of the U.S. patent system in a paper entitled "The Problem with Patents":

> No doubt we are better off with a patent system than without one. Lots of research and invention wouldn't occur without the government's protection. But just because some protection is good, more isn't necessarily better . . . There is growing skepticism among academics about whether such state-imposed monopolies help a rapidly evolving market such as the Internet . . . The question economists are now asking is whether expanded patent protection will do any good. Certainly it will make some people very rich, but that's different from improving a market . . . Rather than unbounded protection, our tradition teaches balance and the dangers inherent in overly strong intellectual – property regimes. But balance in IP seems over for now. A feeding frenzy has taken its place – not just in the field of patents, but in IP generally.[7]

Most recently, Jeffrey Sachs, an eminent economist, stated in his book *Innovation Policy and the Economy*:

> . . . there is an opportunity to re-think the intellectual property rights regime of the world trading system vis-à-vis the world's poorest countries. In the Uruguay Round negotiation, the international pharmaceutical industry pushed very hard for a universal coverage of patent protection without considering the implications for the poorest countries . . . In the conference on the TRIPS agreement, only a few people cast a doubtful eye on the need to have consumers in developing countries to make an effort to acquire core technologies. However, we have witnessed the impact given by the TRIPS agreement on the supply of basic medicines. Currently, the member countries of WTO are at a new negotiation table of the Doha Round, and have already agreed to reconsider the issues of intellectual property rights based on the principle of public health, which is a smart move. The enforcement of intellectual property right protection may slow down the rate of technical diffusion in developing countries, because developing countries in the world have achieved technical diffusion through copycat products and reverse engineering for a long time. Such technical diffusion which should not be hindered for ethical reasons might have been always hampered, and effects to be exerted by the technical diffusion to developing countries might have been unlawfully excluded. The system of intellectual property rights in the global trading system should be put under further observation, political interests, and sustainable research.[8]

Along with the discussions by academics on the patent system, governments, public institutions, and industries of various countries have become concerned about the negative effects brought about by the "alienation" of the patent system.

The Library of Congress pointed out in its report entitled "Patent Reform: Innovation Issues":

> That is, congressional interest in patent policy and possible patent reform has expanded as the importance of intellectual property to innovation has increased. Patent ownership is perceived as an incentive to technical advancement that leads to economic growth. However, growing interest in patents has been accompanied by persistent concerns about the fairness and effectiveness of the current system. Several recent studies, including those by the National Academy of Sciences and the Federal Trade Commission, have recommended patent reform to address perceived deficiencies in the operation of the patent regime. Other experts maintain that major alterations in existing law are unnecessary and that the patent process can adapt, and is adapting, to technical progress.[9]

The Organization for Economic Co-operation and Development (OECD) stated as follows in its annual report entitled "Patents and Innovation: Trends and Policy Challenges":

> Software and services are new subject matter for patents, although to a different extent across countries. The impact of patents on innovation and diffusion in this area has yet to be systematically evaluated, and such evaluation is sorely needed. The quality and breadth of software patents also need to be monitored, and patent offices should keep up their efforts to systematize their experience and knowledge base . . . Economic evaluation suggests that there are further possible directions of change for patent regimes that are worth exploring. Possible avenues for economic-based reforms of patent regimes include a more differentiated approach to patent protection that depends on specific characteristics of the inventions, such as their life cycle or their value; making patent fees commensurate to the degree of protection provided. In the near future, the patent system will be facing even greater challenges than those it has confronted in the past two decades, including increased globalization, the overwhelming use of Internet as a vehicle of diffusion, and expanded innovation in services. Well-informed and more global policies will be needed to prepare the patent system to meet these new challenges, so that it can continue to fulfill its role of encouraging innovation and technology diffusion.[10]

In addition, many countries have become aware that the cost for establishing the legislative and enforcement structure related to the patent system, including the establishment of the patent application and examination system, the judicial trial on infringement litigation as well as administrative enforcement, is high for government. Further, even for the businesses that the patent system is supposed to serve, the cost for implementing patent strategy is also high, as they will have to be equipped with professional legal personnel, establish special management funds and specialized research teams. The cost required for effective operation of the patent system is high in terms of human resources and fiscal resources. In particular, litigation of invalid patents drains the economy of resources that would be better spent on innovation. For example, in the United States, about 100 patent litigations go as far as trial every year. Most of the litigations involve a challenge to the validity of an asserted patent, and 40 percent of the patents at issue are declared invalid. The cost of each patent litigation case usually exceeds $1 million, and in most cases much more. Assuming the average cost of one patent litigation is somewhere between $1 million and $10 million per patent, and assuming that one patent litigation involves more than one patent, the litigation of invalid patents drains the economy of hundreds of millions of dollars per year.[11]

The patent system is not just a means for encouraging innovation. It has become a tool for technology monopoly and market competition, which results in the fact that “occupation” and “enclosure” have become the tendency in patent applications. A so-called patent strategy adopted by developed countries is actually a strategy for maximizing technology monopoly. If our perception of the patent system is still based on a certain kind of naive respect for intangible properties as innovative fruits, or is based on simple recognition of the need to protect an intellectual achievement, we may not be able to deal with threats brought by "defensive patents" and "straw man patents," not to mention the idea of damages to market competition brought by "patent hold-ups" and "patent trolls." "Patentization of technology, standardization of patents and internationalization of standards" has become the operation strategy that businesses use for pursuing maximization of interests. Such competition includes competition of science and technology and control on intellectual property rules. Countries with developed intellectual property rights manage to further promote their control on technology monopoly by using intellectual property rules on the premise of the innovative priorities they possess.

Developed countries have dominated science and technology while controlling international intellectual property rules. According to statistics from the World Bank, 86 percent of R&D expenditure across the world is spent by developed countries including the United States, the European Union (E.U.) and Japan. One-third of the world's population is neither able to perform technical innovation domestically, nor capable of adopting overseas advanced technologies. On the other hand, rich countries which account for about 15 percent of the world's population are entitled to almost all of the achievements of technical creativity.[12] Developed countries have always accounted for 90 percent or more of international patent applications based on PCT. The large number of intellectual property rights they possess has excluded the scientific and technical innovation made by late-developing businesses.

Due to the great difference in technical base, the social effects of the use of a patent system on developed countries and developing countries differ significantly. Countries with developed technologies consider that patent protection is necessary to stimulate economic growth. The encouragement of invention and new technology will translate to agricultural or industrial productivity gains, which will increase domestic and foreign investment, promote technology transfer and facilitate access to a sufficient supply of medicine. There is no reason that the patent system which has functioned in developed countries should not have a similar function in developing countries. However, developing countries are suspicious of the idea that the patent system has an active promoting function. Even in developed countries, many scholars consider that the patent system produces little encouragement of invention in developing countries due to a lack of necessary human resources and technical base. The patent system is incapable of efficiently encouraging development of new products to benefit the poor, because even if the products have been worked out, the poor still cannot afford the products owing to the increase of the costs caused by the license fees. On the other hand, in view of the market acceptability, businesses will try to avoid patent fees, but this will expose them to the risk of legal litigation. A company is obliged to pay for the "questionable patents" under bundling licenses in the face of the patent license policies formulated by the patentees. At the same time, patent protection has prohibited developing countries from the option of introducing technology through imitation. Foreign companies that have obtained a patent license may supply the patented product to the domestic market of the developing countries through importation, instead of producing the patented product within the territory of the developing countries. In other words, the patent system allows foreign companies to get rid of the domestic competition in developing countries through acquisition of patent protection. Further, those systems have increased the cost of importing basic medicines and agricultural products, which has greatly affected the benefits to farmers and to the poor.

Besides the direct influence of restriction of innovation, developing countries may also suffer indirect negative effects, such as being forced to accept patent protection at a higher level, or being put in a passive position in negotiations on technical introduction or licensing owing to a lack of understanding of patent license contracts. Those countries, such as India, Malaysia, and Philippines, which were under colonial rule of developed countries in the past, often unselectively adapt and adhere to the patent system of the ruler. Many other countries were swayed by external pressure when they first established their patent systems. Large companies in developed countries often pressure the government of a recipient country for the technology into establishing or revising patent law, in order to consolidate their market-dominant position.

Technologies licensed by multinational companies are usually secondrate technologies which are easy to imitate; the intellectual property of technical results achieved in research and development organizations established overseas are completely tied to the company in the motherland; less than 10 percent of the profit gained is given to the licensed country, most of which is confined mainly to quality control and minor product adaptation.[13] Therefore, strong protection of intellectual property rights in developing countries will not increase the R&D input accompanied by direct investments made by multinational companies.[14] Further, multinational companies also conduct lock-in for essential technologies in order to prevent the diffusion of sophisticated technology. Multinational companies have established various strategic technical alliances, which form technical networks among multinational companies, to control the development in related technical fields in terms of direction, size, and rate, to win control of production and diffusion of knowledge of science and technology.[15] Those strategic technical alliances are highly concentrated in the United States, the E.U. and Japan, which accounted for 91.24 percent of technical contracts signed between companies in developed countries from 1980 to 1994.[16] Most international technical transfers among developed countries are also concentrated in the United States, the E.U., and Japan.

Introspection: Initiating from the Patentee

In practice, companies with a large number of patents are aware that a complicated patent system has brought about very high risk in competition. Even those companies with strong awareness of intellectual property protection cannot avoid infringement. Those companies have started to review the problems in the operation of the current patent system. Patentees, as "economic men," repackage the bulk of public technologies and expired patents as new patents, which has resulted in so-called "questionable patents." Besides this, the misleading nature and expansion of defense patents also adds fuel to the flames of the current patent "chaos," causing a storm in the current patent scramble. It has been pointed out in a book entitled *Intellectual Property Rights: Discharge of Contents of Intellectual Economy* that "According to a survey on patents owned by multinational companies, 41% of patent applications include defensive patents, 10% of patent applications lead to double patents, 45% of patent applications are filed in order to hinder the production and sales of a similar product by a competitor, and 4% are filed for any other strategic reasons."[17] People are now aware that businesses' patent strategies have become a hindrance to innovation and restrict competition. In 2006, M.W. Schecter, Associate General Counsel of IBM Corporation, stated:

> Patent systems were created to promote innovation. Unfortunately, the U.S. patent system is ill. Innovation is being stunted by the enforcement of invalid patents . . . Alleged infringers are forced to expend considerable resources in their defense, whether they succeed or not. If there is litigation, the expenses escalate. If alleged infringers of invalid patents do not successfully defend themselves, they must pay unnecessary royalties and/or comply with an injunction.[18]

Even IBM, the world's leading patent holder, cannot break free from the spell of patents. In 2006, IBM initiated an online discussion concerning intellectual property, examining how innovation is affected by the quality of patents granted by the patent offices of each country. As was pointed out, patent has become an important "banknote" for creators and users of intellectual properties to create value. However, it takes time to build a healthy basic infrastructure for an intellectual property market, which imposes an excessive burden on a patent system. The uncertainty caused by the situation of a "vacuum" will lead to many problems, including litigation and speculation which are continually increasing. Such acts have hindered the innovative activities that should have been protected by the patent system. Because of this, people are becoming more concerned that the intellectual property market system may not be able to achieve the economic and social objectives of encouraging competition based on innovation, promoting creative ideas based on knowledge and the popularization and expansion of creative expression, rewarding various invention-creations in the economic system, and thereby supporting sustainable development of companies and industry (Nokia, Sun and Panasonic have all expressed similar views).[19] The "open patent" raised by IBM and the "open standard" by Sun Microsystems, Inc. are to a certain degree a reformation toward the patent grant system which may be a countermeasure to the way that "patent thickets" have influenced normal market competition.

In December 2006, the Japanese Fair Trade Commission launched an investigation to identify whether Qualcomm's sales of semiconductor chips to Japanese manufacturers violated the Japanese antimonopoly act. Qualcomm owns a patent for a CDMA chip for mobile phones and collects patent fees. Currently, CDMA chips predominantly prevail in the Asian and U.S. market. Qualcomm is suspected of offering Japanese mobile phone manufacturers a discount on licensing fees for its patented technologies in exchange for the cell phone manufacturers only using Qualcomm products. The Japanese Fair Trade Commission has required the cell phone manufacturers to re-examine the relevant documents regarding the contract signed with Qualcomm and has issued a similar summons against Qualcomm.[20]

In July 2006, semiconductor manufacturers Texas Instruments Inc. and Broadcom Corp. filed an antimonopoly case against Qualcomm in Korea, claiming that Qualcomm had unfairly used its patent rights to collect outrageous patent fees. Korean Fair Trade Commission spokesman Na Yang-ju has announced that mobile phone manufacturers Nextreaming and Thin Multimedia filed similar cases against Qualcomm in 2006.[21]

In October 2006, Texas Instruments Inc. and Broadcom Corp., together with Nokia, NEC and Panasonic, filed a collective lawsuit in the E.U. in Brussels against Qualcomm for restricting competition in the field of 3G mobile phone patented technology.[22]

The current patent system has already illustrated the trends of restricting innovation and fair competition in multinational companies. Meanwhile, because almost all technical fields are already covered by patents, developing countries are forced to concentrate their limited resources on conducting selective innovation in an extremely narrow space. Accordingly, developing countries should examine the social function of the patent system much more seriously and should deal with the challenge of the current international economy from the viewpoint of international rule as well as national strategy.

China's Countermeasure

A patent system is a double-edged sword. As for China, implementing the system in accordance with the economic development of the country is key to the practice of the patent system.

The development of the patent system in China was not driven by internal demand, and therefore it differs from systems in developed countries which were established based on market demand. Under the planned economy, a patent system was not necessary in China. After the reform and opening-up which started in 1978, China had to follow international regulations, in order to open up the domestic market and participate in international trade. When the patent law came into force in China in 1985, the major objective of the law was to meet the demand of the introduction of technologies and the market opening. However, domestic businesses, while making primitive accumulation of capital, were not in great need of patent protection; hence, the Chinese patent system was not highly regarded by most companies, let alone sufficiently used. When Chinese companies completed their primitive accumulation of capital and started to participate in international trade, they began to realize the importance of patent and the demand for protection thus emerged.

China is still a developing country and is still not strong in innovation and the application of patented technologies. So it is necessary not only to establish a system of strong patent protection which conforms to international standards, but also to give consideration to a patent application strategy appropriate for them. But China is not incapable of introducing technologies domestically so she can still benefit from the implementation of the patent system, which requires the market (that the patent system serves) to learn how to make full use of the patent system, that is, to protect others' rights and to protect their own interests.

Patent protection may inevitably lead to restrictions on competition and a certain level of market monopoly, which will restrain the development of the market economy, and which meanwhile damages consumers and free trade. Therefore, when implementing a patent system, the system should be adjusted in order to maximize the profit for social development.

Whether China can use the patent system to effectively promote innovation also depends on national public policies as well as the establishment of an innovative system which conforms to the level of current social development of China. A patent system can promote innovation only by being combined with other systems or mechanisms. Only in a complete and effective creation system can the negative effects of a patent system be restricted and balanced so that it can fulfill the function of promoting creation.

RELATION BETWEEN PATENT PROTECTION AND ECONOMIC DEVELOPMENT

Conclusions Drawn from International Research

As the role of the patent system to promote innovation depends on the social and economic infrastructure and other institutional environments, the same level of patent protection may have different impacts on the economic development in different countries.

In 1997, economists Ginarte and Park found through their research that levels of patent protection are critical, and patent protection merely indirectly promotes economic development. Their paper, "Determinants of Patent Rights: A Cross-National Study", presents the Ginarte-Park patent index, which conducts a horizontal comparison of the differences in patent protection levels among 110 countries for the period 1960–1990.[23] It is assumed that each country had considerable freedom in selecting the level of patent protection during the period. They found that each country started to provide active protection of patents only after their innovative industries reached a certain level. Further, in another paper, "Intellectual Property Rights and Economic Growth," published in the same year, they describe how they found that a patent system indirectly promotes economic development through the promotion of accumulation of R&D and investments.[24]

Later, Keith E. Maskus also conducted a horizontal comparison between countries using the Ginarte-Park patent index. His research, detailed in his report, "Intellectual Property Rights in the Global Economy," found that market scale does not influence patent protection levels. He also holds that patent protection levels in poor but large countries, such as China and India, may not be directly and effectively driven by external pressure. More importantly, Maskus further pointed out that the relation between the strength of a country's patent protection level and its per capita GNP renders a U-shaped curve. That is, the need for patent protection weakens before the per capita GNP reaches a critical point, whereas when the per capita GNP reaches the level of a middle-income country, patent protection will be strengthened; this derives from market demand

and the government will also gradually strengthen patent protection. The higher the income, the faster the need for strengthening patent protection accelerates.[25]

In 2004, Rod Falvey, Neil Foster, and David Greenaway delivered a conclusion based on their findings that patent protection does not play a significant role in promoting economic growth in middle-income countries, providing a better explanation for the U-shaped curve theory.[26] Their paper was based on surveys and researches conducted on a country-by-country basis through critical analysis:

> We investigate the impact of IPR protection on economic growth in a panel data of 80 countries using threshold regression analysis. We show that whilst the impact of IPR protection on growth depends upon the level of development, IPR protection is positively and significantly related to growth for low- and high-income countries, but not for middle-income countries. This suggests that, while IPR protection encourages innovation in high-income countries, and technology flows to low-income countries, middle-income countries may have offsetting losses from reduced scope for imitation.

Therefore, it can be concluded that the bottom of the U-shaped curve exactly corresponds to the middle-income countries.

The intellectual property system has produced pluralistic social effects in high-income countries and middle-income countries, due to great differences in their technical bases.

Background of Entry into Force of Law in China

The U-shaped curve theory demonstrates that developed countries barely have any innovative capacities and therefore do not have problems related to intellectual property protection. A nation tends to adopt a weak protection policy only after its income and technical capacities have reached a middle level, whereas until then it is in most cases focused on imitation and learning. Then, after income and technical capacity have reached a high level, the importance of intellectual property protection starts to be realized.[27] This theory discloses the rule concerning the relation between intellectual property rights and development of the market economy. Intellectual property systems in developed countries are established based on a relatively developed market economy, for which need arises as the result of social development. However, the Chinese intellectual property system is not based on a relatively developed market economy, and under the planned economy China had no need of an intellectual property system. After the reform and opening-up in 1978, the market economy initiated in China, and China itself, had to adhere to international regulations, in order to open up the domestic market and participate in international trade; therefore the intellectual property system was introduced. The patent law which came into force in China in 1985 was introduced mainly for this purpose. R&D conducted in China at that time was mainly based on imitation, which hid the domestic technical gaps. Most companies were in a stage of primitive accumulation of capital, and had virtually no motivation for innovation. Accordingly, the establishment of the Chinese patent system did not stimulate companies' incentives for innovation, and the patent system was not used sufficiently by the companies as subjects of the market economy. After quite some time, universities and public research institutions far removed from the market economy, started to file patent applications in China. It was not until 20 years after the enactment of patent law that pressure from international trade competition forced companies to consider intellectual property-related issues. However, most companies still lack capital and the capacity for implementing an intellectual property strategy.

The revisions to Chinese intellectual property law were often related to international negotiations and foreign trade policies. The first revision to the patent law was pushed by the U.S.–China negotiation on intellectual property rights. The second revision to the patent law, the second revision to the trademark law, and the first revision to the copyright law were all made in preparation for China's entry to the WTO. It demonstrated that the main objective of Chinese intellectual property law reformation was to serve the overall strategy for economic opening-up and to deal with external pressure from international society with respect to China's participation in international trade. The motivation underlying Chinese patent law did not derive from the need for protection from domestic innovative activities; this was clearly different from the way in which the intellectual property system in developed countries was born. In developed countries, the legislation of intellectual property stemmed from the need to develop a market economy. However, China underwent a transition from a planned economy to a market economy, and the country itself is still not fully established as a market economy. But it has to implement an intellectual property system which is closely related to the economy market. China's social infrastructure is insufficient for the implementation of such system.

Empirical Analysis of Patent: Consideration of Innovative Capacities and Consciousness of Patent Strategy in Chinese Companies

The Chinese economy has made great progress through the 30-year reform and opening-up and the move towards a market economy.

Continually since the 1990s, China has sustained an annual average GDP growth rate of no less than 10 percent. Despite this, according to World Bank statistics (World Bank list of economies, July 2008), [28] China is still ranked as a lower middle-income country, with many of its industries categorized as labor-intensive and impoverished, at the bottom in the field of value creation. The most remarkable thing is that there is no support of intellectual property providing for foreign-related trade activities, and intellectual property rights have made no contribution to the growth of its GDP.

The empirical analyses described below focused on the circumstances of patents for inventions in representative large-scale domestic businesses including the telecommunications equipment industry, the chemical pharmaceutical industry, the manufacturing industry, and the automobile industry. In the survey, representative companies from the abovementioned industries were selected as subjects for the research. Huawei represents the telecommunications equipment industry, and North China Pharmaceutical Group Corp. (NCPC) is the largest chemical pharmaceutical company in China. Xuzhou Construction Machinery Group is the largest manufacturer of machine tools, and First Automobile Works is the largest automobile manufacturer.

The author aims to examine the innovative capacities and intellectual property consciousness of Chinese companies by conducting analysis on the innovative capacities and patent situation of those large-scale companies. If even those companies fail to make effective use of the current patent system, small and medium sized companies will definitely lack such a capacity.

The survey is based on publicly-available data. Materials related to sales revenue, etc. come from annual reports, and data on patent applications and patents granted were obtained by patent search (available at http://www.cnipr.com/ (last accessed December 29, 2008)). In this survey, patent refers to patent for invention unless specifically stated otherwise.

Telecommunications company: Huawei

Huawei Technologies Co. Ltd. is a leading global next-generation telecommunications information solutions provider. Today, Huawei's products and solutions are used in more than 100 countries around the world and by 31 operators in the world's top 50 companies; the company serves over 1 billion users throughout the world. Huawei has laboratories in India, the United States, Sweden, Russia, and China (Beijing, Shanghai, and Nanjing), and 48 percent of over 62,000 employees are engaged in R&D. As for the number of patent applications in China, Huawei has topped the list for several consecutive years.

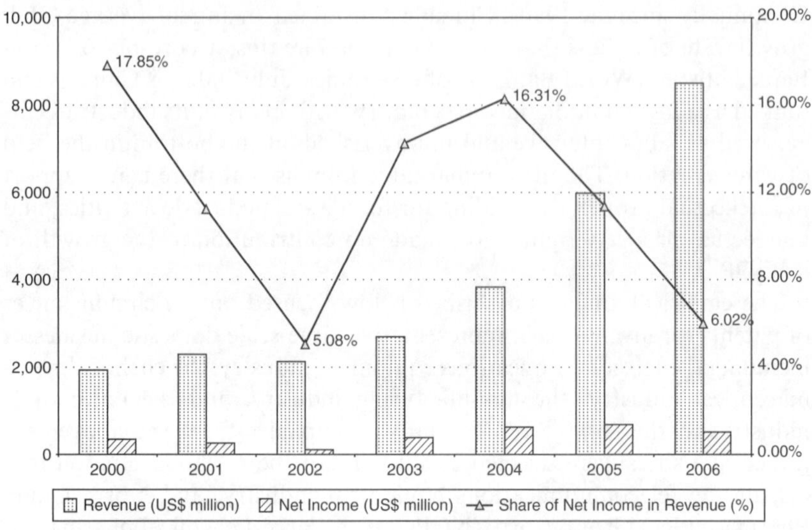

Source: Huawei Annual Report, see http://www.sipo.gov.cn/zljs/ (last accessed December 29, 2008).

Figure 9.1 Huawei: Sales revenue, profit, and R&D expenditure (2000–2006)

Huawei's income mainly comes from business conducted overseas. Although Huawei is one of the large-scale companies in China, their total income amounts to only one-sixth of Nokia's, and one-eighth of Motorola's. Huawei's business income is rapidly increasing, but their profit is not. The ratio between profits and sales revenue sank twice in 2002 and 2006, at a rate of 5.08 percent and 6.02 percent in 2002 and 2006 (see Figure 9.1).

Since 2000, Huawei has seen a large increase in the numbers of patent applications and patents granted. The number of patent applications has increased from 206 in 2000 to 3,508 in 2006, and about 500 patents have been granted every year since 2004 (see Figure 9.2).

At the same time, Huawei started to focus on international patent applications and became a PCT patent applicant as early as 2000. In 2006, Huawei ranked first in the number of published PCT international applications (which numbered 1,743) among developing countries (see Figure 9.3).

Huawei annually devotes about 10 percent of its sales revenue to R&D, about 10 percent of which is spent on high-end research. Nowadays, Huawei is a member of 70 standard-setting organizations. Since 2000,

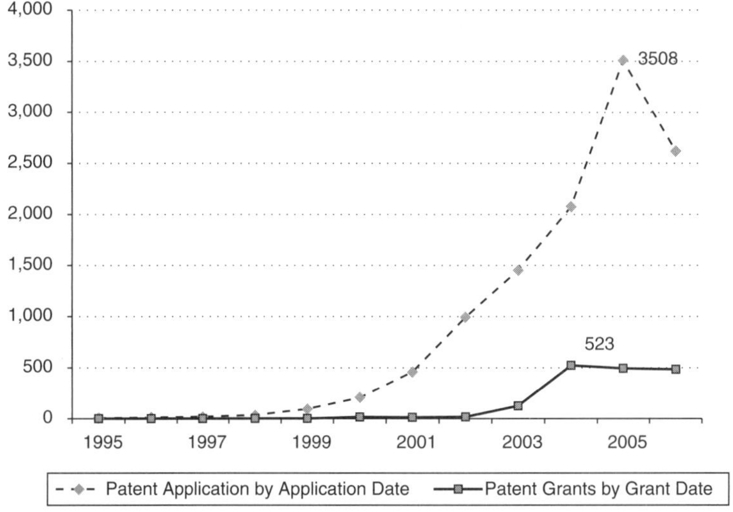

Source: Patent search by the author.

Figure 9.2 Huawei: Number of patent applications for invention and the number of patents granted (1995–2006)

Huawei has constantly ranked in the top three companies for its R&D in the Chinese electronics industry.

Pharmaceutical company: North China Pharmaceutical

North China Pharmaceutical Group Co., Ltd. (NCPC) is the largest chemical pharmaceutical company in China, and has been one of the top 500 largest Chinese industrial companies and companies achieving the best economic results for several consecutive years.

The number of North China Pharmaceutical's patent applications and patents granted was very low compared to Huawei. In 2005, only 17 patent applications were filed, and in 2006, only 11 patents were granted to North China Pharmaceutical (see Figure 9.4).

North China Pharmaceutical, despite being one of the top 500 largest Chinese industrial companies, and the largest medicine exporter in China, filed only four PCT patent applications up to 2006.

Though public material includes no information on the amount of expenditure spent on R&D by North China Pharmaceutical, a related media report says that the company's R&D expenditure accounts for 3–4 percent of its sales revenue. However, foreign pharmaceutical companies usually spend 15–25 percent of their sales revenue on R&D.

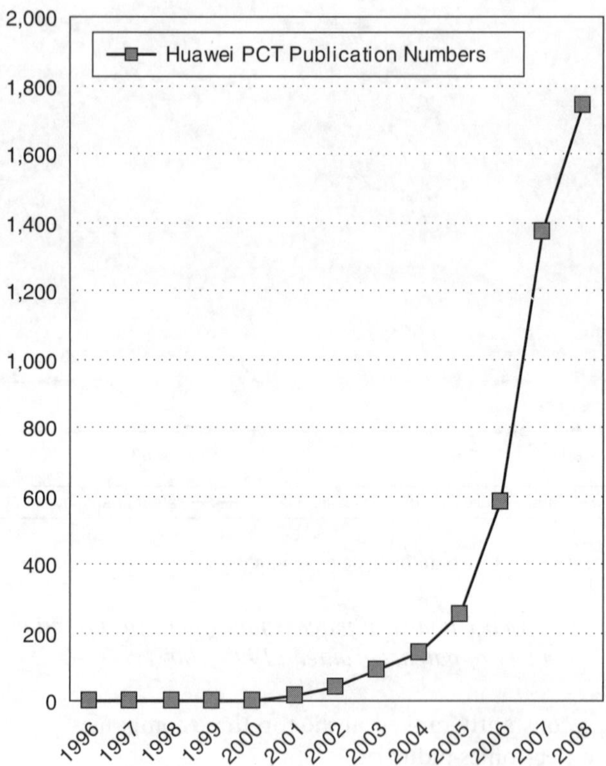

Source: Patent search by the author.

Figure 9.3 Huawei: Number of PCT patent applications (1995–2006)

Manufacturing company: Xuzhou Construction Machinery Group
Xuzhou Construction Machinery Group Co. Ltd. (hereinafter, Xuzhou) is one of 520 national key companies, and is a model company of the 863/CIMS application. In 2006, the company earned sales revenue of CNY 20.26 billion, and became the largest construction machinery developer, manufacturer, and exporter in China. More than 70 percent of Xuzhou's products are in the advanced level domestically, and 10 percent of the products have now reached the world's most advanced level. However, the number of patent applications and patents granted was even lower than North China Pharmaceutical. In 2006, only one patent was granted, and the largest number of patent applications ever filed during a one-year period was only six (see Figure 9.5).

No material was available through public channels on Xuzhou's R&D

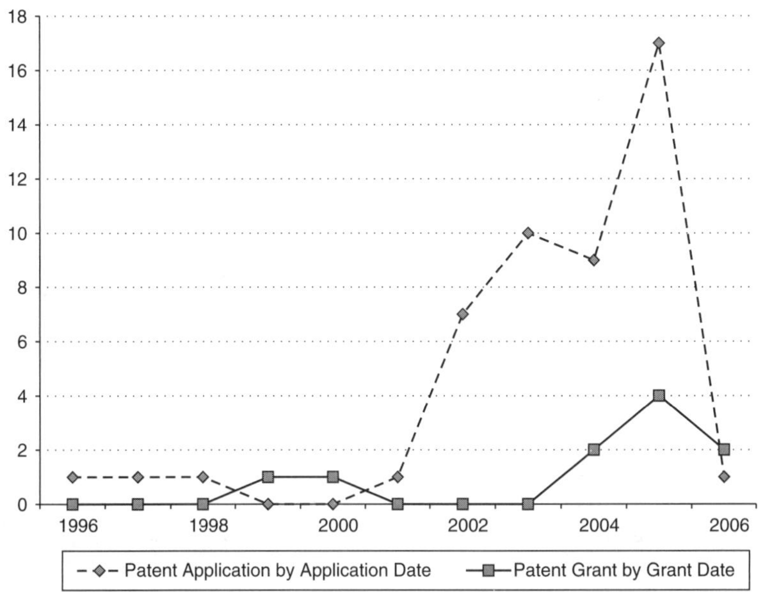

Source: Patent search by the author.

Figure 9.4 North China Pharmaceutical: number of patent applications for invention and number of patents granted (1996–2006)

investment. However, the low number of patent applications and the contracted profit rate imply that the R&D investment of the company is very limited. Indeed, Xuzhou is on the verge of collapse, and still faces many problems linked with the reformation of China's state-owned businesses.

Automobile manufacturer: First Automobile Works

China First Automobile Works Group Corporation (hereinafter, FAW) was ranked 470th in the world's top 500 companies, and ranked first in the top 500 Chinese machinery corporations. In 2006, the company's brand value reached CNY 42.421 billion.

As early as 1995, FAW established a technology center by integrating the Changchun automobile research center, the FAW design center, and the Changchun automobile material research center. The technology center is certified as a state technology center by the State Economic and Trade Commission, State Administration of Taxation, and the General Administration of Customs. It ranked seventh among the 231 company technology centers and led the machinery industry in 1999.

The number of patent applications and patents granted was very low,

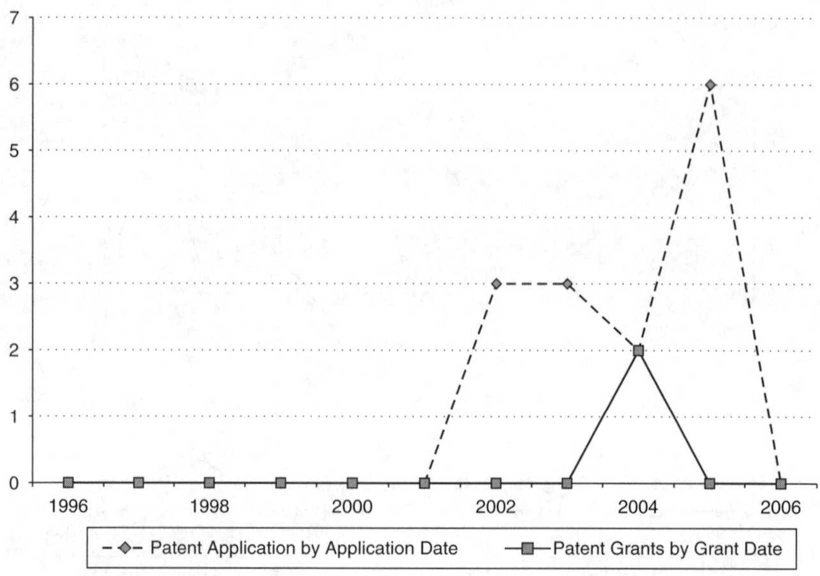

Source: Patent search by the author.

Figure 9.5 Xuzhou Group: number of patent applications for invention and number of patents granted (1996–2006)

just like North China Pharmaceutical. After 2001, FAW enhanced its patent applications, but only 17 patent applications were filed in 2005 and only seven patents were granted in 2006 (see Figure 9.6).

Data concerning FAW's R&D investment is not available through public channels, but it is reported that FAW has already spent CNY 500 million on R&D during the tenth five-year plan period. FAW itself announced that about CNY 1.3 billion has been devoted to R&D every year. However, in view of the number of patents granted to the company, the cost-benefit relationship is imbalanced.

According to general international criteria, it may be difficult for a company to survive when its investment on R&D is less than 1 percent of its sales revenue; a company may manage to survive when it is 2 percent and a company may become competitive only after 5 percent or more of its sales revenue is spent on R&D. Using this criteria, except Huawei, China's large and medium sized companies have been spending at most 0.9 percent of their sales revenues on R&D each year, and even the high-tech industry spends only 1.5 percent at best, which implies that Chinese companies are still in the survival stage. In fact, the survey on companies has shown that

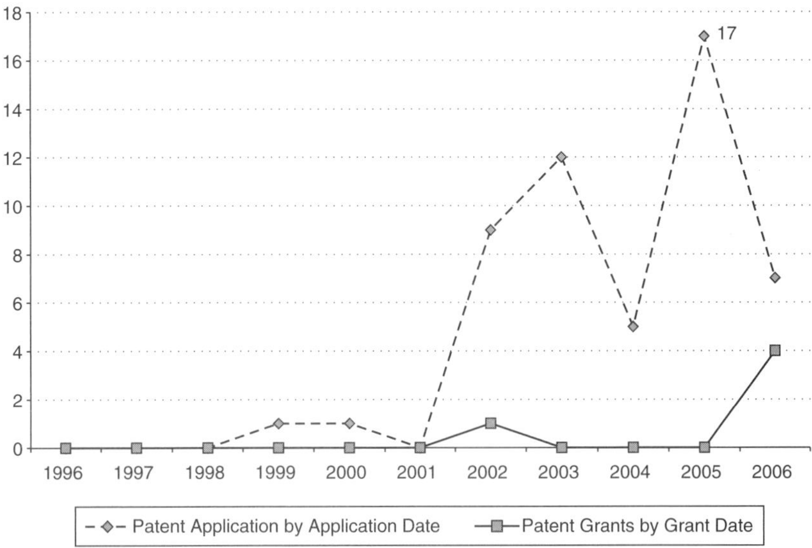

Source: Patent search by the author.

Figure 9.6 China FAW: number of patent applications for invention and number of patents granted (1996–2006)

Chinese businesses usually made significantly less profit in a year when a large number of patent applications were filed. The number of patent applications is increasing in the telecommunications industry, but most of the applications have been filed for defensive purposes. Companies are suffering fluctuations in profit rates due to patent applications, and lack financial stability. In recent years, most companies in the survey have seen their profits drop, which further limits their expenditure on R&D, thus making it difficult to sustain innovative activities.

Survey of international patent applications of China

The development of China's foreign trade mostly derived from comparative advantages and the chaos of price wars rather than companies' innovative advantages. Without the support of self-reliant intellectual property, a problem has emerged caused by the lack of competitive products with high added value. International patent applications and the expansion of foreign trade are completely disconnected. Since 1990, the number of China's PCT international patent applications reached a peak in 2006, which nonetheless accounts for only 2.64 percent of the world's patent applications. Compared with developed countries, there is a large

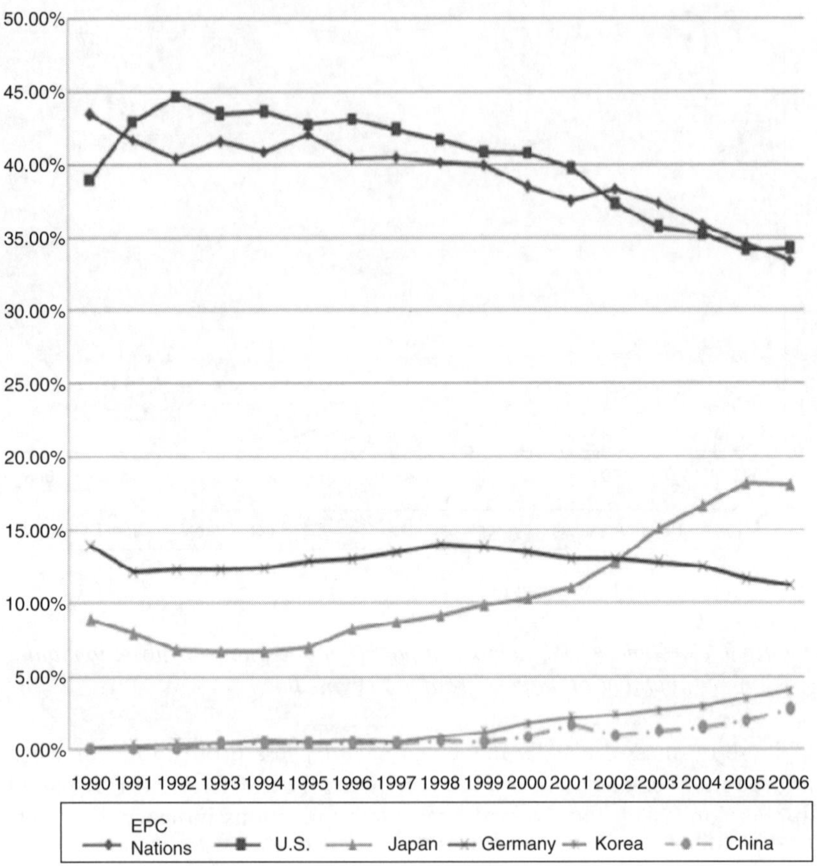

Source: See http://www.wipo.int/export/sites/www/ipstats/en/statistics/patents/xls/wipo_pat_appl_by_route_table.xls (last accessed December 29, 2008).

Figure 9.7 Country-specific ratios of PCT patent applications to total PCT patent applications (1990–2006)

gap (see Figure 9.7) (WIPO, 2007),[29] which is quite incongruous considering the status of China as the world's third largest international trading nation.

Further, taking Sino–U.S. trade as an example, China's trade with the U.S. increased nearly 17-fold from 1991 to 2007. The number of patents granted by the U.S. to China has also increased fairly rapidly, but still is very small in absolute terms (see Figure 9.8).

According to statistics, in 2007, the U.S. granted 6,295 patents to

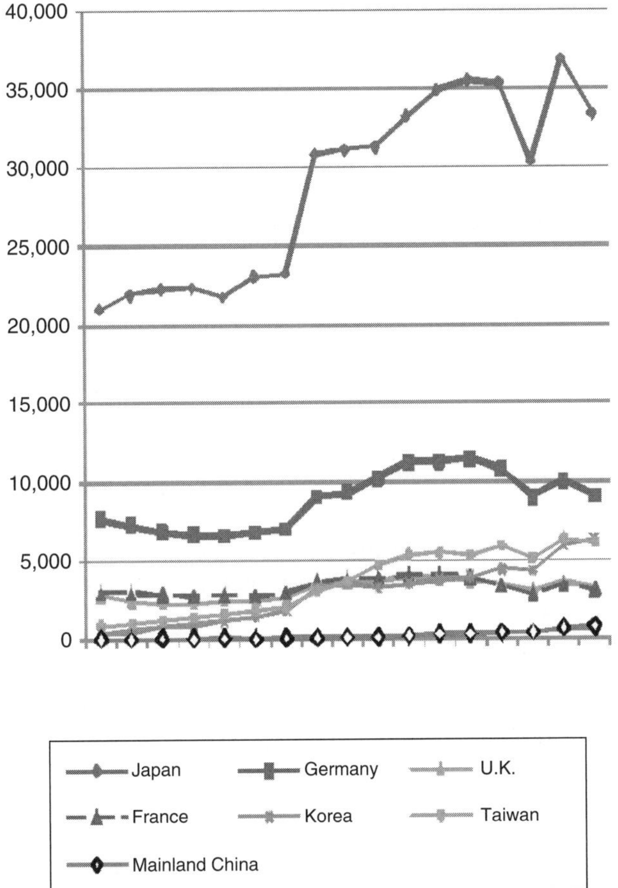

Source: See USPTO, available at www.uspto.gov (last accessed December 29, 2008).

Figure 9.8 Country-specific numbers of patents granted in the U.S. (1991–2007)

Korea, 6,128 patents to Taiwan, and only 772 to Mainland China. The number of patent rights for inventions accounts only for 0.99 percent of the total patent rights for inventions owned by non-American citizens (see Figure 9.9).

As the Chinese economy has become more and more dependent on foreign trade, patents have continually been a cause of trade disputes. In fact, Chinese companies have frequently been accused of being in violation of the USITC's Article 337. From January to June 2003, USITC accepted

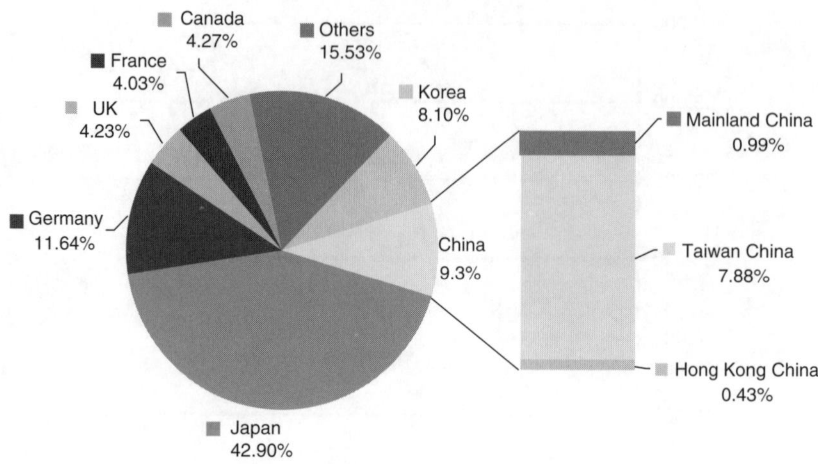

Source: See USPTO, available at www.uspto.gov (last accessed December 29, 2008).

Figure 9.9 Ratio of patent rights granted to China in the U.S. to patent rights granted by non-American Citizens (2007)[30]

11 cases under Article 337, of which 10 cases were related to China, and six cases related to Mainland China. USITC's Article 337 relates to various industries, with enormous profits involved, and the cases were related to products such as tractors, weed cutters, agricultural vehicles, DVDs, wood floors, copier ink, etc.

In conclusion, in the age of economic globalization and in which the Chinese economy is highly dependent on foreign trade, intellectual property has become an important issue restraining the development of the Chinese economy, and it requires the nation's highest concentration and planning from the level of development strategy.

DISCUSSION OF ISSUES RELATING TO THE IMPLEMENTATION OF CHINA'S NATIONAL INTELLECTUAL PROPERTY STRATEGY

Innovation has become a political goal for the pursuit of national economic improvement. The implementation of intellectual property rights strategy has also been raised to the strategic level to promote the rejuvenation of national economic development.

In 2005, China initiated the formulation of a national intellectual property strategy, probing intellectual property policies and measures to promote the country's development. On June 5, 2008, the State Council of the People's Republic of China promulgated the "Outline of the National Intellectual Property Strategy," which provides that:

> By 2020, China will become a country with a comparatively high level in terms of the creation, utilization, protection and administration of intellectual property rights. Given that the legal environment of intellectual property rights is much better, market entities are much better at the creation, utilization, protection and administration of intellectual property rights, the public awareness of intellectual property has increased greatly, the quality and quantity of self-reliant intellectual property are able to effectively support the effort to make China an innovative country, the role of the intellectual property system in promoting economic development, cultural prosperity and social progress in China become very apparent.

Apart from emphasizing the need for perfection of the intellectual property system, the outline particularly provides that:

> We need to guide and support market entities to create and utilize intellectual property through the use of policies related to finance, investment, government procurement, industrial development, energy and environmental protection. Raise the proportion of exportation of goods rich in intellectual property step by step. Promote fundamental changes in the trade growth pattern and optimize trade structure.

The "Outline of the National Intellectual Property Strategy" covers various subjects. However, due to limitations of space here, the author would like to simply discuss the most important issues.

Creation of Intellectual Property Right and "Independent Innovation"

The national intellectual property strategy has as its primary mission to create intellectual property rights and to increase self-reliant intellectual property rights in terms of both quantity and quality. For this reason, since 2008 China started to call for and encourage "independent innovation" in various fields.

The term "independent innovation" is used today in China as a kind of political jargon. "Independent innovation" has three meanings, namely, "original innovation," "integrated innovation," and "re-innovation based on introduction and absorption." "Original innovation" refers to innovation concentrated in the field of basic science and technology and the field of advanced technology, and "integrated innovation" refers to an optimized combination of a large number of new technologies, while "re-innovation based on introduction and absorption" indicates further improvement or upgrade and introduced advanced technologies. "Independent innovation" first calls on self-awareness. The intellectual property rights created can be controlled, without excluding interference with or dependence on the intellectual property rights of others. "Independent innovation" is proposed to encourage learning and renovation based on others' technology, which never excludes introducing or taking note of others' advanced technologies. "Independent innovation" in a sense shares the same meaning as the term "innovation" commonly used internationally. "Independent innovation" is not only reflected in the field of scientific and technical innovation, but also in management innovation. Original equipment manufacturers (OEM) may find that space for scientific and technical innovation is limited, whereas if they can develop a sense of scientific management, they can build their own business brands with the support of borrowed capital and technologies and still create self-reliant intellectual property rights.

"Self-reliant intellectual property rights" is a political term, rather than a new legal term. Many intellectual property rights, in particular, patent rights and copyright, are established based on foundations formed by predecessors. It may be ideal to be entitled to self-reliant technology relating to one product or all key technical links in a certain industry. However, even a large company which has established a monopolistic position may find it difficult to attain exhaustive domination in a certain field. That is why "patent pools" have come into being: a company is given its share say in participating in the formulation of market regulations together with other companies, as long as the company is entitled to certain intellectual property rights regarding certain technical links, which may also be considered as another form of entitlement to intellectual property rights. Technical fields nowadays cannot be fully covered by intellectual property rights entitled to one company. One objective of self-reliant intellectual property rights proposed by China is to guide companies to focus on innovation rather than redundant imitation. Being conscious of innovation may mean that even the slightest improvement may lead to the formation of a new patent right, making the company the owner of a self-reliant intellectual property right. Self-reliant intellectual property rights do not imply complete independence from the technologies or intellectual property rights of others. Self-reliant intellectual property rights should include intellectual property rights purchased from others.

"Independent innovation" is a source of producing intellectual property rights, and the intellectual property system provides an effective guarantee for the realization of independent innovation. One of the objectives of R&D is to create intellectual property rights and to put the rights into practical use. The core of "independent innovation" is intensively demonstrated by self-reliant intellectual property rights. Without "independent innovation," no self-reliant intellectual property right can be created. "Independent innovation" cannot be realized if certain R&D activities in science and technology fail eventually to acquire a self-reliant intellectual property right. Meanwhile, independent innovation also requires intellectual property protection. Lacking effective intellectual property protection will eventually lead to loss of motivation for creation, and therefore, there cannot be independent innovation. In view of this, "independent innovation" and intellectual property rights should foster mutual growth and development, to thereby attain consolidation.

Policy Environment Necessary for the Application of Intellectual Property Rights

To have the ability to create is not equivalent to the entitlement to intellectual property rights. Moreover, the entitlement to self-reliant intellectual property rights is not equivalent to having competitive market power. In order to effectively fulfill the function of intellectual property rights in national development, comprehensive application of the intellectual property system at a high level as well as a well-established systematic guarantee is essential.

There are still some problems in the administration of intellectual property rights in R&D activities conducted in China. The administration of intellectual property rights in R&D activities at universities and institutions is being conducted in a passive, postponing, disorderly, short-term and inefficient manner. "Passive" means that universities, research institutions, companies, and related technologists lack legal consciousness with regard to intellectual property protection during technical innovation. They cannot apply the intellectual property protection to their researches consciously and usually only realize the issue of intellectual property rights after being reminded by administrative staff. "Postponing" means that many research projects do not introduce patent administration into the process from the start, often. not entering into the phase of patent administration until the research results are obtained, which likely causes them to miss the best chance of applying for patent protection. "Disorderly" means that the administrator of a research project neither comprehends nor follows up on the planning in the early stages of the research process, which leaves the intellectual property administration in blind and disordered from the initial stage to the completion of the project. Postponing and disorderly administration is naturally a short-term and inefficient administration, forming a striking contrast with the active, comprehensive, long-term, and highly efficient administration of developed countries.

Even though relevant departments of the state have issued several special regulations in recent years, viewed from the national guidance policy of adopting intellectual property protection in scientific and research activities and the policies and regulations concerning encouraging inventors, oversights and omissions or roughly-shaped policies are also reasons for the disadvantageous intellectual property administration and the failure of organic interaction between technical innovation and intellectual property protection.

The blindness of patent administration can be seen from such issues as the disconnection between intellectual property administration and scientific research in universities and research institutions, the disconnection between patent applications, and the high ratio of abandoned patents after being granted patent rights.

Under a market economy, companies constitute the main focus of innovation. However, many Chinese companies have not yet developed their competence for research, which means that China still has to depend on social power, that is, the creative resources of universities and research institutions, and will have to for quite some time to come. Under these circumstances, the government must provide an effective political environment to promote a favorable situation so that industries, universities and researchers will be jointly initiating R&D projects, creating intellectual property rights and effectively transforming models, thereby promoting the competitiveness of industry.

The national intellectual property strategy of unification of industry, universities, and research institutions has encountered other problems including competition of talent and resources related to innovation against the R&D institutions of foreign companies, as well as the drain of a large number of competitive innovative achievements from universities and research institutions, owing to the purchase of patents by intellectual ventures and intellectual property trading companies and patent renewal during commissioned research. The government should tackle the issue of the drain of innovative resources. In addition, the government should develop a strict contract examination system in universities and research institutions as well as reinforcing the application of patent information, fostering the trading market, and paying more attention to the evaluation of asset of rights.

Balance of Interests in Intellectual Property Protection

Intellectual Property Protection has three aspects, namely, legislation, judiciary and administration.

The third revision to the patent law was made at the end of 2008, but the related legislation will not be put in place for some time. China needs to pay attention to guidance on enforcement and policy.

At present, there are problems in the judiciary regarding intellectual property rights. For example, the standards for the jurisdiction and judgment of defining entitlement of a patent right differ between administrative and judicial trials, which leads to adverse effects including less protection of genuine intellectual property rights holders, costs for protection being too high, and the period in which the state of right is unstable being too long, all of which affect the effect of patent protection.

Further, in the administration, intellectual property protection leans too heavily on "punishment," with little consideration given to positive guidance and support which should be provided to companies. The author proposes that the government should wield its administrative forces over only those cases that may have a serious impact on social and public interests, whereas other cases should be left for the relevant parties to claim protection. The government should work to improve the quality and efficiency of intellectual property protection in serving the companies, establish public resources for intellectual property rights, improve public service propagation, and maintain the justified market competition order by means of public power. Problems may be solved temporarily by simply exerting tighter control, but this is not a fundamental solution. Moreover, it is too costly to continually allow Chinese market subjects to learn lessons from their own experiences. In view of the existing circumstances in China, it is more important to provide an efficient protection mechanism capable of giving correct guidance and focusing mainly on encouragement.

Demand for Talent in the Patent System Capable of Contributing to the Market Economy

Talent in the intellectual property system needs to be diverse and should include high-level professionals with practical experience.

First, there is a need for talent to conduct theoretical research of law and economics as well as perspective research and discussions.

The Chinese intellectual property system, which is still under development, will encounter various new situations and problems; hence, it requires high-level professionals to be engaged in theoretical research and system design by conducting prospective research and discussions on the basic theory of intellectual property rights, the international development trend of intellectual property rights, the national intellectual property system, and measures to promote intellectual property strategy. Since those talents are mainly engaged in design and theoretical research on the intellectual property system, the number therefore may be small but the requirement for comprehensive quality is extremely high. For example, in the field of patents, people are becoming more interested in patent policies and the relation between patent reform and economic development, and this debate is becoming increasingly heated. Patent right is regarded as one of the stimulators to technical improvements which leads to economic growth. Meanwhile, the patent system has been criticized for a long time. Some academics have pointed out that the patent system may be dispensable because market forces alone are capable of driving creativity to an optimal level. The cognition and awareness that the companies hope to gain through timing advantages against their competitors, and the hope that companies that fall behind in technology will be beaten by their competitors, may have provided enough encouragement for promoting invention. In this case, there is no need for more or further stimulation.

Some academics have pointed out that the patent system encourages industrial monopoly, hinders market accession, and often induces speculators, who would like to acquire and control patents rather than put them into social production. In judging whether such opinions are in sharp conflict with each other, it should be noted that we lack strict academic analysis gained through research on the effect of the patent system on the economy. The lack of academic analysis leads to a lack of scientific assessment on the relation between economic development and the patent system in China, failure to make precise adjustments to the patent system from the economic and political point of view, and an incapacity to provide persuasive arguments for the proponents and opponents of the patent system.

Second, the patent system requires senior company staff to use their talent on business administration and marketing decisions.

When senior staff in companies are engaged in the administration of intellectual property rights, they must continuously undertake the crucial responsibilities of, for example, judging the situation and determining strategies. In this respect, their consciousness and level of knowledge of intellectual property rights will directly affect the consciousness and level of knowledge of intellectual property rights of the region. However, many companies in China are at an early stage of development, and lack strategic consciousness with regard to participating in market competition with the use of the intellectual property system. At present, some large-scale high-tech companies have employed intellectual-property-related mechanisms and personnel, but many small and medium sized companies still remain on the back foot in market competition in terms of intellectual property rights.

Third, it is necessary to have enough legal practitioners with knowledge of science and technology in corporate management.

Legal practitioners in the field of intellectual property rights need to be proficient in the knowledge of law, technical administration, and corporate management. There is enormous demand for lawyers, patent attorneys, technical brokers and copyright and trademark agents, who are skilled in intellectual property-related lawsuits and non-litigation affairs.

Fourth, talented people capable of taking part in affairs related to international intellectual property based in foreign languages are needed.

When an intellectual property system conforming to international standards was established, China failed to cultivate and secure the talent necessary for effective implementation of the system. As a result, after joining the WTO, China had to face the problem of a shortage of high-level professionals in the field of intellectual property, construction of public policies, industrial development strategies, and litigation affairs. At the same time, the conflict between developed countries and developing countries in intellectual property protection and economic development is becoming more and more severe; lagging developing countries should seize as many opportunities as possible to take part in international activities. Therefore, developing countries have to plan well to apply for managerial posts in international organizations, and send professionals that have an excellent understanding of foreign languages and a knowledge of domestic and international intellectual property right regulations. This is not only an effective way of cultivating high-level talent for China but also an effective way of participating in international competition to enhance China's influence internationally.

The ancient conception that "success lies not in how fast you do, but in how long you can continue" and that "it takes ten years to grow a tree, but a hundred to rear people" is no longer applicable to the enormous pressures and challenges faced by today's Chinese intellectual property rights. All talent, no matter how much is needed or of what type, is required to participate efficiently in market competition at a high level.

The "Outline of the National Intellectual Property Strategy" reflects the Chinese government's knowledge of the relationship between the intellectual property system and current Chinese economic development. It can be seen that effective implementation of the Outline is a tough task, which requires the practical and feasible deployment of creation, application, protection, and the administration of intellectual property from the national perspective.

THE PATENT GAME IN TECHNICAL STANDARDS: TREND OF OPEN LICENSE IN INTELLECTUAL PROPERTY

When considering the implementation of the national intellectual property strategy, one of the unavoidable problems is the intellectual issues in technical standards, and in particular, the patent policy. China has already witnessed fierce market competition and administration of patent pool problems in the formulation of technical standards, such as the AVS standard (infinite bandwidth net access standard), WAPI standard (digital audio frequency code editing and encryption standard), TD-SCDMA standard (3G mobile phone standard in China), CMMB standard (mobile multimedia broadcasting technology standard in China), and CBSD standard (Blue Light standard in China). Large companies throughout the world with patent consciousness have shown "patentization of technology, standardization of patents, and internationalization of standards." Technical standards have become a competitive means and platform for patentees to pursue maximization of benefits.

There is no way to avoid a large number of patented technologies from being introduced to technical standards. The immediate issue is what kind of intellectual property licensing policy can guarantee the public coordinating function of technical standards. Further, whether or not a standard can be implemented widely and whether or not a fair market competition environment can be sustained after its implementation depends on who is in control of the intellectual property policies with respect to technical standards. With the increasing strengthening of intellectual property protection, technical standards organizations can no longer control the formulation of the standards and the license policy. As a result, intellectual property rights holders hold dominant positions both in the formulation of standards in patent pools and in international standards, causing the technical standards to deviate from the original features oriented toward coordination and public interests, as well as making the technical standard platform a stage, allowing the intellectual property right owners to monopolize the market. In particular, in the Information and Communications Technology (ICT) industry where technical R&D is active, many companies have their own advantages in the patent field and are therefore restrained from participating in standardization activities by taking advantage of their strong position in the market. Patentees have also started to realize there is a need to consider the adoption of a patent license system which will be beneficial for fair competition and healthy development.

Once a technical standard is restrained by intellectual property, there is no way to give consideration to common applicability, coordination, and optimization of the technical standard. In other words, once a technical standard containing intellectual property is promoted and implemented, users of the standard are not only obliged to pay a large sum of patent royalties but also have to face significant restrictions in the application of successive innovation and development of compatible products thereof. A set of technical standards containing patents and copyrights exposes all of the related competitors under the control of the right holder. In addition, a technology standard of basic agreements in the Internet and universal software has made it easier for the intellectual property rights holder to have a monopolistic market position, which not only increases the final users' cost, but also harms healthy competition.

Analysis of Current Patent Policies of Standard-setting Organizations

Until now, most intellectual property policies of the international standardization organizations have been established based on the principle of Reasonable and Non-Discriminatory (RAND) license, that is, based on the principle of fairness and nondiscrimination. However, the RAND principle has an insuperable defect. What is reasonable fairness? No standardization organization has offered an interpretation. What kind of responsibility should be borne by a member who violates the RAND principle? No clear regulations have been set regarding the conditions with respect to patent license, even by such large standardization organizations as ITU, ISO/IEC, IEEE, ETSI, and ANSI. For this reason, a patentee may agree to comply with the RAND principle when entering a standardization organization, and render the principle of RAND meaningless by making use of various restrictive clauses when implementing the technical standard. Such an act will prevent the formulators of the standard from making a correct assessment of the restriction of innovation and competition in the course of setting standards. It can be said that the RAND principle is a merely principled regulation with highly conceptualized and abstracted features and therefore is now facing problems in the process of implementation.

Other than the above, the standardization organizations have announced that they neither interfere with license negotiations nor provide specific license information, and thus the implementers of standards can learn of specific license conditions only through the patentee in the course of selecting the standards, without any reference to the anticipated gross cost of implementing the standards, the slowness in the implementation of standards and the potential risk of "patent war" thus caused. Complete control of license policies by intellectual property rights holders also enables the rights holders to formulate the clauses in license agreements more freely via the favorable standard platform, which further escalates technology and market monopolies and worsens the competition environment. In particular, in the field of the ICT industry, where technical R&D is active, many companies have their own advantages in the field of intellectual property and therefore are restrained in participating in standardization activities by taking advantage of their position in the market. Intellectual property rights holders have also started to realize the need to consider the adoption of an intellectual property license system which will be beneficial for fair competition and healthy development. Many small and medium sized companies are even more anxious to improve the present situation.

In recent years, some companies entitled to intellectual property rights have started to advocate the open licensing of intellectual property rights. The initiation of the "open source movement," the proposal of "open patents" and the establishment of "open standards" all aim at benefiting successive innovation and fair competition, and some large companies have started to promote reformation on intellectual property policies in technical standards. The principle of "fairness and nondiscrimination in ex ante disclosure" (ex ante RAND) proposed by the U.S. company SUN Microsystems, is among the trials. This principle requires companies to disclose, before establishing a technical standard, not only information related to the patent rights and the patent applications but also the substantive requirements for the license, which specifically demonstrates a commitment to the highest license price or the provision of standard license texts and the ex ante commitment on the restricted clauses in the license. As compared with the traditional RAND principle, the merits of the principle of ex ante disclosure lie in the guarantee that a transparent technology competition market can be established before the standard is established, the guarantee that the standardization organization is able to make evaluation on the technical solutions in terms of both technology and cost of use, the guarantee that the user of the standard is able to estimate the anticipated cost for using the standard before the standard is actually implemented, so that resistance against the implementation of the standard and litigations and disputes likely to be caused can be reduced, and a fairly reasonable cost for the user of the standard can be achieved. However, such a new concept of standards can only be applied to those technical standards which contain a smaller number of patents with relatively explicit entitlements. Whether it can be promoted and applied is still under debate. But the principle of ex ante disclosure allows the implementers of the standards to predict the risks and cost of patent application, which conforms to the principle of fair competition.

The author proposes the principle of open licensing of intellectual property rights (hereinafter "open licensing") based on the current open standard, aiming at exploring a certain kind of intellectual property license policy which is operable and predictable for the cost of implementing the standard. The adoption of an open licensing model in formulating standards requires full disclosure of information related to technology and intellectual property. In particular, intellectual property rights holders must avoid false disclosure or bypass disclosure by following the *bona fide* principle. Further, the license policy should enable the implementer to predict the cost of royalties of the intellectual property right in implementing the technical standard. Public interest should also be taken into account after the implementation of the technical standard. Once a patent infringement dispute arises, the judicial authority must give due consideration to issuing an injunction, to avoid patent holdup and royalty stacking, both of which may result in the suspension of the implementation of the standard. The court should also provide reasonable compensation for the patentee based on the license policy announced in advance in the technical standard, in light of the application situation of the compulsory license.

Intellectual Property Open License (IP Open License) in Technical Standards

Open licensing means that intellectual property policies in technical standard activities should comply with the following principles: (1) opening of technical information involved in the technical standard, (2) opening of intellectual property information involved in the technical standard, (3) opening of intellectual property license policies involved in the technical standard, and (4) the predictability of the cost for the use of intellectual property involved in the technical standard.

Above all, the predictability of the cost for the use of intellectual property involved in the technical standard is the core of the principle of open licensing in technical standards, while the opening of technical information and intellectual property information involved in the technical standard serves as the precondition and guarantee respectively.

The principle of IP open licensing is specifically interpreted as follows.

Sufficient disclosure of technical information relating to technology standard

First, technical information in the ICT technical standard should be open, and should not be entitled to intellectual property protection as a trade secret. The same applies to a *de facto* standard. The European Union held in the Microsoft antimonopoly case that as the owner of a *de facto* standard, Microsoft was obliged to disclose inter-operational information necessary for competition. If the technical information of the interface in the operating system of a personal computer was not open, others would be excluded from the market due to the lack of interoperability with Microsoft's products. The European Commission denied Microsoft's allegations that the inter-operational information necessary for competition should be entitled to protection as a trade secret, despite the information meeting the constitutive requirements for trade secrets. Further, where the interface technology and compatible technology relating to a technical standard is a computer program, it should not be entitled to copyright protection either. Constraints imposed on external elements, such as hardware environments, compatibility conditions, efficiency and public domain, lead to a single expression, and therefore they should not be entitled to copyright protection either. As for technical standards of business alliances, the detailed technical information related to the technical standard achieved among companies should also be open. If technical information in a technical standard is not disclosed, a third-party company cannot fairly compete with members in the business alliance by using the technical standard. The business alliance may be suspicious of formulating a technical standard and conspire to exclude competition. At this point, if the technical information in the technical standard is protected as a trade secret by law, what is actually protected by the law is the horizontal agreement concluded among companies for excluding competition.

Next, from the point when the technical standard enters into force, detailed technical information related to the technical standard should be available. During the existence of the *de facto* standard, the owner of the *de facto* standard is obliged to constantly make available technical standard information related to competition. This means that the owner of the *de facto* standard should disclose the technical standard information necessary for competition completely and precisely to all interested parties within a reasonable time before officially launching its product or service when upgrading the technical standard. At the same time, the rights holder should not abuse the dominant market power gained via the *de facto* standard or exclude competition by false disclosure. For example, where a competitor has introduced a new product with an excellent track record, the owner of the *de facto* standard may issue a false announcement in advance to the effect that the owner is also going to provide a new product with the same or similar function and make the consumers wait. In this case, the powerful network effect in the software industry may force the consumers to become familiar with the owner of the *de facto* standard. The so-called "new product" may just be a superficial change to the original technology, but it is quite probable that the competitor will then be excluded from the market.

As for the technical standard of business alliances, technical information related to the completed technical standard should be made open in a timely manner, at least within a reasonable time after the completion of the formulation of the technical standard. In the course of establishing a technical standard, the business alliance may also be justified in not disclosing the nature of the technical information in the standard under formulation. The charter of the business alliance may burden its members with such an obligation. That is because the business alliance employs a membership system, and naturally, no one becomes eligible for technical information related to the established standard in the alliance without becoming a member of the alliance. As a matter of fact, standardization activities means obtaining information related to the development status of the technologies in the related industry, which serves as an important source of information for companies to conduct R&D on competitive technologies. Least of all, if a standard under establishment is opened to the public at an early stage, there is a fear that an outsider of the business alliance may apply for a patent deliberately to ambush the technical standard. Yet, once the technical standard is established, it should be opened in a timely manner. If information related to a completed technical standard can remain unopened until its life cycle has almost come to an end, this would actually be equivalent to admitting the protection of a technical standard as a trade secret, which is probably in violation of antimonopoly law.

The problem concerning the disclosure of technical information in technical standards may generally not occur in a *de jure* standard organization, owing to their close and strict procedure in formulating standards as well as their concerns about the interests of all social parties.

Adequate Opening of Intellectual Property Information Related to Technical Standards

First, intellectual property information related to technical standards should not be entitled to intellectual property protection as a trade secret. The owners of a *de facto* standard should continually open intellectual property information related to competition. They should comply with the principle of RAND. A license agreement that does not provide detailed intellectual property information cannot be regarded as a "reasonable" license agreement. Such an agreement is nothing but a mere tool used by the owner of the *de facto* standard to seek a monopoly price and strategic value.

The basic legal issue for *de jure* standards and the standards of business alliances is whether the regulation of disclosure in the intellectual property policy of the standardization organization is legally binding. There is no doubt that the regulation of disclosure in the intellectual property policy of a standardization organization is legally binding: it requires the members not to claim the entitlement of the intellectual property information related to the standard as a trade secret and thereby cannot seek correspondent legal protection, which should be regarded as a passive legal obligation.

Although intellectual property regulations in standardization organizations are usually rather loose (just requesting the members to fulfill their *bona fide* obligation and to promptly disclose intellectual property information that may be related to the standard) it does not mean that the regulations are not legally binding. Once someone has become a member of the standardization organization, the member should be deemed as accepting the aforesaid intellectual property policies. In this case, if any standard being established or which has been established involves certain intellectual property information about the member's company, the member cannot claim that the information should be entitled to protection as a trade secret. In fact, the disclosure rules in the intellectual property policy of a standardization organization virtually indicate that the act of concealing the entitlement of intellectual property information involved in the technical standard will be regarded as an act of unfair competition.

Next, the intellectual property information disclosed to members of a Standard Setting Organization (SSO) should also be open to the public. An intellectual property policy is not merely a contract among the members or a contract between the members and the standardization organization, but also has an external effect. The implementer of the standard has basic faith in the intellectual property policy of the standardization organization. At the same time, the standardization organization should open the technical information related to the technical standard to the public. If the intellectual property information cannot be opened by the standardization organization, a third party cannot have the same chance of negotiation related to intellectual property licensing as the members of the standardization organization may have. As long as a certain technology property right involved in a certain standard does not constitute a trade secret, the standardization organization cannot claim the intellectual property information which has been disclosed as a trade secret. If a standardization organization knows the members' intellectual property rights have been involved in a technical standard but fails to open those intellectual property rights to the public according to its intellectual property policy, the standardization organization by itself is creating an unfair competitive environment.

Further, the disclosure rules in the intellectual property policy serve as grounds for suing violators for liabilities. Both in Rambus and Broadcom vs. Qualcomm, the court ruled that it was believed that a member of a standardization organization had been burdened with the obligation of disclosure by the intellectual property policy and the member knew that the other members had acted similarly; even the broad regulation in the intellectual property policy is legally binding.

Lastly, the obligation of opening the intellectual property information in the technical standard has an external effect. And legal remedies should also have an external effect. In Broadcom vs. Qualcomm, the court, based on the principle of analogy that the unjustified act conducted by the patentee during patent examination by USPTO should be applied to legal remedies, determined that the patent concealed and remained undisclosed by Qualcomm was not legally enforceable. What was announced in the ruling was that the concealed patent was legally enforceable to all rather than merely to Broadcom which had filed the lawsuit. This means that the court remedied not only Broadcom but also all the companies related to the standard. The court maintains and protects the overall external effects of the intellectual property policies, rather than a private one-to-one relationship; more precisely, the court was enforcing the competition policies represented by intellectual property policies.

Ex Ante Opening of Intellectual Property Licensing Policies in Technical Standards

Intellectual property policies involved with ICT technical standards should be open. In particular, the RAND principle should have objective criteria and the RAND principle in intellectual property policy of a standardization organization should directly serve as legal grounds for filing a lawsuit. If there are no objective criteria for the RAND principle, thus allowing a patentee to define the terms for license, the objectives of intellectual property laws and competition laws, which are represented by the RAND principle, cannot be attained.

In the Microsoft case, several important "objective" criteria were established by the E.U. First, a reasonable price should reflect the market value of the technology, rather than a "strategic value." For a *de facto* standard, a strategic value corresponds to a monopolistic price formed by a monopolistic position, while for a *de jure* standard, a strategic value refers to the value added to the technology after the wide adoption of the standard. If a patentee deliberately concealed a certain technology such as in *Rambus* or *Qualcomm*, the strategic value corresponds to the speculative value acquired by their standard strategy. A reasonable license term respects intellectual property, and demonstrates that the objective of the intellectual property system is the promotion of the increase of the welfare in the whole of society by means of dynamic competition, rather than the maximization of personal profits. Intellectual property is a limited property right, rather than an absolute monopolistic right. Second, if the level of royalty is barely symbolic, it can be directly deduced that such a royalty is reasonable. Third, if the level of royalty is not symbolic, it should be determined in accordance with objective criteria such as the degree of technical innovation, the comparison between the license fee to be collected and the comparable technical license fee in the market.

On the other hand, the commitment of a member of a standardization organization to the RAND principle may serve as legal grounds for filing a lawsuit. In *Qualcomm*, the Third Circuit of the United States Court of Appeals ruled that in a standard-setting environment based on consensus, if a patentee falsely committed to license an essential patent which may be involved in the standard to be licensed based on RAND principle, and the standardization organization adopted such technology in the standard based on the trust of that commitment, the patentee's act in violation of its commitment afterwards is regarded as an accusable anticompetitive act. It can be inferred that the ruling of the court in this case was not a remedy only for Broadcom but also a remedy for the whole of society, just as the remedies for violation of disclosure rules in intellectual property policy mentioned above.

Predictability of Cost for the Use of Intellectual Property Rights in Technical Standards

The situation where a technical standard contains a large number of patents is becoming increasingly common, particularly in the ICT industry. It is no longer possible to predict the cost of implementing one technical standard, which brings enormous legal risks to the user of the standard. Since the rights holder is at the same time the user of a standard, even if a favorable cross-license policy is provided, the patentee has to pay a large amount in the preliminary negotiation process. Such a problem has already been shown in the cases of the DVD standard and the 3GPP standard.

Standard-setting organizations and some companies are making every effort to solve the problem, and have proposed many solutions. For example, the license policy for the 3GPP standard at an early stage referred to the license royalty rate capped at 5 percent, the VITA standard proposed a request for a cap price per patent, the MPEG-2 standard established a standard of $2.50 for royalty fees, the AVS had a targeted royalty of 1 RMB, and the CMMB standard proposed to provide a license free of royalty for two years before charging a small fee. Those solutions were all initiated from the predictability of the royalties for the use of a technology standard. The open-license model proposed by the author does not require a standard-setting organization to adopt a uniformed license royalty rate, but the license conditions should be specifically defined based on such elements as the complexity of various technical fields and standards, as well as the industrial environment. Those license conditions should be taken into consideration during the establishment of a standard, rather than being published in the implementation phase.

Open licensing does not deny the legitimate interests of the intellectual property rights holder. It acknowledges that the right of the intellectual property rights holder should be respected even if the intellectual property is necessary for implementing the technical standard. However, since the intellectual property is implemented based on a common platform provided by the technical standard, and the act of licensing is involved with market competition and public interest, the licensing agreement concluded between the licenser and the implementer of the standard therefore has a social public nature, and thus belongs to an "open right." "Open" here refers to the opening of elements related to market competition under predictable "reasonable" license conditions to unspecified market entities (legal entities) in society.

The more open the license conditions of intellectual property rights in technical standards become, the better it can promote the effective implementation of the technical standard, the accession, penetration and successive innovative activities, the healthy development of industrial ecology, and an increase in social welfare. In other words, the "open license" emphasizes that the licensing act of the rights owner should comply with the requirements with respect to public policy of the intellectual property law and competition law. The "open license" is a "free license with a limitation."

The establishment of an intellectual property license policy whose cost for implementing the technical standard is predictable is key to open licensing.

System Guarantee for Realizing Open Licensing in Technical Standards

The basis for realizing open licensing requires not only an open, transparent, and reasonable license policy established beforehand, but also an ex post judicial guarantee.

Public interests and the application of injunction in implementation of technical standards

The implementation of a technical standard involves innovation and the construction of a fair competition environment, as well as significant public interest. Accordingly, the court should not determine the cessation of infringement on the condition that the standard has already been widely implemented. The rule of injunction came into force in the early stages of patent protection, when the form of objects protected by patent protection was simple, and generally there were only a few cases where one product contained several supplementary patents.[31] However, in ICT technology standards nowadays, technical standard texts defining one system or one facility of the user may contain dozens or even hundreds of intercommunicative or interdependent technical solutions, which are separately entitled to different rights owners under different patents. Those technologies jointly form a chain, and digital communications can perform transmission and processing among the facilities only through the chain. If an injunction is issued by the court, requiring a standard-setting organization to bypass one of those patents, it also requires a critical revision with respect to other solutions related to the patented technical solutions, or even ends with abandonment in some cases. The chain effect thus caused may make the social costs of revising the overall technical solution extremely high and in many cases, infeasible. The so-called "public interests" have a definite legal meaning. Taking the implementation of ICT technical standards as an example, the public interests therein are more obvious compared to traditional industries, because ICT technical standards involve a large number of social groups, as well as unobstructed intercommunicative and compatible information exchanges. The relation between patents in ICT technical standards are complicated and in addition, the number of patents and right owners involved is large, which shows that the members of the industry participating in establishing the technical standard poured tremendous irreversible resources into the establishment. If an injunction is issued, the entire industry will inevitably suffer considerable losses due to the setback in implementation of the technology standard, which will affect many related industries and influence social public welfare.

Even if the court does not issue an injunction, it does not mean that a patentee cannot obtain appropriate compensation. Overseas scholars have already done a great deal of theoretical research on the issue of the rights owner being able to obtain appropriate compensation in the case of not applying the property rule under a patent holdup.[32] The purpose of providing sufficient remuneration for a patentee is to maintain a legitimate right that should be obtained based on innovation. As long as the interests of the rights owner have been provided with sufficient economic compensation in the course of implementing a technical standard, and issuing an injunction would damage public interests, the court should refrain from issuing an injunction, which would give a better result in terms of the balance of interests. The ultimate objective of both technical standards and patent law is to create a system which allows a patentee to receive payment corresponding to their actual contribution. In the case of a patent holdup, the participants in the entire industry have already poured irreversible investment into the early stages of establishing the technical standard, which allows the patentees to hold a trump card, and hence the patentee clearly has an extremely strong bargaining position. In this case, the amount of repayment given to the patentees should be estimated through the application of the obligation principle, namely, presuming the rights owner has licensed his/her patent in the same manner as other owners of the same type of right and the amount of repayment is the royalties or the repayment gained via cross license.

Limitative application of compulsory license and injunction

In cases involving significant public interests, if the court does not issue an injunction in the case of a holdup, and rules that the patentee may gain the royalties in the RAND manner, it produces a legal effect similar to that of the compulsory license.

In China, only the Patent Administration Department under the State Council has the power to determine compulsory licenses. Compared with the case studied in this chapter where an injunction is not issued, both cases involve public interest in terms of substantive requirements, but are completely different in terms of procedures. The laws and regulations including the Chinese patent law (2009), the implementing regulations of the patent law, the measures of compulsory licensing for patent implementation, and the measures of compulsory licensing for patent implementation regarding public health-related issues form a compulsory license system for patent implementation. Chinese patent law devotes one chapter to defining the patent compulsory licensing system.[33] The initiation and implementation of the compulsory licensing system is an administrative procedure in China. However, the aforesaid issue of non-issuance of an injunction is a rule made by a judge based on a judgment of the remedies in patent infringement litigation, which is demonstrated in the case law of other countries.

Laches in implementing standards and application of injunction

Laches is one of the grounds for defense against intellectual property infringement in equity law in the United States. The constitution of laches includes two basic requirements: (1) the rights owner knows or should know his right is being infringed but unreasonably delays the litigation, and (2) the delay causes damages to the infringer. Generally speaking, an infringer with subjective intent is not entitled to the defense of laches. Unlike the time limit for litigation, in the case of laches, such issues as "what is the unreasonable delay," "for how long does a lawsuit have to have not been filed to constitute laches" and "the damage to the infringers is of what kind" should be defined on a case-by-case basis. Further, even if constituting laches, the legal effect varies among the different types of intellectual property rights. In general, if laches is affirmed, the patentee is not entitled to claim for compensation for the damages caused before the litigation, but can still claim for compensation for damages after the litigation and request an injunction. However, in the case of copyright infringement, laches may lead to the court's refusal to issue an injunction on the infringer accused of infringement, which may be transferred to compensation to the rights owner.

In patent infringement litigations in the United States involving laches, the reasonable grounds for a delay in filing litigation generally include: (1) the patentee has already filed litigation against another infringer based on the same patent; and (2) the litigation is delayed owing to license negotiations held between the patentee and the infringer. The damages caused by the delay to the infringer generally include economic damage and damage to the ability to provide evidence, for instance (1) the delay of the patentee significantly affected the possibility that the infringer can defend himself to win the case, such as the loss of an important witnesses, or the loss of important documents; and (2) the infringer had made further investment and expanded the scale of production and management. If the litigation is filed after more than six years (a statutory time limit for claiming for compensation defined by Title 35 of the United States Code), the court will infer that the delay caused damage to the infringer.

As can be seen under the United States Code, in the implementation of ICT technical standards, in most cases, the rights owner can argue based on the defense of laches. Furthermore, even constituting laches, the rights owner is not deprived of the right to obtain the remedy of injunction. From a certain aspect, this means that the rule for the application of remedy of injunction has an independent legal standard, namely the aforesaid four-factor test.

Compared with the United States Code, there is no such "laches" issue in the exercise of rights in China. In order to prevent patentees from sitting on the right, the Supreme People's Court issued "Several Provisions of the Supreme People's Court on Issue Related to Application of Law to Adjudication of Patent Disputes" (entered into force as of July 1, 2001), which provides that:

> the time limitations for patent infringement litigation is two years from the day the patentee or the party of interest knows or should know the infringing act. In a case where the patentee filed litigation after two years, as long as the infringing act still continues at the filing of litigation and the term of the patent has not expired, the People's Court shall rule cessation of infringement for the defendant, and the amount of damages caused by the infringement shall be calculated retroactively through two years from the day the patentee filed litigation with the People's Court.

Even where the patentee failed to file litigation and claim his right in a timely manner, the patentee is still eligible for the remedy of injunction even though the right to recover damages may be limited.

Autonomous Promotion of Rights Owners

Active actions of intellectual property rights holders also serve as important driving forces in promoting open licensing of intellectual property rights. For example, IBM issued the "Interoperability Specifications Pledge,"[34] in which IBM unilaterally committed that they would not claim the essential patent rights in the standards covered by the pledge, and would only reserve a passive right of defense, namely, if anyone alone or in coordination with others claimed an essential patent in the standards covered by the pledge, the aforesaid pledge would be terminated.

Business alliances can also take similar actions. For example, the "Open Invention Network" initiated by IBM, NEC, Novell, Philips, Red Hat, and Sony, licenses the Linux they own on a royalty-free basis on condition that the licensee agrees not to claim its patents against Linux.

The open intellectual property policy is based on openness and transparency in the process of establishing a standard, a clear and precise distribution of intellectual property rights, fair and reasonable license fees for intellectual property rights, and predictability of cost for use of a standard. The open intellectual property policy is further embodied in that an increasing number of software standards are established based on open-source software. Such an open policy is indeed an open policy for intellectual property rights, that is, the licensing of an intellectual property and the payment of fees are not directly demonstrated in the use of technical standards and more companies will take part in establishing and updating the technical standard. The implementation of open technical standards will bring valuable development opportunities to many small and medium sized companies.

Sharing of knowledge has been the basis for the development of human beings throughout history, and the development of the Internet is also inseparable from the spirit of sharing. Imagine a situation in which all of the existing basic Internet protocols were based on patents and copyrights and could not be used without authorization, or could only be available at a high cost; we would never enjoy the civilization and progress brought to us by today's information society.

CONCLUSION: THE PERCEPTIBLE COMES FROM THE INVISIBLE

The above phrase is from "Ode to the Wind" written by Song Yu, a Chinese poet in the State of Chu of the late Warring States Period. Song Yu is said to have been a student of Qu Yuan, and his name is coupled with Qu Yuan as "Qu-Song" in the history of Chinese literature. The direct implication of the phrase is that the wind was generated from the ground and came from far away. Its meaning is somewhat similar to the theory of "the butterfly effect" in chaos theory in the West. Here, a theory in the modern West and the philosophy of an ancient Chinese poet have the same meaning, regardless of the difference in approach. The above phrase reminds the author of the fact that the ancient Chinese civilization contributed to the development of all modern science and culture, but unfortunately, today's China is often labeled as a "culture of theft." However, in view of the idea described above, people around the world may all be more or less involved in "theft." The author concludes this chapter with this phrase which may be interpreted in many ways, leaving his readers to draw their own conclusions.

This is the last chapter of this book. As an author from a country with a late-developing patent system, if I wrote even a little less than the authors from countries with developed patent systems have, I would not feel that I have said enough.

I have been engaged in patent affairs for 23 years since 1986 and 23 years ago, I took part in a team of patent attorneys, starting as a patent practitioner engaged in the patents business. In 1991, I joined an educational and research institution of intellectual property rights. Today, I have realized that the patent system is not as pure and sacred as it was when I first set out. The patent system aims to serve the market economy, whose essential function is to promote technical monopoly. In harsh market competition, what can be seen is a survival market that follows "the law of the jungle," after removing the civilized veil of a patent system. Accordingly, law and academic research should be conducted on the basis of a market economy, as well as research on patent strategies under a market economy environment. That may be considered common sense by the people of developed countries that have already accepted such an idea as a matter of common knowledge. However, in China, it will still take some time to enable the market to understand the essential function of the patent system and to make the best use of the patent system so that it can become a pillar of national economic development. Yet, by using the implied meaning of the phrase of Song Yu, current innovative efforts made by Chinese companies may eventually result in a storm of patents, and the developing objectives of rejuvenation of patent and construction of an innovation-oriented nation may well be realized.

Of course, the author also agrees that knowledge and information should be commonly shared without charge for the sake of all humanity, and intellectual property protection should be limited rather than being used as a tool to frantically pursue profit as it is now. It is merely an intermediate goal to protect patentees' interests, but the ultimate goal of the intellectual patent system is to promote knowledge innovation and expansion amongst all humanity.

I am looking forward to future reformation of the patent system, and also will devote every effort to that goal.

NOTES

1. See Chengsi Zheng, "Intellectual Property Law," *Law Press China*, July 1997, 1st ed., p. 231.
2. Report of the U.K. Intellectual Property Office: "Five hundred years of patents: Tudors and Stuarts," available at http://www.patent.gov.uk/patent/whatis/fivehundred/index.htm: 2008-8 (last accessed December 29, 2008).
3. XuePeng Tang, "False Cause and Effect and True Chance in the Patent Law," 21st Century Business Herald, November 7, 2005, available at http://biz.163.com/05/1107/10/21USG6P500021E8E.html (last accessed December 29, 2008).
4. E. Penrose, *The Economics of the International Patent System*, Baltimore, MD: John Hopkins Press, 1951, pp. 113–115.
5. F. Machlup, "An Economic Review of the Patent System," study commission by the Subcommittee on Patents, Trademarks, and Copyrights of the Committee on the Judiciary, US Senate, 85th Congress, second session, Washington, D.C.: US Government Printing Office, 1958, p. 80.
6. L. Thurow, "Needed: A New System of Intellectual Property Rights," *Harvard Business Review*, Sept–Oct 1997, p. 103.
7. L. Lessig, "The Problem with Patents," *Industry Standard*, April 23, 1999.
8. J. Sachs, "The Global Innovation Divide," in A. Jaffe, J. Lerner and S. Stern (eds), *Innovation Policy and the Economy: Volume 3*, MIT Press, Cambridge MA, 2002.
9. CRS Report for Congress, "Patent Reform: Innovation Issues," available at http://www.opencrs.com/rpts/RL32996_20050715.pdf#search=%22CRS%20Report%20for%20Congress%20Patent%20Reform%3A%20Innovation%20Issues%22 (last accessed December 29, 2008).
10. "Patents and Innovation: Trends and Policy Challenges," OECD, 2004, available at www.oecd.org (last accessed December 29, 2008).
11. See, "Open Collaboration Is Medicine for Our Ailing Patent System," provided by the Intellectual Property Department of IBM China Company Limited, December 2006.

12. International symposium on technical innovation jointly held by the Ministry of Science and Technology of the People's Republic of China and the United Nations University, September 5, 2000, Beijing, available at http://www.gmw.com.cn/0_gm/2000/09/20000908/GB/09%5E18537%5E0%5EGMA3-016.htm (last accessed December 29, 2008).
13. N. Girvan, "TNCs and the Transfer of Technology," *CTC Reporter*, Vol. 19, p. 18 (1985).
14. Survey conducted by Robert Sherwood. See Evelyn Su, "The Winners and the Losers: TRIPS and its effects on developing countries," *Houston Journal of International Law*, Vol. 23 (2000).
15. ZhiJun Feng (lead editor), *Guidelines of Research on National Innovation System*, Jinan: Shandong Education Press, 2000, p. 53.
16. R. Narula and B.M. Sadowski: "Technological catch-up and strategic technology partnering in developing countries," *International Journal of Technology Management*, Vol. 23, Issue 6, pp. 599–617 (2002).
17. P. Ganguli, *Intellectual Property Rights: Discharge of Energy of Intellectual Economy*, translated by JianHua Song et al., Intellectual Property Press, 2004, p. 5.
18. See Manny W. Schecter, "Open Collaboration Is Medicine for Our Ailing Patent System," Intellectual Property Department of IBM China Company Limited, December 2006.
19. *Ibid.*
20. Elaine Chow, "Japan Launches Antitrust Investigation into Qualcomm," Competition Law 360 New York, available at http://www.law360.com/texas/articles/15807/qualcomm-faces-deeper-antitrust-probe (last accessed December 29, 2008).
21. *Ibid.*
22. *Ibid.*
23. J.C. Ginarte and W.G. Park, "Determinants of Patent Rights: A Cross-National Study," May 1997, available at http://www.sciencedirect.com/science/article/B6V77-3SX216B-2/2/b9420f04f58cd371c0324765bc85639e (last accessed December 29, 2008).
24. W.G. Park and J.C. Ginarte, "Intellectual Property Rights and Economic Growth," *Contemporary Economic Policy*, Vol. 15, Issue 3, pp. 51–61 (1997).
25. Keith E. Maskus, "Intellectual Property Rights and Economic Development," *Western Reserve Journal of International Law*, Vol. 32, p. 478 (2000).
26. Rod Falvey, Neil Foster and David Greenaway, "Intellectual Property Rights and Economic Growth", *Wiley Blackwell*, Vol. 10, Issue 4, pp. 700–719 (2004), available at http://www.nottingham.ac.uk/economics/leverhulme/research_papers/0412.pdf (last accessed December 29, 2008).
27. *Ibid.*
28. World Bank, List of Economies (July 2008) available at worldbank.org/DATASTATISTICS/Resources/CLASS.XLS (last accessed July 27, 2008).
29. WIPO Statistics, PCT Statistical Indicators Report, Annual Statistics, available at http://www.wipo.int/pct (last accessed December 29, 2008).
30. See the statistical data regarding patents granted in 2007 which are sorted by state and country of origin, United States Patent and Trademark Office (USPTO), available at http://www.uspto.gov/go/taf/cst_utl.htm (last accessed December 29, 2008).
31. Robert P. Merges, "As Many As Six Impossible Patents Before Breakfast: Property Rights for Business Concepts and Patent System Reform," *Berkeley Technology Law Journal*, Vol. 14, pp. 577–615 (1999).
32. Mark A. Lemley and Philip J. Weiser, "Should Property or Liability Rules Govern Information?" *Texas Law Review*, Vol. 85, p. 289 (2007).
33. "Patent Law of the People's Republic of China", Chapter 6, available at http://www.gov.cn/flfg/2008-12/28/content_1189755.htm (last accessed December 29, 2008).
34. See Interoperability Specifications Pledge, available at http://www-03.ibm.com/opensource/isplist.shtml (last accessed December 29, 2008).

Index